D1330807

WILLIAM WORDSWORTH, SECOND-GENERATION ROMANTIC

William Wordsworth, Second-Generation Romantic provides a truly comprehensive reading of "late" Wordsworth and the full arc of his career from 1814 to 1840, revealing that his major poems after Waterloo contest poetic and political issues with his younger contemporaries: Keats, Shelley, and Byron. Refuting conventional models of influence, where Wordsworth "fathers" the younger poets, Cox demonstrates how Wordsworth's later writing evolved in response to "second-generation" romanticism. After exploring the ways in which his younger contemporaries rewrote his *Excursion*, this volume examines how Wordsworth's "Thanksgiving Ode" enters into a complex conversation with Leigh Hunt and Byron; how the delayed publication of *Peter Bell* could be read as a reaction to the Byronic hero; how the older poet's *River Duddon* sonnets respond to Shelley's "Mont Blanc"; and how his later volumes, particularly "Memorials of a Tour in Italy, 1837," engage in a complicated erasure of poets who both followed and predeceased him.

JEFFREY N. COX is Distinguished Professor of English and Humanities at the University of Colorado Boulder. He is the author and editor of ten volumes, including *Romanticism in the Shadow of War* (2014) and the award-winning *Poetry and Politics in the Cockney School* (1998).

CAMBRIDGE STUDIES IN ROMANTICISM

Founding Editor
Marilyn Butler, University of Oxford

General Editor
James Chandler, University of Chicago

Editorial Board
John Barrell, *University of York*
Paul Hamilton, *University of London*
Mary Jacobus, *University of Cambridge*
Claudia Johnson, *Princeton University*
Alan Liu, *University of California, Santa Barbara*
Jerome McGann, *University of Virginia*
David Simpson, *University of California, Davis*

This series aims to foster the best new work in one of the most challenging fields within English literary studies. From the early 1780s to the early 1830s, a formidable array of talented men and women took to literary composition, not just in poetry, which some of them famously transformed, but in many modes of writing. The expansion of publishing created new opportunities for writers, and the political stakes of what they wrote were raised again by what Wordsworth called those "great national events" that were "almost daily taking place": the French Revolution, the Napoleonic and American wars, urbanization, industrialization, religious revival, an expanded empire abroad, and the reform movement at home. This was an enormous ambition, even when it pretended otherwise. The relations between science, philosophy, religion, and literature were reworked in texts such as *Frankenstein* and *Biographia Literaria*; gender relations in *A Vindication of the Rights of Woman* and *Don Juan*; journalism by Cobbett and Hazlitt; and poetic form, content, and style by the Lake School and the Cockney School. Outside Shakespeare studies, probably no body of writing has produced such a wealth of commentary or done so much to shape the responses of modern criticism. This indeed is the period that saw the emergence of those notions of literature and of literary history, especially national literary history, on which modern scholarship in English has been founded.

The categories produced by Romanticism have also been challenged by recent historicist arguments. The task of the series is to engage both with a challenging corpus of Romantic writings and with the changing field of criticism they have helped to shape. As with other literary series published by Cambridge University Press, this one will represent the work of both younger and more established scholars on either side of the Atlantic and elsewhere.

See the end of the book for a complete list of published titles.

WILLIAM WORDSWORTH, SECOND-GENERATION ROMANTIC

Contesting Poetry after Waterloo

JEFFREY N. COX

University of Colorado Boulder

CAMBRIDGE
UNIVERSITY PRESS

University Printing House, Cambridge CB2 8BS, United Kingdom

One Liberty Plaza, 20th Floor, New York, NY 10006, USA

477 Williamstown Road, Port Melbourne, VIC 3207, Australia

314–321, 3rd Floor, Plot 3, Splendor Forum, Jasola District Centre,
New Delhi – 110025, India

79 Anson Road, #06–04/06, Singapore 079906

Cambridge University Press is part of the University of Cambridge.

It furthers the University's mission by disseminating knowledge in the pursuit of
education, learning, and research at the highest international levels of excellence.

www.cambridge.org
Information on this title: www.cambridge.org/9781108837613
DOI: 10.1017/9781108946698

© Cambridge University Press 2021

This publication is in copyright. Subject to statutory exception
and to the provisions of relevant collective licensing agreements,
no reproduction of any part may take place without the written
permission of Cambridge University Press.

First published 2021

A catalogue record for this publication is available from the British Library.

Library of Congress Cataloging-in-Publication Data
NAMES: Cox, Jeffrey N., author.
TITLE: William Wordsworth, second-generation romantic : contesting poetry after Waterloo /
Jeffrey Cox, University of Colorado Boulder.
DESCRIPTION: Cambridge, United Kingdom ; New York, NY : Cambridge University Press,
2021. | Series: Cambridge studies in Romanticism ; 131 | Includes bibliographical references
and index.
IDENTIFIERS: LCCN 2020049481 (print) | LCCN 2020049482 (ebook) | ISBN 9781108837613
(hardback) | ISBN 9781108946698 (ebook)
SUBJECTS: LCSH: Wordsworth, William, 1770–1850 – Criticism and interpretation. | Wordsworth,
William, 1770–1850 – Contemporaries. | Romanticism – England. | English poetry – 19th century –
History and criticism.
CLASSIFICATION: LCC PR5888 .C69 2021 (print) | LCC PR5888 (ebook) | DDC 821/.7–dc23
LC record available at https://lccn.loc.gov/2020049481
LC ebook record available at https://lccn.loc.gov/2020049482

ISBN 978-1-108-83761-3 Hardback

Cambridge University Press has no responsibility for the persistence or accuracy of
URLs for external or third-party internet websites referred to in this publication
and does not guarantee that any content on such websites is, or will remain,
accurate or appropriate.

This book is dedicated to

Amy

and to our "second generation,"

Julia, Emma, and Claire.

In thanks for all the love and joy you have given me, early
and late.

Contents

Figures

Acknowledgments

This book was a long time in the making, though it finished rather quickly thanks to research support from the University of Colorado Boulder and its Provost, Russ Moore, which gave me time to complete the book as I returned to the faculty after many, many years in administration. It now seems a long time ago that several people helped generate the initial thinking that went into this book. In another century, back in 1997, Jill Heydt-Stevenson, one of the amazing team for the Cornell Wordsworth, asked me to join a panel on late Wordsworth for the conference of the North American Society for the Study of Romanticism. I had never really thought about late Wordsworth and did not think much about him again for years. Then, Julia Carlson asked me to address a special conference on Benjamin Robert Haydon in 2008 where I gave a talk on "Wordsworth, Haydon, and the Cockney School" that first sketched out my thinking about Wordsworth and the younger poets. Other colleagues offered me other moments to contemplate related issues. Nick Roe gave me an opportunity to talk about the Cockney School and *The Excursion* at the Wordsworth Summer Conference of 2010, and Tim Fulford and the 2018 Coleridge Conference allowed me to think through the sonnets on the River Duddon. Many thanks to Tom Torremans for putting on the unforgettable "Transnational Reception of Waterloo in the 19th Century" Conference at Brussels in June 2015, which included a trip to the battlefield on the 200th anniversary of Waterloo and which allowed me to write about Wordsworth's "Thanksgiving Ode."

If these friends gave the initial spark for this book, others were there to keep the energy flowing. The Colorado Romanticism Collaborative – including Thora Brylowe, Jill Heydt-Stevenson, John Stevenson, and Paul Youngquist – form the immediate community of conversation and collaboration that nurtures my work. Our incredible graduate students over the years – including Dana Van Kooy, Terry Robinson, John Leffel, Michele Speitz, Kurtis Hessel, Daniel Larson,

Kirstyn Leuner, and Rebecca Schneider – always inspire me by showing what scholarship can become. Advice, friendship, encouragement, and ideas came in many ways and from many people including Mark Lussier, Greg Kucich, Dan White, Tilar Mazzeo, Julie Kipp, Michael Macovski, Julie Carlson, Sonia Hofkosh, Fran Botkin, Talissa Ford, and Jane Stabler. Closer to home were Chris Braider, Peter Knox, Merrill Lessley, David Mapel, Warren Mottee, and Adam Bradley. Others were there at the end. Devoney Looser – with her sharp intellect and unfailing ear – provided essential advice at a moment when the book threatened to stall out. Michael Gamer offered telling criticisms of the final sections of the book. And then my two amazing recent students, Grace Rexroth and Deven Parker, helped sort out all the final details.

I was still at Texas A&M University when I gave that first late Wordsworth paper, and I still draw upon the vibrant intellectual community there including Susan Egenolf, Margaret Ezell, May Ann O'Farrell, Larry Reynolds, and David McWhirter. I have enjoyed support from the University of Colorado's Center for Humanities and the Arts, including Helmut Müller-Sievers and Paula Anderson. Much of the long gestation of this project took place while I was Vice Provost for Faculty Affairs, and I owe a debt to the provosts I served, to the amazing staff with whom I worked, and to an intellectually lively group of academic administrators including William Kaempfer, Bob Boswell, Mike Grant, Mary Kraus, William Kuskin, Ann Schmiesing, Katherine Eggert, and Michele Moses.

Beyond the talks already mentioned, I shared portions of this book with a number of other supportive audiences at Arizona State University in November 2015; at meetings of the North American Society for the Study of Romanticism in Ottawa in August 2017 and in Chicago in August 2019; at the meeting of the American Society for Eighteenth-Century Studies in Orlando in April 2018; and at the Workshop in Nineteenth Century Studies (WINCS) at the University of Toronto in October 2018. I owe thanks to more people from those events than I can name, but they include Phil Shaw, Chuck Rzepka, Timothy Morton, Ron Broglio, Alexander Regier, Angela Esterhammer, Alan Bewell, Anne Mellor, Marjorie Levinson, Stuart Curran, Jerome McGann, Kevin Gilmartin, and William Galperin.

This is the third time I have worked with Cambridge University Press and its Studies in Romanticism Series, and each time has been a real pleasure. The advice and friendship of Jim Chandler, a true leader in the field, have made my work better. I owe a great thanks to Bethany Thomas for supporting this project and seeing it through to publication. The two anonymous readers gave generous and insightful suggestions; I have tried to do justice to their deep understanding of Wordsworth.

Portions of the first chapter appeared as "Cockney Excursions" in *Wordsworth Circle* 42 (Spring 2011): 106–15, and I draw on it with permission of the journal (© 2011 *Wordsworth Circle*). A version of the second chapter was published as "From Pantomimes to Poetry: Wordsworth, Byron, and Harlequin Read Waterloo" in a special issue, edited by Philip Shaw and Tom Torremans, of *Studies in Romanticism* 56 (Fall 2017): 321–40 (© 2017 Trustees of Boston University; used with permission of Johns Hopkins University Press). Some paragraphs in the Introduction come, with permission, from "Leigh Hunt's Cockney School: The Laker's 'Other'," which appeared in *Romanticism on the Net* 14 (May 1999).

I am finishing this book as we remain in partial quarantine due to the COVID-19 pandemic. We are also facing levels of unemployment not seen since the Great Depression and a rising against racism and in favor of justice, equality, and equity that reminds many of the 1960s. It might seem frivolous right now to publish a book on "late" Wordsworth, but I hope there might be something to learn in this great poet's struggle to prove the power of poetry to speak to his contemporaries and to address the massive destruction of Waterloo and the risings of the era of Reform, not to mention the inescapable realities of aging and death. My own aging has certainly been made more joyous by my many friends and especially by my daughters, Julia, Emma, and Claire, and by Amy, my partner in pandemic as in all things.

Abbreviations

Poetry will be cited by appropriate numbers only (1–2); page numbers will be preceded by p. or pp. (pp. 1–2). For Wordsworth's poetry, I have worked from the earliest print versions, but wherever possible I cite the various volumes of the Cornell Wordsworth, as indicated in each first relevant note. For Byron's poetry, I have drawn on various volumes of *Lord Byron: The Complete Poetical Works,* ed. Jerome J. McGann and Barry Weller, 7 vols. (Oxford: Clarendon Press, 1980–93), which will be cited in each first relevant note. Editions for Coleridge, Hunt, Shelley, and Keats and other materials are listed here.

BLJ	*Byron's Letters and Journals,* ed. Leslie Marchand (Cambridge: Harvard University Press, 1973–82).
CPP	*Coleridge's Poetry and Prose: A Norton Critical Edition,* ed. Nicholas Halmi, Paul Magnuson, and Raimonda Modiano (New York: W. W. Norton & Co., 2004).
CWWH	*The Complete Works of William Hazlitt,* ed. P. P. Howe, 21 vols. (London: J. M. Dent and Sons, 1930–34).
FN	*Fenwick Notes of William Wordsworth,* ed. Jared Curtis (Tirril, UK: Humanities-Ebooks, 2007).
Gill	Stephen Gill, *William Wordsworth: A Life* (Oxford: Clarendon Press, 1989).
KL	*The Letters of John Keats, 1814–1821,* ed. Hyder Edward Rollins, 2 vols. (Cambridge: Harvard University Press, 1958).
KPP	*Keats's Poetry and Prose: A Norton Critical Edition,* ed. Jeffrey N. Cox (New York: W. W. Norton & Co., 2009).
Moorman	Mary Moorman, *William Wordsworth. A Biography,* 2 vols. (Oxford: Clarendon Press, 1957–65).
Reiman	Donald H. Reiman, ed., *The Romantics Reviewed: Contemporary Reviews of British Romantic Writers. Lake*

<table>
<tbody>
<tr><td></td><td>Poets, 2 vols.; Byron and Regency Society Poets [Byron], 5 vols.; Keats and London Radical Writers [Keats], 2 vols (New York: Garland Publishing, 1972).</td></tr>
</tbody>
</table>

Poets, 2 vols.; *Byron and Regency Society Poets* [*Byron*], 5 vols.; *Keats and London Radical Writers* [*Keats*], 2 vols (New York: Garland Publishing, 1972).

SL *The Letters of Percy Bysshe Shelley*, ed. Frederick L. Jones, 2 vols (Oxford: Clarendon Press, 1964).

SPP *Shelley's Poetry and Prose: A Norton Critical Edition.* 2nd ed., ed. Donald H. Reiman and Neil Fraistat (New York: W. W. Norton & Company, 2002).

SWLH *Selected Writings of Leigh Hunt*, gen. eds. Robert Morrison and Michael Eberle-Sinatra, 6 vols. (London: Pickering & Chatto, 2003).

Wordsworth Letters: *The Letters of William and Dorothy Wordsworth*, 2nd ed., ed. Ernest de Selincourt; rev. by Alan Hill, Mary Moorman, and Chester L. Chaver, 8 vols. (Oxford: Clarendon Press, 1967–93). Abbreviations as follows:

WLMY, 1: *The Letters of William and Dorothy Wordsworth, The Middle Years,*
Part I: 1806–1811. Rev. Mary Moorman.

WLMY, 2: *The Letters of William and Dorothy Wordsworth, The Middle Years,*
Part II: 1812–1820. Rev. Mary Moorman and Alan G. Hill.

WLLY, 1: *The Letters of William and Dorothy Wordsworth, The Later Years,*
Part I: 1821–1828. Rev. Alan G. Hill.

WLLY, 2: *The Letters of William and Dorothy Wordsworth, The Later Years,*
Part II: 1829–1834. Rev. Alan G. Hill.

WLLY, 3: *The Letters of William and Dorothy Wordsworth, The Later Years,*
Part III: 1835–1839. Rev. Alan G. Hill.

WLLY, 4: *The Letters of William and Dorothy Wordsworth, The Later Years,*
Part IV: 1840–1853: Rev. Alan G. Hill.

Introduction

It is impossible that any one who inhabits the same age with such writers as those who stand in the foremost ranks of our own, can conscientiously assure himself, that his language and tone of thought may not have been modified by the study of the productions of those extraordinary intellects.

Shelley, "Preface" to *Prometheus Unbound, SPP*, p. 207

. . . all novels of a given historical moment form an argument over the nature of reality and are, to an extent, criticisms of each other.

Ralph Ellison, "The World and the Jug"[1]

But he [Wordsworth] never recognizes Shelley or Keats or any of the following generation as his second self.

Geoffrey Hartman, *Wordsworth's Poetry 1787–1814*[2]

I

Literary history is most often offered as a story of influence, at least as it is embodied in traditional narrative histories and in anthologies. Influence, in that it narrativizes the relation between poets in linear time, helps structure literary history; when conceived as the ability to shape later poetry, influence is also offered as a central criterion for canonicity. We can see the relations between generations of writers (and thus the existence of texts in time) being constructed under the sign of influence, as one generation of great writers is seen following upon another, with the poets of a new age drawing upon tradition and individual talent to perpetuate and to innovate upon their inheritance. It is certainly the case that accounts of the relationship between what we call the "first" generation of romantic writers and the "second" usually rely upon a model of influence and are particularly concerned with tracking the impact of Wordsworth on Keats, most specifically, but also Shelley and even Byron. The extreme version of this common account is found in Harold Bloom who asserts that "poetic history" is "indistinguishable from poetic influence since strong poets make that history by misreading one another, so as to clear imaginative space for themselves."[3] Bloom's account depends upon a notion of poetic oedipal anxiety in which rising poets must always feel constrained by and thus must contest their paternal precursors, which is one way, I guess, to read the Cockney cockiness of Keats and his mentor, Leigh Hunt.

Such a standard literary history – which, of course, scholars have been revising for years – has no room for the Leigh Hunts of poetry; they are simply not "strong" enough to have muscled their way into the canon. This model of cultural history as a series of individual masters speaking to one another across time – always a "great *man*" theory of culture – distorts the relations between Wordsworth and his younger contemporaries in a number of ways, for it forgets that they were contemporaries and obscures the extent to which literary relations are mediated by a larger context of noncanonical figures. That is, the relationship between Wordsworth and the younger poets is not just textual but lived, and it is not just a question of one poet's relation to another but of networks of relations and influences. Wordsworth was not an abstract poetic precursor, a repository of purely literary features to be emulated or corrected. He was an actual acquaintance of Hunt, the painter Benjamin Robert Haydon, Keats, and Keats's friend John Hamilton Reynolds. Wordsworth was someone with whom one might eat dinner or from whom one might receive a letter, and he was also a cultural and even political icon, someone the younger poets might want to praise as an innovative poet but also to attack when they saw him, as with the other Lakers, as a supporter of reactionary culture and policy. Too often, we act as if Wordsworth's poetic life was over before, say, Keats started his. This can be seen in Kenneth Johnston's magisterial and moving *Hidden Wordsworth*, which ends its account of Wordsworth as poet, lover, rebel, spy in 1807:

> Wordsworth's young life is not his whole life, but it is almost all of his Romantic life, and the one he created, crafted, revised, and preserved. We have Wordsworth's warrant for limiting our attention to his youth: 1770–1800 was the only portion of his life he found interesting enough for a poem; he recognized that the rest of his life would not make a good book. Romantic poets are supposed to live short, passionate, unhappy, and self-destructive lives, out of which they produce great poetry. So did Wordsworth, only he survived himself, preserving his Romantic life for

future restoration. . ... Wordsworth the Romantic poet "died" when he read the recently completed *Prelude* to Coleridge in January 1807.[4]

This powerful account is simply not interested in Wordsworth's second life as a "second-generation" romantic poet, living and writing alongside Byron, Shelley, and Keats. If Johnston, among others, has given us the Wordsworth of the French Revolution and the revolutionary war years – Coleridge's Wordsworth – we have yet to understand fully the post-Napoleonic Wordsworth, the Wordsworth known to, admired by, and contested by the Cockney School.

We must not confuse our Wordsworth with theirs. It was not at all certain then that Wordsworth, whose work more often than not was reviled by reviewers and whose reputation was not firmly cemented until the 1820s, would arise as the key poet of his day. At the time, one might have felt more comfortable predicting the immortality of the poet laureate Robert Southey, or the best-sellers Sir Walter Scott and Thomas Moore, or the widely respected Charlotte Smith and Joanna Baillie. Byron famously argued for the merits of Campbell, Rogers, and Moore over Wordsworth, Coleridge, and Southey.[5] Moreover, when the younger poets came to write poems engaged with Wordsworth such as "Alastor" or *Endymion*, they looked not to the *Prelude* – our central Wordsworth poem, which, of course, they never read – or even to *Poems in Two Volumes* of 1807 – which they knew and had absorbed – but to *The Excursion* of 1814, Wordsworth's most important contemporary poem; and while they might continue to look back to "Tintern Abbey" and the "Intimations Ode," they wrote when Wordsworth was offering the "Thanksgiving Ode" and *Peter Bell*.[6] Still, it is clear the young poets made him their leader – a lost leader, perhaps, but still a leader: it is Wordsworth whom they contested most strongly, even if there is clear evidence of Southey's influence on the poetry of Shelley, or if Coleridge sometimes seemed more admired by his younger contemporaries.

I want to challenge the narrative tendency of our model of generational influence by seeing that influence flow both ways – that Wordsworth was affected by his younger contemporaries and rivals, even as they were responding to him. As quoted in one of the epigraphs to this chapter, Geoffrey Hartman noted that Wordsworth "never recognizes Shelley or Keats or any of the following generation as his second self," but Wordsworth does see them as potential competitors. This is clearest when Wordsworth contests the cultural power of the poet whom he saw as demeaning British poetry and society – Byron. But it is also true of the relationship between Wordsworth and Shelley, whose views bothered the older poet yet whom he later regarded as "one of best *artists* of us all."[7] It is also true of Keats, whom Wordsworth viewed as the author of "pretty pieces of paganism" but also "a youth of promise" (letter to Haydon, January 16, 1820, *WLMY*, 2: 578). Shelley, as quoted in another of this chapter's epigraphs, understood these intertwined influences when he wrote in the "Preface" to *Prometheus Unbound*: "It is impossible that any one who inhabits the same age with such writers as those who stand in the foremost ranks of our own, can conscientiously assure himself, that his language and tone of thought may not have been modified by the study of the productions of those extraordinary intellects."

Ralph Ellison, in another epigraph, put it in stronger terms: "all novels of a given historical moment form an argument over the nature of reality and are, to an extent, criticisms of each other." Shelley admits that when we read his verse we might hear the words and thoughts of other poets, and Ellison adds that those echoes create a critical conversation between the texts, an argument over the way things are and how they should be represented in art. Rather than constructing literary history through influence, we need to return influence to the historical contexts where these poets worked with, upon, and against one another. Influence did not stream only in one direction as our tales of poetic "fathers and sons" tend to insist.

Wordsworth, it should not have to be said, was very much an active poet while Byron, Hunt, Shelley, and Keats arose as writers, and I argue that his publications – from the 1814 *Excursion* to the 1819 *Peter Bell* to his last independent volume, *Poetry, Chiefly of Early and Late Years*, published in 1842 – must be read contextually as partly his response to their works, an attempt to define his poetic mission not in the context of the 1790s, when he first came onto the poetic scene, but in the very different era of post-Napoleonic culture. In the simplest terms, Wordsworth created himself as a poet in competition with Cowper and Charlotte Smith, but he had to continue to remake himself in competition with Byron and Hemans.[8] In a sense, the latter, later Wordsworth was, if only by reaction, as much a poet of the age of the second generation of romantic poets, as were Shelley and Keats.

I am not, of course, denying the importance of thinking about the historical differences between being born into one generation and the next – there are crucial distinctions to be drawn between those whose cultural work first began to mature in the 1790s and those who developed in the waning days of Napoleon and the post-Waterloo reaction. What

I am suggesting is that the model of first and second generation romantic poets not only puts too strong a break between these writers – by having Wordsworth in particular "father" the second generation of romantics when their relationship is closer to sibling rivalry – but also asserts too much of an absolute but abstract connection between them as both being generations of *romantic* poets, as if all their differences and rivalries can be subsumed within the word "romanticism." Not forgetting historical differences, we need to reconstruct the relationship between these poets not as a generational development within an abstract romanticism but as a living cultural struggle between the opposing Lake and Cockney Schools, with these schools naming – beyond any reviewer's name-calling – actual gatherings of poets with quite different cultural agendas. The supposedly "natural" relation between generations, often seen as an individual "son" struggling with his poetic "father," must be mediated through the cultural distinction between Lakers and Cockneys. To have a better sense of the lived relationship between Wordsworth and the younger romantic poets, we must first reconstruct their personal relationships and then understand how those interactions could be structured by the larger battle between the Lake and Cockney Schools. Such a resituating of the poetry of the "late" Wordsworth both clarifies his relationship with his younger contemporaries and provides new insights into his writings from *The Excursion* forward.

A body of first-rate scholarship documents the impact of Wordsworth upon his younger contemporaries.[9] Yet few scholars have taken up the possibility that influence moved in the other direction.[10] Tim Fulford in his *The Late Poetry of the Lake Poets*[11] does treat the responses of Wordsworth, Coleridge, and Southey to Byron, noting both what they learn from him and how they work to offer a different kind of Orientalism than that popularized by the younger poet. In his more recently published *Wordsworth's Poetry, 1815–1845* (taken up more fully later in this introduction), Fulford extends his analysis to Wordsworth's responses to Keats's eroticism, which the older poet echoed in order to critique *Endymion* and to "set out a Burkean sexual politics in contrast to an Ovidian nature of desire, rape, and metamorphosis."[12] In such readings, Fulford works, as he puts it in the earlier book, "to revise our understanding of Romantic influence, which has typically, whether seen as a matter of Oedipal struggle (Bloom) or of grateful tribute (Ricks), been studied as a relationship with past poetry – Milton, Shakespeare, Donne, Spenser, eighteenth-century poets."[13] In briefly pursuing these general thoughts, he offers an intriguing blanket statement about the Lake Poets' responses to their younger contemporaries: "Often this ambiguous relationship with younger poets produces a productive tension, resulting in poetry of uncertain voice, when the poet discovered in himself a stylistic affiliation with which he was uncomfortable when it became apparent, or directly associated with his younger predecessor" (p. 18). I find this formulation useful in thinking about moments in Wordsworth where, absent any direct imitation of Keats or Shelley, there still is something in the language that reminds us, and thus probably Wordsworth, of these younger poets. I will show how these sometimes faint echoes within texts signal vital political as well as poetic struggles between authors.

It is often at such moments of "uncomfortable" and "ambiguous" connection, rather than in clear, revisionary echoes, that we find Wordsworth disputing his contemporaries. In another recent book, *Romantic Poetry and Literary Coteries: The Dialect of the Tribe*,[14] Fulford shows how allusion creates a kind of collective language, a tribal dialect. I am interested in moments when these allusions signal tribal warfare, involving Ellison's "argument over the nature of reality." Today's readers may find these allusions to be dubious or stretched, but readers in the period certainly saw poets in each other's works, as when the younger writers collapsed the speakers in *The Excursion* into Wordsworth or identified Wordsworth with Peter Bell. Or, to take a different example, note the difficulty readers (now as well as then) have in separating Byron from Childe Harold or the fact that a reviewer found Lionel in Shelley's "Rosalind and Helen" to be "the labored portraiture of the 'poetic Peer'" (*Gentleman's Magazine* 89 supplement [June 1819]: 625; Reiman, *Keats*, 2: 461). We can find all sorts of literary and lived echoes crossing the works of these poets as they contest one another. We will only understand this poetry – and particularly the "late" poetry of Wordsworth – when we listen to these conversations and arguments.

II

Wordsworth and his younger contemporaries were very much acquainted with one another, both personally and poetically. Although Shelley never met the older poet, most of the figures we identify with the second generation of romantic poets – what I prefer to call the Hunt circle or the Cockney School – did, with even Byron seeing Wordsworth twice, once at Rogers's house, where Byron brought the news of Spencer Percival's assassination (Gill, p. 293). As Nicholas Roe has shown,[15] Keats met with Wordsworth five times in late 1817 and early 1818, and his various encounters with Wordsworth – the reading of the "Hymn to Pan," the "immortal dinner," the non-meeting when Keats went to visit "Lord Wordsworth" at Rydal Mount, only to find to his disgust that the poet was out canvassing for the Lowthers (to Tom Keats, June 26, 1818; *KPP*, p. 252) – are perhaps the best known of the younger poets' interactions with their great living precursor. The Keats–Wordsworth connection has received considerable attention, as Keats is regularly seen as the clearest and strongest inheritor of the Wordsworthian tradition, but there were complex ties between Wordsworth and many of those who would come to be known as the Cockney School.

We might look at the man who created some of the occasions for Keats and Wordsworth to interact: Benjamin Robert Haydon.[16] Haydon met Wordsworth in 1815 through their mutual acquaintance Sir George Beaumont, who had thought his two friends might meet in 1809 when he warned Haydon of Wordsworth's "terrific democratic notions," which Haydon later remarked was "curious," "considering the violence of his [Wordsworth's] subsequent Conservatism."[17] When they finally met years later, they were still talking politics, as the conversation at the breakfast table on May 23, 1815, was of Burke, Fox, and Pitt. By June, Haydon was friendly enough with the poet that he would make a life mask of Wordsworth in order to include his portrait in *Christ's Entry into Jerusalem*; after Wordsworth bore the process "like a philosopher," he joined Haydon and John Scott, the editor of the *Champion* and author of *Paris Revisited in 1815*, for breakfast, where he explained the "principles of his system, his views of man, and his object in writing."[18] That is, Wordsworth presumably set forth the ideas that lay behind both the *Recluse* project and the organization of his poems of 1815. Wordsworth and Haydon became quite attached, sharing a sense of high calling, as Wordsworth called it in his sonnet "To R. B. Haydon, Esq." sent to Haydon and published in the "Thanksgiving Ode" volume. When Wordsworth returned to London in December 1817, he sat for Haydon at least twice, on one occasion reciting "Tintern Abbey" as well as from Milton and on another reading out all of Book IV of *The Excursion* on "Despondency Corrected," a text that was very important to the other poets in Haydon's life.[19] This period of intense interaction culminates, of course, in the famous "immortal dinner" (28 December 1817)[20] where Haydon brought together Wordsworth, Keats, Lamb, and other friends and acquaintances. They dined beneath Haydon's unfinished *Christ's Entry into Jerusalem*, with Wordsworth reciting Milton (at least before his boss Kingston arrived); the young surgeon Joseph Ritchie opening the evening onto the larger world as he talked of the expedition he was joining to find an overland route to the Niger river; Lamb becoming tipsy and attacking Wordsworth for criticizing Voltaire in *The Excursion*; and Keats raising a toast to "Newton's health and confusion to Mathematics."[21]

Keats had known Haydon for about a year at this point, having met him through Leigh Hunt during his early days as part of the Hunt circle in October of 1816. They soon became close friends and mutual advocates. Keats would celebrate Haydon and Hunt along with Wordsworth in his sonnet "Great Spirits now on Earth are sojourning" (*KPP*, p. 56). Keats sent the painter the poem, composed after an evening of feverish talk on November 19, 1816, and Haydon would send the sonnet on to Wordsworth. During Wordsworth's visit to London in 1817, Haydon introduced him to Keats, also just back in town after finishing *Endymion*, a few weeks before the famous dinner, an encounter reported in an almost equally famous account by Haydon decades later:

> When Wordsworth came to Town, I brought Keats to him, by his Wordsworths [sic] desire – Keats expressed to me as we walked to Queen Anne St East where Mr Monkhouse [a relative of Wordsworth's] Lodged, the greatest, the purest, the most unalloyed pleasure at the prospect. Wordsworth received him kindly, & after a few minutes, Wordsworth asked him what he had been lately doing, *I* said he has just finished an exquisite ode to Pan – and as he had not a copy I begged Keats to repeat it – which he did in his usual half chant, . . . walking up & down the room – when he had done I felt really, as if I had heard a young Apollo – Wordsworth drily said
> "a Very pretty piece of Paganism – "[22]

Keats might have expected the older poet to appreciate the stanzaic hymn to Pan from *Endymion* since the passage was inspired by the account of myth in Book IV of *The Excursion*, and Haydon claims that Keats felt the criticism deeply (an assertion Keats's latest biographer, Nicholas Roe, has questioned[23]). Just as Keats's personal acquaintance with Wordsworth came about through the mediation of Haydon, so does our understanding of their relationship continue to be mediated by Haydon's accounts, reliable or not. What seems clear is that Keats placed Wordsworth with Haydon as a kind of hero of the artistic mission but had problems with Wordsworth as well. These concerns were both personal – witness his statement to his brothers in February 1818 that "Wordsworth has left a bad impression wherever he visited in town – by his egotism, Vanity and bigotry" (*KL*, 1: 237) – and political: as Keats wrote his brother Tom, "Wordsworth versus Brougham!! Sad – sad – sad" (June 25–27, 1818; *KPP*, p. 252).

We can again trace Wordsworth's interactions with his younger contemporaries through his relationship to and impact on someone invited to the "immortal dinner" who did not come, John Hamilton Reynolds; the failure to attend would lead to a break between the young poet and the painter. Usually identified solely as Keats's friend, Reynolds – with *Safie* (1814), the Wordsworthian *Eden of the Imagination* (1814), and *The Naiad: A Tale. With Other Poems* (1816) all in print – was, at the time the Hunt circle gathered in late 1816, a much better-known poet than Shelley and the barely published Keats, his fellow "young poets," as Hunt called them in his famous *Examiner* review (*The Examiner*, December 1, 1816; *KPP*, pp. 11–14). Hazlitt, not known for praising contemporary poets, quoted the entirety of one of Reynolds's Robin Hood sonnets at the end of his lecture "On Burns, and the Old English Ballads," published in his *Lectures on the English Poets* (1818). Reynolds was also a voice in the post-Napoleonic poetic chorus, offering his own *Ode* (1815) on Napoleon's first abdication alongside more famous works by Byron or Southey.

Although better known as the author of the "prenatal" satire on Wordsworth's *Peter Bell*, Reynolds was, in his role as an essayist for John Scott's *Champion* from 1815 to 1817, one of the strongest defenders of Wordsworth's poetry at a time when Wordsworth was under a fairly constant critical assault. Reynolds wrote pieces on Wordsworth's early poetry (December 9, 1815), on Wordsworth and popularity (October 9, 1816), and on the "Thanksgiving Ode" volume (October 20, 1816), not to mention praises of Wordsworth in the fanciful "Pilgrimage of Living Poets to the Stream of Castaly" (April 7, 1816), Reynolds's prose *Feast of Poets*. He sent the older poet his *Naiad* volume, dedicated to Wordsworth's admirer Haydon, and Reynolds received a letter (November 28, 1816) of comment and criticism from Wordsworth, along with copies of his "Thanksgiving Ode" volume and his *Letter to a Friend of Robert Burns*.[24]

Reynolds's poetry often shows Wordsworth's influence. "Devon," considered Reynolds's most successful poem and published at the head of the section of shorter "Poems" in his *Garden of Florence* volume (1821), is a tribute to the continuing power of "Tintern Abbey." By 1819 and the *Peter Bell* affair, however, Reynolds had changed his mind about Wordsworth's poetry. Reynolds initially defended *The Excursion* from the *Edinburgh Review*'s famous attack, "This will never do." By 1820, when he rewrote his "Pilgrimage" as "From Living Authors, A Dream" (*Scots Magazine*, August 1820), he attacked the poem for being "egotistical, mystical, and abusive."[25] At a personal level and in his public guise as a poet and reviewer, Reynolds was deeply involved with Wordsworth, and his shifting attitude away from poetic admiration to cultural critique follows a familiar pattern for the Cockney School writers.

Haydon also included Charles Lamb at the "immortal dinner." Lamb was one of a number of long-standing Wordsworth friends, along with Hazlitt and Godwin, who came to identify more with the younger circle of writers. Hazlitt and Wordsworth had broken in 1803 over Hazlitt's sexual conduct, and the poet refused to meet the critic when he was in London in 1815 despite Haydon's attempts to heal the breach between his two friends.[26] Hazlitt's criticism of *The Excursion* provides a kind of roadmap to the younger generation's response to that poem as embodying what Keats would call the "egotistical sublime." Godwin, an old friend of Wordsworth's who was connected to Hunt through the remnants of the old Joseph Johnson circle as well as through the Shelleys, had been appalled by Wordsworth's political views when he visited Rydal Mount in April of 1816 (Moorman, 2: 292–93). Lamb, who continued to be a friend of Wordsworth's and to whom the poet dedicated *The Waggoner* (1819) in the midst of the *Peter Bell* controversy, still teased him over the politics and religious sentiments in *The Excursion*, even though he admired its poetry.[27] This was not just a generational divide, as these members of his own generation also broke with Wordsworth because of his political views.

Not invited to the "immortal dinner" was the central figure in this circle of London writers and artists, Leigh Hunt, even though Haydon had known him since 1807. Shelley was also not invited to the dinner, but then he did not write a poem in praise of Haydon as did Keats, Reynolds, and Wordsworth. The divide between Shelley and Haydon is clear, as they struggled over religion in particular, with Shelley inaugurating a conversation at one of their first meetings with the opening gambit, "As to that detestable religion, the Christian,"[28] and with Haydon penning in his diary in the days before the "immortal dinner" a long refutation of *Queen Mab*.[29] The guest list begins to make sense when we see that Haydon invited friends such as Keats, Reynolds, and Lamb, who he thought would get along with Wordsworth and who shared some of his own views. At the same time, he excluded equally close friends such as Hunt and Hazlitt, or the more controversial Shelley, since they would have either aggravated Wordsworth or himself or both.

Still, the ties between Hunt and Haydon were strong, and the painter did connect Hunt with Wordsworth. *The Examiner* had been an early champion of Haydon's art, and he and Hunt were close if not always peaceful friends. Haydon would visit Hunt and his brother John repeatedly during their years in prison for libeling the Prince Regent, and the brothers would lend money to Haydon even though they themselves were strapped. Haydon, moved by Wordsworth's poetic praise, was in ecstasies over Hunt's celebration of him written in his copy of Vasari in which Hunt compares Haydon to Michelangelo and Raphael.[30] Haydon would bring Wordsworth to see the recently liberated Hunt in the summer of 1815, following the session where he took Wordsworth's life mask.[31] According to Haydon, Hunt, who had praised Wordsworth in the revised version of *The Feast of Poets*, would pay Wordsworth the "highest compliments" at the meeting.

Hunt wrote, of the first meeting with Wordsworth, that the older poet came "to thank me for the zeal I had shown in advocating the cause of his genius."[32] The admiration at this point seemed to be mutual: Wordsworth wrote to Haydon of Keats's "Great Spirits" sonnet that "Leigh Hunt's compliment is well deserved" (January 20, 1817, *WLMY*, 2: 361); and he had written earlier to R. P. Gillies of his "great respect for the *Talents*" (and presumably not the politics) of Hunt as editor of *The Examiner* (April 9, 1816, *WLMY*, 2: 299). However, although he would later in 1820 say of Keats that he was "a youth of promise," (letter to Haydon, January 16, 1820, *WLMY*, 2: 578), perhaps reversing the mocking in *Blackwood's* of Keats as the "Muses' son of promise," he would not disagree with Maga's disapproval of what Wordsworth calls the "sorry company he keeps" – that is, Hunt and his Cockney School. Wordsworth's admiration for Hunt and his circle seems another victim of the increasingly tense ideological war between Lakers and Cockneys, as Hazlitt took on Coleridge, Wordsworth, and above all Southey in the pages of *The Examiner*, as Hunt found the politics if not the poetics of the group disturbing, and as Shelley would inaugurate in his sonnet "To Wordsworth" from his "Alastor" volume the myth of the lost leader. I track some of this growing distance in taking up the "Thanksgiving Ode" volume, where we will see that, early in 1816, Hunt published a number of sonnets by Wordsworth sent to him via Haydon, before turning to attack what he sees as Wordsworth's dangerous political views in "Heaven Made Party to Politics – Mr. Wordsworth's Sonnets on Waterloo" (*The Examiner*, February 18, 1816; *SWLH*, 2: 55–61).

If Haydon was a kind of social go-between, moving from Wordsworth to the Cockney School, in a way he also stood as an artist between the Lakers and the Cockneys. Haydon, who wished to be a kind of Milton of painting just as Wordsworth wanted to be the Milton of modern poetry, was tagged by *Blackwood's* as the "Cockney Raphael" (5 [April 1819]: 97). He has, then and now, suffered from the same misunderstanding as the rest of the Cockney School, for he is, indeed, a Cockney Raphael: that is, someone who offered grand religious and historical paintings that were grounded in the concrete details and the individualized portraiture identified with genre painting. Haydon's direct celebration of the urban life underpinning the energy and swagger of Cockney verse came later, with paintings such as *The Mock Election* of 1828 (Royal Collection Trust) or the Hogarthian *Punch, or May Day* (Tate), which includes a carnival of city types from chimney sweeps to a Bow Street runner. Or consider *Waiting for the Times, the Morning after the Debate on Reform*,[33] where a man, seated in the White Horse cellar in Piccadilly, awaits his turn to read *The Times*, whose editor Thomas Barnes was another graduate of the Cockney School. However, we can locate Cockney tactics even in *Christ's Entry into Jerusalem* (Mount St Mary's Seminary, Cincinnati), Haydon's central work of historical and religious painting (see Figure 0.1).

Figure 0.1 Benjamin Robert Haydon. *Christ's Entry into Jerusalem* (1814–20).
Wordsworth's portrait, with bowed head, appears between the two columns on the right,
next to the sneering Voltaire. 457 x 396 cm. Mount St. Mary's Seminary, Cincinnati.
Photo provided by: The Athenaeum of Ohio in Cincinnati, Ohio, USA

As Robert Woof has shown, Haydon and Wordsworth exchanged letters about the possibility of including an "unfeeling prude who looks with a sneer of cruel self-approbation at the penitent girl" in the painting, but Wordsworth warned against such a figure as belonging to "the higher kinds of Comedy, such as the works of Hogarth" rather than to "a subject of this nature, which to use Milton's expression is 'more than heroic.'"[34] The prude might have been exorcized, but, as Woof points out, the satirical portrait of Voltaire still betrays Haydon's Hogarthian or Cockney tendencies. Even the portraits of his friends Wordsworth and William Bewick, on either side of Voltaire in front of the columns, along with Hazlitt and Keats, in conversation above them, might strike us as odd intrusions into this historical recreation of a key religious event. The attacks upon Haydon's paintings that decried the sentimentality and vulgarity of his efforts at high art echo those against the poetry of the Cockneys. In a sense, the criticism is the same: that one attempts the sublimity of Milton using what Keats calls the "material sublime" ("Dear Reynolds, as last night I lay in bed"; *KPP*, 69); that one tries to create epic art out of modern life and ends up praising Keats's "slippery blisses" (*Endymion* 2: 758) and Hunt's "The two divinest things this world has got / A lovely woman in a rural spot!" (*Story of Rimini*, *SWLH*, 5: 3.257–58).

We might think of Haydon as a painter sitting halfway between the Wordsworth of *The Excursion*, with its grand moral and religious project, and Cockney poetry, with its pursuit of what Keats called a "recourse somewhat human independant [sic] of the great Consolations of Religion and undepraved Sensations – of the Beautiful – the poetical in all things" (letter to Bailey, November 3, 1817; *KPP*, p. 100). We can see Haydon being pulled in both directions in a telling passage in his diary: "If I ever loved any man *once* with a fullness of Soul, it was Leigh Hunt. If I ever reverenced a man, in which virtue, forbearance, & principle were personified, now & formerly, it is *John* [Hunt]. If I ever adored another it is Wordsworth" – but he later returned to the passage to write "not Wordsworth."[35] As with others I have been discussing, Haydon's affection and admiration for Wordsworth seemed to suffer under the tensions that grew between the Cockneys and the Lakers. To understand those tensions, we need to examine how the idea of literary schools was deployed in the period.

III

A reviewer in the *Satirist* complained of a new work in 1813 that it was produced by a member of a "school of sentimental whiners – or affectors of babyish simplicity – of amateurs of pretty touches of nature – of descriptive bardlings." Another, commenting on the same work, contends that the author "combines in a pre-eminent degree the various peculiarities and absurdities of the school of poetry, that his exertions first contributed to establish; his images are in general unnatural and incongruous; his diction uncouth, pedantic, and obscure: he mistakes abruptness for force, and supposes himself to be original only when he is absurd." For one reviewer, the author "is one of a school whose conceptions scorn the bounds of humbler taste," and another accuses the work of "profaneness and absurdity" and of having dangerous moral and religious tendencies.[36]

These might well be reviews of Leigh Hunt's *Story of Rimini* or Keats's *Endymion*, but they are actually all commentaries on Coleridge's *Remorse*, performed and published in 1813. In fact, there is a surprising degree of similarity between the terms used to abuse the Lakers and those later used against the Cockneys. Southey had long been attacked for verse that was seen as marked by the "deprivation of language . . . and . . . the debasement of all those feelings which poetry is designed to communicate," by "perpetual artifice," by "conceit and bad taste," and by "childishness."[37] The *Edinburgh Review* had repeatedly chastised Wordsworth, saying of *Lyrical Ballads* – the key act of anonymous collaborative work that gave substance to the notion of the Lakers as a group – that they were marked by "Childishness, conceit and affectation" as well as "perverseness and bad taste" (11 [October 1808]: 214; Reiman, *Lake Poets*, 2: 428); of Wordsworth's *Poems in Two Volumes* that they demonstrated that the poets of the "new school" are "mannerists" who raid "vulgar ballads and plebeian nurseries for their allusions" (215, 218; Reiman, *Lake Poets*, 2: 430, 431); and of the 1814 *Excursion* that it proved that Wordsworth was "incurable" and that the only thing left for criticism was to protect "against the spreading of the malady" (24 [November 1814]: 2; Reiman, *Lake Poets*, 2: 439). Just to take Wordsworth's key 1807 poems, we find the *Critical Review* calling them "silly" and perhaps "evil" (11 [August 1807]: 399; Reiman, *Lake Poets*, 1: 312). *Le Beau Monde* fumes that the "childish effusions" of *Lyrical Ballads* have given way to the poetry of "that second childhood, . . . though *sans* eyes, *sans* ears, and *sans* teeth, . . . unluckily is not *sans* tongue" (2 [October 1807]: 138; Reiman, *Lake Poets*, 1: 40). *The Cabinet* condemns the poems as "contemptible effusions," "trash," and the "collection of the greatest absurdities, that, under the name of poetry, were offered to the public" (2 [April 1808]: 249; Reiman, *Lake Poets*, 1: 61).

Before the Cockney School attacks were the attacks on the Lake School. Childishness and vulgarity, affectation and artificiality, perversity and plebeian inspiration, blasphemy and disease – these were the same key terms used by *Blackwood's* and others as they attacked the Cockney School.[38] However, one function of the Cockney School attacks, begun in 1817 in *Blackwood's* and echoed elsewhere, is to transfer the terms of censure from the Lakers to the Cockneys, as "Z." opens his first attack, published in October 1817, with an explicit contrast between the two groups: "While the whole critical world is occupied with balancing the merits, whether in theory or in execution of what is commonly called THE LAKE SCHOOL, it is strange that no one seems to think it at all necessary to say a single word about another new school of poetry which has of late sprung up among us . . . [I]t may henceforth be referred to by the designation of THE COCKNEY SCHOOL" (2 [October 1817]: 38; Reiman, *Keats*, 1: 49). "Z." interpellates the Cockneys by calling them into critical being as antagonists to the Lakers. More than that, he works to rescue Wordsworth from the criticisms that had been lodged against the Lakers so that these terms of invective will be available for his attack on the Cockneys. If Wordsworth had been accused of offering emotionally immature poetry – of being childish, babyish, a ransacker of plebeian nurseries – he is now seen as embodying a "patriarchal simplicity of feeling" (2 [October 1817]: 40) so that Hunt, Johnny Keats, and Corny Webb can be infantilized. Where Lake poetry had been found to be vulgar, degrading, and possibly impure and blasphemous, Z. proclaims that "One great charm of Wordsworth's noble compositions consists in the dignified purity of thought" (40); the Cockneys will now be seen as the only peddlers of vulgarity, blasphemy, and voluptuousness. And if the Lakers had been repeatedly taken to task for adopting a mode of poetic experimentation that broke with the canons of poetry, Z. in his later attack upon Keats would proclaim Wordsworth not only the "purest" and "loftiest" but also "the most classical of living English poets" so that he can be contrasted with Hunt, "the meanest, the filthiest, and the most vulgar of Cockney poetasters" (3 [August 1818]: 520). Wordsworth and the Lake School must be praised so that Hunt and the Cockneys can be ridiculed. While one can make the positive assertion that there would have been no Cockney School without the Lake School in the sense that Hunt and his circle are all deeply indebted to Wordsworth, Coleridge, and Southey, it is also the case that the Cockney School is rejected by *Blackwood's* not as the inheritors but as the opponents of the Lakers.

The links between the Lakers and the Cockney School attacks are, however, more complicated than simply Z.'s decision to change the target of critical invective. We can understand *Blackwood's* sudden desire to embrace Wordsworth, who up to that point had been a somewhat risky cultural investment, if we look at the context Z. invokes for his attack on the Cockneys. First, the attacks appear in the midst of a dispute over the nature of poetry. Arguing that "the whole critical world is occupied with balancing the merits . . . of . . . THE LAKE SCHOOL," he must surely be alluding most immediately to the debate aroused by the publication of Coleridge's *Biographia Literaria*: Hazlitt attacked the piece in the *Edinburgh Review* in August 1817 (Reiman, *Lake Poets*, 2: 482–96) while others such as the Tory and High Church *British Critic* (November 1817; Reiman, *Lake Poets*, 1: 149–60) sided with Coleridge in his complaints against the Scotch Reviewers. More generally, Z. must have had in mind what was at this point a more-than-yearlong attack on the Lake School by the group of writers gathered around Hunt.[39] Although Coleridge himself would continue to trouble the *Blackwood's* crew – the *Biographia* received particularly harsh treatment in the same issue as the first Cockney School piece – *Blackwood's* editors seem to decide that. if the gathering of liberal and radical intellectuals around Hunt criticized Wordsworth and the Lakers, *Blackwood's* would defend them: if you are my enemy's enemy, then you must be my friend.

The more immediate object of contention, Coleridge's *Biographia*, was published, after long delay, in July of 1817. In his opening account of the "motives of the present work," Coleridge complains that he has been misrepresented in literary and political commentary:

> It has been my lot to have had my name introduced both in conversation, and in print, more frequently than I find it easy to explain, whether I consider the fewness, unimportance, and limited circulation of my writings, or the retirement and distance, in which I have lived, both from the literary and political world. Most often it has been connected with some charge, which I could not acknowledge, or some principle which I had never entertained.[40]

As the *Biographia* progresses, it becomes clear that this complaint centers on his objection to being grouped as a "Lake Poet" – of having his poetical doctrines identified with the Wordsworth of the preface to *Lyrical Ballads* and his political positions identified with the poet laureate, Southey; as Coleridge puts it, "The solution" to the attacks he has suffered is that "I was in habits of intimacy with Mr. Wordsworth and Mr. Southey!" (1: 55). He had earlier complained in a letter of March 30, 1815 to Byron that he had been treated with what Richard Holmes calls a "watery injustice" in being linked to Wordsworth and Southey: "The cataracts of anonymous criticism never fell of them, but I was wet thro' with the spray."[41] As Coleridge works to castigate reviewers, to defend Southey, to distance himself from Wordsworth's views on poetic diction and the role of the poet, Coleridge clearly has as one of his main goals to establish himself apart from any school, to assert his uniqueness and originality. In his view, he has been criticized unfairly because he has been identified with a group – this "fiction of a new school of poetry," as he calls it (*Biographical Literaria* 1: 69) – in which he claims no membership.

Since the bulk of Coleridge's attacks on reviewers were apparently written in 1815,[42] they would seem to be most directly a rebuttal to the disparagement that *Remorse* had received back in 1813. However, when published in 1817, Coleridge's comments must have struck readers as a rejoinder to the more recent assault launched against him and his fellow Lakers by the Hunt circle in 1816 through *The Examiner*. Coleridge's conclusion to the second volume of the *Biographia* (2: 241–46) gave credence to this by responding directly to Hazlitt's critiques of his most recently published work: the *Lay Sermon, The Statesman's Manual or The Bible the Best Guide to Political Skill and Foresight*, with the literary brawl between Coleridge and Hazlitt helping to define this vexed cultural and political moment, as Robert Keith Lapp has ably shown in his *Contest for Cultural Authority: Hazlitt, Coleridge, and the Distresses of the Regency*.[43]

Hazlitt had ridiculed Coleridge's pamphlet and its use of the Bible to endorse the powers-that-be even before the pamphlet saw print (*The Examiner*, September 8, 1816), later attacking it in both *The Examiner* (December 29, 1816) and the *Edinburgh Review* (27 [1816]). Hazlitt – the "Cockney Aristotle," according to *Blackwood's* (5 [April 1819]: 97) – would follow his attacks on Coleridge with ridicule of Southey during the *Wat Tyler* affair (*The Examiner*, 9, March 30, May 4, 11, and 18, 1817). Wordsworth would also appear at key moments in Hazlitt's essays – for example, his use, to which we will return, of Wordsworth's line from his "Thanksgiving Ode" on carnage as God's daughter in his review of *Coriolanus* – as an emblem of what was wrong with the poetry of the day. Hunt, too, would continue to use *The Examiner* to question the cultural politics of the Lakers, seeing Coleridge and Southey as "advocates of Fire, Slaughter, and Famine" who can support government terror while crying over the Spa Fields Meeting (December 8, 1816; *SWLH*, 2: 78) or arguing that the message of the Lay Sermons is "Hopelessness; – for such is the sum and substance of [Coleridge's] late pamphlet" (*The Examiner*, January 12, 1817; *SWLH*, 2: 88).[44]

These attacks from the Hunt circle point to the political debate that overlaps with the poetical one: even when the Cockneys admire the Lakers' poetry, they criticize their ideology. When it was published in 1817, the *Biographia* was clearly going to be read as part of the post-Waterloo culture wars; it was going to be placed alongside other products of the Lakers during this period, including Wordsworth's "Thanksgiving Ode" volume of 1816 and Southey's *The Poet's Pilgrimage to Waterloo*. The Hunt circle had always been ready to query, humorously and not, the Lakers. Southey's assumption of the laureateship brought on ridicule, Wordsworth's position as Stamp Distributor was commented on, and a recent work such as *The Excursion* was seen as both poetically powerful and politically retrograde, both as one of the three works of the age Keats would glory in and as a piece that for Mary Shelley revealed its author to be "a slave."[45] It was, however, the body of work issued by Lakers in the period between 1814 and 1816 that finally produced a concerted antagonistic response from the Hunt circle, for these poems and pamphlets not only seemed to gloat over Napoleon's defeat – about which Hunt, Hazlitt, and their allies had much more ambiguous feelings – but also to propose that this military victory should announce as well a rout of all the social and cultural forces of the left.

In 1814, we find mutual respect between Hunt and Wordsworth and even Wordsworth and Byron – and, perhaps, a shared sense of relief after Napoleon's abdication. By 1816 the lines of opposition were drawn following the huge losses at Waterloo, after the argument from the right that Wellington's victory meant the defeat of revolutionary ideas and ideals. It was also after Wordsworth, Coleridge, and particularly Southey took public stands in defense of Church and King. There was a cooling in the personal relations between the younger poets and Wordsworth (see Keats's comment, quoted earlier, that "Wordsworth has left a bad impression" during an 1818 visit; letter to George and Tom Keats, February 21, 1818; *KL*, 1: 237). James Chandler explores this shift in attitude in his great essay "'Wordsworth' after Waterloo."[46] I argue further that the Hunt circle becomes a coherent group through its collective engagement with, and ultimately its collaborative attack upon, the Lake School; it is not just *Blackwood's* that defines the Cockneys in opposition to the Lakers, but the Cockneys themselves who – while admiring the verse produced by the Lake School – would challenge their cultural, social, and political vision. In the next chapter, we will see the engagement of Byron, Shelley, Keats, and others with Wordsworth's *Excursion*. Andrew Hubbell has demonstrated that Shelley's *Laon and Cythna* in particular takes on Wordsworth's long poem to establish the model of a struggle between a younger generation and the older Lakers.[47] For the Hunt circle, the work of the Lakers published in the wake of Napoleon's defeat marked a conservative effort to demarcate the shape of culture for the post-Napoleonic age, and thus for the younger writers the Lake Poets came to be reidentified as a group not because of their early poetic revolution but due to their current reactionary politics. In the increasingly polarized cultural scene that was one consequence of the end of the nation's united effort against Napoleon, the Cockneys came together as a group in opposition to what they saw as the older group of poets' betrayal of revolutionary ideals.

My deployment of the idea of a coherent Cockney School in earlier work has been met with some understandable skepticism. One can point to the personal and literary tensions between Keats and Shelley or Byron and Hunt. There are various rows among the group, often involving Haydon, as is likely to occur from time to time among friends and colleagues. One might also note that these complex individuals did not always sit comfortably in any school, as in Coleridge's concerns about being labeled a Laker. These figures do not always sort out into clearly defined camps. We might look at the Pope–Bowles Controversy (1818–24), in which Byron, in his *Letter to John Murray Esq.* (1821), defends Pope as a master of poetic art as opposed to the Lake Poets – he lumps Wordsworth and Southey with Bowles as "Naturals."[48] Keats had offered a quite different poetic critique of Pope in "Sleep and Poetry," and in an unpublished addendum to his *Letter* Byron attacks Keats, Hunt, and "their *under-Sect* – (which someone has maliciously called the 'Cockney School')."[49] Byron places his sometime Cockney allies with the Lakers to make his case for artifice over nature. While this might suggest division in the Cockney ranks, it comes at the same period when Byron was joining with Shelley and Hunt on *The Liberal*. And whatever the slippages among groups of poets in their lived lives, reviewers kept the schools intact on the pages of journals.

Part of this dispute seems to be over the use of the term "school," with Byron fuming that it is "a word which … is never introduced till the decay of art has increased with the number of it's [sic] Professors."[50] The *Edinburgh Review* had made references for many years to a poetic movement lead by Wordsworth and including Southey and Coleridge. In taking up Wordsworth's poems of 1807, Francis Jeffrey states that "[t]he author is known to belong to a certain brotherhood of poets, who have haunted for some years about the Lakes of Cumberland" and goes on to call the group a school (*Edinburgh Review* 11 [October 1807]: 214; Reiman, *Lake Poets*, 2: 429). Again, in discussing John Wilson's *Isle of*

Palms, and Other Poems, the reviewer states that Wilson "is a new recruit
to the company of lake poets" (*Edinburgh Review* 19 [February 1812]:
373). The *Oxford English Dictionary,* however, indicates that the phrase
"Lake School" as opposed to "Lakers" or "lake poets" is introduced in
the post-Waterloo debates. In a review of Coleridge's "Christabel"
volume, the *Edinburgh Review* writer – probably Jeffrey but perhaps
with some help from Hazlitt[51] – offers this attack:

> The other productions of the Lake School have generally exhibited talents
> thrown away upon subjects so mean, that no power of genius could ennoble
> them; or perverted and rendered useless by a false theory of poetical
> composition. But even in the worst of them, if we except the White Doe
> of Mr. Wordsworth and some of the laureate odes, there was always some
> gleams of feeling or of fancy. But the thing now before us, is utterly destitute
> of value. (*Edinburgh Review* 27 [September 1816]: 66; Reiman, *Lake Poets,* 2:
> 473)[52]

Blackwood's key response to Hazlitt's evocation of the Lake School would
come two months later with its famous assault on the Cockney School, and
many similar attacks would follow. Within six months, the *Literary Gazette*
would object to the very idea of a poetic School, "whether . . . the watery,
cockney, be-natural, or sentimental Bards of these times" (4 [April 1818]:
210). Why does the word "school" figure so centrally in these critical
exchanges? Why did Coleridge wish to avoid being part of one, and why
did *Blackwood's* think it important to attack the idea of a Cockney School
rather than the individuals Hunt and Hazlitt, in fact the main targets of
their fulminations?

What is at issue here is an attempt to designate collective literary activity
as somehow tainted, as can also be seen in other terms used to designate
literary groups, such as "sect" and "coterie." Although the term "school"
had for at least a century been used as a positive term to name movements
within the visual arts – for example, the Roman, Venetian, Tuscan, or
Flemish Schools – it was not so readily applied to literary movements. We
might have the "Sons of Ben" or the Scribblerians, but not a School of
Jonson or Pope. It is true that Thomas Warton, in his *History of English
Poetry,* sets aside the idea of organizing his account around the "supposed
respective schools" of poetry, which might suggest concern about the idea
of a literary school,[53] but elsewhere he uses the term "school" neutrally
when discussing a wide range of organizations, from educational institutions to philosophical traditions to the "school of Spenser." Samuel
Johnson famously takes on the metaphysical poets – even at one time

speaking of a metaphysical race – but he does not call them a school. Google N-Gram (https://books.google.com/ngrams) suggests that the term "metaphysical school" does not occur until the 1790s and, even then, on rare occasions. It begins to pick up speed in nineteenth-century periodical accounts of poets such as Cowley.[54] This suggests that the use of "school" as an attack term arises in the romantic period.

Since a "school" is meant, the *OED* tells us, to indicate a "body of persons that are or have been taught by a particular master ... hence, in a wider sense, a body or succession of persons who in some department of speculation or practice are *disciples* of the same master" (my emphasis), the term seems to have been less contentious in the visual arts – where there was a recognition of the need to study certain techniques and styles – than in the verbal arts, where author-ity and thus originality were more central. "School" seems to be used in literary reviewing during the romantic period almost always in a negative way. Beyond the Lake School and the Cockney School, there is the "Satanic" School and also the "Della Cruscan" school used to attack Robert Merry and his fellow writers; later, there would be the "Spasmodic" School and the "Fleshly" School of Poetry. If Harold Bloom imagines great poets fighting off influence so as, finally, to rewrite their precursors, poets who are students at bad schools succumb completely to their masters. And, just as Bloom sees those unable to combat influence suffering from a punning influenza – an "astral disease" as he calls it[55] – so are the inmates of bad schools sick, feeble, and effeminate.

Each round of abuse evidences a fear of a poetic, cultural, and at times political avant-garde; but more than that, I think, we see a desire that the literary be identified with the individual. Although one can repeatedly point to the cooperative and collective nature of much romantic poetry – we need only think of the collaboration on *Lyrical Ballads* or the *Fall of Robespierre*, of the interconnections between the writings of Dorothy and William Wordsworth, or of the ongoing dialogue contained in various poems by Wordsworth and Coleridge, or again of Hunt's sonnet contests, Keats and Reynolds's planned collaboration on a Boccaccio volume, or the works of Byron, Hunt, the Shelleys, and others on *The Liberal* – there was then, as sometimes still now, an attempt to define romantic poetry as the product of the isolated genius. The idea of culture as a group project stood in opposition to the institution of literature as it was coming to be organized in the nineteenth century with the creation of a distinct canon of British literature where authors were admitted as individuals rather than because of their status as a member of any group, class, or category. With the arrival of a full-fledged culture of reviewing where books being appraised rather than simply attacked were typically listed singly by author, and with a focus on reform of the copyright laws that strengthened the sense of the individual ownership of the literary text,[56] literature, like much else, came to be defined as a private enterprise, both an endeavor pursued alone and a cultural product, the value of which was defined by the authority of the individual creating it. This concern about the communal and the collective in cultural production, this turn against sociality in order to protect authority, can be found not only in critical name-calling but also in Coleridge's insistence in the *Biographia* that he be read by himself, in Wordsworth's movement away from the communal practice of the *Lyrical Ballads* to the concern with the individual's ownership through copyright, and in Keats's desire to establish himself as a free-standing poet, having his "own unfettered scope" (letter to Benjamin Bailey, October 8, 1817; *KPP*, p. 99) independent of the influence of Shelley and avoiding being categorized as Hunt's "élève." There seems to be a concern that, while one may be praised as an individual writer, one only gets attacked as a member of a cultural group.

There was at least one person who celebrated the sociability one can find in a school, and that is the person at the center of the Cockney School: Leigh Hunt. As I have argued elsewhere, and as others such as Nicholas Roe have worked to show,[57] there was an actual Cockney School, a lived gathering of poets and intellectuals around Leigh Hunt that needs to be rescued from both the calumnies of *Blackwood's* and the desires of later romantic scholars to separate Keats and Shelley from Hunt. Hunt had announced the arrival of this movement or school a year before the Cockney School attacks, in his "Young Poets" review (*Examiner*, December 1, 1816). It is a typically generous definition that he gives to this school, for it is to include Shelley, Keats, and John Hamilton Reynolds along with Byron and even Byron's old enemies at the *Edinburgh Review*. When Hunt again takes up the theme of the new school in his review of Keats's poems (June 1, July 6 and 13, 1817), he makes it clear that he also wishes to include the older generation of Lake Poets in his new school – even if this inclusion is, as he admits, made "grudgingly ... on some accounts" (June 1, 1817; *SWLH*, 2: 116). He begrudges the inclusion not because of poetic differences – though there are some of those – but because of the increasingly strong sense of ideological opposition between Hunt's London circle and the Lakers. Hunt's inclusive school would soon collapse under the weight of his group's attacks upon the Lakers and of *Blackwood's* successful campaign to isolate the London radical writers as the

Cockney School. Rather than Hunt's broad new school, we get the opposition between Hazlitt's Lake School and Z.'s Cockney School.

One can imagine it having worked out otherwise. While the Cockneys become the Lakers' other, they might have been their brethren. After all, one of the poets often identified as a Laker – Charles Lamb – was by 1816 one of the central members of Hunt's circle. Hazlitt and Godwin were other living bridges between the two groups. Hunt and Wordsworth shared many friends – including Benjamin Robert Haydon, Thomas Noon Talfourd, and Barron Field – and all the young poets included in Hunt's review, even Byron, would echo again and again their older contemporaries' writings. Poetic debt and personal connection might have brought the Lakers and the Cockneys together, but a strong sense of the importance of their ideological differences drove them apart, so that Wordsworth would come to view Byron as insane and dangerous, while Hunt would come in 1819 to see *Peter Bell* as "another didactic little horror of Mr. Wordsworth's, founded on the bewitching principles of fear, bigotry, and diseased impulse" (*The Examiner*, May 2, 1819; *SWLH*, 2: 186). Personal ties did not survive political divides.

IV

Our traditional model of generations of romantic poets not only distorts Wordsworth's relationship with his younger contemporaries but also warps the arc of his own career. In thinking of Wordsworth as a first-generation romantic, we focus on his work up to the 1807 poems, including the unpublished *Prelude* that he had drafted in this period though he continued to revise it. We thus think of him first and foremost as a lyric poet, even though Peter Manning has shown us that the Wordsworth the Cockneys knew – the poet of *The White Doe of Rylstone*, *The Excursion*, and *Peter Bell* – was struggling to establish himself as a narrative poet in a period dominated by Scott and Byron.[58] We admire sonnets included in the 1807 collection, but we are not as attentive to larger sonnet projects that Daniel Robinson and others have taught us to appreciate.[59] We do not spend as much time with Wordsworth's prose or his one play as we might. We have allowed him to remain primarily a psychological poet, a poet of the private life of mind and nature, even though he sought – as Philip Shaw, James Garrett, and others have argued[60] – to become a national poet in writing works such as *The Excursion* and the "Thanksgiving Ode" volume. We see him working to understand nature and the mind, not the end of the

Napoleonic Wars; we have seen him struggling with Milton, not with his contemporaries such as Byron.

Most readers would agree with Arnold that Wordsworth's writing from 1797/98 to 1807/08 forms his great decade, his "golden prime,"[61] but there are various terms used to describe Wordsworth's work after the publication of his 1807 *Poems in Two Volumes*. Critics have been faced with the question of what to do with a large body of verse that – whatever its impact or popularity during Wordsworth's lifetime – has ceased to live for us. As Willard Sperry said of late Wordsworth as early as 1935:

> At this distance . . . there are few persons who habitually reread any consid-
> erable passages written later than *The Excursion*. We no longer assume that
> a poem must be good because Wordsworth wrote it. Indeed, our assump-
> tion is that, unless it antedates 1806–08, it is likely to be poor. Attempts have
> been made to rehabilitate "the later Wordsworth," but they tax the ingenu-
> ity of their authors and the credulity of their public.[62]

Sperry (p. 29) credits H. W. Garrod with the idea of Wordsworth's anti-climax, quoting Garrod's claim that Wordsworth's work over his last forty years presents "the most dismal anti-climax of which the history of litera-ture holds record."[63] In any event, for the last hundred years scholars have sought various ways to characterize the falling off of arguably the greatest poet in the language since Milton.

"Late Wordsworth" is perhaps the most neutral term, except it is odd to describe as late all the work written after 1807, when the poet was thirty-seven, given that he lived to be eighty. Stephen Gill, amongst others, has a more supple view, seeing how Wordsworth's later work – rather than being lumped into one large category defined by lateness – falls into several phases. As we will see, there is a major burst of activity between 1814 and 1820, a turn in Wordsworth's career around 1820, and various other shifts in his work over the remaining thirty years of his life. Tim Fulford has offered a general approach to *The Late Poetry of the Lake Poets* (continued in *Wordsworth's Poetry, 1815–1845*) that empha-sizes how the later works of Wordsworth, Coleridge, and Southey open up new avenues for their poetry, now by creating newly experimental work ("Latest-ness rather than lateness"[64]), now by responding to women writers and younger poets, now by rethinking their earlier work. As Fulford notes, the entire idea of lateness is linked to an "obsession" in the scholarship on romanticism – and perhaps within romantic poetry – with youth,[65] a phenomenon also explored by Clifford Siskin.[66]

Youthfulness moves us from theme to symptom when Sperry suggests, following De Quincey, that Wordsworth was a "Man who was nervously burnt out at forty."[67] He quotes De Quincey at length about William and his sister Dorothy:

> Some people, it is notorious, live faster by much than others, the oil is burned out sooner in one constitution than in another; and the cause of this may be various; but in the Wordsworths one part of the cause is no doubt, a secret fire of temperament too fervid; the self-consuming energies of the brain that gnaw at the life strings forever. . . . There was in both such a premature expression of old age, that strangers invariably supposed them fifteen or twenty years older than they were.[68]

Wordsworth biographer Mary Moorman disagrees, citing Isabella Fenwick and others to demonstrate that, even in the last years of his life, "Wordsworth's health and strength remained almost as vigorous as ever; he was seldom ill" (2: 578). Gill offers a more mixed diagnosis, noting both Wordsworth's physical problems – he had long been bothered by an inflammation of the eyelids usually thought to be trachoma – and his strenuous travel and work schedule (p. 373). As his biographers demonstrate, Wordsworth continued to be active in both life and literature into his last decade, so age cannot be the reason for his supposed decline. Scholars working in age studies have argued that "age" and "old age" are constructed notions, not some physiological absolute; Devoney Looser reminds us that people in the nineteenth century who lived to their twentieth year often lived many decades longer, that the "grand climacteric" that marked the entrance into "old age" was sixty-three, and that aging itself had periods – "'green,' old age and 'feeble' old age."[69] There are interesting ways to think of Wordsworth as an *aging* poet, but old age is not an explanation of some sort of failure of vision.

Sperry considers various possible explanations for Wordsworth's "anti-climax" – mostly biographical ones, from old age to his affair with Annette Vallon, from his complex friendship with Coleridge to the antipathy of Francis Jeffrey.[70] Sperry finally lands upon "The System" as the reason for his failure.[71] His argument here shifts from autobiography to aesthetics or at least aesthetic theory, and I think most critics since Sperry who have seen Wordsworth declining as a poet mean that his writing after 1807 is artistically weaker. Hartman, while finding the late poetry "not uninteresting," still finds that "[a] falling off is painfully obvious."[72] A number of others have challenged this sense of a decrease in poetic power, with both Peter Manning and Judith Page turning to Hartley Coleridge's comments on *Yarrow Revisited* (1835) as Coleridge's son finds this volume of late Wordsworth demonstrating "a decided inclination to the playful, the elegant, and the beautiful."[73] We find one particularly powerful reply to the pervasive sense of aesthetic decline in William Galperin's *Revision and Authority in Wordsworth*. At the heart of Galperin's argument is a sense that Wordsworth's later poetry, far from sacrificing the aesthetic to political and religious authority, instead wages artistic war against authority as such: "Wordsworth does not 'become' an orthodox Christian in his later phase. Instead, his orthodoxy cancels the authority [a 'humanistic or individual authority'] it supersedes so as to cancel *all* authority, including, of course, the authority of orthodoxy itself."[74] I share with Galperin an appreciation for the continuing power of Wordsworth's "late" poetry, though I do not see the poet's aesthetic strength serving to deconstruct the authority of church and state.

Fulford in *Wordsworth's Poetry, 1815–1845* offers a different defense of the aesthetic quality of Wordsworth's later verse as he treats various facets of Wordsworth's "self-fashioning" from 1815 onwards as responses to his literary, cultural, and historical context. Wordsworth, Fulford argues, arrives at the defense of the imagination in the 1815 volume in part as a marketing tool after receiving negative reviews; he moves from a literature arising from and celebrating rural community to a style and vision that spoke to and for members of the landed gentry, as he responds to friends and patrons such as Sir George Beaumont and the Lowthers; and he enters into a conversation with poets from Scott and Hogg to Byron and Keats and Ebenezer Elliott. Illuminating Wordsworth's debts to poetic tradition, poetic contemporaries, and women within his household, Fulford establishes a Wordsworth who finds new power in revisiting the past – whether his own, that of literary culture, or that of historical violence. My study, in contrast, is more fully concerned with how Wordsworth remains an important committed public intellectual by confronting the issues – and the writers – of his day.

As a result, for Shelley or Byron or Hunt, Wordsworth's change was not so much aesthetic as ideological. During his lifetime, the alteration in Wordsworth's work of the second decade of the nineteenth century was most often seen as "apostasy," a turn in his politics that made him into a turncoat, a betrayer of the vision that had inspired Shelley or Hunt or Keats. There is a rich line of criticism that takes up the issue of apostasy, including E. P. Thompson and Charles Mahoney, that can, I think, lead us to a clearer sense of what is at stake in "late" Wordsworth.

Mahoney reminds us: "Apostasy historically names a desertion of one's party, or in medieval times especially of the Church .... Apostasy is a principled, lonely diversion from the mainstream, and can therefore be felt to be courageous and good. But it is also a desertion of a position, or a loyalty formerly held, and can therefore be felt to be a betrayal, a renunciation – at the very least a manifestation of inconstancy in one's character."[75] Julian the Apostate, with his bid to return the Roman empire back to paganism, is the most famous historical example of apostasy and provides Byron with the precedent for his attack on Southey in the "Dedication" to *Don Juan*:

> Meantime, Sir Laureate, I proceed to dedicate,
>   In honest simple verse, this song to you.
> And, if in flattering strains I do not predicate,
>   'Tis that I still retain my 'bluff and blue';
> My politics as yet are all to educate;
>   Apostasy's so fashionable, too,
> To keep *one* creed's a task grown quite Herculean;
> Is it not so, my Tory, Ultra-Julian?
>
> ("Dedication": 17.129–36)

Attacks on the apostasy of the Lake Poets filled reviews and found a particularly strong voice in Hazlitt's prose. It changed the way the younger writers read Wordsworth's verse: they read apostasy into Wordsworth's Solitary in *The Excursion* who deserts his belief in the French Revolution, a turn that the younger poets would continue to interrogate. Shelley, for example, in *Peter Bell the Third* imagines an avatar of Wordsworth betraying his earlier communitarian beliefs – which embraced "the world of all of us, *and where / We find our happiness, or not at all*" (Wordsworth, "The French Revolution as it Appeared to Enthusiasts at Its Commencement")[76] – and converting to the "White Obi" of Christianity.

The events that lead writers such as Hazlitt, Shelley, Hunt, and Byron to find the Lake Poets to be apostates are well known, as the three major older poets were all seen to make compromises with the government: Southey becoming Poet Laureate, Wordsworth accepting a position as Distributor of Stamps, and Coleridge writing for the ministerial papers. Defining moments in the battle between the Lakers and the Cockneys – Southey's accepting the post as laureate, the *Wat Tyler* affair, the debate over Waterloo, Wordsworth's publication in 1819 of *Peter Bell* – provided opportunities for the younger writers to label their older contemporaries as renegades, betrayers of the cause of the Revolution and, more broadly, of the people. These life changes for what Byron termed the "Lakers, in and out of place" (*Don Juan*, "Dedication": 1.6) were seen to be reflected in their writings, with Southey required to pen laureate celebrations of the government, Wordsworth praising the victory at Waterloo in his "Thanksgiving Ode," and Coleridge defending Church and State in periodical work and in his controversial *Lay Sermons*. Against these changes in the views of the older poets, perhaps purchased with the government's gold, Byron, in the passage already quoted, affirms that he has remained true to his political positions, that "I still retain my 'bluff and blue.'" Also, Hazlitt in perhaps his last essay on the "Letter Bell" (1831) can still assert that "I have never given the lie to my own soul" as opposed to the Lakers: "what would not these persons give for the unbroken integrity of their early opinions – for one unshackled, uncontaminated strain."[77]

   E. P. Thompson has provided the strictest reading of Wordsworth's anticlimax (and the decline of Coleridge) in relation to apostasy. In "Disenchantment or Default? A Lay Sermon," he argues that the great poetry of the Lake School arose out of a "tension between a boundless aspiration – for liberty, reason, *egalité*, perfectability – and a peculiarly harsh and unregenerate reality. So long as that tension persists, the creative impulse can be felt. But once the tension slackens, the creative impulse fails. There is nothing in disenchantment inimical to art. But when aspiration is actively denied, we are at the edge of apostasy, and apostasy is a moral failure, and an imaginative failure."[78] Disenchantment with a particular political position – for Thompson's Wordsworth creating a "Jacobinism-in-recoil or a Jacobinism-of-doubt" – does not result in an abandonment of revolutionary hope for some internal quest but an attempt to reground hope against the repeated blows delivered by a "harsh and unregenerate reality."[79] Disenchantment – moving away from an abstract dedication to liberty to a feeling for the people – still produces great poetry. But the apostasy of relinquinshing aspirations for a changed world does not. For Thompson, apostasy is a reactionary turn from lived tensions, "a relapse into received patterns of thought and feeling";[80] for these writers a "capitulation ... to the traditional, paternalistic culture [that] was *in fact* inimical to the sources of their art."[81] For Thompson, political apostasy means poetic death.

   Mahoney's finely nuanced account of apostasy takes up Thompson's seminal article to dispute its reliance upon historical and political reference: "Thompson clarifies early on that romantic apostasy must be understood in terms of reference – more specifically, as a failure of reference."[82] For Mahoney, Thompson – and historicist analysis in general – errs in testing poetry against an external real to which it purportedly refers. For Mahoney, Thompson attacks the Lake Poets for turning to apostasy when they can no longer find anything in their harsh political moment to refer their aspirations to and thus are tempted to retreat from lived historical experience to conventional platitudes and certainties. In apostasy, Mahoney seeks to find some of the same tensions Thompson reserves for disenchantment, but he does so to move the conversation from reference to rhetoric, from social alienation to a "poetics of the verge" (p. 5), from the "language of *power*" as "the institutional expression of the dominant ideology" to the "*language* of power, the sublimity of rhetoric as the force of language" (p. 161). Mahoney explores the "unseemly possibility that rhetoric, the force of language, might 'press' its writer over the verge" from inspiration into ideological betrayal (p. 10). Apostasy remains an uncertain, medial state occupied by not only the Lake Poets but also their central critic, Hazlitt; it gestures toward not an ideological Fall but a perpetual rhetorical falling that remains productive for the imagination.

One of the important implications of Mahoney's subtle reading of apostasy and, particularly, Hazlitt's engagement with it is that he makes clear that the debate between the Lakers and their Cockney critics is finally over the role of literature in life, about the intertwinings of language and power. While Hunt and his allies attacked Southey, Coleridge, and Wordsworth for abandoning their poetic independence for monetary – and thus, ideological – dependence, while they found Lake poetry offering, in Hazlitt's words, "Birth-day and Thanks-giving odes" (*CWWH*, 4: 120) to Church and State, what finally concerns them most is that powerful poetry, particularly that of Wordsworth, might succeed in bolstering established power, that perhaps poetry – Mahoney's rhetorical, figurative turn – always serves power, that to be a poet is to be an apostate.

This equation of poetry with power marks Hazlitt's important review of *Coriolanus* published in *The Examiner* on December 15, 1816: "The language of poetry naturally falls in with the language of power"; "Poetry is right royal" (*CWWH*, 5: 347, 348). I will return to this essay in the first chapter, but here I want to make two points, beyond noting that Hazlitt's analysis of our sympathy with powerful but oppressive figures might apply more to a tragedy such as Shakespeare's play than to the lyrics and romances penned by the romantic poets.[83] First, it is important to recognize that apostate poetry is neither a turn from poetry to politics nor a turn from the political to the transcendental but rather the continued use of poetry as, among other things, a political tool now serving a different politics. Wordsworth in his "apostate" phase is actually more of an explicitly political, engaged poet than he was in his verse of the supposed "Great Decade," and these "late" poems remain experimental, as Fulford, Manning, and others have shown. Again, as Michael Scrivener has suggested, Shelley probably read Hazlitt's review of *Coriolanus* and responded to it in *Laon and Cythna* among other works, but Shelley does not work to free poetry from politics and power but to argue that it can serve democratic politics and the power of the people.[84] Second, all of this is so because for the romantics there is no absolute divide between poetry and politics, aesthetics, and ideology. Poets, the unacknowledged legislators of the world, as Shelley would have it, first imagine all structures of feeling that come to shape human life. Poetry, as a means of providing an order to human life, necessarily generates a political vision. Hazlitt, in pitting aristocratic poetry against democratic prose in his review, essentially argues for the superiority of reason over imagination, prose philosophy over imaginative poetry:

> The understanding is a dividing and measuring faculty: it judges of things not according to their immediate impression on the mind, but according to their relations to one another. The one [the poetic faculty] is a monopolizing faculty, which seeks the greatest quantity of present excitement by inequality and disproportion; the other is a distributive faculty, which seeks the greatest quantity of ultimate good, by justice and proportion. The one is aristocratic, the other a republican faculty. (*CWWH*, 4: 214)

While not mentioning Hazlitt, Jay Cantor, in *The Space Between: Literature and Politics*, explores a similar distinction as he takes up the Platonic debate between philosophy and poetry to explore what he sees as the subordination of poetry to theory in Marxism. He then offers a Shelleyan response, arguing that we need a "confusion of realms, a confusion of art and politics. They are the same activity; art is constitutive of the world at every point – if we only had eyes to see. Politics, work, all human culture is symbol formation, is poetry. . . . All of our works are works of the imagination."[85] We will only appreciate "late" Wordsworth when we return this poetry to the imaginative, political battles it helped to define.

I begin with Wordsworth's *Excursion* and his younger contemporaries' reaction to it to provide a concrete instance of the networks of influence and response that marked their interactions. When we speak of Wordsworth's influence on Keats, we need to take up *The Excursion* even more so than "Tintern Abbey." *The Excursion*, published at the time of Napoleon's 1814 abdication and thus entering into the debate about the shape of post-Napoleonic England, was almost inevitably seen as belonging to the body of work published at the time by the Lake School and its allies, most prominently Southey's laureate poems, *Carmen Triumphale: For the Commencement of the Year 1814* and *Carmen Aulica: Written in 1814, on the Arrival of the Allied Sovereigns in England*. That is, *The Excursion* would have been seen as part of a concerted effort to demarcate the shape of culture for the new post-Napoleonic age. Even though, as in each of the chapters, I want to do justice to what Wordsworth sought to do in his later poetry, I will spend more time showing how Shelley, Keats, Byron, and others read and rewrote *The Excursion* in works such as *The Revolt of Islam*, *Endymion*, and *Childe Harold III* and how this engagement came to define the distance between Wordsworth and his inheritors. One of the key issues taken up in the responses of the younger writers is how to interpret classical myth, the subject of Book IV of *The Excursion*, which deeply influenced them; a coda to this chapter will suggest how Wordsworth's "Laodamia" and "Dion" can be seen as a rebuke in advance of the more eroticized classicism offered by the Cockneys.

The Excursion, reaching readers as they celebrated Napoleon's abdication, offered Wordsworth's most comprehensive published response to the era of democratic revolutions and what he saw as his generation's misguided immersion in the ideals of the French Revolution, with this revolutionary fervor leading to a despondency that could only be overcome through religious belief. In the second chapter, I turn to Wordsworth's response to Napoleon's final defeat at Waterloo in his *Thanksgiving Ode, January 18, 1816, With Other Short Pieces, Chiefly Referring to Recent Public Events*. Scholars have marked the rejoinders of Shelley or Hazlitt to the core ode and its evocation of carnage as God's daughter, but what has not been clear is how Wordsworth's ode and other poems in the volume respond to Hunt's earlier *Descent of Liberty* on Napoleon's abdication and how Wordsworth's volume becomes wrapped up in the evolving opposition between Lakers and Cockneys. Between Waterloo in June 1815 and the publication of Wordsworth's volume in early 1816, we can see the development of a media battle over Waterloo, Wellington, and Wordsworth that shaped the response to the volume when it appeared. We again see Wordsworth remaking his poetry in response to a younger author – in this case, Hunt – and then how his refashioned poetry is read in the midst of deeply divided debates about literature and its relation to violence and power.

Chapter 3 explores Wordsworth's response to Byron, drawing upon various epistolary comments he makes about the noble poet as well as a minor satire on him in which Wordsworth participated. This frame allows us to contemplate Wordsworth's *Peter Bell*, originally written for *Lyrical Ballads* but only published in 1819, as, at the time, a response to Byron and the popularity of the Byronic hero. There is ample evidence in periodical reviews as well as in the response to Wordsworth's poem by Hunt, Keats, Shelley, Byron, and others that contemporaries read the poem as in conversation with Byron. *Peter Bell* provides a key example of how a text's meaning is less dependent upon initial or even final authorial intentions than it is upon the cultural context in which it is issued. The *Peter Bell* controversy – involving a satire by Keats's friend Reynolds and Keats's review of it, reviews of Wordsworth's and Shelley's 1819 publications by Hunt, Shelley's *Peter Bell the Third*, and passages in Byron's *Don Juan* – provides a particularly rich example of these poets in spirited dialogue.

After the furor over *Peter Bell*, Wordsworth, ironically enough, found his poetry selling better. He reissued *Peter Bell* and published the *Waggoner* in 1819, then in 1820 he published his most critically acclaimed volume to date, one which included his sonnet sequence on the River Duddon. This volume is a key moment in Wordsworth's ascent to being declared during the 1820s as the leading poet of the day, importantly over Byron, as in debates on their relevant merits that included John Stuart Mill.[86] However, the *River Duddon* sonnets, largely written before the release of *Peter Bell*, respond not so much to Byron as to Shelley and particularly to his "Mont Blanc," itself a rewriting of poems by Wordsworth and Coleridge. While these sonnets have been seen as, on the one hand, a revitalization of Wordsworth's turn to the nature of the Lake District and, on the other hand, an engagement with literary traditions, they are also an attempt to enter into a debate with Shelley and his allies over whether poetry serves a national or cosmopolitan culture and whether it teaches us skepticism or belief.

The final, two-part chapter on late "late Wordsworth" first analyzes his almost obsessive retrospection and re-collection of his works over time and then takes up his final volume, *Poetry, Chiefly of Early and Late Years* published in 1842, the year before he became poet laureate, and particularly the sequence "Memorials of a Tour in Italy, 1837." Treating explicitly the issue of Wordsworth's age and the issue of the "late Wordsworth," I show how Wordsworth's later volumes involve a recursive retrospective re-collecting of his poetry. The final volume offers an opportunity to confront the key paradox of Wordsworth's later poetry: that during the period of Wordsworth's life when his poetry strikes us as being the least compelling aesthetically, he was probably at his most persuasive as a force within his own culture and society. That is, in what we call the "late Wordsworth" there is a striking case of the disjunction between our aesthetic judgements and estimations of historical importance. I show how the Italian memorials are an opportunity for Wordsworth to assert the power of his poetry in confronting not only a powerful cultural Other in Catholic Italy but also an Other Italy found or invented by Keats, Shelley, Hunt, and particularly Byron, ironically his younger precursors on this ground. I close with a brief post-script on the posthumous publication of Wordsworth's *Prelude* and its impact on his reception history.

Throughout this study I want always to understand what Wordsworth is attempting in his later poetry, to acknowledge the goals he sets as he becomes an increasingly engaged public intellectual. We might not find his assertion of a culture imbued with Christianity and serving the nation much to our liking, but we need to see that he continues to assert that even this more conservative vision is tied to the beauty found in nature and the love we should have for our fellow humans. Still, this later poetry veers from his earlier one in ways to which his younger contemporaries were sensitive. I believe we will finally only understand what Wordsworth tries to accomplish in this later work when we come to see that he is spurred by contemporary events and particularly by the writers we call second-generation romantics. Only when we put Wordsworth in conversation with Shelley, Keats, and Byron will we hear his unique voice. Only when we understand him as a public poet speaking to his contemporaries, including his rival poets, will we get beyond the sense that his later years embody a decline in the quality of a private, lyric poetry. He, too, is part of the second generation of romantic poets dedicated to changing the world through the written word.

CHAPTER I

Cockney Excursions

This will never do.

Francis Jeffrey, *Edinburgh Review* 24 (November 1814): 1

Jeffrey I hear has written what his admirers call a *crushing* review of the Excursion. He might as well set himself upon Skiddaw and fancy that he crushed the mountain.

Southey, letter to Walter Scott, December 24, 1814[1]

I

Receiving a mixed reception at best, *The Excursion* was still recognized as the period's most significant bid to create a major philosophical poem, an epic for the postrevolutionary age. Wordsworth, as the coauthor of *Lyrical Ballads* and the creator of *Poems in Two Volumes*, had established himself as a lyric poet. Had he early on published *The Borderers* (1796–97) or the 1805 *Prelude,* his profile as a poet – and perhaps our sense of romanticism – would have been different: rather than elevating lyric to the heart of his corpus, he would have been seen attempting the two traditionally central forms of tragedy and epic. With *The Excursion* – and with an eye to narrative poets such as Scott, Southey, and Byron – Wordsworth staked his claim to being the epic poet of his day, the Milton of post-Napoleonic Britain. Wordsworth sought to resituate himself in the contemporary literary landscape by moving beyond the lyric poetry that still defines him for us today. Charles Mahoney puts it more sardonically: "In the summer of 1815, Wordsworth was in the midst of a tripartite biblioblitz designed to clarify that he was, incontestably, the contemporary Milton. Having followed up the publication of *The Excursion* (August 1814) with his collected poems (February 1815), Wordsworth would the following year publish the *Thanksgiving Ode* volume (April 1816), the final flourish of his self-aggrandizement as the definitive national poet of his time."[2]

Wordsworth would appear to have been fortunate that *The Excursion*, a work treating the struggle to come to grips with the revolutionary era, was being made ready for print when Napoleon abdicated on April 11, 1814.[3] As Kenneth Johnston tells us, "things seemed to be falling into place for Wordsworth as the poem and the Napoleonic Wars drew to a close together":[4] his commission as Stamp Distributor for Westmorland had come through in April 1813, and he had taken possession of Rydal Mount in May, by which time his family relations and financial matters were in good shape. Put another way, for Wordsworth the personal and the political seemed to be following similarly positive trajectories as he finished *The Excursion*. Publishing his epic and his plan for the *Recluse*, Wordsworth must have felt confident that he was ready to be "duly seated on the immortal hill," as Byron would put it (*Don Juan*, "Dedication": 6.48).[5]

The poem did not, however, achieve the sales for which Wordsworth had hoped. The high price of two guineas for the volume annoyed some lovers of literature (Hazlitt had to borrow Lamb's copy[6]), so Wordsworth hoped the edition would sell out quickly to be followed by a cheaper one, and to that end the Wordsworths asked friends such as the Clarksons to help push purchases.[7] By March 1815, only 300 of the 500 copies printed had been bought; Wordsworth complained to friends about how many copies Scott or Byron could sell, and his resentment of the best-seller Byron would grow. In the end, the timing of the poem's release posed some problems, as its initial reception – marked by Jeffrey's aesthetic judgment, "This will never do" (*Edinburgh Review* [November 1814]: 1; Remain, *Lake Poets*, 2: 439), and Mary Shelley's even harsher ideological one, "he is a slave"[8] – suggests. Arriving when it did, *The Excursion* came inevitably to be read as part of post-Napoleonic and then post-Waterloo literature. Rather than providing a "lone star" shining at "winter's midnight" (to adapt Shelley's "To Wordsworth"), the poem appeared in a summer filled with attempts to illuminate the seemingly bright present and to imagine a brilliant future. There were, of course, public responses to Napoleon's defeat, as I have discussed elsewhere.[9] The festivities following his abdication in the spring of 1814 were lavish, with new fêtes greeting each dignitary who arrived, including the allied monarchs and particularly Wellington, who was met by the Queen when he entered London on June 28. A Service of General Thanksgiving for the Allied Victory was held in St. Paul's on July 7. The government also organized elaborate displays in London's parks, which were opened to the public for daily entertainments and special celebrations such as a reenactment of the Battle of Trafalgar on the Serpentine in Hyde Park (June 20) and a joint celebration of the peace and the Hanoverian Centenary, held in St. James and Green Parks on August 1 – including a balloon ascent, fireworks, and a staging of the Battle of the Nile.[10]

There were many literary responses to the victory as well. Available at booksellers just four months after Napoleon's loss of power, *The Excursion* was one of the first offerings in what would be a booming business in "post"-Napoleonic reflections, standing beside Byron's "Ode to Napoleon Buonaparte" (April 1814) and Hunt's "Ode for the Spring of 1814" (*The Examiner*, April 17, 1814) and *Descent of Liberty* (written in 1814 and published in 1815). Waterloo would provoke a further spate of books including future *Blackwood's* regular George Croly's *Paris in 1815* (1817), Robert Gilmour's *The Battle of Waterloo; A Poem* (1816), Felicia Hemans's *The Restoration of the Works of Art to Italy* (1816), Henry Davidson's *Waterloo; a Poem with Notes* (1816), and Murdo Young's *The Shades of Waterloo! A Vision, in Verse* (1817), not to mention *The Coach that Nap Ran from: an Epic Poem* (1816), a broadside inspired by the exhibition of Napoleon's war coach in London. This explosion of writing suggests that there was a need not just to celebrate a past victory – not just to keep alive both the fight and the fête – but also to consider the future shape of culture and society after the long struggle with France.

Although it may be true, as Johnston memorably put it, that in *The Excursion* Wordsworth "gave his Victorian epic to the Romantics,"[11] at its publication it appeared as very much a poem of its moment, and it would have been read in the context of the attempts to shape the culture of a new, postrevolutionary age by the Lakers and their allies, most prominently Southey's laureate poems, *Carmen Triumphale: For the Commencement of the Year 1814* and *Carmen Aulica: Written in 1814, on the Arrival of the Allied Sovereigns in England*. As would be the case later with *Peter Bell*, a portion of the negative response to *The Excursion* can be seen as arising from the gap between the moment of the poem's original conception and its impact at the point of its publication: Wordsworth wrote *The Excursion* as a cautionary tale for his generation, those who had lost faith in the Revolution when its ideals were threatened from within, as France sought to spread republicanism through arms, as the Terror arose, or as Napoleon kidnapped the Revolution;[12] ironically, the poem came into print as a new literary cohort came of age, those like Shelley and Hunt who witnessed the overthrow of the Revolution from without - as Napoleon was defeated at Waterloo; as the "Holy Alliance" imposed repressive measures throughout Europe; as hopes for Reform in England were during 1816 and 1817 once more suppressed through state violence. *The Excursion*, completed in a mood of triumph as it became clear Napoleon would ultimately lose the war, was unlikely to console a Byron thrilling at the Emperor's return during the hundred days (*BLJ*, 4: 284–85) or a Hazlitt who "seemed prostrated in mind and body" by Napoleon's defeat.[13] In fact, Wordsworth's poem – and the public response to the end of the revolutionary wars – raised profound questions about the possibilities for the poetry of reform these younger writers sought.

The Excursion's impact upon the Hunt circle or Cockney School is best understood within the context of this debate over post-Napoleonic culture in which Wordsworth's poem, however we may interpret it now, was seen as promulgating a conservative position. Today, we can read *The Excursion*, with its Cornell editors, as an open-ended poem, raising more questions than it answers, as the Solitary returns home alone.[14] We can follow William Galperin in finding it a poem that critiques authority, including the poet's own.[15] We can find with Alison Hickey the "impure conceits"[16] of the poem, which lead us to see it less as an ideologically pure poem than one marked by the deployment of mutually revisionary rhetorics.[17] I do not wish to dispute these various strong readings of the poem, but merely to state the obvious – that they were not available to Hunt or Hazlitt or Shelley as they came to read and to rewrite *The Excursion*. I also think that in granting the poem a certain aesthetic knowingness we lose sight of its cultural power: the ability it had, at the time, to inspire and to infuriate. That the younger poets could not ignore *The Excursion*'s poetic power while at the same time they resisted its ideological stance made Wordsworth's poem a key test of poetry's ability to speak in an age of reaction and reform.

II

Interestingly, most reviews of *The Excursion*, including an important one by Hazlitt (*The Examiner*, August 21, 28; October 2, 1814), were largely devoted to the poem's first four books, which are almost read as if they comprised a complete poem in themselves (in much the same way as we read the first book or its earlier version as the "Ruined Cottage" as a separate poem). This was the portion of the poem that intrigued other writers: Lamb called the fourth book "the most valuable part of the poem" (*Quarterly Review* 12 [October 1814]: 106; Reiman, *Lake Poets*, 2: 829). According to Beth Lau,[18] Keats echoed the first four books of *The Excursion* fifty-three times (Book IV alone accounts for thirty-five echoes), while there are only nineteen echoes of the remaining five books; and Mueschke and Griggs indicate that all of the echoes of *The Excursion* in Shelley's "Alastor" are taken from the first four books.[19] Even some twentieth-century critics, including Geoffrey Hartman, tend to focus on the early books of the poem.[20] These four books tell the story essential to *The Excursion* and to the poems that arise to answer it – that of the loss of confidence in the French Revolution and the onset of despondency, here corrected by a return via nature to faith in providence.

We, of course, have largely been interested in the story of Margaret and the "Ruined Cottage," which is closer to "our" Wordsworth than to the poet as understood by the Cockney writers. As Hartman argues, this first book sets up the key problem for *The Excursion*: how do we fully face loss and death without becoming fixated, without losing our "*excursive* power" (4.1259)? As Mary Favret has noted, the poem, apparently set during Britain's American war but also clearly echoing the wars with France, faces in particular the losses identified with war, linking the story of Margaret to that of the Solitary later in the poem.[21] While, as we will see, the younger poets will be concerned with the conservatism they heard in the poem, through Margaret - whose husband "joined a Troop / Of Soldiers, going to a distant Land" (1.709–10) to gain some "Pieces of money" (1.703) to support their family – Wordsworth still echoes his more radical critiques of the 1790s. The Wanderer, who is a Pedlar and becomes the major voice in the poem, has been nurtured alike by natural beauty and by religious fear ("So the foundations of his mind were laid, / In such communion [with nature], not from terror free" [1.148–49; see also 226–39]). The Scottish Church and the natural landscape shaped his ability to appreciate the deep beauty of a world that has been created and that will pass away and to accept that everything – and most crucially ourselves – will die: "we die, my Friend, / Nor we alone" (1: 502–503).

> He had early learned
> To reverence the Volume which displays
> The mystery, the life which cannot die:
> But in the mountains did he feel his faith;
> There did he see the writing; – all things there
> Breathed immortality, revolving life
> And greatness still revolving; infinite;
> There littleness was not; the least of things
> Seemed infinite; and there his spirit shaped
> Her prospects, nor did he believe, – he saw.
> What wonder if his being thus became
> Sublime and comprehensive!   (1.244–55)

He earns an "apprehensive power" (1.185) that enables him to recognize through nature a continuing love of God for the world and its human inhabitants. He is able to sympathize in the loss that Margaret experiences without losing his faith: "In his steady course, / No piteous revolutions had he felt" (1.387–88). He is thus ready to counsel the Solitary, who has undergone the highs and lows brought on by the French Revolution itself.

After the opening book and its account of the sufferings of Margaret, the Poet and his Pedlar friend go to meet the Solitary, who has lost his family and his belief in humanity. A chaplain to a military troop, he met his wife only to lose her and their two children to early graves: "indifferent to delight, / To aim and purpose, he consumed his days, / To private interest dead, and public care" (2.219–21). He was awakened from this initial despair by the events in France: "But now, / To the wide world's astonishment, appeared / A glorious opening, the unlooked-for dawn, / That promised everlasting joy to France! / …. / Her voice of social transport reached even him!" (2.222–25, 229). In the Revolution, he found the communal hope that "Henceforth, whate'er is wanting to yourselves / In others ye shall promptly find" (3.739–40). As the widowed Solitary puts it, "Society became my glittering Bride" (3.743). But when the Revolution turns violent and is overtaken by Napoleon, the Solitary loses "All joy in human nature" (2.312); no longer believing in either individuals or collective action, he retreats into solitude and misanthropy. He is marked by "despondency," which Wordsworth diagnoses as the *mal du siècle* afflicting his generation.

The problem the poem addresses is that faith in the Revolution gives way in the face of revolutionary violence to a "loss of confidence in social Man" (4.262). The Solitary's interlocutors suggest that this collapse was inevitable, as the Revolution was an act of pride: "By their united efforts, there arose / A proud and most presumptuous confidence" (2.249–50); they aspired "Rashly, to fall once more" (4.291). The Solitary's crisis is diagnosed by his companions as a loss of faith in God ("An infidel contempt of holy writ / Stole by degrees upon his mind" [2.264–65]) and as a lack of connection with nature ("languidly I look / Upon this visible fabric of the World" [3.969–70]). As Johnston has argued, "Book IV seeks to energize this languor – his unwise passivity, his positive incapability"; "The Solitary is the absolute perversion of the favorite Wordsworthian formula, Love of Nature leading to Love of Mankind."[22] The solution to his plight offered by his interlocutors might be phrased as the Love of Nature leading from the False Love of Man in Society to the True Love of God: "A piteous lot it were to flee from Man –/ Yet not rejoice in Nature"

(4.574–75). The goal is to reawaken the Solitary's appreciation of a nature that is our best guide to providential order. As the Wanderer says in the opening speech of Book IV, "One adequate support / For the calamities of mortal life / Exists, one only; – an assured belief / That the procession of our fate, howe'er / Sad or disturbed, is ordered by a Being / Of infinite benevolence and power" (10–15). The Wanderer wants the Solitary to learn the lesson one should read in Margaret's fate.

The Solitary, having lost his faith, is not to be moved by appeals to orthodox belief. Instead, the Wanderer and the Poet seek to reconnect him with nature and God through an evocation of pagan mythology, for – as the argument puts it – "Superstition [is] better than apathy." They present the Solitary a comparative account of the Jewish, Persian, Babylonian, Chaldean, and Grecian modes of belief to suggest that they all offered a way for humanity to connect with nature and through nature with God. Myth is a record of humanity's struggle to come to know God, a struggle Christianity fulfills and the Revolution – with its turn to society rather than nature and nature's God – betrayed. Pagan religions saw God through a glass darkly. After the Fall and humanity's subsequent expulsion from Eden and daily communion with God and His angels, God still was present to man through nature:

> And when the One, ineffable of name,
> In nature indivisible, withdrew
> From mortal adoration or regard,
> Not then was Deity engulfed, nor Man,
> The rational Creature, left, to feel the weight
> Of his own reason, without sense or thought
> Of higher reason and a purer will.
>
> (4.659–65)

The Persian was not to be bound within a human world, but, "zealous to reject / Altar and Image and the inclusive walls / And roofs of Temples built by human hands" (667–69), he instead looks to the sky, moon, and stars and comes to see a God in the "whole Circle of the Heavens" (674). Chaldean Shepherds, traversing "trackless fields" (690), see in the pole star "a Guide / And Guardian of their course, that never closed / His steadfast eye" (693–95) and in the movement of the planets found "Decrees and resolutions of the Gods" (700). They can find God in nature because "The Imaginative Faculty was Lord / Of observations natural" (703–704). Our ability to imagine something greater than what is before us is the foundation of faith in a transcendent God, even though pagan worshippers could not yet separate out the divine from the natural. The sublimity within nature still points them outside of the human realm to something beyond.

The imaginative generation of myth is clearest in the Wanderer's account of the creation of Greek myth, which, as Alan Hill reminds us, was Keats's favorite passage:[23]

> – In that fair Clime, the lonely Herdsman, stretched
> On the soft grass through half a summer's day,
> With music lulled his indolent repose:
> And, in some fit of weariness, if he,
> When his own breath was silent, chanced to hear
> A distant strain, far sweeter than the sounds
> Which his poor skill could make, his Fancy fetched,
> Even from the blazing Chariot of the Sun,
> A beardless Youth, who touched a golden lute,
> And filled the illumined groves with ravishment.
>
> (4.847–56)

The herdsman, hearing music in the air as he enjoys the summer sun, combines the two experiences to imagine Apollo as the God of music and poetry. Similarly, a hunter at night transforms the moon into Diana, while a traveler finding a refreshing stream imagines it is guarded by a Naiad. What occurs here is not unlike the account in Blake's *Marriage of Heaven and Hell*, where "The ancient Poets animated all sensible objects with Gods or Geniuses, calling them by the names and adorning them with the properties of woods, rivers, mountains, lakes, cities, and nations, and whatever their enlarged and numerous senses could perceive."[24] Of course, for Blake, this proves that "All Deities reside in the Human breast," while for Wordsworth, the interaction of imagination with nature to create myth is surely a universal experience, but we must come to see that these myths are simply adumbrations of the true God, intimations of the immortality we can earn if we allow the promise found in nature to console us as we confront loss, sorrow, disease, death.

The Hunt circle appreciated Wordsworth's account in Book IV of the creation of myth out of a response to the natural world – witness Hazlitt's praise of "splendid passages . . . tracing the fictions of Eastern mythology to the immediate intercourse of the imagination with Nature"[25] – even as it disagreed with his interpretation of mythopoesis. Ultimately, the Cockneys offer a historicized sense of myth and religion – both paganism and Christianity have had their day – over against Wordsworth's myth of myths in which humanity's half-submissive, half-creative relation to nature always provides the ground for true religion. The remainder of the poem would have struck them as the most conservative and least appealing, for it was here that Wordsworth moved beyond his criticism of the failed revolutionary moment to offer a response to the loss of confidence in social man by insisting upon a kind of institutional identity – one signaled by the presence of the Pastor and his parsonage and ultimately by the appeal to what Johnston calls "Wordsworth's vision of a national or imperial education system"[26] and what Philip Connell has identified as a "receptivity not just to a secular imperialist rhetoric of material 'civilization,' but also to the related, 'providentialist Christian evangelicalism' that was rapidly emerging as 'an important component of Britain's new imperialism.'"[27] There is a social vision in this part of *The Excursion*, but it suggests that community is a question of finding one's place within established institutions. A brand of conservative individualism – resistant to appeals to collective action for remaking future society but defined within traditional collectivities inherited from the past – is born. Of course, one need not share the Cockney's strong opposition to this stance: labeling Wordsworth a Tory humanist, Johnston notes that "there are worse social philosophies."[28]

There was keen interest in *The Excursion* among the Hunt circle. They read and reviewed *The Excursion*; they reread and rewrote the poem, finding there much to praise and to condemn, with Keats famously proclaiming to Haydon that "there are three things to rejoice at in this Age – The Excursion, Your Pictures, and Hazlitt's depth of Taste" (January 10, 1818, *KL,* 1:203) and with Byron writing in *Don Juan* of "A drowsy frowsy poem called the 'Excursion,' / Writ in a manner which is my aversion" (3.94.847–48). Wordsworth's poem had an immediate and lasting impact on the group: Keats turned to revise it first in "I stood tiptoe upon a little hill," which reflects the impact of Hazlitt's critique of *The Excursion's* egotism upon Keats's ideas of poetry; Shelley attempted to engage Byron – the group's corresponding member in exile – with Wordsworth's poem, the merits of which Byron had already debated with Hunt; and the entire circle took up Wordsworth's central theme of "despondency" in poems from "Alastor" to *Manfred*, from "Darkness" to the "Ode on Melancholy."

This mixed response to Wordsworth and his epic plays out in a set of poems produced by the Cockney School that, I want to argue, form a collective response and reworking of *The Excursion*. That is, the reaction of the younger romantics to Wordsworth's epic was not only influenced by their impressions of Wordsworth and his work but also mediated through their engagement with the Cockney School. Thomas Medwin, in his life of

Shelley, claims that "Shelley told me that he and Keats had mutually agreed, in the same given time, (six months each,) to write a long poem, and that the *Endymion* and *Revolt of Islam* were the fruits of this rivalry."[29] Scholars have linked Reynolds's "Romance of Youth," Peacock's *Rhododaphne*, and Hunt's "The Nymphs" to this same moment of collective creativity.[30] Even though Medwin's reports are usually met with justifiable skepticism, I want to suggest that such a competition is a quite plausible extension of Hunt's infamous sonnet-writing contests. However, whether or not we believe that there was a contest with one another, these poets were clearly contesting Wordsworth and the Lake School; the group's engagement with *The Excursion*, as Hunt reconsidered it in late 1816 in preparation for his mythological poems, as Keats studied it perhaps for the first time, as Hazlitt returned to it in a series of attacks upon the Lake School (and the accelerating distinction being drawn between the Lakers and the Cockneys) – all were to lead to a collective effort to rewrite what was the central poem in their Wordsworth canon. This effort involved not only the poems in Medwin's contest but also Peacock's unfinished "Ahrimanes," which figures largely in Shelley's *Laon and Cythna*; Byron's *Childe Harold III*, which the Hunt circle read; and Hazlitt's various treatments of Wordsworth. Such responses reveal how the circle engaged in a collective turn against a poet who, to them, endorsed reaction, with the very joint nature of the enterprise being a response to his Solitary's loss of faith in "social man."

III

The Cockney school reworks *The Excursion* by reframing the central story of the first four books. Faced with a work embodying a poetic power they admired but offering a meaning they abhorred, the Cockneys confronted in rewriting *The Excursion* the possibility that, at their moment, great poetry could only offer an internalized quest romance, that poetry could not serve social reform or renovation. In reworking Wordsworth's epic in their own series of long poems, the Hunt circle sought to resocialize Wordsworth's core story of despondency, to restore a radical intellectual tradition he rejected, and to recreate poetry's experimental ability to disrupt the status quo and to reimagine the future. This is not to say that these writers were being fair to Wordsworth's intentions or his accomplishments: they come to contest Wordsworth, not to praise him.

The Hunt circle's first move in reworking Wordsworth was to suggest that the poet's turn to nature constitutes not an embrace of Providence and a rejection of the false god of society but a fall into the self and away from a community that, in their account, is the only possible Eden for humanity. While Keats's depiction of the "wordsworthian or egotistical sublime" (letter to Woodhouse, October 27, 1818, *KPP*, p. 295) is the most famous version of this attack upon the perceived self-involvement of Wordsworthian poetry, Hazlitt's review of *The Excursion* in *The Examiner* for August 21 and 28 and October 2, 1814, more clearly sets forth the group's concerns. Hazlitt first appears to grant Wordsworth an unmediated vision of nature: "His mind is, as it were, coeval with the primary forms of things, his imagination holds immediately from nature; and his imagination 'owes no allegiance' but 'to the elements'" (*CWWH*, 19: 10). However, Hazlitt then asserts, in apparent contradiction, that Wordsworth's poetry is wholly mediated by the poet's selfhood, for *The Excursion* is "less a poem on the country, than on the love of the country" (p. 10); in fact, "An intense intellectual egotism swallows up every thing" (p. 11). Trapped in a harsh, inhuman nature and with rural life providing none of the city pleasures such as the theater a Cockney would take for granted,[31] the Lake Poet naturally exalts the ego as the only counter to a dead and deadening world: "If the inhabitants of the mountainous districts described by Mr. Wordsworth are less gross and sensual than others, they are more selfish. . . . The weight of matter which surrounds them, crushes their finer sympathies. Their minds become hard and cold, like the rocks which they cultivate" (p. 23). The turn to the self is not a profound epistemological move: selfishness is the natural mode of social life in the country; most simply, "All country people hate each other" (p. 21). The danger is that "where the mind is exclusively occupied with the ideas of things, as they exist in the imagination," then it "must check the genial expansion of the moral sentiments and social affections" (p. 15). What is at stake here is not so much the relationship between self and object; Hazlitt's objection is not that Wordsworth does not allow nature to exist apart from his imagination but that all he sees is himself and nature: "It is as if there were nothing but himself and the universe" (p. 11). The great flaw in Wordsworth's poem, then, is that it lacks other people. Like his Solitary, Wordsworth has rejected society.[32]

The poets around Hunt followed Hazlitt in conflating Wordsworth with his Solitary. This is obviously a reduction of the complex dialogic structure of *The Excursion*: if they had focused on the Wanderer – and particularly his deep, continually reaffirmed care for Margaret in Book I – they might have found a different, more sympathetic figure with whom to engage. However, their reading provides, precisely in being reductive, a powerful revisionary move: in "Alastor," for example, Shelley explores the egotistical sublime through both the poet within the poem and a Wordsworthian narrator. Where Wordsworth's Wanderer chastises the Solitary for turning to society rather than the God of nature, Shelley finds his Wordsworthian poet at fault for turning from society – and particularly the society of women – to seek a life-denying ideal that appears to lie in and beyond nature. The Poet has left human society behind, "left / His cold Fireside and alienated home / To seek strange truths in undiscovered lands" (*SPP*, 75–77); he "lived, he died, he sung, in solitude" (60). In his isolation, he has pursued "nature's most secret steps" (81) but has found no satisfaction, and his quest becomes a longing for a finality not available in this world. This turn from man to nature – the very move urged by Wordsworth's Wanderer – is revealed as a shift not from human blindness to divine insight but rather from life to death. The Poet no longer finds delight in nature: "Whither have fled / The hues of heaven that canopied his bower / Of yesternight" (196–97); "His wan eyes / Gaze on the empty scene as vacantly / As ocean's moon looks on the moon in heaven" (200–202). In a moment we find repeatedly in Keats's poetry, the experience of an idealizing vision leads the poet to denigrate the living world around him.

There does seem another path than that of nature. The poet in "Alastor" receives a vision of a woman whose "voice was like the voice of his own soul" (153) and who combines all of his physical, intellectual, and emotional desires. However, Shelley's Poet pursues not some real woman – say, Manfred's Astarte – but a dream girl sent, we are told, by "The spirit of sweet human love" because he has "spurned / Her choicest gifts" (203–205); that is, the Poet is being driven by dreams of an unattainable ideal love because he has rejected offers of real love – not only the many virgins who "have pined / And wasted for fond love of his wild eyes" (62–63) but most importantly the "Arab maiden" who "brought his food, / Her daily portion . . . / And spread her matting for his couch, and stole / From duties and repose to tend his steps" yet who, ignored, always returned home "Wildered, and wan, and panting" (129–39). Rather than choosing society as his "glittering bride" – and, more tellingly, rather than accepting the Arab maiden as his mate – the Poet has sought not human sympathy but the self. This turn to the ego from others and from the eros that binds us to others is, for Shelley, a death-wish; the Poet now slowly pursues the grave. Shelley makes it clear that the Poet's turn from the Arab maiden to the woman of his dream vision is a turn from an engagement with life to a pursuit of death.

What Shelley's Poet sought in the external natural world and in shared cultural knowledge, he now seeks within, in his dream that denies the social world and suggests that nature is merely a door to death. Arguing that the beauties of nature leave us trapped within the limited, mortal world ("pendent mountains seen in the calm lake, / Lead only to a black and watery depth"), he "eagerly pursues / Beyond the realms of dream that fleeting shade," hoping that "the dark gate of death" will reveal a "mysterious paradise"; this sense that death, not life, will provide human-ity with the answers it seeks leads to despondency, as "The insatiable hope which it awakened, stung / His brain even like despair" (205–22).

The Poet's error in selecting "self-centered seclusion," in attempting "to exist without human sympathy" ("Preface," p. 73), is shared with the Wordsworthian narrator of the poem, so identified by Earl Wasserman and others.[33] Although Shelley's narrator intones his dedication to "our great Mother nature" and salutes "Earth, ocean, air, beloved brotherhood!" (1–2), it is clear (as perhaps is suggested by the absence of Shelley's fourth element of fire found in the "Ashes and sparks" of his "unextinguished hearth" in "Ode to the West Wind" [SPP, 67, 66]) that he has sought nature not as the source of life but as the site of death. Pledging himself to nature, who is "Mother of this unfathomable world," the narrator tells us of his pursuit of nature's "deep mysteries . . . . In charnels and on coffins, where black death / Keeps record of the trophies won from thee" (18, 23, 24–25). Where Shelley hears in nature a "mysterious tongue / Which teaches awful doubt" ("Mont Blanc," SPP, 76–77), his Wordsworthian narrator hopes "to still these obstinate questionings" (26) that once moved the Wordsworth of the "Intimations Ode" and that will always move the skeptical Shelley. It comes as no surprise that this narrator, at the close of the poem, turns away from natural to supernatural solutions, calling for "Medea's wondrous alchemy" or the draught that made Ahasuerus immor-tal or the alchemist's elixir of life (672–86). Although he has claimed, like the Wordsworth of The Excursion, to love nature, this narrator in fact demands a finality (a "tale / Of what we are," 28–29) that nature cannot offer. When he realizes that he, like the visionary Poet, will never complete his quest in this life, he falls into true despondency, "pale despair and cold tranquility," as he finds "Nature's vast frame, the web of human things, / Birth and the grave . . . are not as they were" (717–20). In a closing passage that Shelley later refutes in Adonais, the narrator finds no hope in the Poet's death. Despondency is not a product of failed social action but of a reaction against society in choosing a privatized turn to nature. Wordsworth's Solitary had suffered because "the unexpected transports of our Age /

Carried so high, that every thought – which looked / Beyond the temporal destiny of the Kind – / To many seemed superfluous" (4.263–66); society seemed enough, and thus man turned from God only to find himself in despair when social change faltered. Shelley suggests, rather, that it is the turn from the social to something absolute and purportedly beyond our "temporal destiny" that leads to despondency. In his preface, Shelley defends the hopeful idealist who even when deluded is better than those who are "morally dead" (p. 73) to the call for social amelioration: it is better to have loved and lost the French Revolution than never to have loved at all.

In casting the Poet's choice as that between a real woman and a dream girl, Shelley outlines a second aspect of the circle's revision of Wordsworth: they resexualize Wordsworth's imagery of marriage, not only the Solitary's union with society but also the "spousal verse" sounded in the "Prospectus" to *The Recluse* published with *The Excursion*. Shelley suggests that, had the Poet turned outward to a human romantic, erotic union, he would have been spared his internalized quest into the deathly self. Others perhaps involved in Medwin's contest used the same configuration, though arriving at different conclusions. Peacock in *Rhododaphne* (1818) makes an argument for sexual liberty over a moralizing and restrictive Christianity by posing for his main character Anthemion a choice between different conceptions of love.[34] Again, Reynolds's self-consciously Wordsworthian fragment,[35] "The Romance of Youth," tells the story of a solitary "boy of golden mind," who is so enraptured by tales of glorious romance and so removed from interaction with other people (having "no brother / To link him with mankind – no friend to smother / Fantasies wild and dim" [I]) that he has become completely cut off from external reality, prey to the "solitary mysteries that throw / The mind upon itself" (II): "his lot / Was pain and melancholy" (IX). Significantly, he is not attracted to any of the real beauties that surround him – "He loved no earthly lady" (XXIII). Like the Poet in "Alastor," the Youth encounters a visionary woman, the Queen of the Fairies, who arrives bearing dainties that might look backwards to the land of "Arabie" in "Alastor" and that certainly resemble the much more tangible feast in "The Eve of St. Agnes": there are "chalices of Eastern dew-wine, brew'd / By pearly hands in far Arabian solitude. / And golden berries steep'd in cream"; and fish "from the lonely Mountains of the Moon," "And fruit, the very loveliest and the least, / Came from young spangled trees in gardens of the East" (LVII–LVIII). Reynolds's Youth immediately falls in love with the visionary queen and just as immediately begins to regret his humanity, finding himself "half in gloominess, /

Feeling the fetters of his mortal state, / Which chain'd him to the earth"
(LXVIII). As in "Alastor," the turn from human contact signals a loss of
faith in sexuality that brings one not so much visionary dreariness as
a vision-induced despondency: "the queen had gone, – / And then all
other things were little worth" (LXXV).[36]

This eroticizing turn is perhaps clearest in *Endymion*, a poem long
linked with "Alastor" and *The Excursion*.[37] The poem's very luxurious-
ness – attacked in the press as "the gross slang of voluptuousness" taken
from Hunt (*British Critic* n.s. 9 [June 1818]: 652; Reiman, *Keats*, 1:
212) – sexualizes chaste Wordsworthian nature. In his romance, Keats
depicts another alienated solitary – in fact, he offers an entire society
despondent and turned toward death. Endymion lives, in one sense, in
the Greece depicted in Wordsworth's *Excursion*: the Latmians live amidst
beautiful nature, yet in responding to nature they always look for something beyond it. The hymn to Pan, which apparently did not meet
Wordsworth's approval, could have appeared in *The Excursion* (where
Pan is invoked as "The simple Shepherd's awe-inspiring God" (4.883),
for it provides a pagan apostrophe of the universal God they can only dimly
perceive:

> Be still the unimaginable lodge
> For solitary thinkings; such as dodge
> Conception to the very bourne of heaven,
> Then leave the naked brain: be still the leaven,
> That spreading in this dull and clodded earth
> Gives it a touch ethereal – a new birth:
> Be still a symbol of immensity;
> A firmament reflected in a sea;
> An element filling the space between;
> An unknown.   (*KPP* 1.293–302)

The worship of Pan as an unknown, unknowable something that leads us
to find the earth "dull and clodded" is Keats's negative version of
Wordsworth's natural supernaturalism. The experience of worshipping
Pan takes the mind to "the very bourne of heaven" only to leave the
brain "naked" – that is, bereft of thought. Pan leads us beyond this
earth, which then becomes a dull reflection of some ideal, but he cannot
take us in fact to that ideal. One is reminded of Keats's verse epistle to
Reynolds where the imagination, "brought / Beyond its proper bound, yet
still confined," finds itself "Lost in a sort of purgatory blind" where one
"Cannot refer to any standard law / Of either earth or heaven." Keats there

cries out, "It is a flaw / In happiness to see beyond our *bourn*" (*KPP*, 78–83; my emphasis).

What the hymn to Pan suggests is that the retreat from life experienced by Endymion is not an isolated event but a symptom of his culture's pursuit of an ineffable divinity. As Watkins has noted, it is not only Endymion who seems rather disconnected from the incredibly beautiful physical world that surrounds his people; this entire society seems to be looking beyond life to death and what it might reveal.[38] Endymion's society experiences despondency, as those playing quoits can think only of "the sad death / Of Hyacinthus" (327–28), those competing at archery obsess about "Poor, lonely Niobe!" (339), and the elders sitting with Endymion "out-told / Their *fond* imaginations" (392–93; emphasis added) of those they will meet in death, with "fond" carrying a double meaning of "caring" and "foolish."

As was the case with Shelley's Poet in "Alastor," Keats's Endymion is disturbed by the desire for a kindred spirit. Like his fellow Latmians, Endymion's "fainting recollections" are "riven" by a "cankering venom" that prevents him from enjoying their paradisiacal world (396–97), but we learn that he has been lured away from mortal life by a visionary sexual experience: a tryst with Cynthia, the goddess of the hunt and moon. Like Shelley's doomed Poet, Endymion finds the world unfulfilling after glimpsing his visionary woman: "all the pleasant hues / Of heaven and earth had faded" (1.691–92); in Book Two, Endymion tells us, "Now I have tasted her sweet soul to the core / All other depths are shallow: essences, / Once spiritual, are like muddy lees" (2.904–906). Again, like Shelley's Poet, Endymion, no longer satisfied with life, quests throughout the world for this dream.

Unlike Shelley's Poet, however, Endymion continually encounters his love, who leads him through a series of "bowers" embodying possible ways of configuring the love relationship and the relation between the lovers and the world. Endymion must move beyond the infantilized self-involvement of the wish-fulfillment world of the Bower of Bliss in the Venus and Adonis episode of Book Two. He must learn in Book Three of the need for humanitarian commitment in meeting with Glaucus who has been led by the intensity of his passion into a kind of antisocial captivity that reminds one of "La Belle Dame Sans Merci" and "Lamia" as well as Reynolds's "Naiad" and Peacock's *Rhododaphne*. In the final book, coming forth from the Cave of Quietude, Endymion is ready to confront the choice that undoes Shelley's Poet: that between the real woman before him and the dream maiden ever fading from his view. Endymion, of course, selects the Indian Maid (Keats's version of Shelley's "Arab maiden") only to find that she is in fact Cynthia, the point apparently being that if we embrace the "real" we will find all of the ideal qualities that we have projected onto another realm.[39]

In Keats's clearest argument within the poem for the erotic, the passage he referred to as his "Pleasure Thermometer" and which he hoped was "a regular stepping of the Imagination towards a Truth" (letter to John Taylor, January 30, 1818, quoted KPP, p. 145), Keats followed Hazlitt in linking the vitality of the sensual and the sexual to the viability of the social. In Hazlitt's review of The Excursion, Hazlitt worried that Wordsworth's exclusive occupation "with the ideas of things, as they exist in the imagination or understanding ... must check the genial expansion of the moral sentiments and social affections, must lead to a cold and dry abstraction, as they are found to suspend the animal functions, and relax the bodily frame" (CWWH, 19: 15). This early critique of "the wordsworthian or egotistical sublime" as a rejection of the physical and a pursuit of an abstract and vain intellectuality echoes throughout the work of the Hunt circle, from Keats's cry "O for a Life of Sensations rather than of Thoughts!" (letter to Benjamin Bailey, November 22, 1817, KPP, p. 102) to Byron's description of Juan turning Lake Poet when, incapable of understanding his sexual desire for Donna Julia, he instead embraces a love of rocks and stones and trees (1.90–91), to Percy Shelley's depiction of the Laker Peter Bell as a "moral eunuch" who "Felt faint" when "He touched the hem of Nature's shift" (SPP, 314–16). Linking the "animal functions" to "social affections," Keats's "Pleasure Thermometer" finds that life's "chief intensity" "Is made of love and friendship" (1.800–801) and that sex, often thought the "mere commingling of passionate breath," "Produce[s] more than our searching witnesseth" (833–34). Moving beyond the commonplace notion that erotic love makes the world seem new as it "genders a novel sense, / At which we start and fret" (808–809), Keats grounds our link to nature and society in the fact that men and women "kiss and greet" (842). It is erotic desire that moves us from the self into connection with the world, natural and social.

Although Byron found this passage sentimental, I think Benjamin Bailey was closer to Keats's intent in objecting to Endymion's espousal of "that abominable principle of Shelley's – that Sensual Love is the principle of things."[40] Keats argues not that the external world is somehow dependent upon our erotic drives but that the world will never exist for us if we are not propelled out of the self by desire. Desire, revealing the want or lack within the self, forces us out into the world. When desire finds an object, then we know that there is something outside of the self, something that, in being desired, is found to be valuable: "when we combine therewith, / Life's self is nourish'd by its proper pith" (813–14). It is in this sense that Lionel Trilling can claim that for Keats pleasure is the reality principle – not that Keats sees life as wish-fulfillment but that it is through pleasure that he grasps the world.[41] As I have argued elsewhere about Keats's "I stood tiptoe,"[42] it is through an eroticized blending with the world opposed to the "egotistical sublime" that Keats defeats despondency. Keats argues here – as Shelley does in *Laon and Cythna* or Peacock in *Rhododaphne* – for erotic love as a binding force between people that will reorder a society they see defined by the divisive forces of greed and violence.

IV

If the Cockney writers did not find Wordsworth sexy enough, he might have responded that their eroticism failed to do justice to the fullness and complexity of human interactions as shown in the relationship between the Wanderer and Margaret. It is important to stress that the Cockney turn toward the erotic, which might seem a retreat from the political, is in fact a move to redeem the social. As Hazlitt had suggested, we can regain the "social affections" by reenergizing the "animal functions." Moreover, Keats is careful to place the story of Endymion within a political context established through his proems, where we learn that the despondency he combats arises in part from the "inhuman dearth / Of noble natures" (I.8–9), particularly, as Allot notes, in political life.[43] Keats is writing after the defeat of Napoleon – the "death-day of empires" of the second book's proem (2.34) – and during the "gloomy days" (1.9) of 1817 marked by economic depression and political repression. Of the proem to the third book, Woodhouse tells us, "K. said, with much simplicity, 'It will be easily seen what I think of the present Ministers, by the beginning of the 3ᵈ Book'"; *Blackwood's* found Keats in these lines learning from Hunt "to lisp sedition," and the *British Critic* called them a "jacobinical apostrophe."[44] As Allot notes,[45] Keats's lines (3.1–12) echo Hunt's attacks during August 1817 in *The Examiner* upon the ministry, driven by their pride and "baaing vanities" to destroy England's "human pastures." Allusions to the celebrations following Napoleon's abdication (3.17–18) take up Hazlitt's rejection in his review of *The Excursion* of "Birth-day and Thanksgiving odes" and the "chaunting of <u>Te Deums</u> in all the churches of Christendom" (*CWWH*, 4: 120), as we see the "self-applause" of the rulers being confirmed by celebrations involving "fierce intoxicating tones / Of trumpets, shoutings, and belaboured drums, / And sudden cannon" and staged round "their tiptop nothings, their dull skies, their thrones." The proem to the fourth book, in considering the history of English verse, returns to lament the "Despondency" that besets "our dull uninspired, snail-paced lives" in "these our latter days" (4.18–25). Keats writes his poem to cure the specific despondency of post-Napoleonic England.

An even stronger attempt to rewrite the politics of Wordsworthian despondency is found in the continuing story of the age's best-known solitary, Childe Harold (I will return to other aspects of Byron's poem in the next chapter). Hunt, in his "Young Poets" review, as well as the *Imperial Magazine*, linked *Childe Harold III* to *The Excursion*, the latter claiming "Childe Harold is his noblest work – the third canto is written in the spirit of Wordsworth's Excursion" (3 [April 1821]: 342). The involvement of Byron in *The Excursion* at the time he was composing *Childe Harold III* is a matter of some dispute. Medwin tells us that when Shelley met with Byron during the summer of 1816, Shelley tried to immerse his fellow poet in Wordsworth,[46] and it has often been assumed that *Childe Harold III* should be read as Byron's excursion into Wordsworthianism. However, Jerome McGann has shown that Shelley could have only influenced the end of *Childe Harold III* and a few added stanzas earlier in the canto, since Byron's poem was substantially completed before Shelley arrived in Geneva.[47] Still, there is no doubting Byron's engagement with Wordsworth and *The Excursion*. In a much earlier letter to Hunt (October 30, 1815, *BLJ*, 4: 324–26) thanking him for a copy of his *Feast of Poets* with its praises of Wordsworth, Byron "take[s] leave to differ from you on Wordsworth as freely as I once agreed with you." Byron is particularly critical of *The Excursion*: he argues that "there is undoubtedly much natural talent spilt over 'the Excursion' but it is rain upon rocks where it stands & stagnates . . . who can understand him?"; and he disputes two specific statements in *The Excursion*, one from the description of Greece and Greek mythology in Book IV. Long before he met Shelley, Byron knew Wordsworth's poem well enough to argue with its details.

Childe Harold III is, in fact, framed by two allusions to the section on myth in Book IV of *The Excursion*, though interestingly Byron does not take up the description of Greek religion but the lines on Persian and Chaldean culture.[48] In the first passage, Harold is compared to the Chaldean (see *The Excursion*, 4.690–714) finding the divine in nature: "Like the Chaldean, he could watch the stars, / Till he had peopled them with beings bright / As their own beams" (14.118–20).[49] If Harold, like the Chaldean, could be content in imagining the infinite in nature's finitude, he would have been happy, escaping the slings and arrows of earthly fortune. However, Harold, as the modern solitary, is unable to maintain this innocent but naive faith: "but this clay will sink / Its spark immortal, envying it the light / To which it mounts as if to break the link / That keeps us from yon heaven which woos us to its brink" (14.123–26). As in Keats, Harold can reach the "bourne" or "brink" of heaven but not heaven itself, at which point frustration sets in, along with disgust at the distance between the "spark immortal" we seek both within and without and the fact of our mortality as "clay." The marriage between the mind and the world, between spirit and clay, as promised by Wordsworth, is found to be a false seduction that lures us from the earth without delivering us to heaven. As a result, Harold, already *the* exemplar of *mal du siècle*, now becomes the embodiment of his era's post revolutionary despondency: "Self-exiled Harold wanders forth again, / With naught of hope left" (16.136–37).

While Byron famously has difficulty in establishing Harold as an independent character, Byron's goal is to create a distance between character and narrator not unlike that between Wordsworth's Solitary and his narrator Poet (even if the Cockneys tended to collapse that distance). The difference can be seen through a concluding echo from *The Excursion*, where the narrator identifies himself with a Persian worshipper clearly based on Wordsworth's passage (4.667–71):

> Not vainly did the early Persian make
> His altar the high places, and the peak
> Of earth-o'ergazing mountains, and thus take
> A fit and unwall'ed temple, there to seek
> The Spirit, in whose honour shrines are weak,
> Uprear'd of human hands. Come, and compare
> Columns and idol-dwellings, Goth or Greek,
> With Nature's realms of worship, earth and air,
> Nor fix on fond abodes to circumscribe thy prayer?
>
> (91.851–59)

The narrator seeks in nature what he had earlier hoped to find in the act of creating Harold (stanzas 3–6), an escape from the self; for nature "stirs the feeling infinite, so felt / In solitude, where we are *least* alone; / A truth, which through our being then doth melt / And purifies from self" (90.-842–45). When we experience in nature some spirit greater than ourselves, we escape, if only momentarily, the bonds of self-consciousness or despondency that are part of the human problem addressed in *Childe Harold*. However, if the narrator finds nature a better place than temples to pursue this Spirit because it is less confining and circumscribed, then how can we be certain that nature itself is not finally a limit upon our aspirations? If the tension of the poem is between the soul's spark and the body's clay, then is not the turn to nature just another trap, another reduction of the tragically intertwined aspects of humanity? What the narrator needs, but cannot find, is a point at which spirit and flesh, mind and nature, are united, where he would find "*one* word, / And that one word were Lightning" (97.910–11). In a sense, what the narrator of *Childe Harold* wants is a moment like that given to the Chaldean or the Persian, a moment when – looking at nature – he is able to create the world freely as an embodiment of his own consciousness, when his word would be lightning. Byron's narrator does not believe he has found this creative word that is a thing, but importantly he does not thus despair: "I do believe, / Though I have found them not, that there may be / Words which are things, — hopes which will not deceive, / And virtues which are merciful" (114.1059–62). Qualified with skeptical Byronic hedging, these lines still set forth the same hope found in Shelley's *Laon and Cythna* that, despite personal and social calamities, one should continue to believe in the imagination's ability to connect consciousness with the world through "words which are things," in human goodness and the sympathy that binds us together, and in the pursuit of happiness in this world. Where Wordsworth's Solitary when confronted with such losses despairs and his comforters turn to otherworldly consolations, Byron's narrator keeps alive his hopes for transforming the world.

While the passages on nature in *Childe Harold III* interrogate the Wordsworthian contract between humanity and nature, the mind and the world, Byron, like Keats, places these issues within a thoroughly socialized and historicized context. The despair that is felt in the poem is time-specific, for it is the sense of loss that followed upon the defeat of Napoleon at Waterloo; the canto's answer to that despair is also historicized, for the poem recovers revolutionary history from the attacks of cultural conservatives such as Wordsworth. A major part of Byron's third canto is given over to defending the intellectual inheritance of the Enlightenment that he sees both lying behind the French Revolution and continuing to offer inspiration. Where Wordsworth uses Voltaire as a summary figure of all that is destructive in modern intellectual life and where Coleridge in the *Lay Sermons* of 1816 attacks the Enlightenment (mostly through the figure of Hume), Byron turns to Voltaire himself, to Gibbon, and particularly to Rousseau as modern intellectual giants. Voltaire is praised as the "Proteus" of human talent whose wit was used "Now to o'erthrow a fool, and now to shake a throne"(106.991, 994).[50]

Where Voltaire is seen as undermining political authority, Gibbon – the "lord of irony" – questioned the religious establishment, honing his learning into a "weapon with an edge severe, / Sapping a solemn creed with solemn sneer" (107.1000, 998–99).

Byron's treatment of Rousseau is the most interesting, for Byron sees him as a figure somewhere between the Poet in "Alastor" and Shelley's Rousseau in *The Triumph of Life*. The "apostle of affliction," Rousseau was a man of great passion, "But his love was not the love of living dame . . . But of ideal beauty" (77.726; 78.738, 740); like Keats's Endymion and Shelley's Poet, Byron's Rousseau rejects immediate human companionship as he dreams powerfully of a more abstract love. Warring with foes and friends, finding love and despair to be the same thing, Rousseau turns away from living women to create Julie. However, unlike Shelley's Poet, Rousseau's quest for an ideal does not end in the futile, inward-turning creation of a dream girl, for he imagines out of his love a political ideal:

> Those oracles which set the world in flame,
> Nor ceased to burn till kingdoms were no more:
> Did he not this for France? which lay before
> Bowed to the inborn tyranny of years?
> Broken and trembling to the yoke she bore,
> Till by voice of him and his compeers,
> Roused up to too much wrath, which follows o'ergrown fears?
>
> (81.763–69)

Rousseau is an idealist who is saved from visionary isolation by the fact that others turn his words into things.

Byron, in discussing the French Revolution as growing out of the work of Rousseau and others, including presumably Voltaire, offers a defense of its violence close to Shelley's apologia in the preface to *Laon and Cythna*.[51] Byron sees the Revolution as justified, as it destroyed the "yoke" of "inborn tyranny," but he is concerned that in the "wreck of old opinions" the "good with ill they also overthrew" (82.771, 774). Like Shelley, Byron understands this destruction as the predictable response to years of oppression: "But they, / Who in oppression's darkness caved had dwelt, / They were not eagles, nourish'd with the day; / What marvel then, at times, if they mistook their prey?" (83.784–87). The violence of the Revolution is the natural outgrowth of the brutality of the old regime. The problem for Byron is that the Revolution, in destroying all institutions, ironically made it easier for the older oppressive ones to be rebuilt, for they left "but ruins, wherewith to rebuild / Upon the same foundation, and renew / Dungeons and thrones" (82.775–77). Still, he does not fall into despondency ("none need despair"; 84.394) over this defeat of revolutionary hopes: "But this will not endure, nor be endured! / Mankind have felt their strength, and made it felt" (83.779–80). The people have learned what they can do if they act collectively; next time, they will act not out of rage at past oppression but out of hopes for a better future.

The lesson of the fall of Napoleon and thus of revolutionary France is not that right triumphed over revolutionary evil; rather, it is that humanity is always divided against itself – half-deity and half-dust, in Manfred's words – and can never totally resolve the tension between infinite aspiration and earthbound achievement. Wordsworth's or Harold's struggle to unite the mind with nature is simply another version of this quest. The choice appears to be between utopia and despair – if the Revolution fails, we must lose faith in social man – but *Childe Harold III* argues that we should avoid both the extreme utopian idealism of Rousseau, the French Revolutionaries, and (at times) Napoleon and the cynical despair of those who offer only pietistic resignation and the restoration of Old Corruption.[52] What we must do, then, is to keep hope alive through a particular kind of Byronic discipline: as he closes the poem, the narrator admits that "to feel / We are not what we have been, and to deem / We are not what we should be, and to steel / The heart against itself," that to control "the tyrant spirit of our thought, / Is a stern task of soul"; but he asserts, "No matter, – it is taught" (III.1032–39). We must learn control and caution that will enable us to avoid despair by recognizing the tyrannical, the totalitarian drive of our thought as it demands a final answer. Where Wordsworth's Solitary despairs as he finds the Revolution a flawed political movement rather than an Apocalypse, where Shelley's Poet rejects life when living women cannot fulfill his fantasies of an ideal, the narrator of *Childe Harold III* learns not to abandon his quest: he will write even if he cannot find the Word. He will embrace the world even if he cannot find heaven on earth. And he will fight tyranny even if he cannot create utopia.

V

The Hunt circle took up the challenge of *The Excursion* at least in part because it struck them as powerfully moving verse that represented the vision of a "slave" to power, and thus it threatened their notion that poetry could serve a reformist or revolutionary cause. If *The Excursion* was the great poem of the day, as some felt and others feared, then what does this say about poetry? I have already partially addressed the problem in taking up the accusation of "apostasy" in the Introduction. Is it possible that poetry – in its engagement with tradition or in its pursuit of the extraordinary or in its apparent insistence upon ranking ("Is this as good as Shakespeare?") – necessarily reinforces convention, rank, hierarchy, power? Hazlitt, despondent over the state of poetry as the Lakers became the apparent spokespersons for the current regime, would pose this question to the other members of his group in his "Illustrations of the Times Newspaper" series, where he treats the contemporary culture wars, and in his famous *Examiner* review (December 15, 1816) of a production of *Coriolanus*, mentioned earlier.[53]

Hazlitt found in the Lakers' poetry a central case study for his concern with the uncertain connections between poetry and politics. Simply put, Hazlitt wants to believe, as he puts it in the second *Times* piece, that "[t]he spirit of poetry is in itself favourable to humanity and liberty" (*CWWH*, 7: 142). However, the performance of the Lakers tended to shake this belief, as Hazlitt adds "but, we suspect, not in times like these – not in the present reign." Elsewhere in these essays, Hazlitt seems convinced that poetry, far from being a liberating force, is a servant of established authority: "The language of poetry naturally falls in with the language of power" (5: 347). "The principle of poetry," which might appear levelling in Hazlitt's *Spirit of the Age* (1825) analysis of Wordsworth's verse as it grows out of the French Revolution to eradicate all distinctions in literature's subject matter, is here "a very anti-levelling principle. . . .. It has its altars and its victims, sacrifices, human sacrifices. Kings, priests, nobles, are its train-bearers; tyrants and slaves its executioners – 'Carnage is its daughter!' Poetry is right royal" (p. 348). Hazlitt argues that imagination, needing powerful images to seize upon, naturally turns in sympathy to the powerful. In a rebuke to the Wordsworthian project of seeking poetry in humble subjects, Hazlitt contends that poetry longs for exalted personages, lavish settings, extreme and particularly violent events.

The echo here of Wordsworth's "Thanksgiving Ode" is important, for it suggests that Hazlitt adopts his position on poetry because he feels a true poetry of humanity and liberty has been perverted by Wordsworth, along with Coleridge, Southey, and other former "Jacobins." The first piece (December 15, 1816) on *The Times*, entitled "ON MODERN APOSTATES" and tackling contemporary "literary prostitution or political apostasy" (*CWWH*, 7: 131), lumps Wordsworth, Coleridge, and Southey together with Dr. Stoddart, then the lead-writer of *The Times* and known in Hazlitt's essays and in Hone's satires as "Dr. Slop."[54] Hazlitt reminds these writers of earlier revolutionary sympathies not so much to

argue that they have truly changed their ideological stands – "*Once
a Jacobin and always a Jacobin*" (7: 135) is a motto Hazlitt will repeat[55]
– but to assert that Wordsworth and his friends have always placed the self
above either poetic or political sympathy; Hazlitt writes that the "secret of
the Jacobin poetry and the anti-jacobin politics" of Wordsworth are
linked:

> His lyrical poetry was a cant of humanity about the commonest people to
> level the great with the small; and his political poetry is a cant of loyalty to
> level Bonaparte with kings and hereditary imbecility. . ... [H]e sympathizes
> only with what can enter into no competition with him, with 'the bare earth
> and mountains bare, and grass in the green field.' He sees nothing but
> himself and the universe. . ... The Bourbons, and their processions of the
> Holy Ghost, give no disturbance to his vanity; and he therefore gives them
> none. (7: 144–45)

Echoing his own comments on *The Excursion* (he also used part of this
passage in "On Living Poets"), Hazlitt finds Wordsworth marked everywhere by the egotistical sublime, as the Laker exalts himself now by
selecting paltry poetic subjects, now by endorsing puny political "heroes."

Hazlitt links self-worship back to the glorification of power: "The love of
liberty is the love of others; the love of power is the love of ourselves. The
one is real; the other often but an empty dream" (7: 152). Here, I think,
Hazlitt offers us a way out of his equation of poetry and power. As was
perhaps already suggested by the *Coriolanus* review's theatricalization of
power, oppressive authority is mere show, a fiction, a delusion that "dazzles
the senses, haunts the imagination, confounds the understanding, and
tames the will, *by the vastness of its pretensions*" (7: 149; my emphasis). As
he puts it in treating poets and lawyers as key examples of toadying to
power, "Poetry, like the law, is a fiction" (p. 142). Humanity, which makes
countries along with couplets, grants the power it then worships; we
become the "toad-eating" worshippers of power only when we forget
that all despots reside within the human breast. According to Hazlitt,
writers should not follow the laureate Southey nor the Wordsworth of
the sonnet "November, 1813" ("Now that all hearts are glad, all faces
bright") but the poet/patriot Milton:

> *We* have no less respect for the memory of Milton as a patriot than as a poet.
> Whether he was a *true* patriot, we shall not enquire: he was at least
> a *consistent* one. . ... [H]e was not appointed Poet-Laureate to a Court
> which he had reviled and insulted; he accepted neither place nor pension;
> nor did he write paltry sonnets upon the "Royal Fortitude" of the House of
> Stuart, by which, however, they really lost something.[56]

The function of true poetry, written by true Jacobins, is to unveil the empty delusions of power and to remake the world through love and liberty.

Shelley seeks to create such true poetry, allied to liberty rather than power, in his direct revision of *The Excursion, Laon and Cythna*, written, as Michael Scrivener has argued, as a response to Hazlitt's attack upon literature.[57] It is also part of the collective response to Wordsworth undertaken by the Hunt circle, and it was conceived, as Marilyn Butler has suggested, as an almost collaborative project with Peacock.[58] The link to Peacock is crucial, for his "Ahrimanes" came to embrace the same kind of despair that is at times voiced in Hazlitt's essays.[59] Shelley works to respond not only to Wordsworth but also to those of his circle who would look on Wordsworth's poetic works and despair.

Shelley's and Peacock's poems open in a similar way, with a figure standing on a shore, where a visionary woman tells him of the struggle between freedom and oppression, good and evil. Peacock's central character Darassah himself describes the loss of an idyllic pastoral world, similar to that evoked in *Endymion*. The "Araxian isle" has undergone a sad change, one figured as an explicitly economic one: a golden age – when "spontaneous nature fruits and flowers, / By toil unwrought, with partial bounty dealt" – is destroyed when "one, more daring than the rest, began / To fell the grove, and point the massy pile; / And raised the circling fence, with evil wile, / And to his brethren said: These bounds are mine: / And did with living victims first defile / The verdant turf of Oromazes' shrine" (IX – X). In other words, this Urizenic fall came about from the advent of enclosure, the creation of private property, and the introduction of human sacrifice. The result, of course, is the arrival of inequality and oppression: "common good and common right were made / The fraudful tenure of a powerful few: / The many murmured, trembled, and obeyed. / Then peace and freedom fled the sylvan shade" (XI). While Peacock frames his tale in terms of the struggle between the Zoroastrian Oromazes and Ahrimanes, his portrait of oppression by kings and priests reflects the ideological struggles of the era of the French Revolution.

Darassah learns the world is ruled by Ahrimanes, a precursor of Shelley's Jupiter in that he is a summary figure of all that is wrong in Peacock's own world. Through Ahrimanes, Peacock enacts an inversion of Wordsworth's handling of mythology – of course, including Persian mythology – in *The Excursion*.[60] Where Wordsworth sees all mythology as a flawed attempt to come to terms with the Christian God, Peacock sees all religion as a worship of the figure of evil and oppression, Ahrimanes: "Seeva or Allah – Jove or Mars – they cry: / 'Tis Ahrimanes still that wields the rod; / To him all nature bends, and trembles at his nod" (XXV). All religions are one here, but they are unified by their oppressiveness. Shelley makes a similar point by subjecting Christianity to the same kind of analysis Wordsworth used in accounting for the birth of mythology out of the interrogation of nature, suggesting that Christianity, like the other religious systems Wordsworth describes, is the creation of man's response to the world:

> What is that God? Some moon-struck sophist stood
> Watching the shade from his own soul upthrown
> Fill Heaven and darken Earth, and in such mood
> The Form he saw and worshipped was his own,
> His likeness in the world's vast mirror shewn;
> And 'twere an innocent dream, but that a faith
> Nursed by fear's dew of poison, grows thereon,
> And that men say, God has appointed Death
> On all who scorn his will to wreak immortal wrath.
>
> (*Laon and Cythna*, 8.6.46–54)

As in Hunt's sonnet "To Percy Shelley on the Degrading Notions of Deity," we create God out of our own fears as, in Hunt's words, we "seat a phantom, swelled into grim size / Out of their own passions and bigotries, / And then, for fear, proclaim it meek and sage!" (*SWLH*, 5: 6–8). The imaginative response to nature Wordsworth found in paganism is matched by Hunt's and Shelley's sense that Christianity is a projection of our fears and desires.

In the longer version of "Ahrimanes," Peacock offers through Darassah the tale of an innocent who forgets his love and is corrupted by Ahrimanes, ultimately becoming his sultan, his "viceregent on earth" (p. 286) – in other words, he becomes an apostate to Oromazes. Although Shelley shares with Peacock his analysis of what ails the world and follows his friend in many details, he imagines his hero and heroine remaining true to one another and to their fight for freedom.

Shelley's "Preface" to *Laon and Cythna* seems to invoke Wordsworth as an example of those who first embraced the French Revolution only to despair at its faltering course. Shelley hopes that he lives at a moment beyond Wordsworth's despondency: "Methinks, those who now live have survived an age of despair" (p. 241). As Scrivener reminds us, one reason Shelley could argue for continued revolutionary hope was that he wrote at a time of new potentially revolutionary activity – at Spa Fields, in Pentrich, during the march of the Blanketeers.[61] Like Byron, Shelley seeks to explain the violence of the Revolution as the understandable excess of those who find themselves suddenly in power after having been "dupes and slaves for centuries": "That their conduct could not have been marked by any other characters than ferocity and thoughtlessness, is the historical fact from which liberty derives all its recommendations, and falsehood the worst features of its deformity" (pp. 240–41). He, of course, hopes that reform in England can take another course. Where Wordsworth looked upon the violence of the Revolution and despaired of liberty, where Peacock in "Ahrimanes" looked at the power of those who oppose liberty and despaired of victory, and where Hazlitt looked at Wordsworth's desertion of the revolutionary cause and despaired of literature's ability to escape the allure of power, Shelley seeks to write poetry that speaks truth to power, that reminds us that violence is to be blamed on the oppressor not the oppressed and that poetry preserves hope even in the face of defeat. Opposing the hopeless embrace of the Old Corruption of Church and State, Shelley, in Hunt's words in his review of the poem, offers in *Laon and Cythna* "philosophy, pleasure and justice" (*The Examiner* March 1, 1818: 140; *SWLH*, 2: 159).

Where Wordsworth imagines a Solitary disgusted with the failure of the Revolution and Peacock depicts an advocate of liberty seduced to the side of the oppressor, Shelley provides a character repeatedly propelled into solitude who constantly returns to social engagement. This pattern is already established in the first canto, where it is the narrator who experiences despondency over the Revolution's failure:

> When the last hope of trampled France had failed
> Like a brief dream of unremaining glory,
> From visions of despair I rose, and scaled
> The peak of an aerial promontory. (1.1.1–4)

There the narrator witnesses a battle between an eagle and a snake and is then confronted by a "Woman, beautiful as morning . . . like Love by Hope left desolate" (1.16.136, 144). She admonishes him for his despondency: "To grieve is wise, but the despair / Was weak and vain which led thee here from sleep" (1.21.185–86). She promises to relieve this despair if he will travel with her and the defeated Serpent. During their journey, she offers a history of the struggle between freedom and oppression, between the Serpent and the Eagle, which recalls the similar speech in "Ahrimanes." However, Shelley's version offers a less certain account, as "Much must remain unthought, and more untold" (1.25.218). Where Peacock depicts a struggle between Good and Evil, Shelley merely tells us that there were "Twin Genii, equal Gods" (1.25.224). The Fall occurs when another solitary, "The earliest dweller of the world alone" (1.26.226), witnesses a struggle between these two powers: "A blood red Comet and the Morning Star / Mingling their beams in combat – as he stood / All thoughts within his mind waged mutual war, / In dreadful sympathy – when to the flood / That fair Star fell, he turned and shed his brother's blood" (1.26. 230–34). "Thus evil triumphed" (1.27.235): not as a result of the battle between the two powers, or even because the fair Star fell, but because the solitary, despairing over the Star's defeat, adopted violence as his response. His action, embracing evil's tactics in the defense of good, allows evil to consolidate its power, for evil can now cast the Star as the instigator of violence and corruption, as the Serpent. What we have here is an allegorical representation of the British response to the French Revolution, which is later invoked directly in the Woman's story (see stanzas 39–45): sympathizers with the Revolution watched the great struggle between the principles of freedom and oppression; as the ideals of the Revolution were progressively betrayed, they despaired of them and found violence – the violence of the Terror, even the violence of Napoleon – as the only recourse; and this embrace of violence as a reasonable revolutionary tactic enabled the forces of oppression to demonize the defenders of freedom and to shore up the institutional supports of tyranny – the monarchy and the church – as the only checks upon this "evil."

What the narrator and his audience have to learn – what sympathizers with the Revolution must learn – is not to despair ("despair not" [1.58.522] is the injunction given as we begin to hear the tale of Laon and Cythna) over the defeat of revolutionary hopes nor to turn to the violence that has been used to defeat them. The problem is that we have confronted these defeats in solitude, like the "earliest dweller" standing "alone"; when, filled with anger and despondency, we have turned outward, our response to others has been violence (he "shed his brother's blood"). *Laon and Cythna* insists that revolutionary hope is sustained in community, a communion grounded in love, particularly in erotic contact, the sexuality celebrated in *Endymion* and absent, in the Cockney's view, from *The Excursion*. When Laon begins his narrative in Canto Two, he delights in nature and finds in it solace from the oppression that dominates his society, but it is sympathy with human history – embodied in the ruins of a glorious past civilization he discovers – where he finds hope that "Such man has been, and such may yet become!" (2.12.100). Calling on the word "hope" four times in as many stanzas (13–16), Laon commits himself to remaking his world. Significantly, however, he realizes that he cannot nurture this hope and struggle for it alone; in the love of his sister, Cythna, he finds the support he needs to begin his struggle for freedom.

At the end of Canto Five, Laon has successfully led a nonviolent revolution and has been reunited with his beloved sister Cythna. Canto Six, however, brings the quick counterrevolution and the defeat of the forces of liberty. It is at this moment that one might expect despondency to set in. However, Laon and Cythna find in each other, and in the erotic bond they create, new grounds for hope. Shelley celebrates their union as both innocent and a consolation for what Wordsworth called the loss of faith in social man and Shelley calls the "overthrow / Of public hope." Shelley turns from political failure to the sexual bond that he sees lying beneath all social ties: "A power, a thirst, a knowledge, which below / All thoughts, like light beyond the atmosphere, / Clothing its clouds with grace, doth ever flow" (6.30.263–64, 266–68). Laon and Cythna discover that, when the loving bonds of the larger community are destroyed, one can still find consolation in the sexual ties that link individuals together. They turn from social engagement not to despondent solitude but to one another, recreating the ideal society they have lost in the "communion / Of interchanged vows," the "rite / Of faith most sweet and sacred" (6.39.343–45). Revealing to one another the power of erotic love, recreating the possibility of society by reaffirming the underlying drive that brings people together, Laon and Cythna are now able to confront the recent destruction and to talk "Of the late ruin, swift and horrible, / And how those seeds of hope might yet be sown, / Whose fruit is evil's mortal poison" (6.42.374–76). Even when Laon returns to the city for food and confronts the plague-stricken woman who reveals to him a demonic feast of dead babies, he is able to fight off despair because his love for Cythna gives him strength. In Canto Two, Laon has perhaps been led from love of nature to love of man; but when the love of man leads to failed revolution, he does not despair and turn to the love of God as the only consolation but instead finds in the love he bears for Cythna the promise and hope for a society remade. In this love lies the basis for a new society, for, as Shelley argues in the preface, "Love is celebrated every where as the sole law which should govern the moral world" (p. 247).

Even Shelley's admirers have been rather harsh with *Laon and Cythna/ The Revolt of Islam*, arguing that it failed to transform the public it sought to reach, that it in fact contains the admission that poetry cannot bring about revolution, that Shelley recognizes that if he did awaken revolution-ary ardor, he would only spark new violence.[62] Although it is certainly the case that neither Shelley nor any other poet brought revolution to romantic-era Europe, Shelley does not finally acquiesce to a Hazlittian equation of poetry and power or despair of literature's ability to do good. Shelley well knew that he did not write this poem for a mass audience: he wrote for the educated, liberal readers of journals such as *The Examiner* and of poets such as Wordsworth, and he feared that they were going to despair of both politics and poetry in the face of the failure of the Revolution and the "apostasy" of the Lakers. Just as, within his poem, despairing friends of liberty are presented with depictions of the survival of revolutionary hope, so does the poem itself, as we have seen, offer his audience a fiction of ongoing revolutionary struggle at a moment when reality offered an apparent victory for the forces of oppression.

But how does Shelley work to defend poetry? As Scrivener and Stephen Behrendt remind us,[63] Shelley offers an extension of the Wordsworthian experiments of *Lyrical Ballads*; Shelley contends that like Wordsworth's and Coleridge's book his poem "is an experiment on the temper of the public mind, as to how far a thirst for a happier condition of moral and political society survives, among the enlightened and refined, the tempests which have shaken the age in which we live" (p. 239). The point of the poem is not to inspire revolutionary action among the working classes but to prevent postrevolutionary despondency in the liberal intelligentsia. It is not a model for revolution but an act of poetic renovation. Shelley, like the early Wordsworth he believes now lost, wants to use poetry to enliven, to liberate the imagination, which Wordsworth, Shelley fears, would now bind to conventional and institutional authority. Shelley finds the antidote to despondency in imagination, for it is this power that enables us to envision the world as different and thus to hope: as he puts it in the "Preface," he has drawn on "the harmony of metrical language, the ethereal combinations of the fancy, the rapid and subtle transitions of human passion, all those elements which essentially compose a Poem, in the cause of a liberal and comprehensive morality: and in the view of kindling within the bosoms of my readers, a virtuous enthusiasm for those doctrines of liberty and justice" (p. 239). The extravagance of *Laon and Cythna* – its Eastern exoticism, its evocation of Zoroastrian thought, its use of incest as a sign of a love that shatters all social control, its wild plot – so at odds with Wordsworth's earlier poetic experiment mark Shelley's poem as an attempt to create an imaginative space open to experimentation that lies beyond not only the hackneyed forms criticized by Wordsworth but also Wordsworth's domestication or naturalization of the imagination as well. The very mode of these responses to Wordsworth – the fantastic pagan romances of *Endymion* and *Rhododaphne*, the Eastern quests of "Alastor" and *Laon and Cythna*, even the "romaunt" of *Childe Harold* – announce their distance from *The Excursion*.

This unbinding of the imagination is seen in what is perhaps the oddest, and certainly the most neglected,[64] of these responses to Wordsworth: Hunt's "The Nymphs," published in his *Foliage* volume of 1818 but undertaken as part of the group's response to *The Excursion*'s treatment of myth.[65] Opening with the celebration of the imagination that is able to leave behind "Bigotry's sick eye" and the "*false* philosophy" (*SWLH*, 5: 5, 6) Hunt found besetting the poetry of Wordsworth, "The Nymphs" celebrates the Cockneys' values, with its nympholepsy evoking both their delight in the pagan and their sense of the sensual, the sexual as the ground of the convivial and the communal, what Hunt here calls "social glee" (p. 8). We may remember Byron's travesty of Hunt's poem, but we should also recall Keats's interest in it ("Mr. H has got a great way into a Poem on the Nymphs and has said a number of beautiful things" [letter to C. C. Clarke, March 25, 1817; *KL*, 1: 126–27]) and Shelley's praise of it: "What a delightful poem the 'Nymphs' is! especially the second part. It is truly *poetical*, in the intense and emphatic sense of the word" (letter to Hunt, March 22, 1818, *SL*, 2: 2–3).[66] What Shelley admires about the poem is its free creativity – what he elsewhere calls its originality and intensity – particularly in the second part where Hunt creates his own myth in imagining his own class of nymphs, Nepheliads. As Hunt's sister-in-law Elizabeth Kent put it, "This poet was the first and has hitherto been the only mortal, who has been honoured with the sight of the Nepheliads in person."[67]

Hunt does not follow Wordsworth in analyzing Greek or other myths as a response to nature or take up the line of Shelley and Peacock who suggest that the Christian God is just such another myth; instead, Hunt engages in new mythmaking. Of course, this is exactly what has been denied about the poem, when even one of its admirers, Douglas Bush, criticizes it for being "more esthetic and sensuous ... than religious or mystical."[68] However, what Hunt is doing is creating a myth that refuses both religious allegory and mystical escape from life to embody sensuous experience as he envisions a flock of clouds commanded by beautiful nymphs who swoop down to offer him kisses. It is, as James Thompson notes, a poem in which "the pleasure principle dominates."[69] Hunt's poem is closest to works that resist ready allegorizing, such as Shelley's *Witch of Atlas* or Goethe's *Fairy Tale*, fallen, as Schlegel puts it, "from the heaven of fancy onto the dry earth."[70] Hunt's answer to Wordsworth's subordination of myth to Christian orthodoxy is to make a new myth that cannot be read into any orthodoxy.

It is, however and significantly, a myth dedicated to "the clear thrill of their ['glorious lovers'] hoped age of gold" (261, 263) – that is, another poem of hope and love addressed to an age of despondency. Hunt's poem suggests that one way to answer Hazlitt's concerns about the imagination is to identify the imagination utterly with freedom.

Hunt and his circle found much to admire in Wordsworth and his *Excursion*. They were inspired to rewrite the poem, to offer a series of Cockney Excursions that seek to retell its story so as to diagnose the period's dis-ease of despondency as a retreat from the social. The cure for despair was not natural supernaturalism but an eroticized sociability, and the medicine was not an epic binding of the imagination to the way things are but a series of romances reanimating their readers through the very extravagance and voluptuousness of their verses. As Hazlitt wrote in his review of *The Excursion*, we need not despair of the Revolution's failure. We still can have "the triumph of humanity and liberty" but not "till the many become as united as the *one*, till romantic generosity shall be as common as gross selfishness, till reason shall have acquired the obstinate blindness of prejudice, till the love of power and of change shall no longer goad man on to restless action, till passion and will, hope and fear, love and hatred, and the objects proper to excite them, that is, alternate good and evil, shall no longer sway the bosoms and businesses of men" (*CWWH*, 4: 110). These Cockney Excursions – by resocializing and resexualizing the human project, by reaffirming radical intellectual traditions, and by insisting that poetry can be a way to intellectual liberation – work to engender that romantic generosity, to create that unity, and thus to work toward the triumph of human freedom.

Coda: Laodamia Responds

> Wordsworth's genius is in no respect Bacchic: it is neither epic, nor dramatic, nor dithyrambic. He has deep thought and deep feeling, graceful imaginings, great pathos, and little passion. Withal, his Muse is as decorous as Pamela, much of a Vestal, and nothing of a Bacchant.
> Thomas Love Peacock, "The 'Flask' of Cratinus," 1857[71]

As we have seen, a key issue in *The Excursion* was the proper use and understanding of classical culture and mythology and, more broadly, the interrelations of human interactions with nature, mythopoesis, and religious revelation. We have read the younger poets reworking Wordsworth's particular formulations, and we can catch glimpses of what his response to them might have been in a number of places, with Eric Walker discussing Wordsworth responding to Keats's "Hymn to Pan" in several poems and Fulford finding Wordsworth in "The Haunted Tree" (published in the *River Duddon* volume in 1820) adapting Keats's language of "languorous sensuality" in order to reject it as indulging a possible violence toward women that must be "controlled by a self-restraining masculinity."[72] Wordsworth's most famous retort to Cockney classicism is Haydon's report, noted earlier, of the older poet's comment on Keats's stanzaic hymn to Pan from *Endymion* as a "Very pretty piece of Paganism."[73] I have been as guilty as anyone in seeing this as a narrow-minded, maybe even envious dismissal of a younger poet's revitalization of classical myth by an aging and increasingly conservative older writer. It would seem of a piece with Wordsworth's reported rejection of Canova's statue of Cupid and Psyche, exhibited in London in 1816, as "the dev-ils!" However, scholars such as Geoffrey Hartman, Peter Manning, and Judith Page offer a subtler account of Wordsworth's engagement with the classics that might help us understand how he wanted the literature of antiquity to be read against the work of what Marilyn Butler has defined as a pagan "Cult of the South."[74]

Wordsworth's turn to the classics – or, as Moorman argues, to literary culture more broadly (2: 274) – as a source of inspiration is found in the two poems for Dorothy addressed to "Lycoris" or the "Ode, 1814" (originally "Ode, Composed in January, 1816") from the "Thanksgiving Ode" volume, and it appears most fully in the more obviously classicizing "Laodamia" and "Dion." The first was written in the months after Napoleon's first abdication, the second shortly after Wordsworth completed the "Thanksgiving Ode" volume on Waterloo. While John Paul Pritchard has argued that part of Wordsworth's renewed interest in the classics came from his work in preparing his son John for University, which took the poet back to his own educational encounters with Greek and Roman literature,[75] he also sees Wordsworth's historical moment – the fall of Napoleon – shaping his response to Dion. Jane Worthington established the importance of the links between Wordsworth's readings in the classics and the French Revolutionary period more broadly.[76] Sharon Setzer has understood Wordsworth's reworking of Dion's story, from its place in *The Prelude* to "Dion," as a rethinking of revolutionary history after Napoleon.[77] Judith Page offers a fascinating analysis of "Laodamia" as, in part, Wordsworth's response to the return of Annette Vallon and Wordsworth's child with her into his life: their daughter was to be married and wanted Dorothy Wordsworth to attend, with her plans being interrupted by Napoleon's return. Page, along with these other scholars, illuminates the intense interconnections between Wordsworth's reading, his private life, and his public concerns. As Page puts it, "While Wordsworth's distrust of revolutionary violence and uncontrolled passion was well established by 1814, the poet was still troubled by the conflicts of passion and rebellion that entangled his public and private lives."[78] "Laodamia" and "Dion" take on those conflicts.

If Book IV of *The Excursion* suggested how nature could stimulate culture, "Laodamia" shows how culture might tame nature, or at least a female nature.[79] Wordsworth takes a stand against the erotic poetry of his younger contemporaries, urging his readers to turn from sexual desire to a restrained, rational, and chaste love – from eros to agape. As Christopher Wordsworth put it, the poem depicts the "subordination of what is sensual to what is spiritual, and the subjection of the human passions to the government of reason."[80] Laodamia is the wife of Protesilaus who, knowing the first Greek soldier to set foot at Troy must die, has sacrificed himself. She opens the poem begging the "infernal Gods" (4) to return "my slaughtered Lord" (2).[81] Hermes, "ever-smitten Hermes" in Keats's "Lamia" (*KPP*, 7) but here in his role as the messenger of the gods, leads her husband to her for "three hours' space" (23). The "impassion'd" (25) Laodamia tries to embrace her husband and invites him to the "well-known couch" so she can be "a second time thy bride!" (63–64). Her obvious desire is rebuked by all. Jove "frowned in heaven," the Parcae make Protesilaus seem more corpse-like (65–66), and he chastises his wife, proclaiming "virtue were not virtue if the joys / Of sense were able to return as fast / And surely as they vanish. – Earth destroys / Those raptures duly – Erebus disdains" (68–71). He orders her to "control / Rebellious passion" (73–74). As she recalls instances where the gods have restored life to lovers and argues that love is "mightier far" than military power and martial honor (86), he speaks of an "equable and pure" love experienced by spirits (97–98).[82] He depicts life as a battle between the desire she embraces and the virtue in doing one's duty that he espouses; while he has certainly longed for his life, he has overcome his "old frailties" of the flesh to win a better life hereafter (137). He criticizes her for being "strong in love" but "all too weak / In reason, in self-government too slow" (139–40). He counsels her to yearn "to ascend / Towards a higher object" than physical desire (145–46). Passion, he says, was given in excess to annul the self (149); sex is a "bondage" "opposed to love" (149–50). She does not learn his lesson, however, and when Hermes comes to take Protesilaus back to Elysium, she struggles to keep him for herself, dying as he leaves her. Although Wordsworth, who indicated he had more difficulty with this poem than any other of similar length (*FN*, p. 67), continually reworked the issue of Laodamia's guilt, to which I will turn next, he always ended the poem with an etiological myth involving trees growing from Protesilaus' tomb that wither as soon as they are high enough to view the walls of Troy, stating, "Yet tears to human suffering are due" (164). There is an odd way in which nature, not participating in the moral judgments of men and gods, is able to sympathize with Laodamia whether innocent or not.

Wordsworth worked over the passage on Laodamia's guilt several times. In the original version, she is seen "without crime" (158), though too passionate to be reasonable; in the afterlife she is allowed to "gather flowers / Of blissful quiet mid unfading bowers" (162–63). Later revisions, however, now find her "not without the crime / Of Lovers that in Reason's spite have loved," and she is "doomed to wander in a joyless clime / Apart from happy Ghosts that gather flowers / Of blissful quiet in Elysian bowers" (Ketcham, pp. 151n; 529). Her sexual rebellion against the moral order results in her punishment in the afterlife. While Wordsworth altered some lines upon the suggestions of Landor and added a punishment for Laodamia at the suggestion of his wife, a change revealed interestingly enough to Haydon in 1821,[83] it is also possible that these revisions respond to the odd turn to the classics in Keats's "Isabella; or The Pot of Basil,"[84] where, after Isabella and Lorenzo have consummated their desires in secret, the narrator asks, "Were they unhappy then?" (*KPP*, 89). The answer is "It cannot be," that love, even unlawful love brings pleasures that should be celebrated, "Except in such a page where Theseus' spouse / Over pathless waves towards him bows" (89, 95–96). The next stanza continues to assert that "the little sweet [of love] doth kill much bitterness; / Though Dido silent is in under-grove" (98–99). As I have suggested,[85] Keats appears to be bringing together echoes of Catullus's image of Ariadne abandoned by Theseus in the "Epithalamion of Peleus and Thetis," Virgil's account of Dido in the *Aeneid*, and Hunt's "Bacchus and Ariadne" to celebrate the erotic even if "illicit" or a "crime." Walker and Fulford have found Wordsworth responding to the eroticism of Keats's poetry in other works, so perhaps the hardening of the judgment levied on Laodamia also rebukes the younger poets' "overlusciousness," as Wordsworth later put it.[86]

Hunt, in his volume of classicizing poems including "Bacchus and Ariadne," makes more explicit his endorsement of love over war, as he had already done in his masque *A Descent of Liberty*, which, as we will see in the next chapter, was almost certainly known by Wordsworth: in Hunt's play, a soldier, presumed to be dead, reunites with his wife, unlike

Protesilaus and Laodamia, as Hunt finds peace a time not to celebrate sacrifice but liberty, art, and love. In his 1819 mythological poems, Hunt, rejecting the Jove who would figure as the villain in Shelley's *Prometheus Unbound*, selects Venus, Bacchus, and Eros as his presiding gods.[87] "Hero and Leander" seems to offer a response to the position of a Protesilaus, as the narrator turns from the lovemaking of his characters to chastise those who belittle sexuality: "foolish men still keep / Their vice-creating ways, and still are blindest / To what is happiest, loveliest, best and kindest" (153–55). The poem, of course, tells a story of an overpowering love that leads not to moderated passion but to both Hero and Leander sacrificing themselves for their mutual desire. In "Bacchus and Ariadne," the mortal who, like Protesilaus, leaves his love to pursue glory – here, Theseus who deserts Ariadne to "cut up nations limb by limb" (54) – is seen as a fool, while the god Bacchus, who takes Ariadne as his own, has the proper appreciation for the joys of passion. Again, in another poem in the same volume, "The Panther," Hunt tells the story of a wild cat lured into captivity by "spices and luxury" only to be liberated by Eros (52–56) in a standard Huntian celebration of love over what in *The Examiner* he decried as "money-getting." Hunt offers in these poems a celebration of sexuality that resonates through poems such as *Laon and Cythna* and *Endymion*, as we have seen, not to mention *Don Juan*. These alternative takes on the guilt or innocence of sexual desire suggest that, whatever his intentions, Wordsworth was, in altering Laodamia's fate, also making clear his opposition to the Hunt circle's celebration of an erotic passion he wants controlled, purified, even rebuked. Wordsworth and the Cockneys fight a generational struggle over what Lawrence Lipking has identified in the epic tradition as the requirement that heroes such as Aeneas or Theseus abandon women in order to put their energies into violent war, not sex.[88] Wordsworth's Protesilaus follows in their footsteps, while figures such as Hunt's Leander or Bacchus or Keats's Lorenzo do not.

If "Laodamia" enters into the debate over how sexy the classics actually were, Wordsworth's "Dion" takes up the issue of using ancient history to parse the events of the revolutionary era. "Dion," written in the spring of 1816 when Wordsworth was publishing his "Thanksgiving Ode" volume, appeared with the *River Duddon* sonnets. "Dion" draws, at times quite closely, on Plutarch's life of the Greek student of Plato who came to control Syracuse. In lines later discarded, Wordsworth opens with an image of a swan gliding across the lake at Locarno under a bright moon to suggest Dion's tutelage under Plato, "when the lunar beam / Of Plato's genius from its lofty sphere, / Fell round him in the grove of Academe"

(26–29). His own "natural grace / Of haughtiness without pretence" (21–22) is further developed by Plato's instruction so

> That he, not too elate
> With self-sufficing solitude,
> But with majestic lowliness endued,
> Might in the universal bosom reign . . .   (31–34)

Had he been content to rule as a philosopher king among universal Platonic forms he might have lived a happier life, but he is led by historical events – including his exile – to try to put his lessons into practice by entering into the political life of Sicily. Wordsworth's poem focuses upon the moment in 355 BCE when Dion returns in triumph to Syracuse, as the poet describes the parade of Dion and his soldiers into the city (in a passage that might be compared to the procession that opens Hunt's *Story of Rimini*, published shortly before Wordsworth wrote "Dion"). The people, thrilled with their liberation at Dion's hand, treat him "As if a very Deity he were!" (60).

Such exaltation invites a fall, and the next stanza immediately mourns the loss of Dion: seeing himself as a philosopher king, refusing to restore democracy, and feeling himself forced to murder Heraclides, his sometime ally but long-time foe, Dion is himself then assassinated by the Syracusans. As Wordsworth puts it, he ruled not through "the breath of popular applause, / But through dependence on the sacred laws / Framed in the schools where Wisdom dwelt retir'd" (66–68); further, bowing to evil counselors, he "Hath stained the robes of civil power with blood / Unjustly shed, though for the public good" (75). His guilt over this murder manifests in a figure of a ghostly woman trying to sweep the palace clean of his crimes; her presence also foretells his death by assassination. Wordsworth ends celebrating Dion's "magnanimity" (132) and "native greatness" (135) but sees his death as offering the following moral:

> "Him only pleasure leads, and peace attends;
> Him, only him, the shield of Jove defends,
> Whose means are fair and spotless as his ends."
>
>   (141–43)

This restatement of the notion that the ends do not justify the means may be just advice to living rulers, but none of this matters to Dion, who in dying has found his way to the "universal bosom" (34) where his "hopeless troubles, / . . . instantly dissolved" (137–38) and where he is "Releas'd from life and cares of princely state" (139).

There seems little doubt that Napoleon formed part of the inspiration for this poem whether, with Pritchard, we see a parallel between the exiled Syracusan tyrant who feels compelled to order the murder of the radical Heraclides and the exiled French emperor who had the Duke d'Enghien murdered (an incident brought back into the public eye in March 1816 when his body was disinterred and reburied, sparking a sonnet from Wordsworth included in the "Thanksgiving Ode" volume); or whether we see them as contrasting examples of the difficulties of ruling, as Ketcham suggests in a note; or, with Sharon Setzer, we see the final moralizing lines "as Wordsworth's own epitaph upon the French Revolution itself."[89] In the end, I think Dion must also be at fault because he is a Napoleonic usurper, whatever the crimes of his rivals, Dionysus II and Heraclides: as Setzer argues, the moment when Dion enters Syracuse to be considered a god "reinscribes the idolatry and blasphemy commonly associated with Bonaparte's coronation."[90] As we will see in the next chapter, Wordsworth did believe in waging a just war and was willing to justify the violence needed to overthrow Napoleon, but he wants to make it clear that he does not condone violence used to overthrow the established order with the aim of establishing a "perfect" society, whether one imagined by Plato or one put forward by the theorists of the French Revolution.

Together, "Laodamia" and "Dion" take up issues of personal and political passion, desire and violence – but it is important to see the role of an afterlife, even a pagan one, in the resolutions of these poems. In justifying "Laodamia" to Walter Savage Landor, who had attacked the poem in his imaginary conversation between Southey and Porson,[91] Wordsworth wrote in a letter of January 21, 1824:

> All religions owe their origin or acceptation to the wish of the human heart to supply in another state of existence the deficiencies of this, and to carry still nearer to perfection whatever we admire in our present condition; so that there must be many modes of expression, arising out of this coincidence, or rather identity of feeling, common to all Mythologies. (*WLLY*, 1: 244)

Wordsworth defends his turn to the classics and pagan religion as an imaginative way to think through the afterlife, as he had done in a quite different way in the "Immortality Ode." He goes on:

> This leads to a remark in your last, "that you are disgusted with all books that treat of religion." I am afraid it is a bad sign in me, that I have little relish for any other – even in poetry it is the imaginative only, viz., that which is

conversant [with], or turns upon infinity, that powerfully affects me, – perhaps I ought to explain: I mean to say that, unless in those passages where things are lost to each other, and limits vanish, and aspirations are raised, I read with something too much like indifference – but all great poets are in this view powerful Religionists.

Wordsworth clearly defines himself as a religious poet, but of a particular kind: he writes poetry – whether drawing on nature or the classics – to raise aspirations for a better life by creating moments when "things are lost to each other, and limits vanish." Imaginative power, as we know from the sixth book of the *Prelude*, arises "in such strength / Of usurpation, in such visitings / Of awful promise, when the light of sense / Goes out in flashes that have shewn to us / The invisible world" (532–36).[92] Liu has famously placed these lines on imagination's usurpation in the context of the campaigns of the usurper Napoleon,[93] which offers a powerful way to place "Dion"; and the imagination as an "unfather'd vapour" (527) – that teaches us that "our home / Is with infinitude" (538–39) – might make us think of Protesilaus appearing to Laodamia as an "unsubstantial air" (21) to preach that our true home lies in the afterlife. As in the letter to Landor, the key to all mythologies is that they hold out an afterlife over against this life.

This religious justification of the turn to the classics can be usefully explored through Geoffrey Hartman's consideration of Wordsworth's deployment of classical material. Hartman makes what might seem a startling claim: "I would guess that Keats and Shelley were less radical in their understanding of the classics than Wordsworth."[94] Hartman finds Wordsworth's return to the classics as an element in his poetry "not unlike reintegrating a childhood conceived as the heroic age of the psyche" (p. 182). He allows for the possibility of a kind of bookish inspiration for Wordsworth, similar to that found in Moorman and Manning; but for Hartman, "In Wordsworth's recollection of classical texts there is often something involuntary, a sympathy not agreed to, or painfully hedged about" (p. 183). Coming to the classics through Milton's use of them, Hartman's Wordsworth is recalled to "a more absolute beginning: a point of origin essentially unmediated, beyond the memory of experience . . . . This recession of experience to a boundary where memory fades into myth, or touches the hypostasis of a supernatural origin – as well as complete respect for that boundary – is what occupies the psyche of the poet."[95] If Wordsworth imagined humanity in its "youth" creating myth out of its encounter with nature, if he found in his own youthful "spots of time" moments when the psyche of the poet seems able to generate a humanistic myth out of individual experience, then what if instead it is the core content of the myth – some unmediated primal encounter with the supernatural – that generates memory and thus the self and culture? What if all human creativity resides in the divine breast? If "childhood, the Classics, and divinization" meet in some point,[96] then the historicizing, humanizing moves of the younger writers might strike Wordsworth as masking a more primal experience of the holy other, when imagination returns to its home in infinitude.

I take Hartman's judgment of Wordsworth's use of the classics as radical as arising from a sense that the engagement with the classics poses particular dangers not explored in "Pretty pieces of Paganism," which offer celebrations of the classical past as a zone of erotic freedom. Connell finds the final speech of the Pastor in *The Excursion* offering an "implicit rebuke" to even the Wanderer's "qualified endorsement of pagan myth in Book IV."[97] In another take on comparative religion, "Processions, Suggested by a Sabbath Morning in the Vale of Chamouny" from *Memorials of a Tour on the Continent, 1820*, Wordsworth, as Hartman and Manning have explored,[98] moves through various pagan religious festivals – rites in "Persepolis" (7), a train of "Priests and Damsels" (21) celebrating "Ammonian Jove" (21) in the "Libyan waste" (20), Roman triumphs and feasts – before arguing that they have all been replaced and "subdued" by "Christian pageantries" (37). There is a procession of processions ending in Christian worship. The crux of the poem is its final stanza:

> Trembling, I look upon the secret springs
> Of that licentious craving in the mind
> To act the God among eternal things,
> To bind, on apt suggestion, and unbind;
> And marvel not that antique Faith inclined
> To crowd the world with metamorphosis,
> Vouchsafed in pity or in wrath assigned:
> Such insolent temptations wouldst thou miss,
> Avoid these sights; nor brood o'er Fable's dark abyss!
>
> (64–72)

While Manning notes that this might "recall" Shelley's "Mont Blanc," it strikes me as directly addressing it – Shelley's "secret springs" of human thought become Wordsworth's "secret springs / Of that licentious craving in the mind / To act the God among eternal things" (and I will argue in Chapter 4 that Wordsworth has a fuller response to Shelley's poem in the *River Duddon* sonnets). Wordsworth stands against a poet such as Shelley, who, doubting everything except perhaps man's imaginative capacity, broods in "Mont Blanc" over "Fable's dark abyss" in the cave of the

Witch Poesy and seeks to "act the God" in giving meaning. Shelley falls into the same error as Laodamia, marked by a "licentious craving in the mind" to defy the gods, or as Dion who, as we have seen, is almost deified. They, like a Shelleyan, pursue a belief that they are above the strictures of faith.

In both "Laodamia" and "Dion," I believe we see a Christianized paganism/Platonism being evoked. Both poems are concerned with the nature of the afterlife and what one must do to find redemption through death, as Wordsworth suggested of "Laodamia" to Landor. Where Nietzsche, in "The History of an Error," can see Christianity as a "feminized" version of Plato's positing of a "true" world against the "false" world we inhabit, Wordsworth sees Plato and paganism more generally as offering intimations of Christianity's true sense of moral action – set against false sexual or political revolts – and its reward in the afterlife. This was already the argument of *The Excursion*, but in "Laodamia" and "Dion" Wordsworth explores mythic territory we might associate more with the younger romantics to make the same point. Wordsworth argued, in the Fenwick note to the classicizing "Ode to Lycoris," that one reason to turn to the classics is that the revival of classical learning we associate with the Renaissance was actually part of the Reformation: "Classical literature affected me by its own beauty. But the truths of scripture having been entrusted to the dead languages, and these fountains having been recently reopened at the Reformation, an importance & a sanctity were at that period attached to classical literature that extended, as is obvious in Milton's Lycidas for example, both to its spirit & form in a degree that can never be revived" (*FN*, pp. 121–22).[99] Perhaps the classics (rather than nature?) are God's second book, as in the poem, "A little onward," that sparked Hartman's thoughts, discussed earlier, and that merges Milton's Samson with Sophocles' Antigone and the "Fane of holy writ" with "classic Domes."[100] For Hartman, such a merger suggests that the classics might reach "a dubious and dangerous point" "beyond religious or temporal mediation."[101] I think it more likely that Wordsworth, as in the "Intimations Ode" with its reflection on a Platonic notion of preexistence or as in *The Excursion*, seeks in these classical poems to accomplish what, in the Fenwick note, he sees the great ode doing: he is not trying to "inculcate . . . a belief" but to draw upon ideas that can be "an element in our instincts of immortality" (*FN*, pp. 160–61). What he wants to establish is that there is something greater to which we owe a duty, a duty to repress untoward emotions and desires, a duty to find the correct means. Worthington[102] offers as a gloss on the meaning of "Dion" a sentence from Wordsworth's *Convention of Cintra*, and a slightly fuller quotation might offer some guidance here: "Our duty is – our aim ought to be – to employ the true means of liberty and virtue for the ends of liberty and virtue. In such policy, thoroughly understood, there is fitness and concord and rational subordination; it deserves a higher name – organization, health, and grandeur."[103] Perhaps playing off the revolutionary slogan that the free republic rules through virtue and, if not, terror,[104] Wordsworth wants to find a virtuous means to fight for liberty. This was one of the challenges facing him as he wrote about the violence at Waterloo. The liberated nation also seems to take on some sublime aspect – not just peace and health and "rational subordination" but "grandeur."

This turn to the classics was not, then, ideologically free, as it came to be associated with contemporary battles over poetry and politics. Z., attacking Keats, would, as we have already heard, proclaim Wordsworth not only the "purest" and "loftiest" but also "the most classical of living English poets" so that he can be contrasted with Hunt, "the meanest, the filthiest, and the most vulgar of Cockney poetasters" (3 [August 1818]: 520). While Z. does not here refer to the 1815 "Laodamia," other critics do refer to it in order to establish Wordsworth as a poet who can claim an allegiance to a classical tradition against the "simplified" rhetoric identified in the criticism of the day with the Lakers.[105] In 1820, *Blackwood's*, in taking up the *River Duddon* volume, praises "Dion" for being

> imbued intensely with the spirit of ancient grandeur . . . . It will remind those acquainted with his earlier works, of the *Laodamia,* and satisfy them that have seen that production, how absurdly the charge of "silly simplicity" has been brought against the general tenour either of the thought or the language of Mr Wordsworth. The truth is, that among all the English poets who have written since Milton, there is none, except Gray, who has ever caught the true inspiration of the Grecian Lyre with the same perfect dignity as the great poet of the Lakes. Talking of language merely – we remember nothing in the whole poetry of his contemporaries to be compared with the uniform and unlaboured stateliness of his march in the Laodamia, the "Sonnets to Liberty" and "Dion." (Blackwood's 7 [May 1820]: 208; Reiman, *Lake Poets*, 1: 102)

Similarly, Thomas Noon Talfourd, writing in the *New Monthly Magazine* in 1820, argues that Wordsworth has the "power to grasp the noblest of classic fictions. No one can read his Dion, his Laodamia, and the most majestic of his sonnets, without perceiving that he has power to endow the stateliest shapes of old mythology with new life, and to diffuse about them a new glory," with that glory being the "hints of immortal life" Wordsworth had pointed to in *The Excursion*, and these hopes being offered "with holy disdain of the worldly spirit of the time."[106] Wordsworth's classical poems are read as another salvo in the battle between the Lakers and the Cockneys.

That battle would intensify around Wordsworth's attempt to celebrate Waterloo and in what I will argue can be read as his response to Byron in *Peter Bell* and his answer to Shelley in the *River Duddon* sonnets. In each case, we must do justice to Wordsworth's attempts to wrest religious consolation from his imaginative experiences, but we will only see them clearly when we read him as writing against the young poets who were also busily rewriting him.

CHAPTER 2

Wordsworth's "Thanksgiving Ode"
An Engaged Poetics and the Horrors of War

There is fire, we would almost say an awful strain of piety which pervades the whole . . .

Review of Wordsworth's "Thanksgiving Ode," British Critic
(September 1816): 313

"But thy most dreaded instrument
In working out a pure intent,
Is man, arrayed for mutual slaughter,–
Yea, Carnage is thy daughter!"

What strange and revolting phraseology, to use the mildest term, is this! How utterly at variance with the language of truly Christian devotion. How unmeet an offering.

Review of Wordsworth's "Thanksgiving Ode," by
Josiah Condor, Eclectic Review (July 1816): 6–7

Wordsworth's major poem on Waterloo, his "Ode. The Morning of the Day Appointed for a General Thanksgiving, January 18, 1816," usually referred to as the "Thanksgiving Ode," has been reduced to an ideological bumper sticker. If we happen today to recall this quite complicated piece, where Wordsworth tries to negotiate the use of the ode to discuss difficult public subjects, we are less likely to remember the thrust of the poem than Wordsworth's younger contemporaries' pointed attacks upon its most infamous line, one addressed to God: "Yea, Carnage is thy daughter" (282).[1] Josiah Condor, quoted at the start of this chapter, objects to the phrase on religious terms, but the less devout were also appalled. Shelley, for example, in *Peter Bell the Third*, tells us that Peter/Wordsworth "wrote odes to the Devil; – / In one of which he meekly said: – 'May Carnage and Slaughter, / Thy niece and thy daughter, / May Rapine and Famine, / Thy gorge ever cramming, / Glut thee with living and dead!" (*SPP*, 634–40).[2] Shelley worries that Wordsworth celebrates a God no longer revealed in natural beauty but in the slaughter of the battlefield. Byron would echo the same line in the midst of his "War Cantos":

> "Carnage" (so Wordsworth tells you) "is God's daughter:"
> If *he* speak truth, she is Christ's sister, and
> Just now behaved as in the Holy Land.
>
> (8.9.70–72)[3]

Of course, Byron's entire account in this section of *Don Juan* of the Siege of Ismail can be read as his retort to triumphalist accounts of Waterloo and the poetic responses to the battle by Wordsworth and Southey.

Perhaps most tellingly, Hazlitt quotes Wordsworth's unfortunate line in his great essay on *Coriolanus* published in *The Examiner* (December 15, 1816), which I also took up in the previous two chapters. In the review, Hazlitt worries "that what men delight to read in books, they will put in practice in reality." This disturbs him because he finds that in verse we do not get a reasoned account of politics: "The history of mankind is a romance, a mask, a tragedy" (*CWWH*, 5: 350). He argues that poetry, as opposed to prose, tends to support an aristocratic, authoritarian view of life:

> The principle of poetry is a very anti-levelling principle. It aims at effect, it exists by contrast. It admits of no medium. It is everything by excess. ... Kings, priests, nobles, are its train-bearers; tyrants and slaves its execution-ers – "Carnage is its daughter!" Poetry is right royal. (5: 348)

In the midst of a dispute over how to read Waterloo, in the middle of the expanding struggle between the Cockneys and the Lakers, as Hunt announced a post-Laker gathering of "Young Poets" in the same month as Hazlitt's review,[4] Hazlitt wonders whether poetry itself betrays the writer into serving the state. As an "exaggerating and exclusive faculty" (p. 347), the imagination exalts the powerful to underwrite its aesthetic power. Perhaps a poet such as Wordsworth, when he turns to write of public affairs, must be a political turncoat. It may not just be Southey's or Wordsworth's govern-ment salary that makes them sound like hired spokesmen. Perhaps poetry is power's secret sharer. Perhaps we need not Wordsworth's poetry but Hazlitt's prose to guide us through public debates.

While we have heard these telling attacks without listening again to the ode itself, Wordsworth was not deaf to such concerns in writing his volume on the commemoration of Waterloo. We need to read these poems not simply through the parodic takes of other writers that have almost wholly blocked our view of them; rather, we must place his volume back in its context, in the months following Napoleon's defeat at Waterloo as Wordsworth offered his hymn of thanks amidst a wide range of cultural responses, from the newspapers to the theater to other odes. We must see Wordsworth trying to use poetry to enter the public debate about Waterloo, and we can hear him struggling to write beautiful verses about a violent, ugly event.[5] Philip Shaw has argued that Waterloo was experienced as a traumatic event the significance of which was "overdetermined or unassimilable": an "impossible Thing prior to its domestication as a symbol of national unanimity, of the foreclosure of the international movement for liberty and independence."[6] The scarring reality of Waterloo resisted aesthetic or ideological subordination. Wordsworth, in seeking to enter the public conversation on Waterloo and the wars with France in general, joined others in asking: Can one write an authentic ode to war? How does one debate national policy in poetry? More particularly, I think we better understand Wordsworth's poems if we see that they are written in part as a reply to Leigh Hunt's dramatization of Napoleon's first abdication, his *Descent of Liberty*, a masque or "mask," one of those poetic forms Hazlitt quizzed. Hunt's play and its prefatory ode were themselves written in response to Southey's first laureate ode, his *Carmen Triumphale*, and Hunt uses the ode, the mask, and newspaper prose to formulate his own mode of using literature to speak to public controversies. When we return Wordsworth's Waterloo poems to the context of their composition and publication, we will better understand the interest of what he was attempting in this largely reviled volume, and we will also better understand why it evoked such passionate antipathy. With the "Thanksgiving Ode" volume, we see that "late" Wordsworth was not a poet fleeing from politics into imaginative vision but instead a public intellectual attempting to bend and to bind his imagination to matters of national concern.

I

Wellington issued his official report on the Battle of Waterloo on June 19, 1815; it arrived in London on June 21 and was published as a *London Gazette Extraordinary* on June 22. The painter Benjamin Robert Haydon heard the news from a messenger for the Foreign Office on the night of the 21st, as he was leaving the house of John Scott, editor of the weekly *Champion*, to whom he returned to celebrate the news. Haydon wrote in his diary on June 25 of the impact of the *Gazette* on himself and another editor-friend:

> Read the Gazette again; I know it now actually by heart. Dined with Leigh Hunt. I give myself credit for not worrying him to Death at the news. He was quiet for some time, but knowing it must come bye & bye, so putting on an air of indifference, "Terrible Battle this, Haydon." "A glorious one, Hunt." "Oh, certainly." To it we went.[7]

This anecdote suggests some of the division within the response of the British intelligentsia to the news of Napoleon's defeat. On the one hand, Wordsworth and Southey danced around a bonfire on Skiddaw singing "God Save the King" and eating the standard British roast beef and plum pudding.[8] On the other hand, Hazlitt, who viewed Napoleon's loss as "the utter extinction of human liberty from the earth," was extremely distraught, with Thomas Noon Talfourd finding him "staggering under the blow of Waterloo ... as if he had sustained a personal wrong" and with Haydon describing him as "prostrated in mind and body, he walked about unwashed, unshaved, hardly sober by day, and always intoxicated by night, literally, without exaggeration, for weeks."[9]

The public response was, of course, celebratory if rather muted. On June 23, there were illuminations in London, which *The Times* of the 24th praised as "brilliant" but without "novelty"; "the names of WELLINGTON and BLUCHER shone side by side with magnificence of light," but "We noticed but few transparencies" (*The Times* [June 24, 1815]: 3). By June 26, *The Times* was calling for a national day of Thanksgiving to Almighty God, a fund for Waterloo widows and orphans, and a triumphal arch, made up of the cannon seized at Waterloo and surmounted by an equestrian statue of Wellington as the "Great Conqueror," perhaps at the entrance to Hyde Park (*The Times* [June 26, 1815]: 3). Already on June 29 there was a meeting of the Merchants, Bankers, and Traders of the City of London at the City of London tavern to propose a relief fund. The day of Thanksgiving would, of course, eventually occur on January 18, 1816. It would be 1846 before a statue of Wellington was placed on an arch, not made of cannon and at Green's Park, and by that time, the statue would raise a controversy.[10]

What is perhaps surprising is that the Allies' decisive victory did not prompt the kind of celebrations in London that followed Napoleon's abdication in 1814.[11] Those earlier celebrations were perhaps still too fresh in the public's mind; perhaps 1814's proclamation of "mission accomplished" was a bit of an embarrassment after the Hundred Days; or, more likely, the incredible death toll of Waterloo made such entertainments seem frivolous. Still, there were many sermons preached on Waterloo and particularly its widows and orphans, there were many poems published within a year of the battle – at least thirty-two, according to Simon Bainbridge, and perhaps a hundred or so if we include periodical publications[12] – and there were several Waterloo museums established, including the Waterloo Exhibition, featuring not only artifacts taken from the battlefield but also clothes worn by the emperor and empress, the Waterloo Rooms that displayed Napoleon's charger, and the Waterloo Museum opened by Mr. Palmer at Pall Mall, the advertisements for which focus on the fact that "good fires are kept."[13] There was also a panorama of the battle at Leicester Square, and at Bullock's museum an exhibit of Napoleon's war carriage that would inspire both Byron's carriage for his travels in Europe and an anonymous broadside, *The Coach that Nap ran From: An Epic Poem in Twelve Books* (London: Whittingham and Rowland, 1816). It is notable that the most frequent appearance of the word "Waterloo" in *The Times* during the months following the battle is in advertisements for packet boats taking tourists to Brussels and the battlefield.

The theater, that key cultural venue, acknowledged the battle in some small ways that can help us to understand how Wordsworth would write about Waterloo. On July 3, Astley's Royal Amphitheatre announced in *The Times* a new song, entitled "Waterloo; or Bonaparte Defeated" (*The Times* [July 3, 1815]: 3). An "ADDRESS, In honour of the unconquered Wellington, spoken by Mrs. EDWIN," written by Samuel Arnold and first performed on July 3 at Drury Lane, already raised concerns Wordsworth would share about the ability of the poet to handle such a momentous event:

> Oh! For that "Muse of Fire!" whose burning pen
> Records the God-like deeds of valiant men!
> Then might our humble, yet aspiring verse,
> Our matchless Hero's matchless deeds rehearse.[14]

On July 6, the King's Theatre presented an evening of martial music in celebration of the victory and to raise funds for the widows and orphans; as the advertisement in *The Times* states, the evening included "BEETHOVEN's celebrated Battle Piece," presumably *Wellington's Victory, or, the Battle of Vitoria* (Op. 91), and a new ballet cantata, called *Caesar's Triumph over the Gauls*, with clear historical parallels (*The Times* [July 6, 1815]: 2). Sadler's Wells announced for July 5 a new song by Charles Dibdin called "Waterloo or

Wellington Forever" and offered on August 14 "The Bellerophon, or Nappy napped"; again on October 23, the same theater featured a song performed by Mrs. Charles Dibdin called "The Wonder of 1815," which apparently celebrated the various sensations of the year, including, in the order of the advertisement: the fire-eating lady, presumably Madam Giradelli, who, among other tricks, spat out melted lead marked by her teeth; the Dutch dwarf, Simon Paap, who was seen by some 20,000 people during the year; the Irish Giant, an allusion to the famous Patrick O'Brien, but he had died in 1806, so presumably a reference to the so-called English Giant, James Toller, who sometimes appeared with Paap; the Indian jugglers made famous by Hazlitt; then Waterloo and Wellington; followed by the Maid and the Magpie, a reference to a French play adapted successfully for three different London theaters; and finally, Wilson, the pedestrian – that is, George Wilson, a noted athlete who drew huge crowds to watch him try to walk 1,000 miles at Blackheath in twenty days, with 5,000 pounds bet on his effort and with various attempts to sabotage him (*The Times* [October 23, 1815]: 3). Here, Waterloo appears as just one more item in the sensational news of the day.

Beyond these songs, one finds minor theatrical allusions to the years of war, as when a character refers to the battle of Marengo in *Bobinet the Bandit*, staged at Covent Garden in early December, 1815. We get a more direct account in an anonymous play entitled *The Duke's Coat; or, The Night After Waterloo* that was published but was blocked from performance by the Licenser of plays; apparently this "mere trifle," as the author terms it, derived from a French play, was censored because, the author speculates, "the Licenser may think the Battle of Waterloo too grave and tragical a subject for an Interlude."[15] Whatever the case, no tragedies on the war and Waterloo were forthcoming, but the censor did not prevent the Christmas pantomimes from offering direct representations of the battlefield. We might think of the harlequinades – which often opened with a story from a fairy tale or myth before moving to the traditional pantomimic struggle, staged by two presiding magical figures, between Harlequin and his love Columbine and their opponents including Pantaloon and Clown – as an odd site for reflections on Waterloo, but we also find images such as "The European Pantomime" (see Figure 2.1), where "Mr Boney" as Harlequin takes "a flying leap from the rocky islet of 'Elba'" to the consternation of Louis XVIII as Pantaloon; or we might recall Hazlitt writing of going to the Covent Garden pantomime that Christmas to see the great clown Grimaldi: "There was . . . an ugly report that Mr. Grimaldi was dead . . . . Here indeed he is, safe and sound, and as pleasant as ever. As without the gentleman at St Helena, there is an end of

The European Pantomime
Princeaple Caracters Harliquin Mr Boney Pantaleon Louis xviii Columbine Maria Loutza Clowns &c By Congress

Figure 2.1 Anon. [J. Marks pub.]. "The European Pantomime" (March, 1815?).
Hand-colored etching on paper, 25.8 x 35.5 cm.
© Trustees of the British Museum

politics in Europe; so without [Grimaldi] there must be an end of pantomimes in this country" (*Examiner* [December 31, 1815]). When the
Napoleonic wars are not seen as tragedy, the events of the day are found
descending to political pantomime.

The authors of these pantomimes had to tackle the same problems as the
poets: How does art manage to celebrate a battle while acknowledging the
horrible loss of life? How can one find beauty in the truth of terrible
violence? The more local question for pantomimes is: How does one dare
provide comic entertainments that still engage the most important and
sobering event of the times?

Charles Dibdin, who wrote the Sadler's Wells Waterloo songs, had
opened a pantomime in June at the same theater that, while premiering
prior to the announcement of the victory at Waterloo, clearly provided
a continuing opportunity for audiences to celebrate. It is difficult to
reconstruct much of the play from the extant script, *The Songs Etc. in the
Pantomime Called Harlequin Brilliant; or, The Clown's Capers. Now*

Performing at the Aquatic Theatre, Sadler's Wells (1815). It opens with enslaved workers in a diamond mine somewhere in Asia before the turn to the pantomime proper, where Harlequin Brilliant, backed by the Genius of Consistency, struggles against Pantaloon, supported by the Genius of Riches. The pantomime ranges through various places in Britain before moving to Brighton, where we are told: "Our bustle concluded, away one and all, / Where national Honour and Victory call" (Scene xiii).[16] A British Lieutenant, backed by a chorus, describes a ship, the Britannia Man of War, and by analogy the glories of England:

> How gallantly she bears her port,
>   The Ocean's pride and dread;
> The real Cap of liberty,
>   Adorns her glorious head.
> Her pride is Commerce to increase,
>   In War she is no starter;
> And may she anchor soon in Peace,
>   Her Cable Magna Charta.

Making use of the theater's water tank, the play concludes "On Real Water," with the launching of the ship, followed by the representation of a Naval Temple, with Neptune in his car, as Britannia rises from the waves to the tune of "Rule Britannia" (Scene xiv). Whatever the antics during the pantomimic scenes, featuring clown's capers, the play closes with a celebration of England's military, economic, and political strength.

Harlequin Brilliant, of course, does not depict the realities of war. The Christmas pantomimes are the only two 1815 plays I can find that directly represent the battlefield at Waterloo and thus take on the difficulties faced in creating more famous works of art, even if ephemeral, out of horrific violence. As I have argued elsewhere,[17] these seemingly minor plays are deeply engaged with everyday life – with fads, celebrities, famous sites, and, in these two plays, the recently ended war. The Covent Garden harlequinade *Harlequin and Fortunio; or The Treasures of China* (26 December 1815), like *Harlequin Brilliant,* opens in an Orientalizing mode, with the frame for the harlequinade proper taking place in China; the pantomime scenes bring us to England, first to Brighton, with the Regent's oriental royal pavilion, and then to London before concluding on the battlefield of Waterloo. Harlequin and Columbine are supported by Shing-Moo, the Peaceful Fairy, while their pantomime opponents are backed by Thun-Ton, "the Chinese God of War and Thunder." These supernatural figures agree to put the characters through their pantomimic paces until "on the

Plains of Waterloo, War shall join with Peace, to vex the world no more" (p. 6).[18] Thus, the play offers "An extensive View of the Plain of Waterloo, as it appeared after the Battle" (p. 17), where we find Thun-Ton "contemplating his ravages and devastations." Here, we do see a representation of war's violence, though the *Morning Post* (December 27, 1815) noted that "the absence of the killed and wounded . . . renders the picture incomplete." This sanitized image of war at a distance, to adopt Mary Favret's term,[19] provides a backdrop to Thun-Ton's argument that Waterloo is "Where War gave General Peace!" (p. 12), before the Peaceful Fairy transports the characters to "The Realms of Peace" where a chorus sings the "Song of Peace and Love" (p. 17), providing the kind of celebration found at the end of *Harlequin Brilliant* but largely missing from public events since the battle. Here, the violence cannot dim the brilliance of England's triumph that is seen as ushering in an era supposedly dedicated to peace.

The Drury Lane pantomime reflects the more somber view of the battle. *Harlequin and Fancy; or, The Poet's Last Shilling* was created by Thomas John Dibdin, brother of Charles Dibdin who had been including Waterloo and other contemporary references in his pieces at Sadler's Wells.[20] The pantomime takes up many of the same "wonders" as the brother's song, with George Wilson appearing in a scene with the clown, with multiple references to the rage for Maid and Magpie plays, and with an allusion to (and perhaps an actual appearance by) the Dutch Dwarf and English Giant. The frame of this harlequinade offers a kind of metatheatrical moment, where a poet, contemplating his last shilling, desires to write a tragedy but realizes the unlikelihood of that project bringing him abundant recompense. His shilling speaks to him in the language of the ghost of Hamlet's father, calling upon him to write a pantomime. The poet responds in kind through a parody of *Hamlet*: "To write and what to write, that is the question; / Whether 'tis nobler in the Bard to wield / The Bowl & Dagger of the tragic muse / Or to take arm against a host of Critics / And make a Pantomime" (scene 1). Aided by Fancy, who transforms the poet into Harlequin, and opposed by Satire, the poet as a pantomime character does not so much write as become the harlequinade.

As in the competing piece at Covent Garden, *Harlequin and Fancy* alludes to Waterloo. Referring first to London's touristic celebration of the victory, Dibdin provides a representation of Palmer's Waterloo exhibition, with the theater borrowing "Helmets, . . . Sabres, and Standards" from the "Proprietor of the Waterloo Museum in Pall Mall" (Scene xx). The pantomime also stages one of the celebratory moments from 1814, the kind of festivity absent after Waterloo, a masquerade in honor of Wellington that Watier's club, chaired by Beau Brummel, hosted at Burlington House, with as many as 1,700 people in attendance, including Lady Caroline Lamb and Byron. As always, it is difficult to reconstruct the action in the pantomime scenes Dibdin stages, but we do know that the masquerade involved a giant and a dwarf, perhaps Toller and Paap themselves, as well as an ottoman transformed into a gondola that Harlequin and Columbine use to escape their pursuers. We also know that the masqueraders engaged in a dance, and we know this in part because Byron and his friend Douglas Kinnaird, taking advantage of their positions as members of Drury Lane's governing committee, appeared one night on stage, and the poet later recalled "dancing amongst the figuranti."[21]

Moving to the battlefield, Dibdin recreates the "Triumph of the British Lion over the Eagle" at the "Farmhouse at Waterloo, call'd 'La Belle Alliance,'" the spot where Wellington and Blücher met to signal the end of the battle (Scene xxi). Pride in the British victory is certainly expressed, but where the Covent Garden play celebrates war as the means for securing lasting peace, the Drury Lane harlequinade insists upon the costs of war: we are shown Chelsea and Greenwich pensioners, representing the army's and navy's surviving casualties of war, and a "Waterloo Orphan," the object of all those sermons and fundraisers, who dances a "Military Hornpipe" outside the Waterloo Museum before being "relieved," presumably through charity (Scene 19). Dibdin offers images of sites associated with Waterloo, with the real circulating onto the stage just as Byron, who had been at the masquerade at Watier's, appeared at Drury Lane in its recreation of that famous party. This metatheatrical play with the real is perhaps not surprising when we see a playwright now echoing Shakespeare and now capitalizing on contemporary theatrical hits, such as the Maid and Magpie plays, or upon celebrities of the moment, whether they be the English Giant or Wilson the pedestrian. But Dibdin also seems to have wanted to draw attention to the difficulties in dramatizing monumental historical events such as Waterloo. Although he and his counterpart at Covent Garden were willing to stage the battlefield at Waterloo, Dibdin reminds his audience that the scene occurs in a theater in London, not in the theater of war. Harlequin and Columbine might dance across the field of Waterloo, Clown may perform his tricks amidst the ruins, but Dibdin wants us to remember the tragic reality outside the theater, including the reality of wounded soldiers and widows and orphans. Acknowledging through his poet's opening soliloquy that he is not up to writing a tragedy on the war, Dibdin uses the complex theatrical tools of the harlequinade to ask the question that Wordsworth, too, would take up: how can art best treat the violence and destruction of war?

II

These three long-forgotten pantomimes provide one cultural context for Wordsworth's volume on the Thanksgiving for Waterloo, as we glimpse the lay of the literary landscape Wordsworth would attempt to traverse, from simple celebrations of an unalloyed British victory, through a sense that military might and perhaps even war are necessary to create peace, to a deeper recognition of the loss that attends any triumph won through violence. But there is a more direct dramatic precursor for Wordsworth's poems: Leigh Hunt's *Descent of Liberty, A Mask* of 1815, which Hunt had sent to Wordsworth on May 28, 1815, in response to receiving Wordsworth's *Poems* of 1815. Wordsworth mentions in a letter to Haydon that Hunt's *Descent of Liberty* was a favorite with his wife and her sisters; a few months later, Wordsworth praises Hunt's "Talents" in a letter to R. P. Gillies when announcing the imminent publication of the "Thanksgiving Ode" volume.[22] The initial sonnets dealing with Waterloo that were published during February 1816 in the *Champion* and Hunt's *Examiner* were written between November 1815 and January 18, 1816, when the day of Thanksgiving which gave rise to Wordsworth's ode was celebrated; in other words, he was working on his Waterloo poems at exactly the time the women in his household (and presumably he too) were reading Hunt's *Descent*.

Written during the moment of relief and exhilaration following Napoleon's abdication on April 11, 1814, Hunt's "Ode for the Spring of 1814," which also served as a prefatory poem to the masque, was itself a response to Southey's laureate poem, *Carmen Triumphale* as John Strachan has noted,[23] and it was composed as Hunt was arguing in the *Examiner* against the laureateship in general and criticizing Southey's use of his position in particular. As Greg Kucich has shown, Hunt was concerned about the ways in which literature and politics intersect, about "the strong capacity of literature to collude with or fight against political oppression."[24] Taking up the same issues as Hazlitt did in his *Coriolanus* review, Hunt wants to find a way for poetry to serve liberty and peace instead of power and violence. He saw Southey's writings (and, of greater concern, perhaps Wordsworth's) as the products of a hireling singing the praises of a conservative government he once disdained. Hunt worked to create what Kucich calls an "insolent Cockney aesthetic that would transform poetry and the arts into vital weapons in the struggle against despotic authority" ("Headnote," *SWLH,* 1: 269–70). Hunt's rewriting of Southey, which would then be rewritten by Wordsworth, reveals all three of these poets worrying about the ways the ode, as a form, might address public issues.

On January 1, 1814, Longman, Hurst, Rees, Orme, and Brown published 500 copies of Southey's first laureate ode, *Carmen Triumphale.* Unlike annual poems by earlier laureates, which were relatively short in order to be performed at court and which were often released in periodicals, the ode was long enough to be printed in a quarto of thirty pages and was sold for three shillings.[25] This change in the poem's print status alone raised some hackles. As Southey's editors note, the poet was concerned about having to write the laureate poems, and he wanted to establish himself as a new kind of laureate in part by writing experimental verse, so that formally he links his new work with the innovative verse from the earliest part of his career even as he ideologically departs from his prior views.[26] He also recognized that his ode, which offers a fairly detailed summary of military victories, particularly in Spain and Portugal, might strike some as poor material for a poem. There is also his violent hatred of Napoleon and his disdain for the *Edinburgh Review* (on display in the notes). If Hazlitt saw poetry, as opposed to prose, serving the state, Southey is concerned that his state-sponsored poem might sound like prose. In letters, he referred to the ode as "an oration in verse, rather than a poem,"[27] and, in an attempt to moderate its partisan profile, he agreed with various people with whom he shared the manuscript, including Croker, to delete three final stanzas calling for the assassination of the French Emperor, even though he later published these anonymously in *The Courier* and then with his name attached in *The Times.* Southey's difficulty in finding both the form and content for these public poems would persist, with his *Vision of Judgment* later coming under attack not only for its high Tory argument but also for its experiment with hexameters. And he would, of course, then be answered in verse by Byron not only in his *Vision of Judgment* but also in the War Cantos in *Don Juan* that respond to the kind of laudatory recording of military history in the *Carmen Triumphale* and elsewhere.

Byron's later satiric assaults on Southey owe something to Hunt's earlier response that first came in his review of Southey's ode in *The Examiner* of January 16, 1814, which included a parody of the opening of Southey's ode. Hunt finds some good things in the poem, but he offers a stanza toward the end of the ode as "a specimen of the general poetry, as well as the loyalty, [which] must be very acceptable to those whom Mr. Southey and his friends were formerly in the habit of representing in all sorts of odious and disgusting lights, especially as unfeeling people and lovers of war":

> Open thy gates, O Hanover! Display
>   Thy loyal banners to the day;
> Receive thy old illustrious Line once more!
>   Beneath an Upstart's yoke oppress'd,
> Long has it been thy fortune to deplore
> That Line, whose fostering and paternal sway
>   So many an age thy grateful children blest
>   The yoke is broken now! – a mightier hand
> Has dash'd – in pieces dash'd, – the iron rod.
>   To meet her Princes, the deliver'd land
> Pours her rejoicing multitudes abroad;
> The happy bells from every town and tow'r
>   Roll their glad peals upon the joyful wind;
> And from all hearts and tongues, with one consent,
> The high thanksgiving strain to Heav'n is sent, –
>   Glory to God! Deliverance for mankind![28]

Hunt finds fault with the style here: "In short, his simplicity, as usual, not having strength enough of it's [sic] own, is mixed up with affectation, and composes a most mawkish entertainment" (*SWLH*, 1: 312).[29] It is interesting that Hunt focuses on this stanza, with the return of the British control over Hanover in 1813, perhaps making the point more pertinent to his audience than, say, the lines on Russia. He then parodies the first two stanzas of the poem in order to contest Southey's position as laureate, printing first each of Southey's verses and then his rewriting of them:

> In happy hour doth he receive
> The laurel, meed of famous bards of yore,
> Which Dryden and diviner *Spenser* wore, –
> In happy hour, – and well may he rejoice
>   Whose earliest task must be
> To raise the exultant hymn for victory,
> And join a nation's joy with harp and voice,
> Pouring the strain of triumph on the wind;
> Glory to God, his song, – Deliverance for mankind!
>   . . . .
>
>   In lucky hour doth he receive
> The laurel, meed of bowing bards of yore,
> Which Dryden and obscener Skelton wore, –

> In lucky hour, and well may he rejoice,
> > Whose yearly task must be
> Nothing at Court but what is right to see,
> And have, for nothing but fine words, a voice;
> Wearing bag-wigs and other princely raiment,
> Glory to Kings, his song: – a hundred pounds, his payment!
>
> > > (*SWLH*, 1: 312)

Commenting on this passage, Hunt explains that Spenser was not really a poet laureate, but he allows Dryden as a model for Southey not only as the first official poet laureate but also as someone "who changed his opinions more than once, and who valued himself on being favoured by Charles the Second." He adds Skelton in Spenser's place as the laureate to Henry VIII. He then takes on the second stanza. Southey wrote:

> Wake, lute and harp! My soul, take up the strain!
> > Glory to God! Deliverance for mankind!
> Joy, – for all nations, joy! But most for thee,
> > Who hast so nobly fill'd thy part assign'd,
> O England! O my glorious, native land!
> For thou in evil days didst stand!
> > Against leagued Europe all in arms array'd,
> > > Single and undismay'd,
> Thy hope in Heav'n and in thine own right hand.
> > Now are thy virtuous efforts overpaid,
> Thy generous counsels now their guerdon find, –
> Glory to God! Deliverance for mankind!

Hunt offers his own verses, asserting Southey's "may be better thus!":

> Come, pen and ink! My hand, take up the *notes!*
> Glory to Kings! A hundred pounds to Southey!
> Joy, – for all poets, joy! – who turn their coats:
> > But most for thee, the mouthiest of the mouthy;
> O Robert! O my glorious, natural Bob!
> For thou, before thou knew'st a job,
> > Much of man's OWN freedom didst parade,
> > > Making thy friends afraid,
> Thy hope in truth and in an honest fob.
> > Now are thy worst of verses overpaid,
> Thy bending back hath now official raiment, –
> Glory to Kings, thy song! A hundred pounds, thy payment!
>
> > > (*SWLH*, 1: 313)

With the diminutive "natural Bob" and the rhyming of mouthy with Southey, we can see how Byron drew on Hunt's attack in the "Dedication" to *Don Juan* and elsewhere in that satire, as Paul Magnuson has pointed out.[30] We already get a number of the jibes that will fill critiques of Southey, from the details of the laureateship, including its hundred-pound salary and its requirement to attend court in full dress once a year, to the contrast between Southey's earlier radical poetry and the verse he must write as laureate. The *Wat Tyler* affair looms in the near future.

Hunt offered a more serious response to Southey in his Spring ode on the abdication of Napoleon and then in his masque celebrating the peace. In his ode, Southey emphasizes military victories, as he claims "Force must be crushed by Force" (254). Since for Southey the struggle against Napoleon is a battle of good versus evil, he insists that peace can only be won through war and that any real peace must wait upon "Justice" and "Retribution" (252–53): Napoleon and France must be punished before there can be concord among the nations. Offering a counterview in his ode and mask, Hunt focuses on Liberty and Peace and sees the defeat of Napoleon coming as much from a political awakening, a casting off of mind-forged manacles, as from military action:

> The vision then is past,
>   That held the eyes of nations,
> Swept in his own careering blast,
>   That shook the earth's foundations!
>
> . . . .
>
> We look'd and saw the Wonder on his throne;
> We raised our eyes again, and lo, his place was gone!
>
> (1–4, 10–11)[31]

In *The Descent*, Napoleon is an Enchanter whose spells are easily undone by Liberty: he is a "vision" and a "Wonder" that awed everyone but can be easily set aside as a delusion. If Hazlitt worries that poetry serves power, Hunt demonstrates how power as theatrical show can be easily unmasked by the liberated poet. Rather than focusing on the martial might needed to defeat Napoleon, Hunt emphasizes in his ode the joys that peace brings the soldier, the statesman, the freeman, and the widow (45–55). Rather than following Southey in praising "the Wellesley" as the world's liberator, Hunt suggests that victory was actually brought by a collective understanding of "Experience, Truth, and Conquest of the Will" (21). As in Shelley's much more famous ode, spring is evoked as the time for transformation, when not just Napoleon but also the Allies' "Elder Corruption" (15) will fall before "Liberty! O breath / Of all that's true existence," as a freed captive sees "The green and laughing world ... / Water, and plains, and waving trees, / The skim of birds, and the blue-doming skies" (56–57, 63–66).

As I have argued elsewhere,[32] in *The Descent* Hunt makes the point that it is the people, not the monarchs, who have won the war against Napoleon. In the first scene, a group of shepherds hear on high intimations of the arrival of Liberty, who in the second scene easily defeats Napoleon, an Enchanter floating over a great city on a storm cloud of war. The third scene depicts a procession rejoicing in the victory, but rather than celebrating military heroics it focuses on the possibilities that peace may bring. Thus, while the poem praises the allied nations for the victory, they are instructed to serve Liberty: Prussia, for example, is told to attend to its people – "And acquaint their homes with me, / Triumphant Liberty" (3.274–75) – while Russia is commanded to free Poland (303–25). England, never conquered by the Enchanter Napoleon, is raised above the other nations, but it too is told to tend to Liberty at home now that it has liberated Europe (329–54). Rather than recounting a series of battles, as Southey does, Hunt next introduces Peace, followed by Music, Painting, and Poetry, as the arts serve freedom and amity. In turn, they are followed by a series of allegorical figures such as Experience and Education, Pleasure and Duty (stage directions, pp. 112–13). There is an interlude where the "Sable Genius" worries about the possible return of slavery under the Allies' Restoration (579–739), before a final procession contrasting a "Vision of False Glory," where everyone is enslaved to a Conqueror, to a "Vision of Real Glory," which suggests that victory comes through the work of the people, as armed peasants are joined by artists, "*venerable old men,*" and young couples (stage directions, p. 120). Art, Love, Peace, and above all Liberty are the order of the day. Hunt, in his newspaper parody, ode, and mask, sought a poetry that is not right royal but instead loyal to the people's aspirations. His Cockney literature seeks to grant to the common soldier, to the freeman and the yeoman, to the widow and the young lover a place in poetry and a power within history.

III

I will take this occasion of stating, that it may be agreeable to Mr Hunt to learn that his Mask has been read with great pleasure by my Wife and her Sisters under this Peaceful Roof.
                    Letter to Benjamin Robert Haydon, January 13, 1816;
                                                            WLML, 2: 273

As Wordsworth's reference to it in his letter to Haydon indicates, Hunt's *Descent* must have been on Wordsworth's mind as he composed his poems on Waterloo. Even though I am less concerned with direct allusions to Hunt's poem than I am with the debate into which Wordsworth enters with Hunt about the use of poetry in addressing a national military event, we can find echoes of Hunt's ode and mask in Wordsworth's verses. For example, the first sonnet, "Inscription for a National Monument in Commemoration of the Battle of Waterloo," celebrates the victory over Napoleon's "impious crew" (8), which might echo Milton's *Samson Agonistes* (891) in order to displace Hunt's thrice-repeated praise of the victors over "Conquest's merer crew" (3.268, 288, 310). The second of the sonnets, "Occasioned by the Same Battle," follows Hunt in imagining a bard seeing victory over Napoleon in terms of dispersing clouds – here the mist on the mountains: the appropriate poet for Wordsworth's Waterloo is one "to whom, in vision clear, / The aspiring heads of future things appear, / Like mountain-tops whence mists have rolled away" (ll. 4–6). Throughout the poems, Wordsworth uses images of rising suns and of changing seasons in ways that recall Hunt.

The poem that takes on Hunt most directly is the second of the collection's odes, "Ode, Composed in January 1816." Wordsworth's poet, giving way to Fancy who sits in a Huntian "airy bower" (3), has a vision that offers a "suburban" landscape worthy of the Cockneys, sometimes also thought of as a suburban school: "A landscape richer than the happiest skill / Of pencil ever clothed with light and shade; / An intermingled pomp of vale and hill, / Tower, town, and city – and suburban grove, / And stately forest where the wild deer rove" (10–14). This seems very much to be the landscape of Hunt's *Descent*, where the final triumphal scene takes place on "*A pleasure-ground in the suburbs of a great city laid out in a natural style with wood and turf, the spires and domes appearing over the trees toward the side, and the view opening to the western horizon in front*" (stage direction, p. 97). (The phrase "town and tow'r" also appears in a stanza of Southey's ode that Hunt quoted in his review.) Just as, in Hunt's masque, Liberty appears on a cloud after having dispersed the storm cloud of the Enchanter/Napoleon, so in Wordsworth's poem Saint George appears "in a clouded quarter of the sky, / Through such a portal as with cheerful eye / The traveller greets in time of threatened storm" (18–20). However, Saint George then stages a procession that seems to respond to that which closes Hunt's play: where Hunt celebrates peace, the arts, love, and everyday labor, St. George orders a military parade. Where Hunt's Liberty, having recognized the geniuses of the allied nations, welcomes, as we have seen, "*armed peasants crowned with laurel*" along with "*poets, painters, and musicians*" together with "*venerable old men*" and young lovers (stage direction, p. 120), Saint George calls upon Virgins and Matrons to crown with garlands the returning soldiers, the "Stern Defenders":

> And lo! with crimson banners proudly streaming,
> And upright weapons innocently gleaming,
> Along the surface of a spacious plain,
> Advance in order the redoubted bands,
> And there receive green chaplets from the hands
> Of a fair female train.
>
> (45–50)

And where in Hunt's masque the arts are freed to celebrate love and peace, in Wordsworth's ode art – seemingly confirming Hazlitt's concerns – should be used to create images celebrating victory at war. Since festivals, such as those in both Hunt's and Wordsworth's poems, are passing, Wordsworth calls upon "Sculpture" to forge "imperishable trophies" for this victory; the muses and Mnemosyne should fashion "never dying song" (106), "Chaunting for patriot heroes the reward" (105). He imagines inspired British poets singing of Waterloo so that "future empires" will hear this "bold report, transferred to every clime" (134–36). When we are told that subsequent generations will learn that the battle was won "By works of spirit high and passion pure!" (149), the ode seems to fulfill Wordsworth's desire in his "Advertisement" to celebrate the military, to promote "an assiduous cultivation of martial virtues," not to mention "manly sports among the peasantry." He proposes a standing army and "Institutions, in which, during a time of peace, a reasonable portion of the youth of the country may be instructed in military science" ("Advertisement," pp. 178–79). The entire volume can be read as a stern rebuke to Hunt's paean to peace, liberty, and the arts.

As this suggests, it is not poetic similarities but the poets' ideological differences that are telling. As Wordsworth's advertisement to his volume indicates, he wants to criticize writers such as Hunt who allow "the present distresses under which this kingdom labours" to "interpose a veil sufficiently thick to hide or even to obscure, the splendour of" the "great moral triumph" at Waterloo (p. 178). Wordsworth casts writers such as Hunt who, while criticizing Napoleon, refuse to embrace the Allies, who insist upon focusing on "present distresses" rather than glorious victories, as the ones now marked by despondency, by, in Wordsworth's words, a "morbid satisfaction" as they insist upon cataloguing the losses at Waterloo and upon pointing out what is still wrong with England.

Although our understanding of Wordsworth's volume has largely been determined by its place in the culture wars of the day, we need first to understand the terms upon which he wanted to enter the fray. Wordsworth's "Thanksgiving Ode" volume of 1816 thinks through the difficulty of writing a beautiful poem about a bloody battle, of having imagination, as he puts it in the ode, stoop to the depiction of warfare (163–66). It is not surprising that in a letter to Southey in June 1816 Wordsworth would worry about the form of his ode, wondering whether it is a hymn or whether it needs a stanzaic form; he shares his fellow Laker's apprehensions about writing an ode on a public subject.[33] I think this anxiety about what kind of poem is appropriate for this moment also helps explain the range of forms and styles in the volume, from sonnets to odes, from the visionary turns of "Ode, composed in January 1816," where, as we have seen, Saint George appears to the poet, or "Elegiac Verses, February 1816," where a "Spirit" performs a "mysterious rite" of "pure vision" (35–36), to the sonnets on autumnal nature ("November 1, 1815" and "September 1815"). Again, Wordsworth offers both directly occasional poems in the two sonnets on Napoleon's defeat in Russia or the disinterment of the Duke D'Enghien's body as well as the sweeping historical vision of the Ode, "Who rises on the banks of Seine," where he provides a revelation of France's development from lovely republic to the evil empire of Napoleon. While previously the sonnet had been the main mode for Wordsworth's poetry on the war with France and his dedication to "National Independence and Liberty," here he experiments with both form and mode.

The volume also returns almost obsessively to concerns about whether Wordsworth, the poet writing these poems, is the right poet to compose a poem on Waterloo. For example, the earliest written sonnet included is the "Inscription for a National Monument in Commemoration of the Battle of Waterloo," which imagines the monument called for by *The Times,* that was not built, in order to write an inscription for it, in which Wordsworth proclaims the glory of "death, becoming death" which is "dearer far" than life, as the ultimate sacrifice made by soldiers on the battlefield is justified because they "quelled that impious crew," the French (6–8). But, then, in the next poem in the sequence, "Occasioned by the Same Battle. February 1816," he wonders if there is a bard capable of writing such a poetic inscription that must address both a glorious success and tremendous loss of life, both "this victory sublime" and "the hideous rout," a task, the poem suggests, better left to a chorus of "blest Angels" (11–13). Even as he writes poems of thanksgiving, Wordsworth wonders what sort of poet could give appropriate thanks for such horrifying sublimity. It is thus not surprising that the volume contains the sonnet Wordsworth wrote to Haydon, where he proclaims "High is our calling, Friend!" (1), before worrying about how one can be both "sensitive" and "heroically fashioned" (5–6), how one can keep faith with the "lonely Muse" "While the whole world seems adverse to desert" (7–8), how one can continue to strive to create great art "when Nature sinks" (9). Here, too, belongs the poem to Filicaia, "February 1816," where Wordsworth, amidst writing on Waterloo, longs to be like the Italian poet celebrating more simply King Sobieski's victory during the siege of Vienna. The main ode itself has the poet, while writing a bardic response to the day of thanksgiving, asking for a bard "who to the murmurs of an earthly string / Of Britain's acts would sing" (67–68).

In taking up Wordsworth's "Ode. The Morning of the Day Appointed for a General Thanksgiving. *January* 18, 1816," we must recall, with Simon Bainbridge, that Wordsworth did not write a poem on Waterloo, as did, say, Southey in *The Poet's Pilgrimage to Waterloo* (1816), but on the day of Thanksgiving, and thus the poem is less about the battle itself than how we should interpret its results, how we should read Waterloo.[34] As *The Times* reported (January 19, 1816), January 18 had been "appointed for General Thanksgiving to Divine Providence for the re-establishment of Peace in Europe" with "a particular form of Prayer ... read in all the Churches throughout the Kingdom." In London, a military ceremony – the depositing of the French eagles taken on the field of Waterloo in the Royal Chapel at Whitehall – was joined with a religious one: as *The Times* put it, "The ceremony was conducted with perfect order; and associated as it was with the duties of religious worship, the memory of the contest in which the trophies were won, and the sight of the brave veterans who had survived its carnage, the influence it produced was not of an ordinary nature, but rather approached to a sentiment of sublimity." This service, as perhaps is true of all military thanksgivings, finds God in the role of "God of Battles," as *The Times* would have it, who, in the words of the prayer, "hast again overthrown wicked and rebellious People, and restored to Europe, Peace, Order, and Security."[35] The ceremony conflates God's will with the victory of the nation. Wordsworth certainly links patriotism and providence in his poem, but he does so with a deep appreciation of the distance between God's sublimity and the carnage that marks humanity's actions in this fallen world.

Wordsworth's ode ranges from nature to God to an abstract account of the battle and the role of England, the allies, and France to the final giving of thanks appropriate to the day. The basic tropological move of the ode, which establishes the gap between providence and politics – or poetry, for that matter – is revealed in its first lines. The poem opens with a paean to the sun, rising "In naked splendour, clear from mist or haze, / Or cloud" (9–10) – free, that is, from the meteorological impediments that mark the opening of Hunt's mask. It is a "universal Source of pure delight," universal in that it shines on both the "insensible" and the "rude," on both the "haughty towers where monarchs dwell" and "the low threshold of the Peasant's cell" (1–7). In a move he uses throughout, Wordsworth follows this hyperbole with the opposite figure, litotes: "Not unrejoiced I see thee climb the sky" (8). This negation of a negation is found often in Wordsworth, but here it seems in particular to draw upon the etymological link of litotes to "simple" and its ethical tie to humility. As opposed to the grandiose language of the description of the sun, the position of the poet – "I see thee climb the sky" – is offered in single-syllable words; and he goes on to note that the sun's "naked splendour" dazzles "the vision that presumes to gaze" (9, 13). The same pattern is repeated at the close of the stanza where we learn that the sun with a "splendour" that "dost warm Earth's universal mould" was "*not unadored / By pious men of old*" (30–33; emphasis added). Despite our focus on the hyperbolic summoning of carnage later in the poem, a turn to a simple humility will define the heart of the ode.

While the initial passage opposes the glories of nature with the lowly position of man, we learn that the sun, and the nature it stands for, are, of course, not worthy of such natural piety. The physical world merely shadows forth darkly the true power of God, which is proclaimed as the rising sun is found to provide an appropriate start to this day of Thanksgiving:

> – Well does thine aspect usher in this Day;
> As aptly suits therewith that timid pace,
> Framed in subjection to the chains
> That bind thee to the path which God ordains
> > That thou shalt trace,
> Till, with the heavens and earth, thou pass away! (14–19)

The sun may be an apt emblem of this day of Thanksgiving dedicated to a key event in human history, but we must understand that both humanity and nature are framed by the truly universal history of God's order ending in the final judgment and the end of the natural world. Both the hyperbolic sun and the humble man are "Framed in subjection."

After this opening hymn to the sun, we get a turn to the observing poet, as we might expect, with Wimsatt or Abrams, in a Wordsworth poem. Here, the poet is redefined not as one who "presumes to gaze" (13) at the powerful sun but one whom "All nature seems to hear" (37). If the sun "aptly" shone on the world, the poet now uses "Apt language" (39). The poet offers a spontaneous song of thanksgiving, but again we learn that the local must be subsumed in the universal. While the sun "burns for Poets in the dawning East" (44), the true inspirational source of "this day's sacrifice" comes from a "holier altar" (52) built by God who "fixed immovably the frame / Of the round world" (47–48). God's order will outlive the "fickle skies" and the poets who half-perceive and half-create them (56).

This subordination of both humanity's actions and nature to divine providence sparks what may sound like an outraged response: "Have we not conquered?" (57). The answer will be "yes, but." What follows is a hyperbolic celebration of "Britain," defined as a "loyal band" that follows "their liege Lord, / Clear-sighted Honour" (60–61). Of the many nations, only Britain has stood "Firm as a rock" "To rouse the wicked from their giddy dream" of French liberty (77, 80). But his hyperbolic move is, again, followed by a turn to humility:

> And thus is missed the sole true glory
> That can belong to human story!
> At which *they* only shall arrive
> Who through the abyss of weakness dive:
> The very humblest are too proud of heart:
> And one brief day is rightly set apart
> To Him who lifteth up and layeth low;
> For that Almighty God to whom we owe,
> Say not that we have vanquished – but that we survive.   (83–91)

In discussing the poem in a letter to Southey (probably June 1816, *WLMY*, 2: 325), Wordsworth worried about this "passage which I most suspect of being misunderstood." As Ketcham points out, such abrupt shifts are common to the ode and in particular to Wordsworth's experiments with the form.[36] Garrett argues that readers "might be unprepared for the trap Wordsworth has set" here, as the poem demonstrates that "humility is necessary because the British triumph came only after a long and costly war."[37] The shift seems somewhat less unexpected if we have followed the rhetorical movement from hyperbole to litotes, but it is still striking that Wordsworth asks his readers to set aside their nationalist joy in victory for humility before God. We should be happy that, through God's grace, we survive. We may be hyperbolic in our praise of God or even the abstract nation, but we as individuals must remain humble.

In turning his attention to Britain's opponent, the poem shifts again. Even though the victors should not be too cocky, Wordsworth does not doubt the need to defeat "That Soul of Evil" "from Hell let loose," Napoleon: "How dreadful the dominion of the impure!" (95, 92). What follows is a powerful evocation of the destruction of war, with "desolated countries, towns on fire" (103). To sum up all he feels was threatened by the Napoleonic wars, Wordsworth uses an intriguing phrase that he later changed: "the old forest of civility / Is doomed to perish, to the last fair tree" (109–10). Although he later expanded the passage – "While the fair gardens of civility, / By ignorance defaced, / By violence laid waste, / Perish without reprieve for flower or tree!" (1836–1843; Ketcham, p. 183 n) – the "old forest of civility" provides a wonderfully condensed image of a Burkean appreciation of doxa, of all those unremembered acts of civility and citizenship that Wordsworth sees holding the nation together. The radical Napoleon will uproot every last one of these trees of tradition. This is a struggle of civilization against barbarism.

The next stanza addresses the "prostrate Lands" that have fallen before Napoleon, as their "crouching purpose" and "distracted will" could not oppose the "dark, deep plots of patient skill, / And the celerities of lawless force" that a godless Napoleon unleashed on Europe (124, 111, 115–16). While here Wordsworth, like Southey in his ode (22–32), seems to blame the European nations for having failed to stand up to Napoleon, the next stanza proclaims, "No more – the guilt is banished, / And with the Guilt the Shame is fled, / And with the Guilt and Shame the Woe hath vanished" (125–27). The following stanza (8) indicates that these nations have been redeemed by their final united assault upon Napoleon at Waterloo:

> Wide Europe heaved, impatient to be cast,
>> With *all* her living strength,
>> With *all* her armed powers,
>> Upon the offensive shores.   (150–53)

All of Europe has put forth its power, but it is Britain that leads: "Exalted office, worthily sustained!" (162).

In the midst of this passage, Wordsworth calls upon himself to speak out for the nation he loves, never to "forget thy prowess" (142). This call is answered in the ninth stanza where "Imagination, ne'er before content, / But aye ascending, restless in her pride, / From all that man's performance could present, / Stoops to that closing deed magnificent, / And with the embrace is satisfied" (163–67). Even though, as Wordsworth experienced in writing about crossing the Alps in *The Prelude*, the "awful Power" of the imagination is more likely to usurp human concerns and efforts to reveal "The invisible world," the infinitude that is our "heart and home" (Book Six, 592–605), here imagination is content to celebrate Wellington's victory at Waterloo. In another passage that worried Wordsworth because of "the luxuriance of the imagery and the language ... under so many metaphors,"[38] the news that *"Justice triumphs! Earth is freed!"* (178) echoes from the "sluggish North" to the Andes, from the "vast Pacific" to the deserts of Arabia (179–87). As the world celebrates Napoleon's defeat, even France shall "utter England's name with sadly-plausive voice" (204). As in his second ode, Wordsworth here imagines a global delight in England's triumph.

While the poet notes that the only true monument of thanksgiving is "the labour of the soul" (216), in order to commemorate this stunning victory he contemplates a "new temple" along the Thames (223), much as others urged a monument to Wellington, perhaps, as James Elmes suggested, a replica of the Temple of Theseus in Athens.[39] Wordsworth also calls for regular commemorative services to be held at Westminster Abbey. And if anyone doubt that God will approve of a "martial service" (261) conducted in the churches across the land, he reminds his readers that the "God of peace and love" (260) is also the "Tremendous God of battles" (288): "He guides the Pestilence," "His drought consumes," and "He puts the Earthquake on her still design"; "Yea, Carnage is thy daughter!" (262–82).[40] As we have seen, this final phrase struck writers such as Hazlitt and Shelley as a disturbing celebration of violence as an act of love, but I think that Wordsworth wishes to remind the thankful celebrants again that victory comes at a cost, that one cannot rejoice at the conclusion of war without remembering the violence that was the means to that end: we must recall the "desolated countries, towns on fire" (103).

Wordsworth then turns to the actual day of thanksgiving, the "appointed Day" (290), to imagine both a crowd which "press[es] devoutly down the aisle / Of some old minster's venerable pile" (323–24) and the "humbler ceremonies" (330) he and a few others will hold. Amidst the rejoicing, he again reminds his readers that their "pure delight" is "sprung from bleeding war" (305), that the moment of battle itself was "terrible" (295); the battle is a traumatic spot of time that perhaps nurtures, though its beauty is always underwritten by fear. It is relevant to note that England did not build the Waterloo monument to Wellington as a companion to the Trafalgar monument for Nelson. With Wordsworth, they may have simply felt the loss was too great for such untroubled patriotic triumphalism. In any event, he closes with what we might see as his proleptic version of Demogorgon's final speech in *Prometheus Unbound* where we are taught how to resist tyranny in the future. Imagining, not unlike Byron in Act 2, scene 3 of *Manfred*, that Napoleon – Byron's "Captive Usurper" – might return again as he did for the Hundred Days,[41] Wordsworth concludes by reminding his readers:

> Of warnings – from the unprecedented might,
> Which, in our time, the impious have disclosed;
> And of more arduous duties thence imposed
> Upon future advocates of right;
> > Of mysteries revealed,
> > And judgments unrepealed, –
> > Of earthly revolution,
> > And final retribution, –
> > To his omniscience will appear
> An offering not unworthy to find place,
> On this high DAY OF THANKS, before the Throne of Grace!
>
> 　　　　　　　　　　　　　　　　　　　　(344–54)

Closing with litotes – "not unworthy" and even "unrepealed" – Wordsworth hopes he has found the "spells by which to reassume / An empire o'er the disentangled Doom" (*Prometheus Unbound*, *SPP*, 4.567–68) of any future usurpation by the forces embodied in Napoleon.

Wordsworth's poem attempts to balance a triumphalist tone with tropes of humility. Read within the context of the entire volume, the poem appears as an attempt to balance thanksgiving for a victory with a recognition of that victory's cost; it is written in recognition of the challenge this subject poses to poetry. The volume as a whole seems to want to read the victory of Waterloo as a defeat of evil by God that is so profound, so overwhelming in both its glory and its gore, that it may be beyond the reach of poetry. The volume, called "rhetorical bombast" by Mary Moorman, with J. R. Watson finding that the "language is deliberately inflated,"[42] is, to my ear, more tentative than it might appear: worrying about the role of poetry and the poet in celebrating national might, Wordsworth offers – in recognizing the distance between God's eternal order and the mess of human history – a balance between rejoicing in victory and mourning the humbling loss necessary to earn that triumph.

IV

Wordsworth's volume and its central poem were not read this way by his contemporaries. The entire Waterloo volume upset even Wordsworth's close associates, such as Henry Crabb Robinson, the Clarksons, and Lamb.[43] There was, in fact, something of a media war around Waterloo, Wellington, and Wordsworth in the spring of 1816 between *The Champion*, whose editor John Scott had first celebrated the victory with Haydon, and *The Examiner*, whose editor Hunt had argued with Haydon over the battle.[44] The journals adopted quite different takes on the meaning of Waterloo, with *The Champion* opening the year calling for everyone, even supporters of Reform, to celebrate Wellington, and *The Examiner* offering, like that holiday season's Covent Garden pantomime, an Orientalist fantasy critical of the powers that be.[45] These tensions may have been exacerbated by a rivalry between Scott and Hunt, who both sought to gain the right to publish three sonnets from the Waterloo volume given by Wordsworth to Haydon. At first, Hunt won: Wordsworth's sonnet to Haydon and the sonnet bearing the title "*November* 1, 1815" appeared in both periodicals and "*September* 1815" only in *The Examiner*. Then, after the day of Thanksgiving, Wordsworth sent three additional sonnets directly to Scott: the two on the Waterloo monument and the sonnet to Filicaia already mentioned. Scott promptly published them, only to have Hunt reprint them in a "Political Examiner" article entitled "Heaven Made Party to Earthly Disputes – Mr. Wordsworth's Sonnets on Waterloo" (February 18, 1816).

Drawing on his piece attacking the Holy Alliance from the prior week, Hunt criticizes Wordsworth's willingness to support the Allied sovereigns and their ministers, objecting in particular to Wordsworth's appeals to God to validate his political positions. Hunt had, in the earlier piece, attacked the use of religion to bolster political and military arrangements. He now turns to the use of poetry for political ends, noting that "[p]oetry has often been made the direct vehicle of politics" from Virgil to Dante to Dryden to Tom Moore. He wonders now, given "the state of existing European intellect" and its opposition to the "Holy Alliance," whether anyone can write poetry in support of the monarchs' position (*SWLH*, 2: 56–57). He grants Wordsworth poetic power, dismissing Scott and Southey as bad poets as well as reprehensible political actors; but he goes on: "it would be monstrous, in our opinion, if a Poet like Mr WORDSWORTH . . . *could* accompany such men as the Allied Sovereigns and their Ministers in all their destitutions of faith and even common intellect" (*SWLH*, 2: 57). He contrasts Wordsworth's current support of kings – reminding Wordsworth of his earlier support of the Revolution – with Milton's consistent republican credentials, a tactic also used by Hazlitt in his contemporaneous critiques of the Lake School that took up the issue of apostasy discussed in my Introduction. Hunt understands that Wordsworth's volume, in turning from the battle to its remembrance, wants to argue that "the *results* of the Battle of Waterloo will be as fine as the thing itself" (*SWLH*, 2: 57); and he argues that the actual outcome is not a glorious peace but an unHoly Alliance of Russia, Prussia, and Austria determined to instill "superstitious fear," to deprive the people of their authority, and to support the notion of Divine Right (*The Examiner* [February 11, 1816]). Hunt fears Wordsworth's poems of Thanksgiving give aid and comfort to the Allied rulers in their promulgation of providentially sanctioned oppression.[46]

If Wordsworth's volume had echoed Hunt only in order to refute him, Hunt would offer through his weekly newspaper a counter-intertextual response to Wordsworth's sonnets when he published his own Filicaia poem in *The Examiner* on March 10 and then, anonymously, Byron's "On the Star of the 'Legion of Honour'" in the April 7, 1816 issue where the French tricolor is praised as the "Rainbow of the free," and "When thy bright promise fades away / Our life is but a load of clay" (33, 35–36).[47] Hunt used Byron throughout the months after Waterloo to counter nationalist fervor, from the publication of Byron's "Farewell to Napoleon" published in *The Examiner* on July 30, 1815, until Hunt's farewell at the noble poet's departure to Europe, when Hunt praises Byron's "scorn / Of those who trifle with an age free-born."[48] Hunt puts Byron forward as the anti-Wordsworth.

Byron would offer his own full response to Wordsworth's reading of Waterloo in *Childe Harold III*. Byron's *Childe Harold*, which is often seen as engaging with Wordsworth's ideas of nature and which, as we have seen in the previous chapter, opens and closes with allusions to the fourth book of *The Excursion* on "Despondency Corrected," also argues against Wordsworth's politics as set forth in the "Thanksgiving Ode" volume, to stand not with the Holy Alliance of rulers but with the people, "a proud, brotherly, and civic band, / All unbought champions in no princely cause / Of vice-entail'd Corruption; they no land / Doom'd to bewail the blasphemy of laws / Making kings' rights divine" (64.612–16).[49] Like Wordsworth, Byron is interested not only in Waterloo itself but in its significance, how it should be read aesthetically and ideologically. Like Wordsworth – and for that matter like Dibdin in his pantomime – Byron

self-consciously calls attention to his own role as poet. Byron frames the
third canto of *Childe Harold* with autobiography through an address to his
daughter (stanzas 1–2 and 115–18). While, like Wordsworth, he asks how
history – or nature, for that matter – can be converted into poetry, he also
engages more directly the relationship between his life and his work. Much
as the poet in Dibdin's pantomime becomes Harlequin, Byron the poet
becomes Childe Harold: through Harold he experiences what he would
represent:

> 'Tis to create, and in creating live
> A being more intense, that we endow
> With form our fancy, gaining as we give
> The life we imagine . . .   (6.46–49)

Harold, the "wandering outlaw of his own dark mind" (3.20), is also
a wandering avatar of Byron, who has "thought / Too long and darkly"
(7.55–56). The very slippage between the speaker and Harold constantly
reminds us that we are getting poetry, not some putative reality.

Byron rewrites the Wordsworthian reading of Waterloo, which sees
Napoleon's defeat as the close to and refutation of the revolutionary
period. He does this first in his famous lines on Waterloo and Napoleon
before Harold and he travel to various sites dedicated to liberty. Nowhere is
Byron's distance from the Lakers and their allies clearer than in their
treatment of Napoleon. Where Scott had written stanzas in praise of
Waterloo in Mrs. Gordon's album in Brussels, Byron would set down
the two stanzas of lament beginning "Stop! – for thy tread is on an Empire's
dust" (17.145) to be incorporated in *Childe Harold III*.[50] Where
Wordsworth and Southey might glory at the defeat of Napoleon in
Hazlitt's hated "Birth-day and Thanks-giving odes," Byron continues to
respond to the power of Napoleon even while accepting the necessity of his
defeat.

Coming to Waterloo, Harold looks for a monument, as Wordsworth
and others looked for a Waterloo monument in London. We are told that
this "first and last of fields" needs no memorialization beyond itself, since
the field, in returning to its state prior to the battle, speaks not to the
finality but the fleetingness of this "king-making Victory" (17.153). Byron,
much like Hunt and others in his circle, rejects the idea that Waterloo as
the defeat of Napoleon is also the overthrow of the ideals of the French
Revolution that lay behind him. If anything, the battle should be seen not
as a "combat to make *One* submit" but a struggle "to teach all kings true
sovereignty" (19.165–66): "Shall we, who struck the Lion down, shall we /

Pay the Wolf homage?" (169–70). Byron adopts the position of his intellectual allies that the battle was won by the people, by common soldiers,
not Wellington, and it is telling that the commander is not mentioned,
though the poem does lament the death of Frederick, Duke of Brunswick
(stanza 23), and mentions the Scots forces (stanza 26), though focusing as
much upon their earlier resistance to England as their role at Waterloo.
Byron also mentions his cousin, "gallant Howard," whose father he had
criticized in *English Bards and Scotch Reviewers*, though he is present in part
as a stand-in for the "thousands" who died in the battle (29.261, 256;
31.271).

The high point of the account of Waterloo is not a celebration of
Wellington but the portrait of Napoleon, described as "the greatest, nor
the worst of men," in Byron's own odd litotes. "[A]ntithetically mixed,"
Napoleon is "[c]onqueror and captive of the earth," able to "crush,
command, rebuild" an empire but unable to "govern ... [his] pettiest
passion" (36.316; 37.325; 38.338–39). He is beset by a "fire / And a motion
of the soul which will not dwell / In its own narrow being, but aspire /
Beyond the fitting medium of desire": "This makes the madmen who
have made men mad / By their contagion; Conquerors and Kings, /
Founders of sects and systems, to whom add / Sophists, Bards,
Statesmen" (42.371–74; 43.379–82). Compared to poets and philo-
sophers, Napoleon is presumably linked to Harold-like Byron, in his
Napoleonic coach, and, within the poem to Rousseau, that "apostle of
affliction" (77.726) who receives a parallel portrait in the latter half of the
poem. As discussed in the last chapter, Rousseau, Voltaire, and Gibbon
are all evoked as intellectual founders of revolutionary thought whose
ideas will not be extinguished by Napoleon's defeat at Waterloo. Byron/
Harold praises these monumental figures, and if there is no monument
at Waterloo for Harold to visit, if no Wellington monument yet stood in
London, Harold does visit one dedicated to a military hero of the early
revolution, Marceau, who died in the fourth year of the republic fighting
the Austrians (stanzas 56–57). Although Byron decries Waterloo, we hear
him praise the defense of freedom at Marathon and Morat, a key Swiss
battle for liberty: "While Waterloo with Cannae's carnage vies, / Morat
and Marathon twin names shall stand" (64.608–609). Byron seeks to
revivify belief in revolutionary ideals that conservatives claimed had been
finally killed at Waterloo. He works to keep alive the struggle for
freedom.

Where Wordsworth sees the message of Waterloo and the revolutionary
era as a whole as despondency over politics and humility before God,

Byron, as seen earlier, proclaims that "none need despair" (84.794) over what he sees as the temporary defeat of revolutionary hopes: "But this will not endure, nor be endured! / Mankind have felt their strength, and made it felt" (83.779–80). Where Wordsworth urges his readers after Waterloo to turn from dreams of perfecting "social man" toward humility before God, Byron urges a renewal of a struggle launched by the intellectual break-throughs of Voltaire, Gibbon, and Rousseau. Where Wordsworth humbles even himself as he wonders whether his poetry can capture the sublimity of the God of battles, Byron, urging resistance, will go on to proclaim himself in *Don Juan* the "grand Napoleon of the realms of rhyme" (11.55.440).

While I see Byron offering a strong defense of the possibility of reform and even revolution in Canto III, it is true that *Childe Harold* as a whole can also adopt a more divided, even pessimistic, view of history, as Martin Kelsall and Philip Shaw have shown; Kelsall in particular argues that Byron, a Whig in exile, ends up redefining seemingly perpetual opposition as despair at anything ever changing.[51] Byron's account of Waterloo may reflect a different divided vision than Wordsworth's does, but Byron still worries about the inevitable violence of history while arguing that the particular violence of the revolutionary period does not undermine radical ideals and while still hoping for a progressive politics. I see him as trying to rally resistance even in the face of despair. In addition, Byron's poem comes back to the difficulty of writing a poem on such matters. Before his return to his daughter to close Canto 3, Byron expresses his belief that "there may be / Words which are things," that one might, as he puts it earlier, find "*one word*, / And that one word were Lightning" (114.1060–61; 97.910–11).[52] Wordsworth also seems to want to transform words into things – or at least his poetry into a stone-engraved inscription on a monument to Waterloo. Beyond writing poems that are speech acts – offering a thanksgiving prayer, proclaiming, "Stop – for thy tread is on an Empire's dust" (17.145) – it is almost as if these poets want to escape figurative language into objects equal to memorializing the complex "thing itself," as Hunt called the battle. If Dibdin's pantomime deserves to be ranked alongside Wordsworth's and Byron's poetic reflections on Waterloo, it is because in the pantomime, with words abandoned, the things themselves – the actual helmets and sabers and standards brought from the battle to the theater – stand eloquently silent on stage, representing both the victory and the violence of Waterloo.

Taking up again the issue of finding words that might be things, Byron would return to Waterloo, Wellington, and the Wordsworth of the "Thanksgiving Ode" in the War Cantos, written, as Jerome McGann has argued, under Hunt's influence as Byron worked with Shelley and Hunt on *The Liberal*.[53] As Simon Bainbridge has shown,[54] Byron in Canto VIII, shortly after his line on Wordsworth's carnage quoted at the opening of this chapter, brings together Wellington and Wordsworth (and one could add Southey) as he alludes to pensioned poets and warriors:

> ... Glory's a great thing; –
> Think what it is to be in your old age
> Maintained at the expense of your good king:
>   A moderate pension shakes full many a sage,
> And heroes are made for bards to sing,
>   Which is still better; thus in verse to wage
> Your wars eternally, besides enjoying
> Half-pay for life, make mankind worth destroying.
>
> (8.14.105–12)

Part of Byron's argument throughout the War Cantos is that writers have, whether intentionally or not, provided cover for militarism by glossing over the horrors of war. His attack ranges from epic poets to war reporters, noting that it is "the blaze / Of conquest and its consequences, which / Make Epic poesy so rare and rich" (8.90.718–20) and doubting "if a man's name in a *bulletin* / May make up a *bullet in* his body" (7.21.162–63). His account of the battle is repeatedly interwoven with allusions to poetic and journalistic accounts of warfare, with repeated references to war bulletins and gazettes. In addressing Homer in Canto VII and distancing himself from the traditions of war poetry, Byron reiterates his assertion from Canto I that what separates him from his "epic brethren gone before" is that "this story's actually true" (1.202.1610, 1616):

> Oh, thou eternal Homer! I have now
>   To paint a siege, wherein more men were slain,
> With deadlier engines and a speedier blow,
>   Than in thy Greek gazette of that campaign;
> And yet, like all men else, I must allow,
>   To vie with thee would be about as vain
> As for a brook to cope with Ocean's flood;
> But still we Moderns equal you in blood;
>
> If not in poetry, at least in fact,
>   And fact is truth, the grand desideratum!
>
> (7.80–81.633–43)

Again, in Canto VIII, Byron asserts, "But then the fact's a fact – and 'tis the part / Of a true poet to escape from fiction / When'er he can" (8.86.681–83).

For Byron, poetry on public events can only avoid cant by remaining true to the violent facts of history, by getting to the "thing itself." For him, if Southey's *Carmen Triumphale* or Wordsworth's "Thanksgiving Ode" sound false, it is because they have failed to use poetry to see into the life of the things that make up history.

Most of us today prefer Byron's anti-militarism to Wordsworth's faithful nationalism, but we must be clear that Wordsworth's "Thanksgiving Ode" volume, whether we like it or not, is the work of an engaged poet, of a public intellectual striving to find the correct literary tools to speak to and for the nation. This is not imaginative retreat. It is not simply a form of "displacement" where "the actual human issues with which poetry is concerned are resituated in a variety of idealized localities."[55] Byron and Wordsworth may have had opposing views, but they agreed on the necessity of poetry speaking to the public and to contemporary events, and they both recognized the difficulty of versifying the violence of history. Still, in publishing this volume, with its rewriting of Hunt and its turn against liberal critics of the government, Wordsworth threw down a gauntlet to writers such as Hazlitt, Hunt, and Byron that they willingly took up. Primed by this publication, the Hunt circle would be ready for a fight when Wordsworth, in that complex year of 1819, issued *Peter Bell*, which – as we will see in the next chapter – could be read as a rebuke to the poet who, at the time, most worried Wordsworth: Byron.

CHAPTER 3

"This Potter-Don-Juan"
Peter Bell *in 1819*

"Do you call that [Byron's 'The Prisoner of Chillon'] beautiful?" says
Wordy. "Why, it's nonsense" . . . .. Muloch said there was a very deep
and very fine meaning in it. Wordsworth flew into a rage, and from
words they almost came to blows.

Edward Vaughan Kenealy, Memoirs (1908)¹

I

A poem's meaning does not rest solely with its author, nor is it fixed by its
moment of creation. When a poem enters into the world, no matter when
it was written, readers see it as speaking to both the present moment and
contemporary writers. Wordsworth's *Peter Bell* provides an important test
case of how the moment of publication can alter the understanding of
a poem.

Wordsworth began *Peter Bell* in 1798 as part of the work that would come
to be *Lyrical Ballads*. John Jordan has traced in his Cornell Wordsworth
edition the history of the composition and publication plans of *Peter Bell*,
reminding us of the moment in 1814 when Wordsworth, preparing to issue
The Excursion and to publish his collected poems, imagined a volume of
narrative poems including *The White Doe of Rylstone*, *Peter Bell*, and
Benjamin the Waggoner.² *Peter Bell*, from the perspective of its conception
and revision, belongs with Wordsworth's great work of the late 1790s, or
perhaps with that key moment of self-fashioning in 1815 when he sought to
establish himself as the poet – particularly the narrative poet – of the post-
French revolutionary period.³

However, I want to argue, following James Chandler, that the poem
became something quite different when it was published in 1819. In his
essential "'Wordsworth' After Waterloo," Chandler has argued that by 1819
Wordsworth's political persona had been completely fixed by attacks from
Hazlitt, Hunt, and others; by the *Wat Tyler* affair that had embarrassed

Southey; and by Wordsworth's electoral support of the Lowthers. Thus, Shelley in writing *Peter Bell the Third* read even this work of the young Wordsworth as the production of a "Renegade": as Chandler puts it, "The assault on *Peter Bell* in 1819 offers powerful evidence to suggest that the young Wordsworth of *Lyrical Ballads* was not being read the same way after Waterloo as he had been, say, four years before."[4] Both Byron and Shelley draw attention to the gap between the poem's composition and its publication. In the dedicatory verses to *The Witch of Atlas* (1820; published 1824), Shelley notes that "Wordsworth informs us he was nineteen years / Considering and retouching Peter Bell; / Watering his laurels with the killing tears / Of low, dull care, so that their roots to hell / Might pierce" (*SPP*, 4.25–29). Byron, wishing "Peter Bell / And he who wrote it were in hell / For writing nonsense for the Nonce," notes: "'It saw the light in Ninety-eight,'/ Sweet babe of one and twenty years!" He goes on to make the standard critique of Wordsworth as an apostate:

> He gives the perfect work to light!
> Will. Wordsworth – if I might advise,
> Content you with the praise you get
> From Sir George Beaumont, Baronet,
> And with your place in the Excise.[5]

Far from being a "leveling" poet from the radical 1790s, Wordsworth is now seen as a government lackey and a toady to the nobility.[6]

Yet it is not only a question of Byron or Shelley reading Wordsworth differently; Wordsworth himself changed the meaning of the poem by releasing it at the time he did. This is not to say that Wordsworth did not continually wish to assert the continuity of his corpus – in assembling his poetry in the collected 1815 edition, in imagining *The Excursion* within the never-finished *Recluse*, in placing poems from the "Thanksgiving Ode" volume with earlier "Sonnets Dedicated to Liberty" from *Poems in Two Volumes* to form "Poems Dedicated to National Independence and Liberty," and in Wordsworth's late acts of retrospection and re-collection I will take up in the Chapter 5. We might thus see his decision to print a poem from the days of *Lyrical Ballads* as an assertion of his belief in his earlier poetry despite years of attack, as Gill suggests of *The Waggoner*, originally written in 1806 and published after *Peter Bell* in 1819: "Dedicating the poem to Lamb, Wordsworth once again reminded critics that this was the work of an earlier period, 1806. Since the publication of *Poems, in Two Volumes* in 1807 had destroyed what reputation he had had, this was a coolly defiant gesture" (p. 332). Still, Wordsworth knew that he

published *Peter Bell* in a very different moment than that of its composition, and his "coolly defiant gesture" is not just a reach across time to prove
he is not an apostate or renegado but also a stand in the present against
what he sees as poetic and political dangers to demonstrate he speaks to
current concerns.

As Scrivener notes, "As political action, Wordsworth's *Peter Bell* is . . .
'ultra-legitimate.'"[7] *Peter Bell* appears now as a "Tale in Verse" rather than
a lyrical ballad, with a dedication to "Robert Southey, Esq. P. L." – which,
Hunt would explain, "does not stand for *Precious Looby* but *Poet Laureat*"
(*The Examiner* May 2, 1819; *SWLH*, 2: 189).[8] In this guise, the poem was,
I believe, a key attempt by Wordsworth to wrest the definition of narrative
poetry from Scott, Hunt, Moore, and particularly Byron; as we will see, it
contests the idea of poetry being put forth by the younger poets identified
with the Cockney School. I want to argue that the moment of *Peter Bell's*
publication significantly alters the meaning of the text. *Peter Bell* gets read,
and I think should be read, as interacting not with the poetry of the 1790s
or as taking a place within Wordsworth's recollection of his poetry around
1815 to shape his own corpus but as in dialogue with his immediate and
younger contemporaries, with Byron in particular visiting or haunting this
poem at its point of publication. *Peter Bell* needs to be read alongside
various poems of 1819 such as Hunt's *Hero and Leander and Bacchus and
Ariadne*, Shelley's *Rosalind and Helen*, and Byron's *Don Juan*, as well as
lesser-known poems such as *The Vestriad* sent to Wordsworth by its author
Hans Busk or *Ode to the Duke and Wellington and Other Poems* by Byron's
acquaintance Robert Charles Dallas. The younger writers certainly took
Peter Bell as a poem of the moment. The extent of the Hunt circle's attack
upon *Peter Bell*, involving Hunt's review of Wordsworth's tale, Reynolds's
"antenatal" poem (and Keats's review of it) along with his satiric sequel of
Benjamin the Waggoner (at the last minute, retitled simply as *The
Waggoner*), as well as Shelley and Byron's responses,[9] suggests that
Wordsworth's younger contemporaries felt the need to answer the poem,
that it was seen as challenging their poetry. The *British Critic* (2nd series, 9
[June 1819]: 592; Reiman, *Lake Poets*, 1: 169), for example, certainly read
Wordsworth's poem as a rebuke to contemporary poetry (I offer conjectures as to specific targets in brackets). Praising *Peter Bell*, the reviewer says
that Wordsworth's "writings are devoted to the cause of religion and
morality, and in that holy cause we scarcely know a more zealous, a more
fearless, or more eloquent advocate; it is quite refreshing to turn from the
tawdry voluptuousness of one contemporary poet [Hunt?], or the gloomy
misanthropy of another [Byron?]; the vague aspirations of this man

[Keats?], the cold scepticisim of that [Hazlitt? Peacock?], or the shocking blasphemy of a third [Shelley?], to the pure, manly single-minded morality of Wordsworth." Within this context, I read the figure of Peter Bell in 1819 as an anti-Byronic hero, as an attempt to redefine the villain-hero as simply a villain.

On a number of occasions, Wordsworth defines his status as a poet in contrast to that of Scott (whom he admires as a man) and particularly Byron (whom he seems truly to despise) as writers not deserving of the title of "poet." We need to remember that during this period Wordsworth was still struggling to get his poems read and to rise above the critical abuse heaped upon him by such key publications as the *Edinburgh Review*; he is clearly and understandably jealous of Scott's and Byron's enormous success. In a letter to Samuel Rogers (May 5, 1814, *WLMY*, 2: 148), he mentions he is publishing *The Excursion*, noting, "I shall be content if the Publication pay its expenses, for Mr. Scott and your friend Lord B. flourishing at the rate they do, how can an honest *Poet* hope to thrive?" Writing to R. P. Gillies, a poet and *Blackwood's* contributor (November 23, 1814, *WLMY*, 2: 169), he calls Byron a "bad writer"; in labelling him "bold bad Bard Baron B." in a letter to *The Champion's* editor John Scott (February 25, 1816, *WLMY*, 2: 283), Wordsworth clearly still envies the praise granted liberally to both Byron and Scott. He complained to Tom Moore that Byron in *Childe Harold* plagiarized "his style and sentiments," particularly from "Tintern Abbey."[10] Writing in 1814 to Sara Hutchinson (December 10, 1814, *WLMY*, 2: 176), he labels Byron the "crack-brained, skull-bearing Lordship" (he also spoke to Henry Crabb Robinson of the insanity in the Byron family and believed "Lord Byron to be somewhat cracked"[11]). About a decade later, he would speak to J. J. Taylor "with deserved severity of Byron's licentiousness and contempt of religious decorum."[12] Perhaps most strikingly, Wordsworth lashes out against Byron in another letter to John Scott (April 18, 1816, *WLMY*, 2: 304): "The man is insane; and will probably end his career in a mad-house. I never thought him anything else since his first appearance in public. The verses on his private affairs excite in me less indignation than pity. The latter copy is the Billingsgate of Bedlam." Most tellingly, he calls upon Henry Crabb Robinson to urge the *Quarterly Review* to attack Byron after the publication of *Don Juan*:

> You will probably see Gifford, the Editor of the Quarterly Review; tell him from me, if you think proper, that every true-born Englishman will regard the pretensions of the Review to the character of a faithful defender of the

institutions of the country, as *hollow*, while it leaves the infamous publication Don Juan unbranded ... by some decisive words of reprobation, both
as to the damnable tendency of such works, and as to [the] despicable
quality of the powers requisite for their production. What avails it to hunt
down Shelley, whom few read, and leave Byron untouched?

I am persuaded that Don Juan will do more harm to the English character, than anything of our time. (late January 1820, *WLMY*, 2: 579)

Although I am clearly interested more generally in arguing that
Wordsworth's publishing efforts during the years of the Cockney School
disputes should be understood in the context of the Hunt circle's considerable successes, it is Byron against whom Wordsworth most clearly defines
himself.

Interestingly, Wordsworth was part of an earlier poetic response to
Byron engineered by an admirer of Southey's, Miss Mary Barker of
Keswick. *Lines Addressed to A Noble Lord; (His Lordship will know why)
by one of the Small Fry of the Lakes* (London: Pople, 1815) included about five
stanzas written by Wordsworth out of its total of sixteen.[13] This is one of
any number of contemporary satires and critiques of Byron's poetry. In
fact, while we think of parodies of Wordsworth around the publication of
Peter Bell and *The Waggoner* in 1819,[14] at the same time we find attacks on
Byron in, for example: *Don Juan: with a Biographical Account of Lord Byron
and His Family; Anecdotes of his Lordship's Travels and Residence in Greece,
at Geneva, &c. Including also a Sketch of the Vampyre Family* (London:
William Wright, 1819; perhaps by the miniaturist George Perfect
Harding), where we get a preview of the "Satanic School" attacks in the
labeling of Byron, Polidori, and the Shelleys as "Vampyres" (pp. 141–42);
A Poetical Epistle from Alma Mater to Lord Byron (Cambridge: Deighton
and Sons, 1819; perhaps by E. Goode), where Byron is the "Degenerate
Son" of his university, "pand'ring to the genius of the times" so that "maids
and striplings hail with loud applause / The Wand'ring Child, Soft Thief,
and Blue Bashaws" (pp. 3–4); and Wordsworth's and Coleridge's old
acquaintance Joseph Cottle's *An Expostulary Epistle to Lord Byron*
(London: Cadell and Davies, 1820), where we find a Napoleonic Byron
"Climbing to heights the *Gallic Fiend* ne'er trod, / Thou lift'st thy front
against the Throne of God! / Heading the Atheist's Crew!" (175). Along
with dramatizations of Byron's poems and the setting of a number of his
lyrics to music, these texts attest to the ways in which Byron's poetry
dominated the popular culture of this moment.

Wordsworth did not want Byron to know his involvement in Mary
Barker's satiric poem, though he assumed his poetic opponent would

blame both him and Southey (letter to Sara Hutchinson, December 10, 1814 (?), *WLMY*, 2: 175–76). The poem, apparently inspired by an attack upon the Lakers in a letter from Byron to James Hogg,[15] suggests that Byron give up his "insane career" (11) and learn about nature and God in the Lake District: "To unlearn thyself, repair / Hither" (188–89). The poem finds Byron marked by "Vanity" and "Remorse" and headed for "Annihilation" (5–7); such moralizing terms fill the satires on Byron, and Cottle at least joins Barker in remarking on Byron's famous skull cup, in her poem a "goblet skull" filled with "Many a foul, Avernian draught" (15, 17), and for Cottle, "his Father's Skull!" from which Byron "spurn'd of Nature, callous more than dull, / Can quaff libations" (43–44). The main objection seems to be that Byron casts Gothic villains as heroes – that is, Byronic heroes:[16] he has found that "The viler Wretch the better Lover" and that "the nature the most odious / Is best theme for verse melodious!" (25, 27–28). Byron's morally mixed characters are contrasted with the simple morality and modest lives of those who live in the Lake District. If Byron will later in the "Dedication" to *Don Juan* wish that Wordsworth, Coleridge, and Southey would change their lakes for ocean, Wordsworth finds his "PONDS" more poetic than Byron's "dishonour'd Seas, / With their shores and Cyclades, / Stock'd with Pachas, Seraskiers, / Slaves, and turban'd Buccaneers; / Sensual Mussulmen atrocious, / Renegadoes, more ferocious" (167–73). Wordsworth and his coauthors make fun of the Byron of *Childe Harold I* and *II* and of the "oriental" tales, filled as they are with "Heroes suited to the trances / Of thy crude, distemper'd fancies" (174–75). With this satire on Byron in mind, I want to suggest that the publication of *Peter Bell*, even though the poem was written in 1798 long before Byron published or Wordsworth objected to him, could be considered in 1819 as a corrective to Byron.[17]

II

In Wordsworth's poem, Peter has not visited the Cyclades, but he has been "a wild and woodland rover" (217);[18] several stanzas are given over to detailing his journeys from Wales to Scotland. Where Barker's lines hoped that a visit to the Lake District would transform the wayward Lord, Peter has remained unchanged by the natural beauties he encounters. While "He rov'd among the vales and streams," "Nature ne'er could find the way / Into the heart of Peter Bell" (251, 254–55); unlike the Lake Poet who can dance with daffodils, for Peter, "A primrose by a river's brim /

A yellow primrose was to him, / And it was nothing more" (258–60). We can almost imagine the key description of Peter coming from a Byronic send-up of the Byronic hero:

> Of all that lead a lawless life,
> Of all that love their lawless lives,
> In city or in village small,
> He was the wildest far of all; –
> He had a dozen wedded wives.
>
> (286–90)

Although Wordsworth cannot explain how Peter won all these wives, the fear attached to women's response to Peter Bell (295) suggests he has some of the villainous charisma that marks the Corsair or the Giaour; in 1819 his promiscuity might well have reminded one of the Giaour and his peers, who were seen in contemporary reviews as wild womanizers,[19] or even of Don Juan (the first two cantos of which were published on July 15, 1819) as when one reviewer (perhaps George Croly) referred to Wordsworth's character as "this Potter-Don-Juan" (*Literary Gazette* May 1, 1819: 284; Reiman, *Lake Poets*, 2: 598). Peter Bell's outlaw status again would have reminded readers of the Byronic figure ("The hero of Lord Byron's poems ... is always a man that has defrauded the gallows, whether he be a Giaour, a Corsair, or a Renegado"; *British Review* 7 [May 1816]: 453, Reiman, *Byron*, 2: 429), particularly as a figure such as the Corsair had already in a way been domesticated back to England. Peter Manning and David Erdman remind us of how the defense sought to use lines from the *Corsair* in explaining how Isaac Ludlam fell under the influence of Jeremiah Brandreth, the leader of the Pentridge uprising, lines that include a description of Conrad oddly close to that of Peter Bell:

> What is that spell that thus his lawless train
> Confess and envy, yet oppose in vain;
> What should it be that thus their faith can bind,
> The power, the nerve, the magic of the mind.[20]

Such evocations of Byron in such a context suggest that one could have read Wordsworth's poem as an attack upon Byron at a time when Byron's poetry was so clearly open to broad cultural applications.

Peter's story proper begins when, during his wanderings, he enters – not unlike Dante – a "thick wood" (351) and then comes upon a stray ass refusing to leave the bank of the river in which his master has drowned. (It is amusing to note with Carlo Bajetta that the narrator of *Peter Bell* begins, like the narrator of *Don Juan*, *in medias res* before acceding to his audience's request to "begin with the beginning."²¹) Since Peter's Byronic disease has not been cured by nature, stronger measures are necessary: the shock of seeing the dead man's body rise from the water, the shriek of what we learn is the dead man's son, a sudden and apparently miraculous shaking of the ground, and a hellfire sermon from a Methodist preacher. The narrator makes it clear that Peter, alone in a countryside that does not move him to natural piety, is susceptible to doubts and fears. When the ass refuses to move, he assumes "There is some plot against me laid" and then proposes that "Some ugly witchcraft must be here!" (442, 452). As Peter struggles with "demoniac power" (514) to compel the ass to go with him, he suddenly sees "a startling sight" (539). The narrator gives a long series of speculations on what Peter has seen – is it a reflection of the moon, an image of a coffin or the gallows, some pagan idol "hewn in stone" (546)? Or, in lines that would shock Hunt and Shelley:

> Is it a party in a parlour?
> Cramm'd just as they on earth were cramm'd –
> Some sipping punch, some sipping tea,
> But, as you by their faces see,
> All silent and all damn'd! (556–60)

Of course, what Peter actually sees is not some supernatural vision but the all too natural body of the dead man.

Peter, shocked by the sight of the corpse, decides to follow the ass's lead in order to find the dead man's cottage. As they make their way, there is suddenly a "burst of doleful sound! / And Peter honestly might say, / The like came never to his ears / Though he has been full thirty years / A rover night and day!" (656–60). We are, as with the rising of the drowned man, told what is not present ("'Tis not a plover of the moors, / 'Tis not a bittern of the fen; / Nor can it be a barking fox – / Nor night-bird chamber'd in the rocks – / Nor wild-cat in a woody glen!" [661–65]). The sound, apparently having no natural source, appears so ghastly and ghostly that the narrator has to reassure his listener, Bess, that this is the cry of the "Wood-boy" whose father has died. Unaware of this, Peter again engages in inward-directed speculation. "That lamentable noise . . . wrought in him conviction strange":

> A faith that, for the dead man's sake
> And this poor slave who lov'd him well,
> Vengeance upon his head will fall,
> Some visitation worse than all
> Which ever till this night befell. (704–10)

Closed to nature's beauties, he continues to find disturbing interpretations of natural events.

Peter then crosses a frightening gothic landscape, where rocks "Build up a wild fantastic scene; / Temples like those among the Hindoos, / And mosques, and spires, and abbey windows" (727–29); in the midst of this eclectic religious landscape (which might recall the passages of comparative mythology in *The Excursion*), a sudden rolling of the earth leads Peter to believe that the "earth was charg'd to quake / And yawn for his unworthy sake" (893–94), but the narrator makes it clear that it is not hell opening up for Peter but the aftershock of gunpowder being set off by miners. Still, believing that he is being pursued for all his evil deeds, Peter is ready when he overhears the call of a Methodist preacher to repent. In a poem offered to prove that one does not need the supernatural to create imaginative poetry,[22] earthly events – a corpse surfacing in a pool, a controlled explosion in a mine, even a rocky landscape – are seen as open to a supernatural interpretation. Proffering an explanation of Peter's reactions, the beginning of the third part of the poem suggests that we are all subject to "Dread Spirits" (811), later called "Spirits of the Mind" (966). The narrator indicates that he has experienced visitations from such "Dread Beings!" (824), telling us of a "gentle soul, / Though given to sadness and to gloom" (786–7) who suddenly sees appear on the page of a "pious book" (792) a "ghostly word" (806) outlined in light against a background of darkness. He never told anyone what the word was, but "It brought full many a sin to light / Out of the bottom of his heart" (809–10). Presumably this is the kind of "Fear" and "Sorrow" that, according to the proem to *Peter Bell*, can lead to "Repentance" (151–53), so the narrator asks that these spirits "From men of pensive virtue go, / ... / and your empire show / On hearts like that of Peter Bell" (823–25). However, while the "gentle soul" has his piety to instruct his understanding of these spirits and while the narrator presumably has nature to guide him, Peter experiences signs he cannot interpret. At times he seems to stray toward superstition or some folk or pagan notion, but then the Methodist preacher fixes Peter's understanding: he is one of the damned unless he repents. Hearing the sermon, Peter "melted into tears" (1010) and, we later learn, "after ten months' melancholy, / Became a good and honest man" (1184–85).

Even though some have argued for the comedic and even satiric thrust of *Peter Bell* – which would be an interesting way of seeing the poem as responding to the Byron of *Beppo* and *Don Juan*[23] – I believe we need to take seriously Wordsworth's attempt to provide a religious understanding of the imaginative interaction with the natural world. In a letter to Benjamin Robert Haydon in late April 1820 (*WLMY*, 2: 594), Wordsworth indicated that he was preparing a new volume of his collected works that would include *Peter Bell* and notes, "In more than one passage their publication will evince my wish to uphold the cause of Christianity." Interestingly, in 1820 Wordsworth added a note to the poem's lines that describe the sign of the cross marking the ass's shoulder to indicate that they are an homage to Haydon's painting of *Christ's Entry into Jerusalem*, making a direct link to the life of Christ and perhaps to the *encomium asini* tradition, as Leah Marcus and Carlo Bajetta have suggested.[24] As Peter begins to experience his conversion, we are told that "A holy sense pervades his mind" and that "man's heart is a holy thing" (1103, 1122). The "spirits of the mind," described earlier, and the emotions evoked by the natural world serve God's purposes. In the section on comparative religion in the fourth book of *The Excursion*, which, as we have seen, the younger writers admired, Wordsworth had already rewritten what are essentially spots of time into intimations of the Almighty. But in *Peter Bell* he draws not on Greek mythology or Middle Eastern religion but on Methodism, calling forth the denunciation of Hunt's circle.

III

As Hunt's review of *Peter Bell* indicates, he and his circle doubted that Wordsworth truly believed in the religious salvation offered to Peter. Hunt would have agreed with the *Monthly Review* (2nd Series, 89 [August 1819]: 419; Reiman, *Lake Poets*, 2: 760), which compares *Peter Bell* to Hannah More's *Cheap Repository Tracts,* suggesting this is conservative propaganda "intended for the reformation of the lowest of the lower orders." The turn to Methodism was one of the things the Cockneys most hated about the poem.[25] Calling the poem "another didactic little horror of Mr. Wordsworth's," Hunt quoted the lines on the damned party in the parlor in his *Examiner* review (May 2, 1819: 282–83) and exclaimed, "What pretty little hopeful imaginations for a reforming philosopher! Is Mr. Wordsworth in earnest or is he not, in thinking that his fellow-creatures are to be damned? If he is, who is to be made really better or more comfortable in this world, by having such notions of another? If not, how wretched is this hypocrisy?" (*SWLH*, 2: 189). Shelley, apparently quoting the lines from Hunt's review,[26] uses the same passage as an epigraph to *Peter Bell the Third* and satirizes it in the body of the poem (*SPP*, 217–221, 353–72).

Hunt's review attacks what he sees as the "weak and vulgar philosophy" of the poem. He notes that Peter Bell's reformation is brought about by both his sense of the donkey's attachment to his dead master and by "the sound of a Damnation Sermon, which a Methodist is vociferating from a chapel. The consequence is, that after a melancholy of eleven months, he is thoroughly reformed, and has a proper united sense of hare-bells and hell-fire" (*SWLH*, 2: 187). While *Blackwood's* (5 [May 1819]: 135); Reiman, *Lake Poets*, 1: 95) praised the "singular versification of methodistical eloquence" in the poem (and also quoted the passage on the damned party with apparent approval), Hunt finds here "the philosophy of violence and hopelessness" (*SWLH*, 2: 187): it is, in other words, the philosophy of despondency, of the brutality and loss of faith that marked the postrevolutionary era. Methodism is for Hunt merely a tool of tyranny. He had long attacked Methodism, here "founded in hopelessness, and that too of the very worst sort, – namely, hopelessness of others, and salvation for itself" (*SWLH*, 2: 187). One of Hunt's earliest series in *The Examiner* had dealt with Methodism, reprinted as *An Attempt to Shew the Folly of Methodism In a Series of Essays, First Published in the Weekly Paper Called the Examiner, And Now Enlarged with a Preface and Additional Notes By the Editor of the Examiner* (London: John Hunt, 1809). In that work, Hunt argued for his usual doctrine of cheerfulness, contending, "All the best feelings of the heart are as naturally open to a chearful piety, as the flowers to Heaven's sunshine"; "But who will discover these feelings in Methodism? Who will discover the artlessness of childhood, or the romantic generosity of youth, or the pity, the humility, and the universal charities of CHRIST, in the worldly gloom, the violent passions, and the unavoidable hell of Methodism? It is a religion unfit for the young and the benevolent, and when I say this, I say it is not the Christian Religion" (p. 39). As is the case with Peter Bell, Methodists, according to Hunt, are converted only by extreme situations and extraordinary discomfort: "Thus their religion is at war even with their health, and nothing can be more contemptible than their repeated boasts of the beautiful effects of sickness. Fever and accidents make the great majority of Methodists: they are converted not by the sunshine but by the tempest: stomach-aches, rheumatisms, and catarrhs, a constitution destroyed by debauchery, and a mind debilitated by ignorance, become *precious helps to a communion with God*" (pp. 40–41). For Hunt, Wordsworth's *Peter Bell* is in perfect accord with the religious sect Hunt had attacked for its religious gloominess and its political quietism.

Hunt was not alone in finding fault with Methodism and Wordsworth's use of it. Not that there were no poetic defenders of Methodism. Jane Taylor in her interesting "Poetry and Reality" criticizes any poet, presumably including Wordsworth, who rather than attending church on the Sabbath "seeks his own sequestered bower," where he does not have to hear so "unpoetical a word as sin," "Confounding picturesque with moral taste" (22, 79, 131).[27] The Cockneys would have none of this. Hazlitt took on Methodism in his *Round Table* essay "On the Causes of Methodism" (originally in *The Examiner* October 22, 1815). Jeffrey in the *Edinburgh Review* (24 [November 1814]: 4; Reiman, *Lake Poets*, 2: 440) spoke of *The Excursion* as repeating the "mystical verbiage of the methodist pulpit" "till the speaker entertains no doubt that he is the elected organ of divine truth and persuasion." Horace Smith also wrote an attack upon Methodism called "Nehemiah Muggs," part of which appeared in the *London Magazine*. Smith offers a parody of a hellfire sermon (3 [February, March, June, 1821]: 280–81); I offer a long selection from this little-known poem:

> "Viler than vilest of vile sinners!
> Ye who at fairs or alehouse dinners
> Sup on your reprobate Welsh rabbit;
> Ye who love skittles, bowls, and dice,
> And make disorder'd nights of vice
> Your regular and daily habit: –
> What! will ye still, ye heathen, flee
> From sanctity and grace,
> Until your blind idolatry
> Shall stare ye in the face?
> Will ye throw off the mask, and show
> Thereby the cloven foot below?
> Do – but remember you must pay
> What's due to you on settling day;
> For Heaven's eye, it stands to sense,
> Can never stomach such transgressions;
> Nor can the hand of Providence
> Wink at your impious expressions. –
> The profligate thinks vengeance dead,
> And in his fancied safety chuckles,
> But Atheism's hydra head
> Shall have a rap upon the knuckles. –
> The never blushing cheek of vice
> Shall kick the bucket in a trice;
> While the deaf ear that never pray'd,
> Shall quickly by the heels be laid." –[28]

The "unconverted congregation" greets this "display of declamation" with roars of laughter. Jane Taylor again offers a contrasting vision, praising the "the poor Itinerant," a Methodist preacher, who finds a barn in which "To preach – or if you will, to rant and roar" "'That gospel news [the "christened heathens"] never heard before'" (201, 204–205). Methodism is also part of the landscape Shelley discovers in "Hell … a city much like London – / A populous and a smokey city":

> There is great talk of Revolution –
>   And a great chance of despotism –
> German soldiers – camps – confusion –
> Tumults – lotteries – rage – delusion –
>   Gin – suicide and methodism.
>
> (*SPP*, 147–48, 172–76)

Scrivener has reminded us that "Methodism has long been considered as a form of social control over the poor" and that following the Peterloo Massacre, referred to in Shelley's poem, the Methodists were the "only organization with a plebeian following that congratulated the authorities."[29] In 1819, Wordsworth's turn to Methodism was bound to be seen as a reactionary move, an appeal to a sect to which many of the "lower" orders but not he belonged.[30]

In other words, *Peter Bell* is seen as an attempt to frighten people who hold beliefs that Wordsworth himself does not share. For the Cockneys, Wordsworth has moved from his positive argument for religion in *The Excursion* (still praised, at least for contrast with other Wordsworth poems, by Keats in his review of Reynolds's *Peter Bell*) to the use of religion as a weapon against those who might threaten the status quo. Methodism is for Hunt, Hazlitt, and Shelley a kind of institutionalized despondency, the theological analogue to the Lakers' poetry of despair.

Another line of attack by the younger poets on Wordsworth was to conflate him with his creation. Just as Shelley and his fellow writers had linked Wordsworth with his Solitary, as we saw in Chapter 1, so do Hunt and then Shelley identify Wordsworth with Peter Bell. Hunt describes Peter as "a potter, who has rambled about the country, and been as wilful, after his fashion, as any Lake poet" (*SWLH*, 2: 186–87). Shelley more closely identifies Peter Verbo-vale (534) with his creator Wordsworth, tracing the poet's career through that of his creation.[31] Shelley's poem thus offers a compendium of the Hunt circle's criticisms of Wordsworth as Peter. Although Peter's early verse is both powerful and dedicated to freedom, even there his titanic egotism overwhelmed everything:

> All things that Peter saw and felt
> Had a peculiar aspect to him;

And when they came within the belt
Of his own nature, seem'd to melt
    Like cloud to cloud, into him.
. . . .

He had a mind which was somehow
    At once circumference and centrear
Of all he might or feel or know.

(*SPP*, 273–77, 293–95)

Shelley pursues the same critique of Wordsworth as Keats does in his comment on the "wordsworthian or egotistical sublime" or as Hazlitt in his review of *The Excursion*. This egotism is linked to a lack of erotic joy, of sensual pleasure, as Peter/Wordsworth is described as a "moral eunuch" who "Felt faint" when "He touched the hem of Nature's shift" (314–16) and as a "Male prude" (331) who cannot love the sexual aspect of nature with the passion of Burns. Peter Bell is no Tam O'Shanter, even if in Wordsworth's defensive sonnet, "On the Detraction which Followed the Publication of Certain Poem," he compares Peter to Burns's Rob Roy and to Robin Hood. Shelley echoes Hazlitt and Byron in their sense of Wordsworth's desertion of the erotic.

Shelley's Peter takes to writing poetry, inspired by a Coleridge-like figure who is "A subtle-souled psychologist" who "might have turned / Hell into Heaven," "But he in shadows undiscerned / Trusted, – and damned himself to madness" (379, 383–87), as Shelley takes up some of the same criticisms of Coleridge that Byron set forth in *Don Juan*. Clearly Peter/Wordsworth is a Lake Poet who "could speak of rocks and trees / In poetic metre" (421–22), and still his "verse was clear, and came / Announcing from the frozen hearth / Of cold age, that none might tame / The soul of that diviner flame / It augured to the Earth" (433–37). This intimation of mortal divinity rouses the Devil's ire, and he thus calls for the reviews to damn Peter's books much as they had Wordsworth's early volumes. Shelley then tracks Peter's/Wordsworth's decline, as Peter tries to defend himself in prose (513–17), as he becomes a "solemn and unsexual man" who embraces the "*White Obi*" of Christianity (550–52), and as he comes – in direct opposition to the Hunt circle's embrace of cheerfulness and sociality – to believe "That 'happiness is wrong'" (573): "His morals thus were undermined" (579).[32] Shelley criticizes the "enormous folly" of *The Excursion* with its "Baptisms, Sunday-schools and Graves" (614–15) and the patriotic posturings of the "Thanksgiving Ode" volume with its praise of

Carnage as God's daughter (634–52). Shelley, knowing that *Peter Bell* was written in 1798 but finding it in 1819 to reveal the "apostate" Wordsworth that had written *The Excursion* and the "Thanksgiving Ode," locates the source of Wordsworth's problems even in his early verse. Now that Peter/Wordsworth is willing to sing "The folly which soothes Tyranny" (622), Peter is praised by the reviewers and awarded a government post. But having betrayed freedom and the imagination, he is condemned to dullness, the aesthetic counterpart of despondency. Wordsworth has become the problem he wrote *The Excursion* to cure.

IV

The disagreement between the younger writers and Wordsworth over *Peter Bell's* political and religious messages is matched by a struggle over the means by which poetry should treat such issues. As with the response to *The Excursion* or the debate over how to respond to Waterloo, these writers differ over the kind of poetry best suited to tackle contemporary concerns. Wordsworth frames *Peter Bell* with a proem in defense of what we know as "natural supernaturalism," what Lamb in reviewing *The Excursion* called Wordsworth's "Natural Methodism" (*Quarterly Review* 12 [October 1814]: 105; Reiman, *Lake Poets*, 2: 828). Barker's lines to Byron, discussed earlier, opened with an attack upon his "Pegasus," "one / Such as Demons ride upon" (1–2). *Peter Bell* famously opens with Wordsworth's rejection of the winged horse as he journeys forth in his winged boat ("There's something in a flying horse, / . . . / But through the clouds I'll never float / Until I have a little Boat" [3–4]).[33] These lines may originally have been offered as an argument for Wordsworthian lyrical ballads, but they were read differently in 1819. They could appear as a rejection of the verse taken up by the younger poets and identified with the Cockney School. Finding that "Temptation lurks among . . . [the] words" (121) offered by the flying canoe, the narrator of the poem rejects visionary poetry to focus upon "What on the earth is doing" (125). The narrator then relegates heroic tales to the past:

> There was a time when all mankind
> Did listen with a faith sincere
> To tuneful tongues in mystery vers'd;
> *Then* Poets fearlessly rehears'd
> The wonders of a wild career.   (126–30)

He thus urges the boat to "Take with you some ambitious Youth" for "The common growth of mother earth / Suffices me" (133, 138–39). Visionary poetry is perhaps fine for younger poets and for humanity as a whole in its "youth," but the mature, adult poet finds, as in the "Prospectus" to *The Recluse,* that there are no "nobler marvels than the mind" (148). To the younger poets, this might read like an admonition against their entire poetic mission.

Thus, in *The Witch of Atlas,* which Shelley calls a "visionary rhyme" (8), Shelley took Wordsworth's lines as almost a personal rebuke, and he objects to *Peter Bell* in his dedication "To Mary," but the earlier joint satire on Byron's Pegasus suggests that it is Jeffrey's poet of "visionary reform" who would have seemed a more likely target.[34] In Ebenezer Elliott's *The Giaour. A Satire. Addressed to Lord Byron* (1823), the noble poet is hailed as "thou dread of Wordsworth's Ass" (33), and we are told he "Hates Wordsworth's ass" (515), while the *Edinburgh [Scots] Magazine* (2nd Series, 4 [May 1819]: 429; Reiman, *Lake Poets,* 2: 863) reads *Peter Bell's* dedication to Southey as perhaps including a "hit at Lord Byron." Byron certainly responded to Wordsworth's opening lines in *Don Juan,* where he attacks both *The Waggoner* and *Peter Bell*:

> He wishes for "a boat" to sail the deeps –
>   Of ocean? – No, of air; and then he makes
> Another outcry for "a little boat,"
> And drivels seas to set it well afloat.
>
> If he must fain sweep o'er the ethereal plain,
>   And Pegasus runs restive in his "waggon,"
> Could he not beg the loan of Charles's Wain?
>   Or pray Medea for a single dragon?
> Or if too classic for his vulgar brain,
>   He fear'd his neck to venture such a nag on,
> And he must needs mount nearer to the moon,
> Could not the blockhead ask for a balloon?
>
>   (3.98–99.350–361)[35]

It is not just the content of the poem that bothered the younger poets but its formal opposition to their more extravagant verse, the experiments of *Childe Harold* or *Manfred,* of *The Revolt of Islam* and *Endymion* and even Hunt's "Nymphs," poems that use avant-garde forms to open a speculative space beyond Wordsworth's own poetic experiment of *Lyrical Ballads.* Wordsworth presumably saw himself continuing that experiment in *Peter Bell,* but the younger poets believed he has bound the imagination here to what Hunt would call the "oldest tyrannies and slaveries" (*The Examiner* May 9, 1819: 302; *SWLH*, 2: 192.

While Wordsworth's reformed villain can certainly be read as a response to the popularity of the Byronic hero – and while his decision to finally publish his long-delayed poem could be seen as his attempt to answer Byron's poetry – the vision or ideology of the poem was contrasted by Hunt with that of Shelley (and thus with his own), and it would of course be Shelley who would offer the group's strongest response to Wordsworth in *Peter Bell the Third*.[36] As early as 1818, in reviewing Shelley's *Revolt of Islam* for *The Examiner* (February 22, 1818), Hunt juxtaposed Shelley both with Southey and with the Wordsworth of the "Thanksgiving Ode," noting that Shelley preaches hope where they embrace despair. Hunt suggests the Lakers could learn from Shelley "how it becomes an antagonist to talk; and how charitable and consistent the mind can be, that really inquires into the philosophical causes of things":

> Mr. Shelley does not say that Mr. Southey is "no better than a housebreaker" [as Southey had said of reformers in the *Quarterly Review*]; nor does he exclaim with Mr. Wordsworth, in the ill-concealed melancholy of a strange piety, which would be still stranger if it were really chearful, that "Carnage is God's daughter." He is not in the habit, evidently, of begging the question against the low and uneducated; nor has he the least respect for that very seeping lady, Miss Theodosia Carnage; – but stop; we must not be violating the charity of his philosophy. (*SWLH*, 2: 155)

Hunt makes the contrast even sharper in reviewing Shelley's *Rosalind and Helen* (*The Examiner* May 9, 1819) the week after attacking *Peter Bell*:

> This publication, in form and appearance resembling the one we criticised last week, presents a curious contrast with it in every other respect. It is in as finer a moral taste, as *Rosalind* and *Helen* are pleasanter names than *Peter Bell*. The object of Mr. Wordsworth's administrations of melancholy is to make men timid, servile, and (considering his religion) selfish; – that of Mr. Shelley's, to render them fearless, independent, affectionate, infinitely social. You might be made to worship a devil by the process of Mr. Wordsworth's philosophy; by that of Mr. Shelley, you might re-seat a dethroned goodness. The Poet of the Lakes always carries his egotism and "saving knowledge" about with him, and unless he has the settlement of the matter, will go in a pet and plant himself by the side of the oldest tyrannies and slaveries; – our Cosmopolite-Poet would evidently die with pleasure to all personal identity, could he but see his fellow-creatures reasonable and happy…. Mr. Wordsworth has become hopeless of this world, and

therefore would make every body else so; – Mr. Shelly is superior to hopelessness itself; and does not see why all happiness and all strength is to be bounded by what he himself can feel or can affect. (*SWLH*, 2: 192–93)

Hunt echoes all of the arguments the Cockney School raised against Wordsworth and the Lakers, endorsing a cosmopolitan sociality of philosophical reform over against the narrow despondency of the egotistical sublime. Hunt offers Shelley as the antidote to the poisonous despair he sees the Lake Poets injecting into society's common life.

Hunt also suggests that the "form and appearance" of *Rosalind and Helen* and *Peter Bell* are alike. They are both octavo volumes. Both include one major narrative poem with shorter poems – sonnets in the case of *Peter Bell* and Shelley's Ozymandias sonnet, along with "Hymn to Intellectual Beauty" and "Written Among the Eugenaen Hills" in *Rosalind and Helen*. Both begin with a prose introduction to the main poem. And, interestingly, both volumes include lengthy advertisements for other books at the end of the volume, with Wordsworth's publisher Longman et al. promoting a wide range of texts, from a *General Commercial Dictionary* to Anna Maria Porter's *Fast of St. Magdalen* to volumes of poetry by Tom Moore and Southey. In contrast, the Olliers' list in Shelley's volume is more or less a catalogue of the Cockney School, with volumes by Percy and Mary Shelley, by Hunt, and by Barry Cornwall. These similar-looking books announce themselves as coming from opposite ends of the literary scene.

The battle over *Peter Bell*, then, was not just a battle of books. It was a battle in which both sides argued that books matter, that words matter, that the way we write and read changes the way we think and live. Wordsworth believed the stakes were high: as we have seen, he called upon Henry Crabb Robinson to urge the *Quarterly Review* to attack Byron after the publication of *Don Juan* (late January 1820, *WLMY*, 2: 579). Hunt would counter that Wordsworth would reduce that character to hopelessness. This battle of the books was nothing less than a battle for the soul of the nation.

It was also a battle that demonstrates that textual meaning is not just contingent upon its moment of creation; as I have argued, the delayed publication of *Peter Bell* changed the way it was read and received. When published, the poem inevitably competed within a literary marketplace that included Shelley and Byron. As we will see in the next chapter, this moment of controversy actually had a positive impact on Wordsworth's sales. In 1820, he would bring out a new volume of poems to much acclaim, and if the battle over *Peter Bell* was decidedly public, I will argue that in his *River Duddon* sonnets Wordsworth contends almost silently with one of his powerful younger contemporaries.

CHAPTER 4

Thinking Rivers
The Flow of Influence, Wordsworth–Coleridge–Shelley

> ... yet still I cannot help being afraid of encouraging emulation – it
> proves too often closely akin to envy . . .. My own case is, I am aware,
> a peculiar one in many respects, but I can sincerely affirm, that I am
> not indebted to emulation for my attainments whatever they be.
>
> Wordsworth, letter to Charles Wordsworth, March 12, 1846;
> *WLLY*, 4: 765

I

In 1820, Wordsworth published a volume with a long – and largely long-forgotten – title: *The River Duddon, A Series of Sonnets: Vaudracour and Julia: and Other Poems. To Which is Annexed a Topographical Description of the Country of the Lakes in the North of England.*[1] It was available in late April, about two months before the appearance of Keats's *Lamia, Isabella, The Eve of St. Agnes and Other Poems* and about three months before Shelley's *Prometheus Unbound: A Lyrical Drama in Four Acts, with Other Poems.* Wordsworth's collection also appeared after he had seen the scandal around *Peter Bell* turn into a publishing success that led him, as we have seen, to issue quickly *The Waggoner* in 1819 as well. In 1820, after the positive reception of his volume of sonnets, he would issue another edition of the sonnets in a uniform Volume III of his *Poems*, a new edition of *The Excursion* in the same format, and a separate four-volume *Miscellaneous Poems of William Wordsworth*. It was an intense period of publication for him as he reached a larger audience and as the *River Duddon* volume received near unanimous critical acclaim. Stephen Gill sees this flurry of publications around the sonnet volume as marking the end to a key phase in Wordsworth's work as a poet, with the *Ecclesiastical Sketches* begun shortly thereafter inaugurating a new stage (pp. 330–37, 344). Placing the *River Duddon* volume within the context of Peterloo, the Six Acts, and the death of George III, Brian Bate has also explored the volume as bringing about a major shift in Wordsworth's reputation as he becomes *the* English poet of the moment.[2]

Wordsworth's *River Duddon* volume would seem to have little to do with Shelley's and Keats's more famous books of the same publishing season beyond the fact that they all include "other poems." However, I think we need to read these poets as being part of the conversation about what constituted poetry in 1820. Reviewers certainly stressed the place of the sonnet sequence on the contemporary literary scene. *Blackwood's* (7 [May 1820]: 206; Reiman, *Lake Poets*, 1: 99–107), for example, identifies Wordsworth along with Scott, Byron, Southey, and Coleridge as the contemporary poets to be reckoned with, and the *London Magazine* ends an account of the various schools that informed English poetry with a recognition of Wordsworth as the greatest living poet (*London Magazine* [Golds] 1 [June 1820]: 618–27; Reiman, *Lake Poets*, 2: 617–26). Most relevant for my argument, the *British Review*, while finding much to praise about Wordsworth, argues that those who have followed him – "men of low standard and presumptuous claims" – have demeaned poetry. As the reviewer rehearses various choruses from the Cockney School attacks, he can at least be relieved that Wordsworth's sonnets are above the "quantity of flippant colloquial trash, which at the present period claims to be poetry" (*British Review* 16 [September 1820]: 46; Reiman, *Lake Poets*, 1: 247–55). To reviewers, many of whom go out of their way to belittle *Peter Bell* once more, the *River Duddon* volume redeems not only Wordsworth's reputation but contemporary poetry itself.

It probably did not strike his younger contemporaries so. As we have heard, Leigh Hunt had in 1819 compared Wordsworth's *Peter Bell* to Shelley's *Rosalind and Helen* volume, pointing out that the latter "is in as finer a moral taste, as *Rosalind* and *Helen* are pleasanter names than *Peter Bell*";[3] we could imagine him contrasting the sound of "Lamia" and "Prometheus" with "Duddon" – a title that, in fact, the *Eclectic Review*[4] complained "stands boldly forward, indeed, in defiance of all ludicrous associations." More importantly, in praising Shelley's *Rosalind and Helen* at Wordsworth's expense, Hunt contrasted the conservative Wordsworth with his friend as "our Cosmopolite-Poet," and it is around the issues of national and cosmopolitan culture that I might put these volumes together.[5] It is indeed striking, given Hunt's appellation for Shelley, how often reviews of the *River Duddon* volume praise Wordsworth's "Englishness": for *Blackwood's*, Wordsworth is "a pure and reverent worshipper of the true majesty of the English Muse" (7 [May 1820]: 211; Reiman, *Lake Poets*, 1: 105); the *British Critic* (15 [February 1821]: 118; Reiman, *Lake Poets*, 1: 184–95) finds his style "very English." Wordsworth is a true English poet, then, unlike someone such as Shelley with his turn to

Greek literature, Keats with his evocations of Italian and classical texts, and most definitely Byron, the most cosmopolite poet of them all.

I think Gill is correct in seeing 1820 as a moment of summation on Wordsworth's part, as he seeks to establish himself as *the* key national poet of the post-Napoleonic moment, as the de facto poet laureate for a victorious Britain. However, a sequence of sonnets on the River Duddon would not at first appear to be much of a salvo in the battle of the books that raged around *Peter Bell*. For example, the *Blackwood's* review quoted already, probably by John Wilson, sees the sonnets as stepping away from the experimental verse of *Lyrical Ballads*; he argues that in the sonnet sequence "not a few of his customary singularities of style and manner are unquestionably less prominent than in any of his former publications" and, quoting from "Dion," included in the volume, finds that Wordsworth is the only poet since Milton and Gray to capture "the true inspiration of the Grecian Lyre," hardly the hallmark of Lake School poetics (207, 208). The *British Critic* praises the sonnets as examples of Wordsworth's "meditative nature": "We may observe, too, that the demand which descriptive poetry makes upon the imagination for dress and colouring of language, has seemed to divert him from that unaccountable addiction to a frigid and creeping idiom, halting between prose and verse, in which the class of writers to which he belongs is so prone to indulge" (*The British Critic* (16 [September 1820]; Reiman, *Lake Poets*, 1: 247–55). Again, the *Literary Chronicle* ([July 1820]; Reiman, *Lake Poets*, 2: 585–87) discovers in the sonnets "all the beauties and very few of the defects of this writer." Geoffrey Jackson, in editing the poems, strikes a similar stance, arguing that "part of Wordsworth's project is to impose a kind of classical order and poetic decorum on the transient flux of impressions and associations."[6] The *River Duddon* volume would seem to these reviewers to signal Wordsworth's retreat from the cultural battlefield and the war over the definition of poetry that erupted around *Peter Bell*. We might find here a truly late Wordsworth.

The *Eclectic Review* disagreed. While finding the *Duddon* volume "ample atonement for his last offence" of *Peter Bell*, it thus reminds readers of the attacks on that poem, further complaining that "the Author of the Excursion is almost forgotten in the Author of Peter Bell" (*Eclectic Review*, 2nd series, 14 [August 1820]; Reiman, *Lake Poets*, 1: 394–401). The reviewer goes on to point out that Wordsworth himself has embedded the *Peter Bell* controversy in the *River Duddon* volume by including "On the Detraction which Followed the Publication of a Certain Poem." Based on Milton's sonnet beginning "A Book was writ of late called 'Tetrachordon,'"

Wordsworth's sonnet notes that "A Book came forth of late, called 'Peter Bell.'" The author complains that, despite what he claims are its appropriate style and good subject matter, "a harpy brood" "Waxed wrath, and with foul claws" "On Bard and Hero clamorously fell" (1, 7–8). The *Eclectic's* reviewer is puzzled by what he sees as Wordsworth's move from humor to a "very sober earnest" address to Peter in the sestet. It also queries why Wordsworth would echo Milton's poem, unless it is because Wordsworth has "a sort of half-concealed fidgety ambition to be taken for a cousin-german of the great patriot bard."

This review, hostile as it is, reflects more accurately than the others, I believe, Wordsworth's intentions in the *River Duddon* sonnets. The sequence may take up a river rather than the Lakes themselves, but, of course, the Duddon is in the Lake District, and in the *Topographical Description of the Country of the Lakes in the North of England* printed with the poems Wordsworth parallels the "vale of Duddon" with "the long lake of Winandermere" and the "vale of Coniston" with its mere; all are seen as a series of "spokes from the nave of wheel," the center of which is a spot on a "cloud hanging midway" between Great Gavel and Scawfell.[7] The *River Duddon* volume also lacks the more polemical dedication to Southey in *Peter Bell* (the 1820 volume is offered to his brother, Christopher), but it does, as we will see, include a postscript linking the sequence to the other major Laker, Coleridge. Beyond the sonnet on *Peter Bell*, Wordsworth's own continued positioning of himself against his younger imitators and antagonists is suggested by the fact that he announced he would place the *Duddon* sonnets in a fourth volume of his poetic works with the "Thanksgiving Ode," *Peter Bell*, and *The Waggoner*[8] – that is, the most controversial poems Wordsworth published during the post-Waterloo cultural battle between the Lakers and the Cockneys. *The Excursion*, also reissued, was a poem that inspired both poetic imitation and political opposition from Keats, Shelley, Hunt, Byron, and others, and the "Thanksgiving Ode" and *Peter Bell* had, in particular, enraged them as they saw the greatest poet of their day "plant[ing] himself," as again Hunt put it, "by the side of the oldest tyrannies and slaveries."[9]

I think the *Eclectic* reviewer is also correct in seeing Wordsworth comparing himself to Milton. If *The Excursion* was Wordsworth's bid to be the Miltonic epic poet of his day and if poems such as *Peter Bell* represented his attempt to contest the nature of narrative poetry with Byron and Scott, as Peter Manning has noted,[10] then Wordsworth's sonnets – the earlier sonnets on liberty and now the sonnets to the River Duddon – constitute his bid to be Milton's inheritor in this form as well.

In all these genres, Wordsworth claims his right to chair the feast of poets in 1820, but he does so not in disengaged solitude but in conversation with others at the table.[11]

We need, then, to understand the literary ambition of these sonnets that have been seen as offering a more limited "period charm."[12] Written over the course of many years,[13] the sequence on the River Duddon is organized around an imagined hike down the river on a single day. As Stewart Wilcox, Joseph Phelan, Lee M. Johnson, John Wyatt, and James M. Garrett[14] have all pointed out, the sonnets are sequenced around several overlapping patterns of growth and development. As Wilcox puts it:

> the sequence observes the unity of time, beginning at dawn and ending before sunset; man's life is but a day. And through personification the Stream, at the start a "child," is associated with the stages of man's development. By means of these devices the river is affiliated in the memory with both Man and Nature, bringing them together imaginatively and uniting the sonnets structurally.[15]

Thus, as the series tracks the river from its source to its destination on the coast, it also moves through the stages of human life. In Sonnets II–VI as the poet follows the river from its origins on Wrynose Fell, he evokes the early years of life, as the Duddon is the "Child of the clouds!" (II.1), taken care of by "Thy hand-maid Frost" (II.5), who tends the river's "cradle" (II.6), and by "thy Foster-mother, Earth!" (III.14). Sonnet III evokes "thy beginning" and "the spot that gives thee birth" (7, 9). As the "cradled Nursling of the mountain" (IV.1), the river is appropriately attended by "ruddy children" who "sport through the summer day, / Thy pleas'd associates" (V.11–13). As the "Rill" that is the Duddon has "grown / Into a Brook" (IX.1–2) in the second quarter of the sequence, the poems move from childhood to adolescence and particularly adolescent love. Mapping history onto the sequence, Wordsworth first evokes the river as it was before man came on the scene and then tracks its presence until the current day. Initially, Duddon is "remote from every taint / Of sordid industry" (II.1). It has existed "Thousands of years before the silent air / Was pierced by whizzing shaft of hunter keen!" (II.13–14). As the poems shift from childhood to adolescence, they also track the development from prehistoric times to "the Man who roved or fled, / First of his tribe, to this dark dell" (VIII.1–2). As the river flows onward and as we move from adolescent romance to the work of shepherds and others along the river, we learn of various phases of human history in the vale involving Druids, Danes, Romans, and medieval knights. The sequence closes, as the river

reaches the sea, with the contemporary power of British commerce and its
military (XXXI). Part of the appeal and charm of the sequence is this easy
linking of the river's growth, the development of a human being through
the stages of life, and the evolution of culture through history.

However, if one looks more closely, the parallels between the river's
natural flow, the course of human life, and the passage of history also call
attention to the status of the sequence itself, the way in which the sonnets
operate as points along the fluvial movement of the series. *Blackwood's*[16]
argued that the *Duddon* sonnets "should be considered as forming something not unlike one poem," but in fact what we experience in reading is
the oscillation between the sonnets as individual poems, as, if you will,
individual pools,[17] and the sequence as a coherent literary whole, as a river.
This toggling highlights the highly wrought nature of the *River Duddon*
sonnets. We see such a self-conscious move in Sonnet VI, the first one to
bear a separate title, "Flowers," which additionally draws attention to itself,
for it doubles back on the course of the river the sequence is tracking: in
Sonnet V, Wordsworth celebrates "green alders" that shade the river (6);
Sonnet VI opens, "Ere yet our course was graced with social trees / It lacked
not old remains of hawthorn bowers" (1–2). As Daniel Robinson and
others have noticed, such moves draw attention to the flow of the poems
rather than the flow of the river.[18] In making us think of the poems as
poems, such tactics also raise questions about the sequence's literary
inheritances: "Flowers" is accompanied by a note that acknowledges
Wordsworth's debt in lines 9 and 10 to the Rev. Joseph Sympson,
a friend of the Wordsworths who, despite Wordsworth's claim that he
"ought to find a place in the History of Westmorland," is almost completely obscured in literary history.

Scholars have thus long recognized that Wordsworth's highly wrought
sequence is self-consciously literary with Robinson pointing to its reflections on the sonnet,[19] and William Galperin seeing the entire series as
demonstrating the gap between poetry and the objects it seems to present
to us: "What is most mimetic about these poems turns out to be the
impossibility of representation."[20] Galperin finds the phenomenal world
frustrating both tradition, with its conventions for representing the world,
and individual genius, which seeks to impose a new vision on that world.
Galperin's Wordsworth reworks both literary conventions and his own
modes of literary authority in order to gesture to a world that always
escapes poetry. Galperin is interested in the ways these sonnets explore
the limits of art, offering what he sees as a key example of a "repudiation of
the 'greater romantic lyric'" (217). Robinson is more interested in how

Wordsworth engages the sonnet tradition itself. Robinson notes for example that, in writing a sequence on the River Duddon, Wordsworth adopted "one of the most common symbols in the eighteenth century sonnet – the river – prevalent as a symbol for the flow of human life in sonnets by Thomas Warton, Anna Seward, Smith, Bowles, and many others."[21] Again, Robinson argues that the first sonnet "announces its literariness" (456) through its allusion to literary portrayals of other rivers and that the seventh poem "reintroduces the amorous tradition of the sonnet" (457). Although these scholars demonstrate just how self-conscious Wordsworth's Duddon sonnets are, the volume is not only engaged with the literary in the abstract or the literary tradition but also very much aware of contemporary poetry.

In order to understand Wordsworth's goals in the *River Duddon* sequence and the complex interconnections between the overlapping generations of romantic poets, this chapter traces what I believe are hidden influences in Wordsworth's sonnets. While Wordsworth might appear to be linking these poems back to 1797, in a sense erasing the time during which the younger poets wrote, he also calls our attention to 1817, a pivotal year in the post-Napoleonic culture war between the Lakers and the Cockneys. Wordsworth will invoke Coleridge as an inspiration for his poems, but in doing so, if we follow the flow of influence, he leads us to the presence of another poet, Shelley, who had in "Mont Blanc" sought to rewrite Coleridge and Wordsworth and whom Wordsworth now seems compelled to rewrite in turn. By thinking about the ways in which these poems think about rivers, we can, I think, come to a clearer understanding of how these writers were, in Ellison's terms from my opening epigraph, penning criticisms of one another.

II

In the *River Duddon* sonnet volume, Wordsworth does not engage his contemporaries in any direct or confrontational way. There is no polemical preface or dedication here as in the "Thanksgiving Ode" volume and *Peter Bell*. There is a postscript, which indirectly shows how Wordsworth positions himself in the literary landscape. In order to establish the tradition of imagining that a loco-descriptive poem was written within a particular short time sequence, Wordsworth refers to Dyer's "Ruins of Rome" and William Crowe's 1788 "Lewesdon Hill," with Crowe claiming to "finishing the whole [of his poem] on a May-morning, before breakfast" (p. 76). Then, to establish the role rivers play in inspiring poets,

Wordsworth turns to Virgil, Burns, and the poet/physician John Armstrong, the last of whom praised rivers – and their "gelid reign" – in his *Art of Preserving Health* (1744).

While the postscript evokes poems on rivers, it does not take up the tradition of the sonnet, though Wordsworth certainly did so elsewhere. He makes a number of comments on the form of the sonnet, and, of course, he also penned sonnets, most famously "Scorn not the Sonnet," that speak self-consciously about the form. In such observations, Wordsworth works to establish himself as an inheritor of Milton, noting that he turned to sonnet writing after his sister in 1802 read to him Milton's sonnets, after which he adopted a Miltonic form, preferring the Italianate octave-sestet over the English quatrains and couplet but enjambing the break between them.[22] As intimated above by the *Eclectic Review*, if Wordsworth wanted to be the epic Milton of his day, he also wanted to be a Miltonic, not a Shakespearean, writer of sonnets.

At the same time, Wordsworth obscures from view his debt to key figures in the revival of the sonnet during the romantic period, most importantly Charlotte Smith and William Bowles, but also such sonneteers as Mary Robinson, Anna Seward, and Helen Maria Williams, not to mention his earlier comrades in poetry: Lamb, Charles Lloyd, and Coleridge himself. As Daniel Robinson has pointed out, Wordsworth owes a deep debt to Smith's enlargement of the sonnet's emotional scope as well as to Bowles's use of the sonnet to offer a loco-descriptive account of a river, but he does not want to be seen as continuing their tradition. As Robinson puts it, "Wordsworth never publicly acknowledged any debt to Smith, ... Bowles, or other sonnet writers of the eighteenth century, claiming instead Milton as his precursor in order to distance himself from a practice that he believed had become hackneyed by the end of the century."[23] Burying references to such contemporary influences, Wordsworth also avoids acknowledging the work done in the sonnet by his younger followers, even though he surely knows of at least some of the work of Keats and Hunt in the sonnet, and he clearly knew Byron's one famous sonnet on Chillon.[24] While pointing to obscure poets such as Crowe and Armstrong, Wordsworth prefers to be seen as part of a great tradition that includes Milton but not Smith or Hunt.

The living poet that Wordsworth does mention in his postscript is Coleridge, and here, again, we get a clue to how Wordsworth is imagining his place in the pantheon of poets in 1820.[25] In establishing the tradition of writing about rivers, Wordsworth notes that his friend had intended to write "a rural poem, to be entitled 'The Brook'":

May I not venture, then, to hope, that instead of being a hindrance, by anticipation of any part of the subject, these Sonnets may remind Mr. Coleridge of his own more comprehensive design, and induce him to fulfill it? – There is a sympathy in streams, "one calleth to another;" and, I would gladly believe, that "The Brook" will, ere long, murmur in concert with "The Duddon." (pp. 76–77)

The mention of Coleridge's poem, proposed as early as their first collaborations in 1797, points toward the past as well as beyond the sonnets he is writing, again perhaps masking that tradition. Wordsworth argues, "I have further kept from encroaching upon any right Mr. C may still wish to exercise, by the restriction which the frame of the Sonnet imposed upon me, narrowing unavoidably the range of thought, and precluding, though not without its advantages, many graces to which a freer movement of verse would naturally have led" (p. 76). That is, Coleridge could have written a blank verse epic, like *The Excursion*, or perhaps a locodescriptive poem, similar to "Tintern Abbey" or Coleridge's own "Hymn Before Sun-rise, In the Vale of Chamouny." In any event, just as the dedication to *Peter Bell* highlighted Wordsworth's ties to Southey, this "Postscript" reminds readers of the alliance of Wordsworth and Coleridge. It is as if he wanted to reassert his membership in the Lake School despite years of attack and in the face of the rising and opposing Cockney School.

A Lake School reunion does not seem to have been Coleridge's desire in telling his own readers about the planned poem. As Wordsworth reminds us, Coleridge had given a "sketch" of "The Brook" in "a recent publication" – that is, the 1817 *Biographia Literaria* where, as I suggested in the Introduction, even the opening paragraph forecasts Coleridge's desire to be considered as distinct from the Lake School and Wordsworthian poetics in particular. Fulford has shown how Coleridge seeks, in the contemporary volume of verse, *Christabel; Kubla Khan, A Vision; The Pains of Sleep*, to create a performative poetics of reverie set against the definition of poetry in the "Preface" to *Lyrical Ballads*. Fulford argues that these three poems of the 1790s are redefined in print as "late" poems written to defend Coleridge from the attacks on the Lake School and to challenge Scott and Byron.[26] Similarly, while "The Brook" was projected in the 1790s and is invoked by Wordsworth in 1820, its only print existence occurs in 1817, in the midst of poetical and political struggles over the shape of the supposedly postrevolutionary world.

It is important to remember how contentious a literary year 1817 was. The previous, 1816, ended with Leigh Hunt's "Young Poets" essay, as we have seen, announcing a post-Laker school of poetry into which Hunt enlists Byron as well as Keats, Shelley, and John Hamilton Reynolds. The pirated edition of *Wat Tyler* would appear in February, embarrassing Southey and leading to an attack on him in Parliament by William Smith, not to mention a scathing *Examiner* review of Southey's response. Hazlitt would also take on Coleridge for his *Lay Sermons*. By October 1817, *Blackwood's* would respond by launching the Cockney School attacks. The *Biographia* thus appeared at a time of intense cultural controversy.

Coleridge, however, had earlier disputes in mind. He describes the projected "Brook" at the end of his recounting of the "Spy Nozy" incident, to explicate his landlord's response to a local, patriotic "Dogsberry" investigating the poet, as the landlord explains that Coleridge has been wandering over the countryside toward the channel not to spy for the French but because he was planning to write a poem "to put Quantock and all about here in print" (1.195). Dissatisfied with Cowper's *The Task*, Coleridge wanted to find

> a subject, that should give equal room and freedom for description, incident, and impassioned reflections on men, nature, and society, yet supply in itself a natural connection to the parts, and unity to the whole. Such a subject I conceived myself to have found in a stream, traced from its source in the hills among the yellow-red moss and conical glass-shaped tufts of bent, to the first break or fall, where its drops first become audible, ... and thence to the peat and turf barn ... to the sheepfold ... to the lonely cottage and its bleak garden won from the heath; to the hamlet, the villages, the market-town, the manufactories, and the seaport. (1: 195–96)

Much as in the *Duddon* series, "The Brook" was to trace the course of a river from source to sea in order to think about the lifespan of men and women. For Richard Holmes, "the water imagery here" not only links to the "flowing thematic of the entire *Biographia*" but also evokes "the unwritten philosophic epic of Coleridge's letter to Wordsworth, and perhaps signals the recovery of 'Kubla Khan,' that miniature epic of the 'sacred river' originally written at the same time."[27] That is, Holmes sees Coleridge bringing together his writings on rivers in order to think about the flow of his life, thought, and work.

In any event, while Coleridge tells us that "circumstances, evil and good" prevented him from completing the project, he notes sarcastically, "Had I finished the work, it was my purpose in the heat of the moment to have dedicated it to our then committee of public safety as containing the charts and maps, which I was to have supplied the French Government in aid of their plans of invasion" (1: 195–96). As Kenneth Johnston argues, Coleridge's retelling of the "Spy Nozy" incident here seems designed to separate him from not only his earlier political positions but also from partisan politics – which he goes on to attack – in general. His youthful, radical days are reduced to a humorous anecdote as he prepares himself, in Johnston's words, to "re-start his career" in a post-Napoleon world, to separate himself from his earlier politics and poetry, to offer himself as England's "sage,"[28] no longer working on projected poems such as "The Brook" but on tomes such as the *Biographia*. Following Johnston and Fulford, we can see Coleridge's considerable publishing efforts in 1816–18 – as he releases not only the *Biographia* and the "Christabel" volume but also the *Lay Sermons* and *Sibylline Leaves* which included a reprinting of "Hymn Before Sun-Rise, in the Vale of Chamouny," a poem I turn to later – as *his* bid to the writer of the moment. Wordsworth, undergoing in 1820, as Gill suggests, a turn in his career, evokes Coleridge's earlier career makeover. Both are trying to make their way in a post-Napoleonic political, social, and cultural world free from worries of a French invasion, but also a literary scene that had been invaded by the Cockney School.

III

Percy Shelley's "Mont Blanc" – written most likely between July 22 and August 29, 1816 – appeared in print at the close of Mary Shelley's 1817 *History of a Six Weeks' Tour*, which itself, with its strong evocations of Rousseau, whom Coleridge called "crazy," and Byron, whom Coleridge referred to as the "wicked lord," might be seen as another salvo in the literary wars of that year.[29] It has long been recognized that "Mont Blanc" evokes Wordsworthian and Coleridgean poetry in order to rework the greater romantic lyric created by the Lake Poets, including "Tintern Abbey," "Kubla Khan," and the "Hymn Before Sun-Rise," but we need a better sense of how these allusions function. In addition, what I think has not been recognized is that Wordsworth perhaps seeks to answer in turn Shelley's great river poem "Mont Blanc" in the sonnets on the River Duddon, as influence flows both ways.

If the everlasting universe of things rolls through the mind at the opening of Shelley's poem, it is the poetry of Wordsworth and Coleridge that rolls through the poet's mind.[30] Shelley had already taken up the Lake poets in his "Alastor" volume, with its famous sonnet on Wordsworth, with its engagement in "Alastor" itself with *The Excursion*, "Tintern

Abbey," and the "Intimations Ode," and with "O! There are spirits of the air," according to Mary Shelley, addressing Coleridge.[31] Again, *Laon and Cythna*, printed about the same time as the *History of a Six Weeks' Tour*, clearly seeks to rewrite Wordsworth's response to the revolutionary era in *The Excursion*. "Mont Blanc" was written and published, then, during a period when Shelley was actively seeking to define himself in relation and in reaction to the Lakers.

"Mont Blanc" replies most directly to Coleridge's "Hymn Before Sun-Rise, in the Vale of Chamouny," a work that was, of course, not written there and adapted from a poem by Friederike Brun. Coleridge's "Hymn" was first published in the *Morning Post,* and, as Charles Robinson has established, Shelley read the poem when it was reprinted in *The Friend* in 1809 (it was then collected in 1817 as a "Meditative Poem in Blank Verse" in *Sibylline Leaves*).[32] Robinson has also shown the degree to which Coleridge, as well as Wordsworth, was a subject of conversation between Byron and Shelley in the summer of 1816. Indeed, Shelley wrote to Peacock on July 17, "Tell me of the political state of England – its literature, of which when I speak Coleridge is in my thoughts" (*SL*, 1: 501). Robinson and others have pointed to Shelley's echoes of Coleridge's hymn as well as of "Kubla Khan," that other key river poem. More recently, Richard Adelman has placed "Mont Blanc" in a line of poems on the "idle mind" stemming from Cowper's *The Task*, which Coleridge had hoped to respond to in "The Brook," and including Coleridge's "Eolian Harp" and "Frost at Midnight," which Adelman sees Shelley engaging in a more sympathetic way than other critics have seen him treating the "Hymn."[33] I want to suggest that the interplay between these echoes helps to define Shelley's stance toward his older contemporaries.

There is little doubt Shelley wishes to reject the explicit religiosity of Coleridge's celebration of Mont Blanc. Shelley presumably did not read Coleridge's Joyce Kilmeresque "only God can make a tree" proclamation in the note that accompanied the poem when it first appeared in the *Morning Post*, but we can imagine what he would have thought of Coleridge asserting that

> the whole vale, its every light, its every sound, must needs impress every mind not utterly callous with the thought – Who *would* be, who *could* be an Atheist in this valley of Wonders![34]

Shelley – that lover of mankind, that democrat, that atheist of hotel registries – could be, as Curran reminds us.[35] In particular, Shelley seems to echo in order to refute in particular Coleridge's lines from the hymn,

"And they too have a voice, yon piles of Snow, / And in their perilous fall shall thunder, GOD!" (*CPP*, 62–3). Shelley's "great Mountain" also "hast a voice" but it is used "to repeal / Large codes of fraud and woe" (*SPP*, 80–81). Shelley might, in looking at Mont Blanc, be in a "trance sublime and strange" (35), but unlike Coleridge who "entranc'd in prayer / . . . worshipped the Invisible alone" (*CPP*, 15–16), Shelley "muse[s] on my own separate phantasy" (*SPP*, 36) as he moves to the "cave of the witch Poesy" to seek "some faint image" (46–47) of the power that "comes down" in "likeness of the Arve" (16). Rather than bow before an invisible God, Shelley in his third stanza provides a series of images, a range of thought experiments about the meaning of Mont Blanc. To simplify his complex exploration, he asks whether, as Coleridge suggests, Mont Blanc, as the "dread Ambassador from Earth to Heaven" (*CPP*, 82), has "unfurled / The veil of life and death?" (*SPP*, 53–54). Or, if we prefer a psychological to a theological explanation, perhaps this is a site where dream and waking life come together. Or myth might explain what we see: "Is this the scene where the old Earth-quake daemon taught her young / Ruin?" (72–73). Or, should we turn to science to find an explanation of the mountain in terms of volcanic action, a "sea / Of fire" (73–4)? Where in Coleridge's poem both the entire natural landscape and the poet answer a series of questions with one proclamation – "GOD" – in Shelley's poem, "None can reply" (75) to the question of the origin and meaning of the mountain. In place of Coleridge's vocal faith we have silence and skepticism. At the close of his poem, Shelley seems to return to the opening of Coleridge's "Hymn"; Coleridge looks at Mont Blanc rising "how silently"(*CPP*, 7) and sees again "thine own calm home, thy crystal shrine, / Thy habitation from eternity!" (11–12) until the mountain "Did'st vanish from my thought": "I worshipped the Invisible alone" (15–16). In his final stanza, Shelley – echoing specific words from Coleridge's "Hymn" such as "calm" or "silently" – also takes another look at Mont Blanc that "yet gleams on high" (*SPP*, 127), but it is not to have the mountain vanish into the Invisible but to reassert its physical presence, not some abstract Power, not Coleridge's "awful Form" (*CPP*, 5), but the "power of many sights / And many sounds, and much of life and death" (*SPP*, 127–28). Where Coleridge finds the mountain an emblem of eternity, Shelley replaces eternity with the "infinite dome / Of Heaven" (140–41), which might in other hands be an attribute of God but here appears as a description of the everlasting universe of things of the poem's opening, a physical world without beginning or end, a world not in need of a creator. And, of course, where Coleridge ends with worship, Shelley concludes with a question, offering not atheism in place of theism but, as Colin Jager has suggested, an opening of thought beyond both religion and secularism.[36]

It is easy to see Shelley rejecting the vision of Coleridge's hymn, but what are we to make of his use of poems such as "Tintern Abbey" or "Kubla Khan" or "The Eolian Harp" with which he would have much more sympathy? What I want to suggest is that Shelley echoes earlier poems by Wordsworth and Coleridge to suggest the gap that has arisen between the Lakers' poetry of the 1790s, which Coleridge would in a sense disavow in his 1817 *Biographia*, and the poetry they are producing now, in Coleridge's "Hymn," reissued in 1817, or in the 1814 *Excursion*, or in Wordsworth's "Thanksgiving Ode" that was published in early May 1816 as Shelley left for Europe and the famous 1816 summer. The Lakers of the present moment find God clearly proclaimed in the sublimity of a mountain, even in the terrifying carnage of war. The earlier writings of these poets offered more tentative essays and effusions. "Tintern Abbey," which Shelley clearly echoes in the opening of "Mont Blanc," might be seen to offer a merger of a natural world half-perceived and half-created by humanity where loss – from the loss of leaving a place, to the loss of leaving behind one's earlier self, to the loss of life – can find abundant recompense in what Keats called, in words I quoted before, "a recourse somewhat human independant [sic] of the great Consolations of Religion."[37] "Kubla Khan," which Shelley alludes to in his fourth section, might be read as speaking of the power of human creativity that can build a "pleasure dome" in spite of the "caverns measureless to man" (*CPP*, 2, 4), just as Shelley's "human mind's imaginings" (*SPP*, 143) might offer meaning to a powerful if amoral nature. The "Eolian Harp," echoed in Shelley's final question, might be recalled for its pantheistic speculation "what if all of animated nature / Be but organic Harps diversely framed" (*CPP*, 36–37). The self-questioning mode[38] of the greater romantic lyric is pitted against the certitudes of the late poetry of the Lake poets.

This use of old radical writings to embarrass a current Laker is a common tactic in Cockney critiques of their older contemporaries, from Shelley's own "To Wordsworth" – where the "Poet of Nature" has betrayed the "truth and liberty" of his earlier work (*SPP*, 1, 12) – to Smith's attack on Southey in Parliament, where he quoted from both *Wat Tyler* and a recent reactionary Southey essay in the *Quarterly Review*. We might think here of the satire on Southey, "The Laureate Laid Double," published in *The Examiner* (August 4, 1816) where passages from the *Lay of the Laureate* are placed next to parodies recovering Southey's Jacobin past, or Hazlitt's excoriations of the Lake Poets as apostates taken up by both

Charles Mahoney, as we have seen, and by Kevin Gilmartin in his book on Hazlitt as political essayist.[39] The attempt by Wordsworth and Coleridge as well as Southey to redefine themselves as post-Napoleonic writers of a triumphant England is called out by Shelley and the other Cockneys as self-betrayal. It apparently stung, as we can see in Wordsworth's letter to Henry Crabb Robinson of June 24, 1817, where he protests that Smith's labeling of Southey as a "Renegado" works so that the "*act of change* is stigmatized";[40] he objects that evolution or reformation is seen as deformation. I am not claiming that the Cockney accusations are fair or right but simply that, in the charged atmosphere of cultural battle following the defeat of Napoleon, in a moment that reviewers defined through the opposition of Lakers and Cockneys, every piece of writing converses with and contests opposing pieces. It is clear that both sides see even the simplest literary gestures as potential attacks that must be answered. And I hear Wordsworth answering Shelley in his sonnets on the River Duddon.

IV

I cannot say for certain that Wordsworth ever read Shelley's "Mont Blanc." It would have made sense for him to have consulted Mary Shelley's travelogue when he was contemplating a trip to Europe with Southey in 1817 but did not go until 1820. In that later trip, as Dorothy Wordsworth indicated in her *Journal of a Tour on the Continent* (1820), "Switzerland was our end and aim,"[41] while William wrote to Henry Crabb Robinson in late January 1820 (*WLMY*, 2: 579) to tell him of his plans to go to Switzerland in the summer. In the same paragraph, he has Shelley on his mind as he tells Robinson that he thinks it more important to attack Byron than "to hunt down Shelley." Chester and Alice Shaver indicate in *Wordsworth's Library: A Catalogue*[42] that Wordsworth owned several volumes of Shelley's poetry along with Mary Shelley's *Rambles in Germany and Italy in 1840, 1842, and 1843*, but none of these was published before 1829. Duncan Wu, the author of *Wordsworth's Reading*, has suggested to me that an entry in Wordsworth's list of books he had loaned out might refer to Mary Shelley's *History of a Six Weeks' Tour* where "Mont Blanc" appears, but Wu added that it is more likely a reference to Shelley's *Rambles*.[43]

Wordsworth might have been led to at least parts of "Mont Blanc" by reviews of the *History of a Six Weeks' Tour* that have been explored by Benjamin Colbert.[44] Although the *Monthly Review* had only a brief mention, the *Eclectic Review* (2nd series, 9 [May 1818]: 470–74) – which we know Wordsworth sometimes read – gives more time to the book, including quoting the opening lines of "Mont Blanc," with their clear echoes of "Tintern Abbey." It seems even more likely that Wordsworth would have read the July 1818 issue of *Blackwood's* – he wrote in 1819 that the publisher had sent him the journal when it began – and that he would have given it some attention. The April issue, for example, reports on Hazlitt's lectures on English poetry, and the May issue takes up Moore and Byron and includes a "Letter from Z. to Leigh Hunt, King of the Cockneys"; the Cockney School attacks continued in the July issue, which, more importantly, opens with the first in a proposed series of "Essays on the Lake School of Poetry." This review of Wordsworth's *White Doe of Rylstone* begins with the pronouncement "The three great master-spirits of our age, in the poetical world, are Scott, Wordsworth, and Byron" (3 [July 1818]: 367; Reiman, *Lake Poets*, 1: 78). After declaring that the current age of poetry is equaled only by that of the Elizabethans, the author gives short accounts of Scott's and Byron's poetic genius before focusing on Wordsworth, concluding that "the 'White Doe of Rylstone' is a tale written with a singularly beautiful simplicity of language, and with a power and pathos that has not been often excelled in English Poetry" (381). Further into the issue, Wordsworth could have read a review of Mary Shelley's *History* that might have caught the eye of someone longing to visit Europe, and at the conclusion of the review is the third stanza of "Mont Blanc," which the reviewer describes as "a little poem by the husband, which, though rather too ambitious, and at times too close an imitation of Coleridge's sublime hymn on the vale of Chamouny, is often very beautiful" (416). This link to Coleridge and the surrounding arguments about the Lake and Cockney schools surely could have drawn Wordsworth's attention.

Given these factors, I think it likely that Wordsworth did know "Mont Blanc," at least in pieces, but even if he did not I think we can hear language akin to Shelley in the *River Duddon* sonnets. Of course, the only regularly cited echo of the younger romantics in this sequence is not from Shelley but from Keats, and it has been severely queried. Ernest de Selincourt and Mary Moorman both hear in line 10 of Wordsworth's sonnet "The Resting Place" – "Or if the Fancy, too industrious Elf" – an echo of Keats's "Ode to a Nightingale": "Adieu! The fancy cannot cheat so well / As she is fam'd to do, deceiving elf" (*KPP*, 73–74). Wordsworth published his poem before Keats issued his, but they point out that Haydon could still have sent a copy of the ode published in the *Annals of Fine Arts* for July 1819 to Wordsworth, who in early 1820 wrote the painter about "Keates . . . a youth of promise too great for the sorry company he keeps."[45] Rebuffing this argument, Geoffrey Jackson conjectures that Wordsworth's sonnet was completed by early June 1819 and thus could not echo Keats.[46] I am less interested in whether Wordsworth is offering what de Selincourt sees as a "subconscious reminiscence" of Keats or, according to Moorman, a "conscious tribute" to Keats than I am in the fact that Wordsworth is using language we, and I believe knowing readers of the period, identify with Keats.[47] Again, as we have seen, Sonnet VI, "Flowers," in reversing course draws attention to its status as a poem and also offers a note citing the poetry of the Rev. Joseph Sympson. If we read the passage Wordsworth highlights by these tactics, we might hear what sounds like Keats, for in this hawthorn bower, where bees hum, one can catch:

> . . . the fragrance which the sundry flowers,
> Fed by the stream with soft perpetual showers,
> Plenteously yielded to the vagrant breeze.
> There bloomed the strawberry of the wilderness;
> The trembling eye-bright showed her sapphire blue,
> The thyme her purple like the blush of even;
> And, if the breath of some to no caress
> Invited, forth they peeped so fair to view,
> All kinds alike seemed favourites of Heaven.   (6–14)

Reading both Wordsworth's and Keats's volumes in 1820, one would have heard them speaking to one another; Keats writes:

> I cannot see what flowers are at my feet,
>   Nor what soft incense hangs upon the boughs,
> But, in embalmed darkness, guess each sweet
>   Wherewith the seasonable month endows
> The grass, the thicket, and the fruit-tree wild;
>   White hawthorn, and the pastoral eglantine;
>   Fast fading violets cover'd up in leaves;
>   And mid-May's eldest child,
> The coming musk-rose, full of dewy wine,
>   The murmurous haunt of flies on summer eves.
>   (*KPP*, 41–50)

Or perhaps we might hear another poem which Wordsworth truly could not have known, as Cupid and Psyche enjoy the "eye-dawn of aurorean love" "'Mid hush'd, cool-rooted flowers, fragrant-eyed, / Blue, silver-white, and budded Tyrian" (*KPP*, 20, 13–14). Of course, one can find instances of this lush writing elsewhere in Keats, or in Hunt or others of the Cockney School. The lines from Wordsworth's sonnet – "The trembling eye-bright showed her sapphire blue / The thyme her purple like the blush of even" – sound more like a Cockney than the chaste Wordsworth who in "Guilt and Sorrow" remembers another riverside scene, a "little croft" along the Derwent, "a plot of corn, / A garden stored with peas, and mint, and thyme."[48] This simple catalogue is what we expect of Wordsworth, not these Keatsian lines where every rift is loaded with ore.

And if we do not hear Keats, then why not Hunt: if we return to "The Resting Place," we find Wordsworth writing of a visit to a "Half grot, half arbour" when "Mid-noon is past; – upon the sultry mead / No zephyr breathes" (7, 1–2) in language that sounds not unlike Hunt infamously describing in *The Story of Rimini* "The two divinest things the world has got, / A lovely woman in a rural spot" (*SWLH*, 5: canto 3: 257–58) where his lovers meet "on a summer afternoon" (504). And what of the striking close of Wordsworth's sonnet, where a "stealthy prospect" from the grot "may tempt / Loose Idless to forego her wily mask"? (13–14). Wordsworth often uses the words "idle" and "idleness," but this is the only appearance in his poetry of "idless," which happens to appear twice in *Childe Harold*, by the author of *Hours of Idleness,* for example, at the close of the second canto where Byron addresses Harold, who "Hast soothed thine idless with inglorious lays": "Soon shall thy voice be lost amid the throng / Of louder minstrels in these later days" (94.884–85), a reference to the struggle between contemporary poets that Byron would continue to address in *Don Juan.*[49] The point is the one Shelley made in the "Preface" to *Prometheus Unbound*: even if we set aside conscious and unconscious echoes, contemporary poets still use enough common language and poetic tactics to be heard conversing with and contesting each other.

We hear Shelley, too, in the *Duddon* sonnets when, in the first of the sonnets, we read of "Alpine torrents thundering / Through icy portals radiant as heaven's bow" (7–8). We might think of Shelley's alpine poem that brings together river, ice, and rainbow. In Sonnet II, the Duddon is guarded by a "ruthless Power! Who would not spare / Those mighty forests" (II.9–10), and we might hear Shelley's overwhelming "Power in likeness of the Arve" (*SPP*, 16). Again, when Wordsworth in Sonnet XV comes upon a rock formation, "In semblance fresh, as if, with dire affray, / Some Statue, placed amid these regions old / For tutelary service, thence had rolled" (5–7), we might recall Shelley's "unsculptured image" (*SPP*, 27), where a waterfall has shaped the rock. And when Wordsworth asks of his statue, "Was it by mortals sculptur'd? – weary slaves / Of slow endeavor! or abruptly cast / Into rude shape by fire, with roaring blast / Tempestuously let loose from central caves? / Or fashioned by the turbulence of waves, / Then, when o'er highest hills the Deluge past?" (9–14), it is hard not to hear Shelley: "Is this the scene / Where the old Earthquake-daemon taught her young / Ruin? Were these their toys? or did a sea / Of fire, envelope once this silent snow?" (*SPP*, 71–74). Shelley's answer – "None can reply" (75) – seems to echo in another poem, Sonnet VIII, where Wordsworth asks about the man who first walked along the River Duddon before asserting "No voice replies" (9); and in that sonnet, which goes on to praise the stream whose "function was to heal and to restore, / To soothe and cleanse, not madden and pollute" (13–14), we find a natural world that never did betray the heart that loved her, not the nature of "Mont Blanc," where the River Arve is a creator and a destroyer, both the "breath and blood of distant lands" and a "flood of ruin" (*SPP*, 124, 107). I cannot demonstrate that "Mont Blanc," so clearly shaped by "Tintern Abbey," in its turn provoked these lines from Wordsworth, but it is clear that Wordsworth uses the same kind of language and rhetoric to address his river as it flows from the mountains to the sea as Shelley does in taking up the River Arve as it flows from the Valley of Chamonix at Mont Blanc to Lake Geneva and, then, as the Rhone to the Mediterranean (*SPP*, p. 100n). At some level, Wordsworth and Shelley are in conversation.

V

To what end might Wordsworth be echoing Shelley or drawing on Shelleyan language? As I suggested earlier, we can hear what strikes me as a direct echo and response to Shelley's "Mont Blanc, Lines Written in the Vale of Chamouni" in the poem from *Memorials of a Tour on the Continent, 1820* entitled "Processions. Suggested by a Sabbath Morning in the Vale of Chamouny," obviously written in response to the same landscape. Again, in the last stanza of that poem Wordsworth seems to echo the first stanza of "Mont Blanc" when he writes of the "secret springs / Of that licentious craving in the mind / To act the God among external things" (64–66). While, in Wordsworth's poem, Christians and even pagans see God revealed in grand landscapes, Shelley – a licentious, radical Cockney – seeks to "act the God among external things" by finding in the "human mind's imaginings" the meaning of the "Silence and solitude" of nature (*SPP*, 143–44). In the *River Duddon* sequence, Wordsworth seeks to strip nature of all those imaginings, all what he calls in "Processions" "Fables dark abyss!" (72). If we avoid our blasphemous cravings, we will hear God speak in the silent solitude of the world.

Wordsworth's opening sonnet sets a key theme of the sequence, most baldly put, that the native, homey River Duddon – which, in his

comments to Isabella Fenwick, he compares to the Ganges and the Nile
(*FN*, p. 98) – provides all the inspiration that others seek in the wide world:

> Not envying shades which haply yet may throw
> A grateful coolness round the rocky spring,
> Bandusia, once responsive to the string
> Of the Horatian lyre with babbling flow;
> Careless of flowers that in perennial blow
> Round the moist marge of Persian fountains cling;
> Heedless of Alpine torrents thundering
> Through icy portals radiant as heaven's bow;
> I seek the birth-place of a native Stream. –
> All hail ye mountains, hail thou morning light!
> Better to breathe upon this aëry height
> Than pass in needless sleep from dream to dream;
> Pure flow the verse, pure, vigorous, free, and bright,
> For Duddon, long-lov'd Duddon, is my theme!   (1–14)

One need not turn to ancient Rome, or the exotic East, or the sublime Alps
for "pure, vigorous, free, and bright" poetry that arises instead from contemplating the English countryside. While the most obvious literary allusion
here is to Horace, with his Sabine farm on the Bandusia,[50] we might
remember that, at the time, the turn to Italy was identified with Hunt in
particular but also such Cockneys as Keats, Shelley, Reynolds, and Cornwall;
we might also hear echoes of the evocation of Eastern lands in Byron and,
again, of Shelley's Alpine imagery.[51] Then, after closing Sonnet XI, a "Faëry
Chasm," with Shelleyan questions, Wordsworth, in his next poem, "Hints
for the Fancy," calls upon his "loitering Muse" (1) to move down the river,
and to leave behind a whole series of imagined foreign scenes, "Niagaras,
Alpine passes," and "Abodes of Naïads" that appear to the poet in miniature
as he looks at stream: he calls to "Leave them – and, if thou canst, without
regret!" (5, 6, 14). The very first sonnet establishes both that Wordsworth,
eschewing the globe-trotting cosmopolitanism of his younger contemporaries, writes of a "native stream," and that, from this position of homeland
security, he will be able to write not the kind of voluptuous, "smart ass"
poetry of the Cockneys but poetry that is "pure, vigorous, free, and bright."
As his reviewers noted with praise, he is a distinctly English poet.

    Although Wordsworth, in my reading, wants to turn from Shelley, the
Huntian cosmo-polite poet, to reground poetry on native ground,
I recognize that one could argue that Wordsworth is actually responding
to Shelley's prototype, Coleridge's "Hymn Before Sun-Rise." After all,
Coleridge tells us in a letter from 1819 that Wordsworth had complained

about his poem on Mont Blanc, finding it an example of the "Mock Sublime," perhaps objecting that Coleridge's hymn, an adaptation of Brun's poem in German, was not actually about Mont Blanc but Scafell.[52] Coleridge responds to Wordsworth's charge by saying there had been "no Mockery" in his "image and utterance of Thoughts and Emotions" (*CPP*, 196n), but Wordsworth's phrase may not so much suggest derision as fakery: it is not so much that the religious feelings in the poem are covertly being ridiculed – as we might say they are being overtly derided in Shelley's counterpoem – as they are being simulated. Coleridge claims to write a powerful hymn to an awe-inspiring mountain, but he never saw the mountain and his hymn is mediated through Brun's images, thoughts, and emotions. Coleridge is so swamped by influence from the German text that De Quincey would see it as plagiarism, though in such matters we need to ensure we follow Margaret Russett's finely tuned account of plagiarism and literary identity in *Fictions and Fakes*.[53] Wordsworth, resisting influence and the mock sublime arising from imitation, stands against the imposition of foreign culture on native ground.

In self-consciously turning from various influences as they are embodied in literary conventions, Wordsworth also tries to strip away any foreign or artificial impositions on nature (as De Man, Garrett, and Galperin in different ways suggest) to arrive at, if not an unmediated vision, what we might call a self-consciously de-institutionalized one, a nature from which we have sought to remove the screen of culture. Asking in the third poem, "How shall I paint thee?" (1), Wordsworth repeatedly queries the issue of representation, but to me it appears that Wordsworth's "pure, vigorous, free, and bright" verse strives not to give us the object itself but, in a slight revision of Galperin's view, the object freed of both the traditional conventions of a Horace and the modern innovations of a Shelley. While at first in this third sonnet Wordsworth asks that his verse might be "a speaking monument" (3) – the kind of merger of word and thing, speech and object that I explored in Chapter 2 on Waterloo poems – at the close of the sonnet, where he looks to the source of the Duddon, he asks for something simpler:

> To dignify the spot that gives thee birth,
> No sign of hoar Antiquity's esteem
> Appears, and none of modern Fortune's care;
> Yet thou thyself hast round thee shed a gleam
> Of brilliant moss, instinct with freshness rare;
> Prompt offering to thy Foster-mother, Earth! (9–14)

We cannot see the Bandusian stream without thinking of Horace's monument to it. If we hear of the Arve, we also hear Coleridge and Shelley. However, if we set aside both modernity ("modern Fortune's care") and antiquity ("hoar Antiquity's esteem") – that is, if we set aside all influence – we might glimpse not a monument but "moss, instinct with freshness rare." We might think here of Hazlitt's reflections on Wordsworth's *Excursion*: "Such is the severe simplicity of Mr. Wordsworth's taste, that we doubt whether he would not reject a druidical temple, or time-hallowed ruin, as too modern and artificial for his purpose. He only familiarizes himself or his readers with a stone, covered with lichens, which has slept in the same spot of ground from the creation of the world."[54] We see this again in Sonnet V, where Wordsworth is the "Sole listener" to the "breeze that play'd / With clear voice," and he is thus able to catch "the fitful sound / Wafted o'er sullen moss and craggy mound" (1–3).

Yet, culture immediately imposes itself between the speaker and nature, as Earth is personified as a "Foster-mother" (III.14). In Sonnet IV, the river becomes "Protean" (3), reminding us of the power of classical culture over our accounts of nature. Humbler interpreters of nature appear in Sonnet V, as children sport along the river, watched by their mother. Sonnet VII, as Robinson notes (p. 457), draws attention to the tradition of the Petrarchan love sonnet as a "love-sick Stripling," whose frustrated love is too much with him, cries out, "Change me, some God, into that breathing rose!" (2, 1). After the lover imagines himself a rose on Laura's breast, as Petrarch is evoked, or the bird in his cage, as Catullus and the tradition of Latin love poetry is suggested,[55] Wordsworth turns from these hackneyed versions of eros, these "Too daring choice[s]" (10), to celebrate again the simple world of the river's ecosystem:

> There are whose calmer mind it would content
> To be an unculled flow'ret of the glen,
> Fearless of plough and scythe; or darkling wren,
> That tunes on Duddon's banks her slender voice.   (11–14)

In its rejection of the conventions that inform the history of the sonnet, this poem recalls the sequence's first, with its turn from poetic accounts of foreign rivers.

I could multiply examples of this turn to and away from convention and tradition perhaps most obviously with the sonnet "American Tradition," suggesting the power of indigenous myth to write over the landscape, just as the flood imagined in the poem rushes over the earth; or the poem

"Tradition" that offers a local legend of a lovelorn woman who commits suicide before celebrating the "lonely Primrose," "Untouched memento of her hapless doom!" (13–14) where the poet tries to locate memory in the flower, not the story. Moving away from strictly literary traditions, Garrett has offered a strong reading of the closing sonnets of the sequence as offering local nature against the urban seat of empire by setting the humble Duddon against "sovereign Thames ... / Spreading his bosom under Kentish downs, / With Commerce freighted or triumphant War" (XXXI.12–14).[56] Already in Sonnet II, Wordsworth imagined the Duddon standing remote "from every taint / Of sordid industry" (1–2); again, Sonnet XXVIII notes that "No record tells of lance opposed to lance" along the Duddon, no histories of "doubtful combat issued in a trance / Of victory" (1, 5–6). The poems work to free the Duddon from the increasingly imperial history of combat and commerce just as they suggest it stands beyond the reach of local legend, of international myth, and of the literary tradition. We may not ever reach the thing-in-itself, but we may be able to range beyond the conventions that have defined the thing for us.

As the sequence ends, the River Duddon yet glides below. What remains if we try to strip from nature's silence and the solitude the history of human imaginings, the history of cultural influence? I offer two speculative answers to the question of what Wordsworth wants to achieve here. First, we are left with a Bloomian "strong poet" who can rise above influences, admitting to drawing on a William Crowe or John Armstrong or the Reverend William Sympson but working to silence the voices of Smith or Shelley. As Wordsworth congratulated himself, "My sonnets to the river Duddon have been wonderfully popular,"[57] and I want to suggest that they were in part popular because they subsume ancient and modern traditions to release his unique voice. He is not the poet of the "mock sublime," simply echoing others, but of a true sublime speaking into nature's silence. Second, we are left with the proper subject for such a poet, the God praised by Coleridge and queried by Shelley. As Robert Ryan has shown in *Charles Darwin and the Church of Wordsworth*, Wordsworth's increasing readership after 1820 "was recruited, much of it, from those who found the religious content of his poetry to be of special interest."[58] After Sonnet XVII, where Wordsworth invokes a time when the Romans "bent the knee to Jove and Mars" and Druids worshiped at a "mystic Round" (11–12), he then turns to "Seathwaite Chapel" to invoke "Sacred Religion" (1) and to praise at

least one tradition, both lived and written, the one that is offered in
service to the "holy lamp" of religion's "truth":

> Truth's holy lamp, pure source of bright effect,
> Gifted to purge the vapoury atmosphere
> That seeks to stifle it; – as in those days
> When this low Pile a Gospel Teacher knew,
> Whose good works formed an endless retinue:
> Such Priest as Chaucer sang in fervent lays;
> Such as the heaven-taught skill of Herbert drew;
> And tender Goldsmith crown'd with deathless praise!
>
> (7–14)

"Sacred Religion," as the "mother of form and fear" (1), replaces the earlier
Wordsworthian nature that nurtures alike by beauty and by fear. As the
"Mother of LOVE" (XVIII.6), Sacred Religion might end the constant
substitution of religions – from Druid to Roman to Catholic – the changing of "rites" "to please the fickle worshipper" (XVIII.3, 4). Wordsworth
hopes that, at least in this protected vale, "Truth's holy lamp" prevails
(XVIII.7). This right religion is exemplified by a "Gospel Teacher"
(XVIII.10), who in a lengthy note we learn is Robert Walker (1710–1802),
a clergyman known as Wonderful Walker. Wordsworth devotes twenty
pages of prose to Walker, with the sequence only taking up thirty-three
pages; some reviews spend as much time on the memorial of this clergyman
as they do on the poetry.[59] In the note, we learn of why we should admire
Walker, as various witnesses are brought forward to attest to his piety and
particularly his frugality. In his own comments, Wordsworth praises
Walker's thrift, simplicity, and hard work: "What contrast does this life
of this obscurely-seated, and, in point of worldly wealth, poorly-repaid
Churchman, present to that of a Cardinal Wolsey!" (p. 95). In what reads
almost as if it were a reply to Hazlitt's complaints in his review of *The
Excursion* that the narrowness of country life creates mean-spirited
people,[60] Wordsworth writes:

> It might have been concluded that no one could thus, as it were, have
> converted his body into a machine of industry for the humblest uses, and
> kept his thoughts so frequently bent upon secular concerns, without
> grievous injury to the more precious parts of his nature. . . . But, in this
> extraordinary man, things in their nature adverse were reconciled; his
> conversation was remarkable, not only for being chaste and pure, but for
> the degree in which it was fervent and eloquent; his written style was
> correct, simple, animated. Nor did his *affections* suffer more than his
> intellect. (p. 93)

Where Hazlitt worried that a constrained country life deadened the intellect, the emotions, and the senses, Wordsworth finds Walker exemplifying both intellectual and emotional power.

It is a letter by Walker himself quoted in Wordsworth's notes that makes clearest why he appears in this sonnet praising a steadfast belief:

> I am situated greatly to my satisfaction with regard to the conduct and behavior of my auditory, who not only live in the happy ignorance of the follies and vices of the age, but in mutual peace and good-will with one another, and are seemingly (I hope really so) sincere Christians, and sound members of the established church, not one dissenter of any denomination being amongst them all. (p. 89)

While Wordsworth wants to distinguish between fidelity to doctrine and bigotry, he does note that Walker "was indeed most zealously attached to the doctrine and frame of the Established Church" (p. 94). This portrait of Wonderful Walker closes on a typically Wordsworthian vignette of Walker and his wife laid to rest: "We have been dwelling upon images of peace in the moral world, that have brought us to the quiet enclosure of consecrated ground, in which this venerable pair lie interred" (p. 95). Opposed to this peaceful churchyard in the mountains is a "mill for spinning yarn" erected on Seathwaite Brook near the parsonage: "it is a mean and disagreeable object, though not unimportant to the spectator, as calling to mind the momentous changes wrought by such inventions in the frame of society – changes which have proved especially unfavourable to these mountain solitudes" (p. 96). Wordsworth's sonnets are devoted to celebrating the unchanging aspects of both these solitudes and of the religion Walker espoused.

Walker had already appeared in *The Excursion*, and, while Johnston links the sonnet sequence to the larger *Recluse* project, and Wordsworth himself, as we have seen, connects it to Coleridge's unfinished poem, "The Brook," the *River Duddon* sonnets also return to the arguments of Wordsworth's key published long poem, particularly that explored in *Excursion* Book IV where, as we saw in Chapter 1, Wordsworth offers a history of religion as various clouded versions of the truth pursued through the ages by Sonnet XVIII's "fickle worshipper[s]" (4). Walker appears in Book VII as the characters visit the Churchyard among the Mountains. He is praised for "temperance" (342), "industry severe" (343), "Stern self-denial" (345), and

> Forbearance, charity in deed and thought,
> And resolution competent to take
> Out of the bosom of simplicity

> All that her holy customs recommend,
> And the best ages of the world prescribe.   (348–52)

The Pastor, noting that Walker's title of "Wonderful" is better than that of various "Emperors and Chiefs" (363, 362), admits that "An unelaborate Stone / May cover him" (371–72), but that opens up an attack upon embellishment, even that of poet:

> – Noise is there not enough in doleful war –
> But that the heaven-born Poet must stand forth
> And lend the echoes of his sacred shell,
> To multiply and aggravate the din?
> Pangs are there not enough in hopeless love –
> And, in requited passion, all too much
> Of turbulence, anxiety, and fear –
> But that the Minstrel of the rural shade
> Must tune his pipe, insidiously to nurse
> The perturbation in the suffering breast,
> And propagate its kind, where'er he may?
> – Ah who (and with such rapture as befits
> The hallowed theme) will rise and celebrate
> The good Man's deeds and purposes; retrace
> His struggles, his discomfiture deplore,
> His triumphs hail, and glorify his end?
> That Virtue, like the fumes and vapoury clouds
> Through fancy's heat redounding in the brain,
> And like the soft infections of the heart,
> By charm of measured words may spread through fields
> And cottages, and Piety survive
> Upon the lips of Men in hall or bower;
> Not for reproof, but high and warm delight,
> And grave encouragement, by song inspired.   (VII.380–403)

Just as in the sonnet, religion shines through the "vapoury atmosphere" (XVIII.8) that seeks to obscure "Truth's holy lamp," so here Virtue should be attended by the "fumes and vapoury clouds" that poetry, with its "charm of measured words," devotes to subjects other than piety. Just as the Walker passage in *The Excursion* turns to a statement on poetry, so does the sonnet on Seathwaite Chapel call attention to itself as a piece of poetry.[61] If there is a possible echo of *The Excursion*, there is a direct quotation in the first line from Samuel Daniel's *Musophilus, or Defence of all Learning* (1599). As de Selincourt and Jackson point out, while Wordsworth puts quotation marks around "mother of form and fear," in fact the whole line comes from Daniel.[62] There are also direct references to

Chaucer's *Canterbury Tales*, Herbert's *A Priest to the Temple or The Country Parson, his Character and Rule of Holy Life* (1652), and Goldsmith's *Deserted Village* (1770). This is just one instance of what Daniel Robinson has called the ways the sequence "announces its literariness" (p. 456), but Wordsworth evokes the literary to query it. Why should poets write of war or love? As in *The Excursion*, here in the *River Duddon* sequence, Wordsworth wants us to celebrate not lovers or warriors but Walker: the various modes of poetry identified with the sonnet should be rejected to celebrate the simple Duddon and its Wonderful Priest. We may never escape the mediations of art, but Wordsworth at least wants to gesture toward a fresh vision by eschewing inherited poetic conventions to embrace living religious ones.

Although *The Excursion* is very much present here, the sequence's famous final poem evokes for me not so much Wordsworth's published epic but his unpublished *Prelude*. Just as Coleridge and Shelley take one last look at Mont Blanc, so Wordsworth now casts his eyes "*backward*" on the river which he had imagined as "past away" as it flowed into the sea. Always in motion, the river still remains: "The Form remains, the Function never dies" (6) – a more abstract formulation of the moment in Book Six of the *Prelude* where imaginative vision can grasp "The immeasurable height / Of woods decaying, never to be decay'd, / The stationary blasts of water-falls" (VI: 556–57).[63] As we all know, this moment in Wordsworth's crossing of the Alps comes after his own visit to Mont Blanc and the "wondrous Vale / Of Chamouny" (456–7), where the overlay of tradition, of cultural influence, prohibits him from truly seeing the mountain. The mock sublime of the touristic experience of Mont Blanc gives way to the sublime of an imaginative apocalypse.[64] At the end of the Duddon sequence, there is still an evocation of the power of poetry – the ability of "something from our hands [to] have power / To live, and act, and serve the future hour" even as "tow'rd the silent tomb we go" (10–11, 12). But we should not speak into that silence Shelleyan questions that seek to repeal large codes of fraud and woe, but instead voice a faith in the cardinal virtues evoked in the sequence's final words: "Thro' love, thro' hope, and faith's transcendent dower / We feel that we are greater than we know" (13–14). If we see nature in the act of stripping from it influence and tradition, we see through it so that we can "in calm of mind / And soul . . . mingle with Eternity!" (XXXII: 13–14)

Wordsworth sees such beliefs as answering Byronic despair, Keatsian "overlusciousness," and Shelleyan atheism.[65] As we read these sonnets, we may admire some of Wordsworth's stances; we may find some reactionary.

But the point is that in turning to and away from the past he is trying to change the present. Wordsworth engages contemporary poetry because he wants to shape his own moment; in taking up his younger contemporaries he is debating with them not just about rhyme or rhetoric but about the ways we think culturally, theologically, and politically.

The sequence's closing evocation of a spiritual tranquility won through faith, hope, and charity is quite beautiful, but it is not how Shelley would have concluded: in "Hymn to Intellectual Beauty," another poem of the summer of 1816, he created his own virtues, of "Love, Hope, and Self-Esteem" (37), of eros, a radical opening to the future, and a faith in our humanity. This is not just playing with words; if Shelley rewrote Coleridge and Wordsworth, if Wordsworth seeks to find a true sublime beyond Coleridge or Shelley, they all do so because they believe in the power of poetry to, in Wordsworth's words, "live, and act." The stakes in this battle over literary influence and tradition are not simply matters of literature. If these poems are criticisms of each other, it is because that critique can change minds and actions. How we think and write about rivers has an influence on how our lives flow through the world.

CHAPTER 5

Late "Late Wordsworth"

I: Retrospection and Re-collection

> That Man descends into the VALE of years;
> Yet have I thought that we might also speak,
> And not presumptuously I trust, of Age,
> As of a final EMINENCE, though bare
> In aspect and forbidding, yet a Point
> On which 'tis not impossible to sit
> In awful sovereignty – a place of power –
> – A Throne, which may be likened unto his,
> Who, in some placid day of summer, looks
> Down from a mountain-top
>
> (*The Excursion* 9: 50–59)

Up to 1820 the name of Wordsworth was trampled under foot; from
1820 to 1830 it was militant; from 1830 to 1835 it was triumphant.

De Quincey, "Autobiography of an English Opium Eater,"
Tait's Edinburgh Magazine 2 (1835): 543

I

Before I started this project, if I had an image of Wordsworth in 1820 it was
of an old, rather reactionary and querulous man, prone to egotism. He was,
as we have seen, a vigorous, active fifty-year-old, publishing multiple
volumes of poetry, fully engaged with family and friends, and traveling
to the continent. Scholars of age studies have shown us that the idea of old
age is socially constructed and thus varies, and that a man of fifty would not
have been considered old in Wordsworth's day.[1] In particular, he would
not have reached one benchmark of old age – the "grand climacteric" of
63 – until 1833 when he traveled for the third time to Scotland and wrote

most of the poems about that tour to be included in his *Yarrow Revisited* volume. He would publish his final original volume, based in part on an 1837 trip to Italy, in 1842 when he was seventy-two. No matter how "late" Wordsworth's poems become or seem, he did not strike people as "old" until very, very late in his life.

It is not that Wordsworth ignored the fact that he was aging. He constantly notes the passage of lived time – think of "five long winters!"[2] – and gestures to the aging process in any number of poems. For example, in an 1816 poem addressed to his daughter Dora, "A little onward lend thy guiding hand," he refers both to the fact that his daughter (and thus he) is older and to the immediate circumstance of his recovery from his recurring inflammations of his eyes; but he also asserts that Time has not "enrolled me yet, / Though not unmenaced, among those who lean / Upon a living staff" (8–10).[3] He defines himself as middle aged, which he was by most standards at forty-six. By the time of the very late "At Vallombrosa," to which I will return, he admits he is now, at sixty-seven, in the "winter of age" (27).

Wordsworth has seemed preternaturally old to us because of the early deaths of Keats, Shelley, and Byron. Born in 1770, if he had been Keats he would have died in 1795 having written almost nothing and would most likely not have made it into our literary histories. If, like Shelley, he had died before his thirtieth birthday, he would have lived to publish *Lyrical Ballads*; perhaps we would have then seen him as another Keats, the "Muses' son of promise,"[4] who wrote some juvenilia and one great book, with additional impressive work, including the beginnings of the *Prelude*, later being discovered in manuscript as was, say, "The Fall of Hyperion." Byron lived to thirty-six, so if Wordsworth had died at that age in 1806 he still would not have seen the publication of the 1807 *Poems in Two Volumes*, which, when released posthumously, might have been reviewed differently than it was. The fact is, when I was taught Wordsworth, an age ago, we essentially did not progress beyond that 1807 volume except to glance at the "Extempore Effusion on the Death of James Hogg." Had he died at Byron's age, Wordsworth might have gone down as another great poet who perished too young. Having written "Tintern Abbey," "Michael," and the "Intimations Ode" among many other stunning lyrical poems, he would not have become the poet of *The Excursion*, the "Thanksgiving Ode," the sonnets in defense of capital punishment – all poems we do not love or perhaps loathe. We would not have had to grapple with "late" Wordsworth.

The fact that Wordsworth long outlived his younger contemporaries does not make him "old" in 1820 or even 1833, but I do think we can learn something about late "late Wordsworth" if we draw on Devoney Looser's introduction of the idea, adapted from Hester Lynch Piozzi, of "retrospection" as a marker of "late" poetry. She points to the varying ways that women writers such as Piozzi, Edgeworth, Barbauld, and Jane Porter use a "retrospective lens": "To have been through it – and to have looked back through it in writing – is a creative or narrative approach that many aged writers used, communicating self-awareness about the inherent differences of life in one's advanced years."[5] Even though attitudes toward aging are distinctly gendered, Looser's ideas still apply here, at least in part because there is perhaps no poet more given to such retrospection than Wordsworth – and he didn't have to wait until old age to engage in it: as Geoffrey Hartman observed, one might give Wordsworth's "Peel Castle" and, by extension, every Wordsworth poem the title "X Revisited," even though few of us spend much time with the one so named, "Yarrow Revisited."[6]

This retrospective turn is particularly pronounced in the volumes Wordsworth published after the *River Duddon* sonnets – we only need think of such titles as *Memorials of a Tour on the Continent, 1820* (1822) and "Memorials of a Tour of Italy, 1837" (1842). Retrospection is also a hallmark, as Stephen Gill has so clearly shown, of Wordsworth's incessant rewriting as he issued his poems in new and varying editions (and we can add the Fenwick notes as another kind of retrospective turn).[7] For example, the four-volume *Miscellaneous Poems of William Wordsworth* of 1820 offered "all of the poetry he wanted to preserve, in a reconsidered order, in a fully revised text, complemented by the theoretical prose. Wordsworth was very consciously reviewing and representing all that he had done" (Gill, p. 336). Gill notes that in part Wordsworth responded to criticism by others, dropping "Alice Fell" because Coleridge had found it to be a failure in the *Biographia Literaria* and cutting lines from *Peter Bell* that had annoyed Henry Crabb Robinson, among others. Again, in preparing the five-volume *Collected Works* in 1827, Wordsworth did more than simply incorporate poems written since the 1820 edition – *Ecclesiastical Sketches* and *Memorials of a Tour on the Continent, 1820*: "every poem was freshly scrutinized, right down to commas and semicolons. *The Excursion* was revised with particular care. . . . Newly revised, each collected edition was a re-presentation of the whole, still-evolving corpus, not a mere augmenting of the old by addition of recent work" (Gill, p. 367). Again, if we look at the copy of the *Yarrow Revisited* volume held at the British

Library (Ashley MS 2262) that Wordsworth used to prepare the fifth volume of his *Poetical Works* (1836–37), we see Mary Wordsworth along with the poet not only emending particular lines but even making notes for the composition of pages, as when run-on lines in sonnets are to be set as single lines or when "Stanzas Suggested in a Steam-Boat off St. Bees' Heads" should be printed with "three stanzas on a page, without being numbered."

Each edition was an opportunity to return to and to revise earlier works, to "re-collect" them in the present, the kind of effort examined by Michael Gamer who, in *Romanticism, Self-Canonization, and the Business of Poetry*, takes up editions of *Lyrical Ballads* and the first collected works of 1815. In the latter, Gamer argues Wordsworth already tries to bring his works into a meaningful whole: "The result is a collection deliberately structured and determinedly alive: composed by a living poet; comprised of an allegorical life continually renewing itself; and closing with a poem [the 'Intimations Ode'] that returns readers to childhood and the collection's beginning"; again, "three corpuses (the body of the poet, the body of the collection, and the body of the nation) must line up aesthetically like planets and, if possible, become metaphors for one another, residing within a single authorial entity."[8] Each of Wordsworth's re-collections reconfigures his work into a new whole. Our dismemberment of Wordsworth's corpus – the division between early and late, the discovery of a decline or anticlimax – is particularly striking since no poet strove more furiously to assert the unity of his entire body of work.

I will focus in the second part of this chapter on Wordsworth's final retrospective act of writing, "Memorials of a Tour in Italy, 1837," included in the intensely retrospective collection *Poems, Chiefly of Early and Late Years*, and I will do so in part because we find in that volume that his "retrospective lens" allows him *not* to see those younger contemporaries he outlived. His poems on Italy not only convert the Italian landscape and culture into something more English; they also noticeably elide the presence of Keats, Shelley, Hunt, and Byron, all deeply connected with the representation of Italy in the period. However, I first want briefly to suggest how other volumes of this period contribute to Wordsworth's retrospective attempts to re-collect and to recreate his career.

II

If in 1820 Wordsworth had published the *River Duddon* volume and included in it his *Topographical Description of the Country of the Lakes in the North of England* (itself a revised version of the earlier *Guide through the District of the Lakes*), in 1822 Wordsworth published not only *Memorials of a Tour on the Continent, 1820*, with its obvious link to that pivotal year,[9] but also a separate edition of the *Topographical Description* as *A Description of the Scenery of the Lakes in the North of England*, and a new sonnet sequence, *Ecclesiastical Sketches*. The opening poem of this volume returns self-consciously to the *Duddon* series:

> I, WHO descended with glad step to chase
> Cerulean Duddon from his cloud-fed spring,
> And of my wild Companion dared to sing,
> In verse that moved with strictly-measured pace;
> I, who essayed the nobler Stream to trace
> Of Liberty, and smote the plausive string
> Till the checked Torrent, fiercely combating,
> In victory found her natural resting-place;
> Now seek upon the heights of Time the source
> Of a holy River, on whose banks are found
> Sweet pastoral flowers, and laurels that have crowned
> Full oft the unworthy brow of lawless force;
> Where, for the delight of him who tracks its course,
> Immortal amaranth and palms abound.
>
> (I. "Introduction"; 1–14)[10]

This poetic "Introduction" stretches back to the beginnings of Wordsworth's work in the sonnet. First, perhaps unconsciously, he cites his often occluded precursor, Charlotte Smith, who, as Geoffrey Jackson notes, uses the phrase "palm and amaranth" in her sonnet to "Mrs. ——," where the "bloom[s]" of the "bowers of Fancy" are left behind for the palm and amaranth that lead us through the tomb to "Faith's consoling voice."[11] Wordsworth also brings together all his own previous work on the sonnet, linking the *River Duddon* sequence to the earlier "Sonnets Dedicated to Liberty" from *Poems in Two Volumes* (which had, in a different retrospective move, been linked with the poems of the "Thanksgiving Ode" volume when they were collected together in his poetical works as "Poems Dedicated to National Independence and Liberty"). Adding a new sonnet sequence to his corpus, he urges us to see it as one of a series of sequences, as a poetic series in a series of series. As in his revisions for new editions, he gathers together his newer and his older poetry. And as he links the forward movement of his life to a retrospective recollection of all his work, he also forges, as Gamer suggests of the 1815 works, a connection to the history of the nation, from "Liberty" "fiercely combating" against Napoleon to the "victory" at Waterloo. Of course, what he is going to add in this series is a chronicle of the English church, explicitly delineating a history of faith only gestured at in the *River Duddon* series in poems such as "Seathwaite Chapel" (Sonnet XVIII), with its evocation of Chaucer, Herbert, Goldsmith, and Wonderful Walker. It is worth noting that in the "Advertisement" to this volume, where Wordsworth says he believes "that certain points in the Ecclesiastical History of our Country might advantageously be presented to view in Verse," he also notes that Southey is "writing a concise History of the Church *in* England" (p. 137), thereby bringing the Lake School together in its current efforts, as he had in the dedication to *Peter Bell* and the "Postscript" to the *Duddon* sonnets.

The volume thus could again be read as a riposte to Wordsworth's less devout rivals in the Cockney School. Several reviewers commented on the link to Southey, with both the *Journal of Belles Lettres* (March 30, 1822: 191; Reiman, *Lake Poets*, 2: 609) and the *Literary Chronicle* (December 14, 1822: 791; Reiman, *Lake Poets*, 2: 588) further tying Wordsworth's volume to the controversy around Southey's *Vision of Judgment* and Byron's famous reply. Most reviews noted that Wordsworth explicitly stated that his poems were written in the context of the debate over the Catholic Question, and several objected to the series' theological and political message, with the *General Weekly Register* finding that "The object of Mr. W seems to be the excellence of clerical power," by urging his readers "to seek the deity in pieces of painted wood, gilt crosses, and priestcraft" (May 5, 1822: 184–85; Reiman, *Lake Poets*, 2: 551–52) and with the *Monthly Repository* arguing that, "In truth since Wordsworth changed his politics, his writings have lost much of their charm" (17 [June 1822]: 361; Reiman, *Lake Poets*, 2: 694). *Blackwood's* extensive praise of the volume might most clearly suggest by way of contrast the response of Byron or Shelley or Hunt. The reviewer, perhaps John Wilson, opens by applying Wordsworth's line about Milton, "His soul is like a star, and dwells apart," to Wordsworth himself (August 12, 1822): 175; Reiman, *Lake Poets*, 1: 108). Shelley, drawing a quite different comparison, had adapted the line in "To Wordsworth" where the older poet in his youth "*wert* as a lone star" before he betrayed his dedication to "truth and liberty" (*SPP*, 7, 12, emphasis added); as elsewhere in the Cockney School response, Milton is used to bury late Wordsworth, not to praise him. *Blackwood's* goes on to proclaim Wordsworth "the most ORIGINAL POET OF THE AGE" and to claim that all other poets, including Scott, Moore, and Hunt, are all indebted to him, asserting that Wordsworth even "taught Byron how to look on a mountain, and how to listen to a cataract or the sea" (175–76; Reiman, *Lake Poets*, 2: 108–109).

I think it unlikely that the younger poets would have seen themselves so influenced by a poet revising his poetry away from natural supernatural-ism toward the Established Church, as *Blackwood's* praises Wordsworth's embrace of "Christianity, and great Establishments for the preservation of its doctrines pure and unsullied," noting that "never was the alliance between church and state so philosophically illustrated" (185–86; Reiman, *Lake Poets*, 2: 118–19). Wordsworth, again, is setting forth a vision set in opposition to his younger contemporaries, including those now dead.

Even more strongly, *Yarrow Revisited, And Other Poems* of 1835, the next independent volume Wordsworth released, has the "appearance of a memorial volume," as Stephen Gill puts it (p. 376); it is "retrospective and elegiac" (p. 377):

> Dedicated to an even older poet, Samuel Rogers (1763–1855) . . . it opens with a note to *Yarrow Revisited* which describes the poem as a "memorial" to a day spent with Scott and reminds the reader of "the Author's previous poems suggested by that celebrated Stream," the Yarrow. With the back-ward glance already established, the opening stanza, which directly invokes the first poem in the series, dwells on the years that have passed between each of Wordsworth's visits. Next comes *On the Departure of Sir Walter Scott*, now given a meaning by Scott's death which it did not have in 1831 when it was composed. This poignant sonnet is followed by another, *A Place of Burial in the South of Scotland*, and by many others which maintain the retrospective mood . . . . (Gill, pp. 377–78)

When "Extempore Effusion upon the Death of James Hogg" was issued with its mournful evocations of Hogg, Scott, Coleridge, Lamb, Crabbe, and Hemans (but not, of course, Byron, Shelley, or Keats), Wordsworth's sense of outliving his contemporaries became even clearer. While Gill goes on to note that seeing this volume as "only elegiac or wistfully retrospect-ive" (p. 378) distorts its political message, to which I will return, he signals the degree to which this gathering is involved in a mode of retrospection that seeks to bind together Wordsworth's entire career, even as we have continued to insist on the break between his early, pre-*Excursion* work and the "late" poetry that follows.

"Yarrow Revisited," a poem celebrating "a day of happy hours, / Our happy days recalling" (23–24), allows Wordsworth to make a number of links across the years. In its title and headnote, it obviously recalls his "Yarrow Unvisited," written in 1803 and published in *Poems in Two Volumes*, as well as his "Yarrow Visited," written in 1814 and published the next year. The opening lines – "The gallant Youth, who may have gained, / Or seeks a 'Winsome Marrow'" (1–2) – echo the opening stanza of "Yarrow Unvisited" and its reference to Dorothy Wordsworth as his companionate "*winsome Marrow*" (6), itself an echo of "the exquisite Ballad of Hamilton" (headnote).[12] Lines 73–81 describe the situation of "Yarrow Visited," where Wordsworth journeys to see the river even though he fears that seeing the actual sight will destroy his imaginative rendering of it, as he "Beheld what I had feared to see, / Unwilling to surrender / Dreams treasured up from early days, / The holy and the tender."

Evoking himself, "Yarrow Revisited" also links Wordsworth to a number of writers who were his companions – Dorothy and Coleridge traveling with him when they failed to visit Yarrow, James Hogg on the trip in 1814, and most fully, Scott – as the poem is offered as "a memorial for a day passed with Sir Walter Scott and other Friends visiting the Banks of the Yarrow under his guidance, immediately before his departure from Abbotsford, for Naples" (p. 490). Providing another river poem to give his volume a title, Wordsworth also refers back to the *River Duddon* series, and, as in that sequence, the flowing of the stream allows the poet to think over the course of human life:

> Brisk Youth appeared, the Morn of youth,
> > With freaks of graceful folly, –
> Life's temperate Noon, her sober Eve,
> > Her Night not melancholy,
> Past, present, future, all appeared
> > In harmony united,
> Like guests that meet, and some from far,
> > By cordial love invited.   (25–32)

The inviting closing simile provides the kind of link across one's life that is also offered in "Tintern Abbey." However, where in that poem the link occurs through a mixture of memory and imaginative thought, here it is "cordial love" that binds the phases of one's life, as perhaps are also bound together the various "guests" associated with his thinking about the Yarrow.

As a poem linked to other poems and poets, "Yarrow Revisited" then turns to poetry, which is found to provide a continuity within culture that the Yarrow offers in nature. If the Yarrow "Did meet us with unaltered face, / Though we were changed and changing" (35–36), we need not fear that "natural shadows" will "spread / Our inward prospect over" (37–38), because the "Muse, / And her divine employment" "trains" humanity to enjoy "hope and calm enjoyment" in the face of "sickness" and "Care"

(41–48). At the middle point of the poem, Wordsworth then apostrophizes Scott as a poet who has to leave his native land for Italy due to poor health, but who can still draw on "native Fancy" to "Preserve thy heart from sinking" (55–56). Part of the hope is that Scott, having been inspired by the Yarrow, the Tweed, and the Teviot, may now glory in the Tiber: "For Thou, upon a hundred streams, / By tales of love and sorrow, / Of faithful love, undaunted truth, / Hast shed the power of Yarrow" (65–68). As Looser remarks on writing in old age such as Scott's or Wordsworth's, "to have looked back through [life] in writing" is to assert that one has "been through it" so that one's experiences flow from earlier ones.[13] This is a core source of power in Wordsworth. In describing "spots of time" in the twelfth book of *The Prelude*, Wordsworth celebrates how "remembrances" of a place grant any return to that locale a "radiance more sublime": "So feeling comes in aid / Of feeling, and diversity of strength / Attends us, if but once we have been strong" (11: 324–28).[14] An older man, as he discovers new strengths from having experienced all he has been through, Wordsworth can also recollect the strength of his younger self, the gift he wishes for the aging and ill Scott.

As Wordsworth moves into the final section of the poem, he mimics the Shelleyan questioning of nature ("And what were thou, and earth, and stars, and sea, / If to the human mind's imaginings / Silence and solitude were vacancy"; *SPP*, 142–44) posed at the close of "Mont Blanc." Wordsworth writes:

> And what, for this frail world, were all
> That mortals do or suffer,
> Did no responsive harp, no pen,
> Memorial tribute offer? (81–84)

There is a way we can see Wordsworth giving a Shelleyan answer to this question. If Shelley asserted that poets are the unacknowledged legislators of the world, Wordsworth finds that even "mighty Nature's self" needs help from "the poetic voice / That hourly speaks within us" (85, 87–88). If Shelley found love to be the secret of morals, Wordsworth, too, finds love as the binding force in bringing together past and present, guest and host, friend and family.

There is, however, a Wordsworthian turn to these thoughts. The particular form of poetic and affective connection he puts forward is "localized Romance" (89). Jill Rubenstein, noting that Wordsworth alludes to Scott's *Lay of the Last Minstrel* (1805) set in Newark Tower whose ruins Wordsworth and his fellow poet visited (97–104), has usefully analyzed

Wordsworth's relation to aspects of Scott's poetics, and she more broadly sees Wordsworth offering "an intellectually acceptable and emotionally satisfying alternative for the aging poet who now seeks, like Scott, the reassurance that spiritual continuity and historical permanence need not imply stagnation."[15] This is one way to understand the agenda of the "late" Wordsworth. The poem revises Wordsworth's earlier union of imagination and nature, subject and object, as Rubenstein also suggests. The balance in "Tintern Abbey" between mind and world where we "half perceive and half create" tilts now strongly toward the "poetic voice" that must speak into the silence and vacancy of nature. We get not so much things that inspire the poet's words or words that aspire to be things (discussed in Chapter 2 in relation to the "Thanksgiving Ode") as things that need to be put into poetic words:

> Flow on for ever, Yarrow Stream!
>   Fulfil thy pensive duty,
> Well pleased that future Bards should chant
>   For simple hearts thy beauty,
> To dream-light dear while yet unseen,
>   Dear to the common sunshine,
> And dearer still, as now I feel,
>   To memory's shadowy moonshine!   (105–12)

The unity of past, present, and future is now offered as a progress quite different from the growth of the poet's mind in "Tintern Abbey." There, we move from "glad animal movements" that have the immediacy of a total immersion in nature to a moment when nature is apart but still "all in all" for consciousness to the time when the poet has "learned / To look on nature, not as in the hour / Of thoughtless youth; but hearing oftentimes / The still, sad music of humanity" (75, 76, 89–92).[16] Simply put, we must transform from animals in nature to humans apart from nature but still linked to it through the thought created by memory and imagination. In almost a reversal of this pattern, the earliest phase of "Yarrow Revisited" is one of pure imagination, unclouded by visiting the actual Yarrow – the "dream-light dear while yet unseen" – and we move to the "common sunshine" of directly experiencing nature and then to a memory of it that will last into the future. Beginning not with nature but the imaginative mind, Wordsworth does not fear losing nature here, so there is no need for abundant recompense: Scott and other great poets who have written over the landscape demonstrate that poetry can last as long as the river it celebrates. Ironically, at a moment when many feel Wordsworth's "poetic voice" is less imaginative, he professes more strongly than ever the imaginative power of poetry.

Yet, perhaps what troubles us is that this power no longer appears as an archetypal revelatory confrontation between subject and object that creates in all of us the imaginative experience that may give rise to poetry. As Manning puts it in discussing Wordsworth's "Pillar of Trajan," to which we will return, "Meanings once inscribed on the natural landscape in 'Poems on the Naming of Places' now shelter in art."[17] A universal experience of the world we call "poetic" gives way to the institution of "poetry," with, for example, different schools being identified with the "classic Fancy" and the "native Fancy" (54–55). Where the *River Duddon* series still seemed to work to dis-establish the institutions that stand between us and nature, this poem, following upon the *Ecclesiastical Sketches'* celebration of the established Church, rejoices in the establishment of canonical poetry.[18] To adapt a distinction I have used elsewhere, we get a canon of collected masterpieces rather than a pantheon open to new vision,[19] and one might object to a canon of Wordsworth and Scott rather than Shelley and Keats. But perhaps the real problem is, as again Rubenstein suggests, that the institution of poetry must then be subordinated to the institution of religion, with the state church obviously being allied to the state, as *Blackwood's* noted in its review of Wordsworth's *Ecclesiastical Sketches*. In an odd way, love of nature leads to love of God, which leads to love of church and state that are seen as serving God.

Even though such ideas had already been adumbrated in the "Thanksgiving Ode" and elsewhere, Wordsworth seems more strident in another poem from the Yarrow collection, "The Warning," where the poet, thinking of his new grandson, worries over England's future after the passage of the Reform Bill of 1832: though to be clear, one person's stridency is another's urgency as the power of poetry is called upon to address national crises. As Wordsworth noted in his prose "Postscript," the poems in the Yarrow volume have included "opinions . . . upon the course of public affairs," "uttered . . . in the spirit of *reflective* patriotism" (*Prose*, 3: 240; my emphasis), another form of retrospection. Drawing upon his experiences during the French Revolution, having seen "on the soil of France / Rash Polity begin her maniac dance" (65–66), he worries that the "labouring multitude," "trained to theoretic feud" (112, 111), like the French people led on by *philosophes*, will "In bursts of outrage spread your judgments wide, / And to your wrath cry out, 'Be thou our guide'" (119–20). He hopes that the people will find "saving skill / . . . in forbearance, strength in standing still" (149–50). In such a time of "adverse Change" (7), the steady and steadying institutions of poetry, church, and state are ever more needful. It is this apparent quietism that formed the sense of ideological betrayal that some have found in this later poetry: John Haydn Baker has argued that it is this specific call for acceptance of the way things are that led Browning, following Shelley, to attack Wordsworth in the "Lost Leader" as betraying the revolutionary hopes he once inspired, as he "boasts his quiescence" and bids the people "crouch whom the rest bade aspire."[20] Of course, Wordsworth offers himself as the poetic leader of a distressed nation, not of poets such as Shelley or Browning, stressed by his political beliefs.

With its grandfather's prayer for a newborn and with its return to Wordsworth's experiences during the Revolution, detailed in the yet unpublished *Prelude*, "The Warning" is another attempt to find unity in Wordsworth's life and work. As Rubenstein points out,[21] the last poem in the "Yarrow" group, "Apology," also works to pull together all these poems, even though they were not directly presented as a sequence as were the *River Duddon* and *Ecclesiastical* sonnets:

> No more: the end is sudden and abrupt,
> Abrupt – as without preconceived design
> Was the beginning, yet the several Lays
> Have moved in order, to each other bound
> By a continuous and acknowledged tie
> Though unapparent . . .   (1–6)

The second half of the poem offers one such link, by returning to Scott's departure for his health while recognizing that he is now dead:

> Nor will the Muse condemn, or treat with scorn
> Our ministration, humble but sincere,
> That from a threshold loved by every Muse
> Its impulse took – that sorrow-stricken door,
> Whence, as a current from its fountain-head
> Our thoughts have issued, and our feelings flowed . . .   (17–22)

Wordsworth wants to argue that the poems all proceed from the inspiration he received from visiting Yarrow with Scott and from bidding his old friend a fond farewell. Two other important links can be found in these final lines. First, a phrase in the passage just quoted, "Our ministration," makes an obvious connection between Wordsworth's poetic consolations and those offered by those ministering within the Church (and perhaps links back to Coleridge in *Lyrical Ballads* and the "ministrations" of nature found in "The Dungeon" or the more famous "secret ministry" of "Frost at

Midnight"). The link between poetic imagination and religious faith is reasserted. Second, the political valence of the sequence and the volume – seen most starkly, again, in "The Warning" – is alluded to as Wordsworth notes that "every day brought with it tidings new / Of rash change, ominous for the public weal" (28–29). These public threats shadow his poetic musing with "dejection," again evoking both Coleridge and the "despondency" analyzed in *The Excursion*. He binds together the group of poems as poetic and religious consolations to both an ailing fellow poet and to the sickly public sphere.

Peter Manning has brilliantly explored the lines that make up the rest of the first half of "The Apology," as Wordsworth compares his gathering of poems with a relief at Persepolis. Wordsworth has argued, again, that his poems are "bound / By a continuous and acknowledge tie":

> Though unapparent, like those Shapes distinct
> That yet survive ensculptured on the walls
> Of Palace, or of Temple, 'mid the wreck
> Of famed Persepolis; each following each,
> As might beseem a stately embassy,
> In set array; these bearing in their hands
> Ensign of civil power, weapon of war,
> Or gift, to be presented at the Throne
> Of the Great King; and others, as they go
> In priestly vest, with holy offerings charged,
> Or leading victims drest for sacrifice.   (5–16)

Manning has shown how interest in Persia was intensified by the struggle with Napoleon over this vital land link between Europe and India and how in the 1830s there continued a fascination with Persian figures, art, and culture. He suggests that this web of historical allusions defines Wordsworth's late style:

> the bookishness of the late Wordsworth suggests to me a poet done with the autobiographical involvement of the *Prelude* and the "Moods of his own Mind," and turning outward to the span of history, at once to present events and to time not merely personal. . . . "Tintern Abbey" produces complexity by its supple syntax, [its] hesitations and qualifications . . . . The "Apology" gives instead the sculptured, concrete, material image a fixed visual form and an almost liturgical gravity of style that seem the very opposite. Yet when one looks closely the fixity dissolves: the indeterminate bearings of the image, the shimmer of various possible connections and the question of how to read the image that they set in motion, produce a different sort of complexity, a complexity of temporal, spatial, and historical suggestiveness. In this late manner, Wordsworth finds a style that releases multiple perspectives on east and west, past and present, the enduring and the contemporary,

above all, on the poet's immersion in, and resistance to, the history on which he meditates.[22]

Offering our best understanding of how history informs Wordsworth's late style, Manning also suggests how these poems serve a "liturgical" and political or ideological purpose, as Wordsworth goes on to show in the rest of the poem. As again Gamer suggests, Wordsworth maps the history of his life not only on the development of his own work – as he recounts both lived trips to and poetical representations of the Yarrow – but also on the history of his society, particularly its political and religious history.

There is one more link here – perhaps an unacknowledged one – that I think will help us to understand the project of the very late "Memorials of a Tour in Italy" (1842). For, as Wordsworth describes the imagined parade of figures on the walls of a ruin in Persepolis, he might also be describing a more famous procession, available for viewing in London: the Parthenon frieze, and the famous poem that, among many other works of art, takes up that relief:

> Who are these coming to the sacrifice?
>   To what green altar, O mysterious priest,
> Lead'st thou that heifer lowing at the skies,
>   And all her silken flanks with garlands drest?
>
>   (KPP, 31–34)

Wordsworth's language resembles Keats's, with echoes of "sacrifice," "drest," and "priest" in "priestly." Just as we might hear Shelleyan questions sounding in "Yarrow Revisited" only to be given non-Shelleyan replies, and just as we might recall Byron versifying history in *Don Juan* as Wordsworth does for very different ends, here we might hear Keats's contemplation of a frieze, albeit one that arrives at a very different sense of love, beauty, and truth than the Lake poet who preceded and followed him. What is interesting about Wordsworth's final 1842 Italian "Memorials" is that they provided the older poet with an easy, direct way to contemplate, to complement, and to combat these younger writers, a path he ultimately did not follow.

II: Contesting Italy

> Who would keep
> Power must resolve to cleave to it through life,
> Else it deserts him, surely as he lives.
>   Wordsworth, "Musings Near Aquapendente," 115–117

I

When, in 1837, Wordsworth traveled with Henry Crabb Robinson to Italy – to Rome, Florence, and Venice – he followed in the footsteps of countless Englishmen who had made similar trips. When, in 1842, he published poems evoking Italy and Italian culture, he also traversed ground crossed by many English poets – from Chaucer and Shakespeare to Byron and Hemans. Dedicated to his *"Companion"* ("To Henry Crabb Robinson," 1), the poems on his Italian trip, then, might appear ready to be diagnosed not only for the anxiety of influence but also for what Dean MacCannell and James Buzard have taught us to see as the anxieties of tourism that are finally the vicissitudes of modernity as such. Yet, for Wordsworth, I will argue, the "Memorials" were an opportunity to assert the power of his poetry in both confronting the cultural influence of Italy and turning away from the Italianate poetry of Hunt, Keats, Shelley, and particularly Byron, ironically his successors who had preceded him to this ground.

It is a paradox that during the period of Wordsworth's life when his poetry strikes us as being the least aesthetically convincing, he was probably at his most compelling as a force within his own culture and society. As Gill puts it in *Wordsworth and the Victorians*, "At a time when indisputably Wordsworth's creative powers were waning, his importance grew."[23] That is, in what we call the "late Wordsworth" there is a striking case of the disjunction between our aesthetic judgments and estimations of more direct cultural impact. My attempt to reanimate Wordsworth's late work, to stitch back together the body of his early and late poetry, might appear the work of a historicist Victor Frankenstein, who promises to overcome through historical recovery the death of most of Wordsworth's poetry only to bring to life a corpus where the yellow skin of scholarly writing barely covers the work of ideological argument. But then again, perhaps there is something important to be learned from this uncannily unlovely body of poetry I am calling late "late Wordsworth."

The 1837 trip fulfilled a lifetime dream of Wordsworth's, though he believed that it was, ironically enough for my discussion, too late in his career to have the same kind of transformative effect it had had on Shelley and Byron. Wordsworth wrote to his family toward the end of the trip: "I have, however, to regret that this journey was not made some years ago, – to regret it, I mean, as a Poet . . . [M]y mind has been enriched by innumerable images, which I could have turned to account in verse . . . in a way they now are little likely to do" (July 5, 1837; *WLLY*, 3: 423). Departing in

March, Wordsworth and Robinson traveled from Paris, through Lyon, Toulon, and Nice, for Genoa. They then went via Massa, Luca, Pisa, Volterra, and Sienna to Rome. In Rome, they mingled with the considerable expatriate community there, including Dr. John Aitkin Carlyle, Thomas Carlyle's brother; William Collins, Wilkie Collins's father; and Christian Karl Josias von Bunsen, a German polymath and diplomat to the Vatican who was a follower of the classical scholar Barthold Georg Niebuhr, whom Wordsworth addressed in several poems. They spent a considerable amount of time at the home of Frances Mackenzie (younger daughter of Lord Seaforth), whose guests included the historian and political theorist Sismondi and his wife, Jessie Allen (whose sister was married to Sir James Mackintosh), and the American Hispanist George Ticknor and his wife. Wordsworth and Robinson also mingled with the lively Roman artistic colony, including the Liverpool sculptor John Gibson, protégé of William Roscoe and an acquaintance of everyone from Blake to Canova; the Danish sculptor Bertel Thorvaldsen, who showed them his sculpture of Byron; and Joseph Severn, with whom Wordsworth discussed "poor Keats."[24] The eagerness of all these figures to meet Wordsworth signals his cultural status at this point in his life. These visits also suggest the kind of cosmopolitan community of which Wordsworth could have been a part. After their time in Rome, the threat of cholera in Naples prevented them from traveling south as planned. They instead headed to Florence, after visiting the "Tuscan sanctuaries" at Laverna, Camaldoli, and Vallombrosa, and then to Bologna, Milan, and, through Verona, Vicenza, and Padua, to Venice. They left, crossing the Alps into Germany before heading home in August.

Although he worried to his family about whether this trip would inspire him to write, in fact he came to compose thirty-some poems for his "Memorials of a Tour in Italy, 1837." Despite the date in its title, almost all the poems were written as recollections in tranquility during 1840 and 1841. Only the "Cuckoo at Laverna" was composed during the trip; there were also two translations from Michelangelo, perhaps drafted as early as 1805, and two poems added to the grouping in the new edition of *The Poems of William Wordsworth* of 1845, "Composed on May Morning, 1838" and "The Pillar of Trajan," which was written in 1825–26 and previously published in 1827. Despite fine work by Manning, James Chandler, and Bruce Graver, this is a little-read collection – with the exception, perhaps, of "Musings near Aquapendente." But, nonetheless, this gathering of late poems strikes me as, on its own terms, a powerful, final expression of Wordsworth's poetic project.

"Power" is a term we rarely apply to "late" Wordsworth. Yet, in 1840 and 1841, when he wrote the bulk of the Italian "Memorials," he was arguably experiencing the most successful moment of his career. His poetry, which had never sold as well as his friend Scott or his rival Byron, was reaching a wider audience, and he had increasingly fervent admirers, as my earlier epigraph from De Quincey suggests. Stephen Gill suggests that in 1840, "As he entered his last decade Wordsworth knew from overwhelming evidence that his poetry had comforted, strengthened, and encouraged many people" (p. 399). As Robert Ryan argues, there arose what he refers to as "the Church of Wordsworth," "the remarkably large and ecumenical congregation of believers who considered Wordsworth their priest, prophet, or spiritual advisor. It was the power and range of his religious influence, surpassing and then surviving the cultural authority of the professional clergy, that made him an especially effective counterforce to Darwinian science."[25] Rydal Mount had become almost a pilgrimage site, with even the Queen Dowager visiting in July 1840. Wordsworth was celebrated by various learned organizations, and Durham University conferred upon him the honorary degree of Doctor of Civil Laws in 1838, with Oxford awarding him another degree the next year. He was involved in public debates on copyright reform, capital punishment, and the extension of the railroads to Windermere. He was asked to stand as a conservative candidate in 1841 – a post he refused – and was offered in 1843 the Poet Laureateship, a position he finally accepted. The 1845 single-volume edition of his collected poems identifies him as "William Wordsworth, D.C. L., Poet Laureate, Etc. Etc.," linking him to his public recognitions and paralleling his dedication of *Peter Bell* to Southey as "Robert Southey, Esq., P.L., &c. &c." We may feel that this broader knowledge of Wordsworth's work was purchased by a loss of poetic power; or, to put it in the terms that had been used ever since he had accepted the Stamp Distributorship, he could be seen as gaining various forms of institutional approval because he had been bought by the government. Gill, however, argues that such political squabbles had long been forgotten, that Wordsworth's rise in reputation "was . . . allowed to go unchallenged by the work the second-generation Romantics might have produced" (p. 396); in other words, outliving the generation that might have criticized his political choices and threatened his cultural power, Wordsworth is seen communicating an uncontested legacy.

As all this suggests, the volume containing the poems from his trip to Italy were written and published when his fame was at its greatest, when he might well feel his voice would be most widely and clearly heard. As always, he wanted his work to be heard in its entirety, as a unified whole. This unity was presented rather prosaically in the title of this volume, *Poems, Chiefly of Early and Late Years* (1842), the last independent volume of poems he was to offer, which contains pieces from across more than four decades, including early works such as *The Borderers* (begun in 1796) and late pieces such as the "Sonnets upon the Punishment of Death" (written between 1839 and 1841). In the brief prose note to the Italian series, he also links back to earlier poems on European locations, "in particular, 'Descriptive Sketches,' 'Memorials of a Tour on the Continent in 1820,' and a sonnet upon the extinction of the Venetian Republic" (p. 741).[26] It is interesting that the early poems have been "rescued" by Wordsworthians from their locus of publication in this extremely late volume to be returned to their early scene of composition; presumably works such as "Guilt and Sorrow" or *The Borderers* exhibit an aesthetic quality not found in the late poems that surround them in this volume. However, I wonder to what extent our aesthetic distinctions within the Wordsworth canon rework in order to obscure a different division that would have been apparent to Shelley, Byron, Hazlitt, Keats, and Hunt – or, to cite a rising poet of the late 1830s, Browning, the author of "The Lost Leader" in 1845 – for whom Wordsworth's fall was not an aesthetic anticlimax but an ideological apostasy, as I have argued in my Introduction. Did Wordsworth publish the early *Borderers* together with the late sonnets on the death penalty to demonstrate a coherent poetic project, or to show that he had maintained – unlike his friend Southey who had suffered through the *Wat Tyler* affair – a consistent, if solidifying, ideological position?

Presumably both. Insisting upon the continuity of his work in the interestingly named "Prelude" to this volume, Wordsworth seems to subordinate the aesthetic to the ideological as he argues that his early and late poems, simple lyrics and exalted verse, are united in their service to a social, didactic end.[27] The poem opens with what will become a long simile. Wordsworth, wandering in a typical "*desultory walk*," describes listening to a thrush that sings at the start of a "*vernal storm*" to assure the traveler that a calm is to follow (1–10). Wordsworth hopes that his current book, written in the midst of what he clearly sees as the stormy days of the 1840s, will provide a similar glance of future tranquility. His book has, for him, a clear social purpose:

> . . . *now, my Book!*
> *Charged with those lays, and others of like mood,*
> *Or loftier pitch if higher rose the theme,*

> *Go, single – yet aspiring to be joined*
> *With thy Forerunners that through many a year*
> *Have faithfully prepared each other's way –*
> *Go forth upon a mission best fulfilled*
> *When and wherever, in this changeful world,*
> *Power hath been given to please for higher ends*
> *Than pleasure only ...*   (14–23)

As with all these retrospective volumes, Wordsworth hopes to join his latest volume to its "Forerunners," arguing that his earlier poetry has paved the way for his "late" style. There is no break but only the "progress" evoked in the poem's final line (55).

However, part of this development is now to find that poetic or aesthetic power aims higher than pleasure. While Wordsworth had argued as early as the "Preface" to *Lyrical Ballads* that his poems served "a worthy *purpose*,"[28] there he also argues that poetry serves the principle of pleasure, the "naked and native dignity of man" (*Prose*, 1: 140). In this "Prelude," pleasure may remain, but it is clearly subordinated to "higher ends." More particularly, in these "*days* / *When unforeseen distress spreads far and wide* / *Among a People mournfully cast down,* / *Or into anger roused by venal words*" (42–45), Wordsworth hopes his book will "*console* / *And reconcile*" both "*young and old*" (51–52). While he makes clear in the Fenwick Note that he is thinking in particular of the debate over the Corn Laws ("the discontents then fomented thro' the country by the Agitators of the Anti-Corn Law league"; *FN*, p. 162), Wordsworth had, of course, been distressed by any number of changes in the 1830s and what he saw as the dangers of the 1840s. He had been on the losing side of the two great issues of the day, Reform and Catholic Emancipation, and he was so distressed by what he saw as the decline of England that he was willing to believe that "a course of affliction," such as the cholera epidemic of 1831, was necessary to "bring back this Nation to its senses" and to see the "necessity of sacrificing liberty to order, probably under a military government" (letter to Robinson, May 5, 1833; *WLLY*, 2: 585). This "Prelude," then, takes up some of the same issues as "The Warning," discussed earlier. Finding, again, in the Fenwick note that contemporary problems evoke recurring threats, that "the particular causes of such troubles are transitory but [the] disposition to excite & liability to be excited are nevertheless permanent & therefore proper objects for the Poet's regard" (*FN*, p. 162), his response to the difficulties of the moment still calls upon the central powers of his poetry:

> *A Voice devoted to the love whose seeds*
> *Are sown in every human breast, to beauty*
> *Lodged within compass of the humblest sight,*

To cheerful intercourse with wood and field,
And sympathy with man's substantial griefs ... (37–41)

His is a poetry devoted to love and beauty, to communion with humanity and nature; yet, rather than the progression being the love of nature leading to the love of humanity, here, intercourse with nature and sympathy with other people lead to *"thoughtful gratitude / For benefits that still survive, by faith / In progress, under laws divine, maintained"* (53–55). The evolving state and traditional religion are what will save us from these days of "unforeseen distress." Although we may find this abstract and unappealing, Wordsworth believes that the church and state he embraces are made lovely by beauty and by love. We may see this as a conservative turn, but for him, I think, it continues to be a move to link his affirmation of institutions to the continuing sources of his poetic power – the *"Power* [that] *hath been given to please for higher ends,"* the power we deny late Wordsworth.

However, a gathering of poems on a journey to Italy would hardly seem a promising subject for an assertion of cultural power. Italy, having long served as both England's Other and its secret sharer, as both a kind of anti-England full of Machiavellian princes, popish plots, and Gothic horrors as well as a source of inspiration and illumination, might overwhelm the British observer. Part of the complexity of any English response to Italy arises from the fact that Italy could stand in for or mediate a whole series of others. Nearer than Greece, Italy could evoke the entire classical past. Home to Rome, it could stand for Catholic Europe. Historiographically, it could embody a vaguely "Gothic" past, a more clearly defined medieval age, or a not-yet-defined "renaissance" – in any event, a post-classical age that was not the present. Italy presented through its paintings, statues, monuments, and literature a vast cultural archive offering such a surfeit of inspiration that one's imagination might fail. The poet might be inundated by influence, able to offer only the "mock sublime" Wordsworth purportedly found in Coleridge's "Hymn Before Sunrise" (as discussed in Chapter 4). Struggling to avoid the "burden of the past" that Walter Jackson Bate sees besetting the modern poet who seeks to absorb the rich cultural inheritance of both the ancient and early modern worlds,[29] Wordsworth, in claiming to find so much in Italy disappointing, actually frees his imagination to see beyond touristic Italy. Wordsworth, "tired" of "churches and pictures and statues" (letter to Mary Wordsworth and Dora Wordsworth, May 6, 1837; *WLLY*, 3: 399–400), can, he finds, imaginatively recover English rocks and stones and trees.

Wordsworth's Italian tour and the series of poems on it are, in important ways, linked to the eighteenth-century Grand Tour. Of course, the Grand Tour was for young men, and Wordsworth notes that he is too old for this kind of traveling: "I am too old in head, limbs and eyesight for such hard work" (letter to Mary Wordsworth and Dora Wordsworth, 6 May 1837; *WLLY*, 3: 400). Again, he tells Henry Crabb Robinson that he should have taken the trip earlier, that it is now "too late": "I have matter for volumes had I but youth to work it up."[30] The Grand Tour was not only not a country for old men; it was also, we are told, itself too old-fashioned, languishing during the Napoleonic Wars and put to its final rest by one of the first post-Napoleonic tourists, Byron.[31] James Buzard describes the function of the Grand Tour in the eighteenth century:

> Among its many offices, the Grand Tour had performed the forthright ideological work of cementing the solidarity of the British ruling classes and providing them with a pseudo-historical legitimation. While English gentlemen refined their statecraft in Paris or in Amsterdam, it was in Rome that they found the richest message for their own era and class, and writers such as Addison, Lord Lyttleton, and James Thomson forged a pedigree for Augustan England by imagining their nation as the heir to the great but fallen Roman imperial tradition.[32]

However, Buzard notes, "Little of this complacency could be mustered in the post-Napoleonic period," and he finds Byron offering, in the place of the routines of the Grand Tour, "accredited anti-touristic gestures that were performable *within* tourism."[33] Bruce Redford, too, finds first William Beckford and then Byron radically transforming the Grand Tour, "abandon[ing] all conceptions of the Tour as a training-ground for public life, and all literary conventions that were designed to instruct and improve. In their place, they offer a solipsistic autobiographical enterprise, which subordinates the external world to the troubled consciousness of a traveler whose primary quest is directed inward."[34] J. R. Hale has also provided a detailed account of how European travel after Waterloo "saw the gradual outnumbering of Grand Tourists by travelers who might, though anachronistically, be called Cook's tourists."[35] Things continued to change in the years between the rush of post-Waterloo travel and Wordsworth's trip in 1837. Buzard goes on to note how mid-century writers such as Dickens began to parody the Byronic version of European travel, and Peter Manning, in writing of Wordsworth's "Memorials" in particular, analyzes how Wordsworth counters Byron, seeing "the tour poems as a deliberate anti-*Childe Harold*."[36] We can better understand how Wordsworth challenges both conventional and Byronic tourism if we place the two poets in relation to the eighteenth-century Grand Tour as outlined clearly and cogently by Redford in *Venice and the Grand Tour*, where he labels the goals of the tour as learning to look, learning to govern, and learning to quote.[37]

Byron may be anti-touristic but *Childe Harold IV* is much more of a travel poem than Wordsworth's "Memorials." For Redford, "Canto IV of *Childe Harold's Pilgrimage* smells not of the lamp but the guidebook."[38] Byron visits and describes any number of famous sights, making other places necessary stopping points for travelers who followed him; the lengthy notes to the poem, not to mention Hobhouse's companion volume of *Historical Illustrations of the Fourth Canto of Childe Harold*, suggest how engaged Byron is with Italian sights and the histories behind them.[39] We get, for example, famous set pieces describing Venice ("I stood in Venice, on the Bridge of Sighs; / A palace and a prison on each hand"; 1.1–2); the fountain of Egeria ("Egeria! sweet creation of some heart / Which found no mortal resting-place so fair / As thine ideal breast"; 115.1027–29); St. Peter's in Rome ("Thou seest not all; but piecemeal thou must break, / To separate contemplation, the great whole"; 157.1405–06); and the Coliseum ("This long-explored but still exhaustless mine / Of contemplation"; 128.1150–51). By contrast, Wordsworth, Robinson tells us, was not much taken with the conventional sights, expecting "no great pleasure from such things": "Wordsworth is no hunter after sentimental relics."[40] Thus, while Wordsworth was apparently quite taken with St. Peter's Basilica, his poem "Near Rome, In Sight of St. Peter's" does not follow Byron in giving us a sense of the place; instead, viewing the dome from a natural spot nearby, he contemplates the crowing of a cock and thinks of the betrayal of Jesus by he "whose name the Papal Chair / And yon resplendent church are proud to bear" (13–14). He later added to the series a poem on "The Pillar of Trajan" which might be compared to Byron's description of the same sight in *Childe Harold IV*, stanzas 110 to 111. Byron, while celebrating Trajan's military conquests and asserting "still we Trajan's name adore" (111.999), describes the pillar to assert the power of time and of historical displacement, as he notes that Trajan's pillar is surmounted by a statue of St. Peter. Wordsworth, too, has been concerned with the passage of time and the loss of the past, particularly as he sees Niebuhr and his followers destroying our belief in the fables of Rome's earliest history.[41] He celebrates Trajan's pillar as rising above a cityscape where "Towers are crushed, and unforbidden weeds / O'er mutilated arches shed their seeds" (1–2). Gazing on the frieze that winds round the pillar and inspired by the "Muse" (23),

Wordsworth is able to "commune with the mind and heart / Of him who thus survives by classic art, / His actions witness, venerate his mien, / And study Trajan as by Pliny seen" (25–28).

Wordsworth's celebration of art can be linked to one of key goals of the Grand Tour: to instruct young Englishmen in the art of viewing art, to turn them into connoisseurs, as treatises on the tour indicated which paintings, statues, and buildings to see and how to judge them properly.[42] Byron claims, at least, to disdain such moves: dismissing the need to learn to look, he leaves it to "The artist and his ape, to tell and tell / How well his connoisseurship understands" as they attempt to "describe the undescribable" (53.470–71, 473); again, while celebrating any number of literary figures, Byron still mocks the quotations of the learned Grand Tourist, "he, who will, his recollections rake / And quote in classic raptures, and awake / The hills with Latian echoes" (75.670–72). Byron again demurs from the usual Grand Tour acquisition of political knowledge, mixing ancient with modern rulers, drawing not (as a Macaulay might) just on ancient Roman figures such as Numa but also on Cromwell, Napoleon, and George Washington, and finding that the only lesson to be gained from history, the "moral of all human tales," is decline and fall (108.964). As a counter to Byron, Wordsworth offers his own revisionary Grand Tour, but he strives to rework rather than to disregard the lessons of travel.

Wordsworth still wants to learn to look, but with a key difference. Part of Wordsworth's power is that he not only knows *how* to look – he also knows what one should look *at*, and, in the end, one should not focus one's gaze on the celebrated works of Roman and Italian art. He names only one sonnet in the Italian sequence for a work of art, "Before the Picture of the Baptist, By Raphael, in the Gallery at Florence," but then offers not a description of the painting but instead the narrative of John the Baptist. Wordsworth is concerned, then, less with learning the self-confirming practice of connoisseurship – where one proves oneself a judge of art by judging in accordance with the standards of one's rank, education, and taste – than with overcoming the self-alienating practice of tourism. Wordsworth often seems a reluctant tourist. As Moorman notes, "He was 'indifferent to mere sights,' although he regarded sightseeing as a duty" (2: 523). He missed England and home, writing at one point that "Venice will be the last spot in Italy thank God where we shall be detained. I never was good at sightseeing, yet it must be done" (May 30, 1837; *WLLY*, 2: 408). Still, whatever strains travel brought, he was throughout his life an inveterate sightseer.[43] Wordsworth, as Charles

Norton Coe established, read a great deal of travel literature and echoed some sixty different travel books in his poetry.[44] Six sequences of poems refer to a "tour" in their title, and he wrote various versions of his prose *Guide to the Lakes*; and, when we note with Alan Liu that Wordsworth began his career with touring works such as "Descriptive Sketches taken during a Pedestrian Tour among the Alps," his entire corpus takes on the shape of a Memorial Tour, linking travel with Looser's retrospection. Tying Wordsworth to tourism, we might think of the importance of travel to *The Prelude* or of the fact that Thomas Cook's main venue for information and advertisements was called *The Excursionist*, begun in 1851.

Still, Wordsworth, no less than Byron, objected to the stance of the typical tourist. The much-maligned institution of tourism is itself a struggle for a kind of cultural power – in part, the ability to see correctly. As MacCannell puts it, "touristic shame is not based on being a tourist but on not being tourist enough, on a failure to see everything the way it 'ought' to be seen."[45] The tourist is caught in a double bind: the tour is undertaken in order to escape from the mechanical, the boring, the deadening trials of everyday life and is thus a quest for the new, the exciting; yet the tour is comprised of sights that are attractions exactly because they have already been constructed by someone else, in fact predigested by guidebooks and other accoutrements of the tour telling one what one "ought" to see. Touristic experience is always belated, mediated, inauthentic. Sadly, the sight never appears as it "ought" to look because it has lost some of its attraction precisely in becoming an attraction.

Wordsworth confronts this sense of touristic disappointment in the second sonnet of the Italian "Memorials" called "At Rome":

> Is this, ye Gods, the Capitolian Hill?
> Yon petty Steep in truth the fearful Rock,
> Tarpeian named of yore, and keeping still
> That name, a local Phantom proud to mock
> The Traveller's expectation?   (1–5)

As he explains in the Fenwick note, "when particular spots or objects are sought out disappointment is I believe invariably felt" (*FN*, p. 181).[46] As so often in Wordsworth – we need think only of "the soulless image on the eye" produced by Mont Blanc in Book VI of the *Prelude* that "usurp'd upon a living thought" (454–55) or his concerns in the Yarrow poems, discussed earlier – the expectation exceeds the sight; here, Rome offers mere phantoms of its famed locales, as "what men see and touch" "Destroy the ideal Power within" the "living thought" (7, 6).[47]

Of course, what appears as touristic angst over the failure of the sight to attract is also an escape from what might be the power of the sight to overwhelm: if Rome were all it was cracked up to be, Wordsworth would be reduced to admiring silence. The sonnet, written years later, arises out of the attraction's failure to captivate, out of Wordsworth's ability to see *through* the sight. While when we see the sought-after sight, "our wish obtained, deeply we sigh" (9) in disappointment, there is abundant recompense: "Yet not unrecompensed are they who learn, / From that depression raised, to mount on high / With stronger wing, more clearly to discern / Eternal things" (10–13). As in the Simplon Pass passage in the *Prelude*, disappointment in the external world of the tourist gives way to a revelation of the eternal power of the imagination.

And what does Wordsworth see beyond Italy? While "Eternal things" here might suggest that we see into a Christianized version of the "life of things," what Wordsworth envisions through Italy is, more often, England. If, for Redford, Byron sees himself, Wordsworth sees home. In the poem that precedes the one on his disappointment with Rome, he describes his entry into the Eternal City, where he finds that "the whole majesty of Rome" is "supplanted" (12) by a single pine with an English association: "when I learned the Tree was living there, / Saved from the sordid axe by Beaumont's care, / Oh, what a gush of tenderness was mine!" (6–8). (As Wordsworth wrote to his family, his lifelong friend Sir George Beaumont had purchased a stone-pine on Monte Mario "that it might stand as long as Nature would allow.")[48] Again, when Wordsworth goes to Vallombrosa – one of what he refers to as the Tuscan Sanctuaries – it is neither its Italianate nor its religious significance that impresses him,[49] but the presence of Milton: "for his Spirit is here" ("At Vallombrosa," 10). Composing the place-specific "Cuckoo at Laverna," the only poem actually begun on the tour, he praises the cuckoo – called the "Voice of the Desert" (103) – and speaks of listening to bird song in exotic locales – "among files / Of orange-trees bedecked with glowing fruit" and "the lightsome Olive's twinkling canopy" (16–17, 21); yet, what really moves him is that such sounds remind him of the Nightingale or Thrush "as in a common English grove" (23). Here, at Laverna, "assemblages of new and old, / Strange and familiar" (25–26) (including the assemblage of his old and new works) can be made through "a sweet fellowship with kinds beloved, / For old remembrance sake" (15–16).

In such poems, Wordsworth reworks touristic disappointment. The tourist flees home but finds only the homilies of the guidebook. Surmounting touristic disappointment, Wordsworth discovers there is no place like home, or, more exactly, the new place has value insofar as it imaginatively resembles home. As he had hoped for Scott in "Yarrow Revisited," the imaginative power gained through "native fancy" rescues the disappointed traveler on classic ground. It is thus fitting that it is at home that Wordsworth is able best to recollect Italy and offer his retrospection in tranquility. In "Composed on May-Morning, 1838," a concluding sonnet which he added to the sequence in 1845, Wordsworth can, amidst "you, dear Hills" of the Lake District, truly celebrate their "rival image brought / From far" (1–2), as he delights in an Italy that is not an Other but the same as England. Any disappointments in Italy's artistic sights are made up for by the remembered natural glories of England.

As Redford indicates,[50] the Grand Tour's lessons in art were always connected with political instruction, as the young English gentleman toured the continent in order to learn how to govern. One gained a wider vision through travel, but, more importantly, one learned to appreciate the superiority of England's social system. For example, Gilbert Burnet, whose late seventeenth-century *Travels* Wordsworth echoes in the sonnet "At Rome,"[51] argued that the purpose of the tour was to teach the superiority of the English government over continental absolutism, of Protestantism over Catholicism, of English enterprise over European decadence.[52] Although Byron, as noted, seems to reject this part of the touristic mission, Wordsworth, like grand tourists before him who hoped to learn how to govern, also finds in Italy proof of the superiority of English society – its Church, its government, its economy. If Byron learns any lesson from Italy about governing Britain, it is that the fall of sea-conquering Venice presages the fall of Britain, ruler of the waves (*Childe Harold IV*, stanza 17). Wordsworth, though troubled by his England, still conforms Italy to English precedent, thus showing how Italy can avoid the counterexample of revolutionary France: through his verses, he hopes to teach how "Vexed and disordered" ("Musings," 365) England can be ordered better. Wordsworth pursues throughout the "Memorials" two public themes that might, unkindly, be described as Robinson did in writing to Landor: that Wordsworth had strong "moral and religious feelings added to a spice of John Bullism."[53]

First, there is a commemoration of what Wordsworth calls in the first poem "Christian Traditions." There is, for the opponent of Catholic

Emancipation, a great deal of sympathy for Catholicism here, even for a peasant's prayer to the Virgin, which, he notes, "may lack / The heavenly sanction needed to ensure / Its own fulfillment" (VIII, 9–11). However, it is not Italian Catholicism that Wordsworth finally wants to celebrate; instead, it is the English Oxford Movement that arose between the visit and the publication of the verses and that Wordsworth praised in a later 1845 note to the opening verses for taking "for its first principle, a devout deference to the voice of Christian antiquity" (p. 790).

Second, there is a celebration of national liberty as he invokes images of Republican Rome and decries Italy's current loss of liberty under Austrian control; but, in the Fenwick note, he makes it clear that he supports no revolutionary action, as he praises "the Carbonari, if I may still call them so" for having learned "patience" and for turning their efforts to "spreading knowledge actively but as quietly as they can" (*FN*, p. 186). He supports nation, not revolution or Reform. The Englishman in occupied, Catholic Italy should learn to appreciate his national liberty and his nation's Church. The Italian should learn from the Englishman true piety and patience.

That Wordsworth sees himself here as the voice for his people is made clear in a sonnet about "Dante's favourite seat" at Florence, where – recalling that "the mighty Poet bore / A Patriot's heart" (XVI, 11–12) – Wordsworth "for a moment, filled that empty Throne" (14), taking on Dante's role of poet/prophet/patriot. As Graver has argued, Wordsworth's assuming Dante's seat is a complex action that indicates his dedication to Italian unification, his hope that Italy will avoid the violence of the French Revolution, and perhaps his homage to Italy's greatest poet of the era, Giacomo Leopardi, who died in the cholera epidemic Wordsworth avoided; as Graver puts it, "Leopardi's death left the throne of Dante, as Wordsworth understood it, empty. When 'for a moment' the English poet fills that throne, it may be a quiet tribute to the passing of the author of 'All' Italia' and "Risorgimento.'"[54]

As the turn to Dante reminds us, learning to quote, to find literary precursors in the Italian landscape, is the third goal of the Grand Tour, and again Wordsworth makes a telling revisionary move. While Wordsworth invokes a conventionally textualized Italian landscape, quoting the right authors – particularly in citing classical sources as when he hopes to reach Naples, "that delicious Bay, / Parthenope's Domain – Virgilian haunt / Illustrated with never-dying verse" ("Musings Near Aquapendente," 264–66) – what truly interests him are the echoes of English precursors – Sir George Beaumont and his pine tree at Rome, Milton at Vallombrosa.

It is therefore striking that he makes no mention of his younger contemporaries who were so strongly linked to Italy. Other writers certainly
did. Samuel Rogers, to whom Wordsworth dedicated the *Yarrow Revisited*
volume, included a lengthy tribute to Byron in his extremely successful
Italy, which included an apostrophe: "BYRON, thou art gone, / Gone like
a star that through the firmament / Shot and was lost, in its eccentric
course / Dazzling, perplexing."[55] John Chaloner in his *Rome* of 1821 finds
that "the tide of Byron's lofty lines" (353) on the Coliseum overwhelm even
the poetry of Ovid and Virgil. In an imitation of *Childe Harold* written in
Spenserian stanzas and providing passages parallel to Byron on, for
example, Egeria and the Coliseum, John Edmund Reade offers in *Italy:
A Poem, in Six Parts* (1838) another portrait of Byron, mentions Shelley,
and quotes Hunt in his notes.[56] William Edmondstoune Aytoun,[57] in his
"Lament for Percy Shelley," imagines Byron and Hunt on the Italian shore
watching Shelley's body burn and recounts his own visit to the graves of
Shelley and Keats in Rome. Robert Montgomery, author of the very
popular *Omnipresence of the Deity* (1828), also closes the first part of *The
Age Reviewed* (London: William Carpenter, 1827) with celebrations of
Keats, Shelley, and particularly Byron but attacks Hunt and most other
writers of the day. Published the same year as Wordsworth's "Memorials,"
Margaret Keogh's *Herculaneum, Pompeii, and Other Poems* (taking up the
sites Wordsworth missed due to the cholera) offers tags from Byron on her
title page and before each of the titular poems.[58] Also in 1842, Andrew
Alexander Knox, who, oddly enough, traveled with Mary Shelley to Italy
that year, published *Giotto and Francesca, And Other Poems*, providing – like
Keats and his friend Reynolds – a versified version of a tale from Boccaccio
that seems to echo both Keats and Byron, and he uses a motto from
Shelley's *Hellas* for "The Phantom Viracocha, A Story of the Incas."[59]
Wordsworth's "Memorials" might have memorialized Keats and Shelley,
dead on Italian soil, or celebrated Byron and Hunt, who had stirred so
much interest in things Italian.[60] Unlike his own English countryside of
the Lake District, which could serve him as a vast memory place for his
own experiences, this landscape echoed with the lives and verses of the
younger poets.

As Peter Manning has convincingly argued in his account of Scott's
presence in "Musings Near Aquapendente," Wordsworth surely had at
least Byron in mind as he toured Italy.[61] There were traces of the younger,
dead poets wherever Robinson and Wordsworth went. For example, taking
a boat out to view Genoa, Wordsworth, troubled by the rough waters,
thought of how "Shelley and Byron – one of them at least, who seemed to

have courted agitation from any quarter – would have probably rejoiced in such a situation," in the words of the Fenwick Note (p. 142).[62] He pursued in reverse the itinerary of *Childe Harold IV*, moving from Rome to Florence to Venice, including a visit to the fountain of Egeria (letter to Mary Wordsworth, 6 May 1837; *WLLY*, 2: 399), one of the most memorable of the sites evoked in Byron's poem. Wordsworth also visited Pisa, home to the "Pisan triumvirate" of Shelley, Byron, and Hunt, where Wordsworth perhaps found relief from the blasphemy of the so-called "Satanic School" in the fact that the graveyard in the Campo Santo was composed of "sacred earth / Fetched from Mount Calvary" ("Musings," 15–59; p. 798n). In Rome, he and Robinson were at first "agreeably lodged in the Piazza di Spagna," the center of British tourism in the city (Hale, p. 89) and the site, of course, of Keats's death, and Wordsworth met with Joseph Severn and talked at length of Keats.[63]

Wordsworth had textual traces available to him as well. Even though, as we saw in Chapter 4, one should query whether Wordsworth had read, for example, any of Keats's odes before publishing the *River Duddon* sonnets – and while I have had to argue he could have known of Shelley's "Mont Blanc" from reviews – there is no doubt that he was aware of his younger contemporaries' works when he traveled to Italy and wrote the poems inspired by that tour. He had long owned a copy of Keats's 1817 *Poems*, sent to him by the author, and he later also possessed a copy of the 1829 Galignani edition of *The Poetical Works of Coleridge, Shelley, and Keats* along with Mary Shelley's four-volume 1839 edition of *The Poetical Works of Percy Bysshe Shelley*.[64] He owned a number of volumes by Hunt, from *The Descent of Liberty* to the 1832 *Poetical Works of Leigh Hunt* (133).[65] He could have read widely in these poets. That he paid attention to them, at least in these later years, is confirmed by various comments he made, which were increasingly positive. For example, while in 1820 Wordsworth worried to Landor about *The Liberal*, founded by Hunt, Shelley, and Byron, fearing it would "be directed against everything in religion, in morals and probably in government and literature, which our Forefathers have been accustomed to reverence," Robinson wrote, "I have head Wordsworth speak very kindly both of the writings and person of Leigh Hunt."[66]

Again, Wordsworth had corresponded with Haydon earlier in his life about Keats, and Robert Perceval Graves, the curate at Windermere for around thirty years ("partly through the intervention of Mr. Wordsworth"), later reports that Wordsworth was pleased to note the similarities between his own "Praised be the Art" and Keats's "Ode on a Grecian Urn." This comment was, apparently, made around 1840, in the period when he was working on the Italian "Memorials."[67] Sara Coleridge reports another comment from the same time frame: "Mr. Wordsworth used to say of Shelley and Keats that they would ever be great favorite with the young, but would not satisfy men of all ages," an interesting remark from a poet who long outlived them.[68] Coleridge's comments on the two poets suggest some of the difficulties Shelley and Keats posed for a religious reader such as herself and, perhaps, for Wordsworth. Writing to Aubrey de Vere about his review of Keats, Shelley, and Tennyson, she notes that "You are more displeased with Shelley's *wrong* religion than with Keats's *no* religion," before quoting Wordsworth's friend Isabella Fenwick on Keats: "'Oh, he was dark, very dark,' said Miss Fenwick to me one day about Keats, and I heard her say it with pain. 'He knew nothing about Christianity.'"[69]

According to Trelawney (not exactly a reliable source), Wordsworth moved from disdain for Shelley's poetry to strong admiration. Trelawney claims to have met Wordsworth in Switzerland in 1819 (it must have been 1820), shortly after a local bookseller had introduced him to Shelley's poetry. Trelawney says that he asked Wordsworth what he thought of Shelley: "'Nothing,' he replied . . . . 'A poet who has not produced a good poem before he is twenty-five, we may conclude cannot, and never will do so.'" Trelawney then claims that "in after-years, Shelley being dead, Wordsworth . . . admitted that Shelley was the greatest master of harmonious verse in our modern literature."[70] Others recorded similar comments. As Edith Batho tells us, "In 1826, J. J. Tayler records, '[Wordsworth] told us he thought the greatest of modern geniuses, had he given his powers a proper direction, and one decidedly superior to Byron, was Shelley, a young man, author of *Queen Mab*, who died lately at Rome.'"[71] Again, William Ewart Gladstone recalled that Wordsworth "thought Shelley had the greatest native powers in poetry of all the men of this age."[72] Henry Crabb Robinson, too, indicated that Wordsworth placed Shelley above Byron as a poet, and Christopher Wordsworth tells us that the older poet found that "Shelley is one of the best *artists* of us all: I mean in workmanship of style."[73] Giving evidence of Wordsworth's reading in Shelley, Robinson reports that Wordsworth thought *The Cenci* to be the "greatest tragedy of the age," and there are several indications that he praised Shelley's "To a Sky-lark."[74] Of course, Wordsworth's admiration of Shelley's poetry did not extend to Shelley's politics and religion, finding that the younger poet "looks on all things with an evil eye" and had an "ill-humour toward established opinions and institutions."[75] It is worth noting that Shelley's *Peter Bell the Third* was finally published by

Mary Shelley in 1839 (in an edition sent by Moxon to Dora Wordsworth)[76] and that, at the time Wordsworth was preparing to publish his *Poems, Chiefly of Early and Late Years* with Moxon, Wordsworth feared that his publisher might go bankrupt as result of a prosecution for blasphemous libel after he issued an unexpurgated version of *Queen Mab*; Wordsworth's friend Talfourd defended Moxon, who lost but was not sentenced. Behind any aesthetic admiration, there was always ideological disagreement, even disgust.

It was surely Byron who would have been most in Wordsworth's mind while he toured Italy, not least because it was Byron who had always bothered him the most, as we have repeatedly seen. Wordsworth appears to have known more of Byron's poetry than he sometimes allowed. In Wordsworth's comments on Byron gathered by Markham Peacock, Wordsworth seems to have a thorough knowledge of all four cantos of *Childe Harold* as well as of poems from "The Prisoner of Chillon" to *Don Juan*, from *Vision of Judgment* to Byron's "Ode to Napoleon Bonaparte."[77] As Manning has noted, Wordsworth could not escape Byron's fame in the 1830s, with the publication of Tom Moore's *Letters and Journals of Lord Byron* in 1830 and in 1834 the first six of the seventeen-volume *Works of Lord Byron: With His Letters and Journals and His Life, By Thomas Moore.*[78] Wordsworth was, quite early on, engaged in thinking about and responding to Byron, and, in 1834, in the midst of Moore's and Murray's reassertion of Byron's place in the literature of the day, Wordsworth tells us that he wrote some lines in one of his "Evening Voluntaries" ("Not in the lucid intervals of life") "with L. Byron's character as a Poet before me" (*FN*, p. 147). As in the earlier joint satire on Byron discussed in Chapter 3, the noble poet is found to lack a true feeling for nature, even though he possesses "words / Which practiced Talent readily affords" (7–8).[79]

Then, just as Wordsworth was preparing to leave for Italy in March 1837, Byron – and particularly Byron's own attacks upon Wordsworth – must have just reentered the older poet's consciousness, for, at the close of 1836, Walter Savage Landor published what Robinson insisted was an imitation of Byron, *A Satire on Satirists, and Admonition to Detractors*, where Wordsworth is portrayed as a detractor, unable to appreciate the verse of any other poet, even his friend Southey. It is striking that Robinson begins his account of the trip to Italy by recounting the contretemps over Landor's *Satire*.[80] A mini-crisis had ensued, with Robinson discussing the dispute with Samuel Rogers on February 23, 1837, writing several times to Landor, and intercepting a copy of the poem intended for Southey; Wordsworth wrote to Southey to assure him that he admired him and had never spoken ill of him.[81] Barron Field in his draft life of Wordsworth devotes his third appendix to "A Quarrel of the Poets," where he, too, details the row, including Robinson's attempt to convince Landor to suppress the poem on the grounds of a lack of originality.[82] Field notes that in 1842, when Wordsworth was publishing his Italian poems, Landor once again attacked, this time in a new "Imaginary Conversation between Porson and Southey" published in *Blackwood's*, where, in Field's words, Landor "pull[ed] to pieces all the prosaic and simple passages of Mr. Wordsworth's poems, as the Edinburgh Review had done thirty years before."[83] Field reminds us that Wordsworth's son-in-law, Edward Quillinan, responded with his own imaginary conversation between Landor and the editor of *Blackwood's*. Clearly, the long battle with Byron would have been fresh in Wordsworth's mind as he and Robinson traveled in March toward Italy, where they would again hear of Byron on May 17, when at least Robinson visited Severn Thorwaldsen's studio in Rome and saw his statue of Byron, and where Chevalier Bunsen told Wordsworth that Byron thought he was the offspring of a demon.[84]

Landor, attacking *Blackwood's* along with Wordsworth and praising Lamb, Hazlitt, Shelley, and Keats, repeats in his satire many of the criticisms the younger poets of the Cockney School had launched against their Laker precursor. As Robinson would point out in rebuking Landor, his *Satire on Satirists* owed specific debts to Byron's "Dedication" to *Don Juan* and his "Observations upon an Article in *Blackwood's*," published posthumously in 1833, which also joins criticism of *Blackwood's* with an assault upon Wordsworth.[85] Robert Super indicates that Landor had also received from Keats's friend Charles Brown "a collection of scurrilous quotations from *Blackwood's* which he planned to use in his biography of Keats."[86] This, perhaps, lead to the line, in the midst of praise of the satirist Charles Churchill, "he stabb'd no Keats" (l. 125), which has a note attached indicating that "Lamb, Keats, Hazlitt, Coleridge, all in short who, recently dead, are now dividing amongst them the admiration of their country, were turned to ridicule by the worthy men employed by Mr. Blackwood" (p. 221n). He also celebrates Hunt, hoping that "Hunt's Cold-bath-field may bloom with bowers, for him" (l. 128), perhaps conflating Hunt's famous prison-cell bower at Horsemonger Lane with the Coldbath Field Prison where his brother John was incarcerated. Shelley is included in a passage on Byron where we hear "with you [Byron] / Shelley stands foremost" (176–77).

Landor treats Byron and Wordsworth at greater length. Attacking the Scottish critics at *Blackwood's*, Landor recalls Byron's earlier response to

Scotch reviewers. Finding that "In Satire's narrow strait he swam the best" (171), Landor seems to argue that Byron's own limited ability to appreciate Keats or even Shelley, let alone Southey (175–82), can be traced back to those attacks: he "From Scottish saltiness caught his rapid thirst" (174). Still, "Byron was not *all* Byron; one small part / Bore the impression of a human heart" (167–68). He could escape from being only a detractor. Wordsworth comes in for the longest assault. He is once more discovered as the poet of the egotistical sublime, moved by his own poetry but not, for example, his friend Talfourd's *Ion* (223–35) and contending, in words quoted from Byron, that Southey's poetry was not worth five shillings (284–85). Landor urges Wordsworth to learn to appreciate Moore and Campbell, Dryden and even Byron. Landor further endorses, against the very English Wordsworth, a cosmopolitan canon which includes Goethe, Lamartine, Chateaubriand, and Beranger (264–83 & n.). Wordsworth's own poetry is taken to task, as Landor pokes fun at the *Duddon* sonnets and returns to the controversy over the "Thanksgiving Ode":

> No more on daisies and on pilewort fed,
> By weary Duddon's ever tumbled bed,
> The Grasmere cuckoo leaves those sylvan scenes,
> And, percht on shovel hats and dandy deans,
> And prickt with spicy cheer, at Philpot's nod
> Devoutly fathers Slaughter upon God.   (236–41)

If Wordsworth's late volumes attempted to re-collect his life's work, Landor regathers the years of critical assault the Lake Poet had suffered.

As David Chandler has argued in his fine "Lines Crossed: Walter Savage Landor and Wordsworth," Landor's deepest argument with Wordsworth is over how to respect and foster a literary tradition, how to honor one's heritage and pass on something to one's heirs. In the terms of the Grand Tour, how does one learn to quote? As Chandler describes Landor's view, the

> tendency of Wordsworth to disparage some of his leading precursors in English poetry, to be loftily condescending about his English contemporaries, including a friend like Southey, and ignorantly rude about German poetry, made him ... a very bad heir to the great tradition of European poetry. Wordsworth could not be trusted to value properly the treasures of the past he had inherited. Worse, the Lake poet understood the legacy he would bequeath in terms of his own increasing fame rather than a willingness to nurture the talents of younger poets.[87]

Chandler goes on to quote from the close of Landor's poem, where he calls upon Wordsworth to give up the "starts of jealousy" that mark "youth" and to "let age / Rest with composure on another's page. / Take the hand of the timid, rear the young" (330–32). Landor wants the aging Wordsworth not only to turn a retrospective eye on his own career, re-collecting only his own works, but also to do justice to those with whom he has striven, whether consciously or not, in song. It is illuminating that in a letter to Robinson back in 1821, one filled with comments on literature – from John Scott's death in a duel over *Blackwood's* critical attacks to concerns about the continued denigration of the Lake School – Wordsworth, in a discussion of the Cockney Poet Barry Cornwall's tragedy *Mirandola*, exclaims, "As to Poetry I am sick of it – it overruns the Country in all shapes of the plagues of Egypt . . . . But let us desist or we shall be accused of envying the rising generation."[88] Where Landor wants the kind of mentoring relationship between the generations that Jane Spencer has studied between older and younger men, Wordsworth offers more opposition than advice.[89]

In Field's and in Robinson's own account, it is Robinson (and then Quillinan) who dealt with the testy Landor, but we might also hear Wordsworth directly responding to Landor's poem in the Italian "Memorials." Of these, the only poem written in Italy itself was "The Cuckoo at Laverna," perhaps a reply to Landor's designation of him as the "Grasmere Cuckoo"; and when Wordsworth wrote of the woods at Vallombrosa, he conceivably recalled Landor's lines: "Sooner shall Tuscan Vallombrosa lack wood / Than Britain Grub-Street, Billingsgate, and Blackwood" (30–31). In fact, the Fenwick note to "At Vallombrosa," with its account of the difficulties in offering praise to "great & good men" since "the objects of admiration vary so much with time & circumstances" (pp. 182–83), reads like a thoughtful response to Landor's demand that Wordsworth now praise famous poets. While Landor would say that Wordsworth could not admit within his poems these richly remembered poets because he was incapable of appreciating the poetry of anyone but himself, it is not envy but ideological opposition to these Cockney poets and aristocratic rebels that shapes Wordsworth's response. The fundamental point is made most clear when we see that Wordsworth was more than able to celebrate another poet in the most powerful of the poems in the series, the opening "Musings Near Aquapendente, April 1837."[90]

As Manning has shown,[91] whatever repressed references there may to be to Byron in these verses, Wordsworth hails Sir Walter Scott as a key poetic precursor on Italian ground. After some opening musings to which we will return, Wordsworth wonders whether there is another with whom he can share his delight in the landscape near the town and falls of Aquapendente: "One there surely was, / 'The Wizard of the North'" who "with anxious hope [was] / Brought to this genial climate, when disease / Preyed upon body and mind" (56–59). Wordsworth then devotes a long passage to Scott, in which he remembers climbing Helvellyn with him in 1805 and visiting him at Abbotsford in 1831 before Scott's own departure for Italy in a futile search for health, already taken up in "Yarrow Revisited," as already discussed. What is striking here is that Scott seems to be valued because he knows the value of Wordsworth's poetry. First, Wordsworth wonders whether, despite his illness, "yet not the less / Had [Scott's] sunk eye kindled at those dear words / That spake of bards and minstrels" (59–61) – that is, the lines included just above in Wordsworth's poem, where he describes various locales within the Lake District:

> Places forsaken now, but loving still
> The muses, as they loved them in the days
> Of the old minstrels and the border bards   (50–52)

Isabella Fenwick reports that Wordsworth recalled: "His, Sir W. Scott's, eye did in fact kindle at them for the lines 'Places forsaken now' & the two that follow were adopted from a Poem of mine which nearly 40 years ago was in part read to him & he never forgot them" (*FN*, p. 176). As Curtis notes (797n), these lines were in a draft of "Michael" that Scott heard and remembered, even though they did not appear in the printed version. Wordsworth, claiming to imagine what he has in fact experienced, can ratify Scott's imaginative powers, because Scott responded fulsomely to his "dear words." He rejoiced in Wordsworth's poetry and in their shared experience in the Lake District, where they, along with Humphrey Davy, climbed "old Hellvellyn's brow" (62) in 1805 (*FN*, p. 176).

As Wordsworth turns to Scott's departure for Italy, announced in "Yarrow Revisited," we find that Scott did even better, for, in turning to Italy, Scott demonstrated that he too knew *how* and *whom* to quote. Wordsworth writes, "He said, 'When I am there, although 'tis fair, / 'Twill be another Yarrow'" (76–77), as Scott is said to have quoted "Yarrow Unvisited," from a passage that enacts the dilemma of touristic disappointment:

> Be Yarrow stream unseen, unknown!
> It must, or we shall rue it:
> We have a vision of our own;
> Ah! why should we undo it?

> The treasured dreams of times long past,
> We'll keep them, *winsome Marrow*!
> For when we're there, although 'tis fair,
> 'Twill be another Yarrow.   (49–56)

In "Musings," Wordsworth claims that this "Prophecy" of Scott's disenchantment was "more than fulfilled" by Scott's tour to Italy where "Her
splendors" were "seen, not felt" (77, 82), a point he expands upon in the
Fenwick note (p. 177). Scott, the knowledgeable traveler, ready with his
Wordsworth quotation, cannot escape touristic disappointment: he found
another Italy, fair but not the one of his dreams.

This complex act of self-quotation by way of Scott offers, in Manning's
words, "Wordsworth's covert self-endorsement,"[92] as Wordsworth uses the
far more popular poet's quotation as a kind of blurb for his new collection
of poems. Moreover, it enables Wordsworth to shift on to Scott all the
vicissitudes of tourism, which Wordsworth can then be found to escape.
Wordsworth gives thanks in the next passage that, while Italy, filled with
"Nature's loveliest looks, / Art's noblest relics, history's rich bequests, /
Failed to reanimate and but feebly cheered / The whole world's Darling,"
he, unlike Scott, is "free to rove at will" as he acquires inspiration for new
verse (95–98). And he is able to do so because Italy is for him "another
Yarrow" in a different sense, not a disappointing simulacra of itself but
a means of recovering, through the imagination, the home landscapes
Wordsworth loves, including Yarrow. As the Apennines evoke the landscape of the Lake District, Italy is recovered as another Yarrow, another
England.

This turn is made even clearer if we recognize an earlier act of self-
quotation at the opening of "Musings." This poem opens on Redford's
issue of learning to look or, more precisely, the difficulty in seeing correctly, though, this time, the fault clearly lies with the viewer. Wordsworth,
naming himself "an Islander by birth, / A Mountaineer by habit" (3–4),
claims to discover an answerable style for the magnificent landscape before
him, composed as it is of the Apennines and two coastlines. In
a manuscript version of the poem (DC MS 143), Wordsworth wishes to
summon an "instant power" so that he can "resound your praise / In
measure equal to your claims" (Curtis, p. 742n). But Wordsworth immediately drops this assertion as a "presumptuous thought": "it fled / Like
vapour, like a towering cloud dissolved" (7–8). As Curtis notes (p. 796n),
Wordsworth, at lines 35–36, quotes from the eighth book of the unpublished *Prelude*,[93] but he also seems to be drawing in the opening lines of

"Musings" on Book VI of *The Prelude* and its famous account of hiking through the Alps, with its ur-scene of touristic disappointment before Mont Blanc. In that passage, after having failed to realize he has crossed the Alps, the poet is again confronted by "that Power," "Imagination! lifting up itself / Before the eye and progress of my Song / Like an unfather'd vapour," which, if not presumptuous, exhibits "strength / Of usurpation" (VI: 527, 525, 532–33). The link between the two passages seems particularly strong when we remember that in *The Prelude,* after the passage on the imagination, Wordsworth returns to see, among other things, "The stationary blasts of waterfalls" (558), just as here he turns from the imaginative heights to describe Aquapendente ("hanging water"): "Yon snow-white torrent-fall, plumb down it drops / Yet ever hangs or seems to hang in air" (10–11). Wordsworth is again halted, as the scene is able "to fix and satisfy the mind / Passive yet pleased" (25–26). Seeing correctly here would seem to be a kind of "wise passiveness," a willingness to be pleased by the scene without the aid of touristic or artistic embellishment.

Except that Wordsworth again blanks out the scene before him and unleashes his imagination, so that he may once again leave Italy behind to discover his true subject, England. The "Broom in flower / Close at my side" (26–27) carries him back to the English countryside. Here, we get the other borrowing from the *Prelude,* already noted, as he is "Transported over that cloud-wooing hill, / Seat Sandal" to "Helvellyn's top" (35–37). At this point, he is granted "visual sovereignty" – the power he sought in the opening lines – as he views "hills multitudinous, / (Not Apennine can boast of fairer) hills / Pride of two nations, wood and lake and plains" (40–42): the mountains between two seas are replaced by the hills between two nations, but he now has the power to see it steady and to see it whole. England replaces Italy; Wordsworth's singular voice supplants any other influence.

The complex evocation of Scott (and of Wordsworth himself) also serves to cover the precursors Wordsworth does not wish to honor. We might imagine the ailing Scott replacing Keats, who also traveled to Italy for health, for Scott had the good sense to sum up his trip through a quotation of Wordsworth.[94] And when Wordsworth writes of Scott in Italy as the "whole world's Darling" (98), he uses Scott to displace that more famous and even more favored Italian tourist, Byron, for, again as noted by Manning, it is finally the Byron of *Childe Harold IV* that Wordsworth seeks to answer most directly in this poem and in the "Memorials" as a whole. It is striking that in the sonnet added to the "Memorials," "Composed on May-Morning 1838," Wordsworth, in thinking back to

the May of his Italy trip, especially remembers "the famed Egerian Grot"
and the "sunny, shadowy, Colyseum" (7, 11), two spots particularly identified with Byron. Wordsworth, the good Englishman longing for home,
offers himself in place of Byron, the cosmopolitan, who opens the first two
cantos of *Childe Harold* with a quotation from *Le Cosmopolite* that suggests
his voyage was inspired by hatred for his native country. Byron, "A ruin
amidst ruins" (IV.25.219) meditating upon Italy's, and presumably
England's, decline, gives way to Wordsworth, "Frail as the frailest" who
is still granted the power to see beyond fallen Italy to an empowered
England. Byron had stood at St. Peter's and said, "Thou seest not all;
but piecemeal thou must break, / To separate contemplation, the great
whole" (IV.157.1405–1406). Wordsworth, in contrast, claims "visual sovereignty." Although he is initially concerned in "Musings" about his pre-
sumption in assuming power, he now believes that God "who guides and
governs all" and who demands that we "look / Beyond these transient
spheres" still allows us to "wear a crown / Of earthly hope" (107–10).
Wordsworth thus asserts, "Who would keep / Power must resolve to cleave
to it through life, / Else it deserts him, surely as he lives" (115–17). He is
willing now to compare himself not to the failing Scott nor to Keats's
baffled Balboa masquerading as Cortez but to the most renowned traveler
of them all, Columbus.

Through Wordsworth's "Memorials," a particularly dangerous Italy is
put to rest, buried. Where Shelley and Byron found in Italy the opportunity to "court . . . agitation from any quarter" (*FN*, p. 178), Wordsworth
longs for the calm of home. Home to pagan and Catholic temptations
alike, Italy is rendered safe by Wordsworth for the good Protestant; the
Oxford Movement gives a name to his sense of returning to the Tuscan
Sanctuaries, to Christian antiquities, as a non-Catholic pilgrim.
Revolutionary fervor is to be contained by gradual reform. Cockney
experimental poetics are answered by the arch-Tory Scott. It is here, in
Wordsworth's rejection of his radical rivals, that we find him using the tour
to learn how to govern or, more precisely, how to teach England good
government. The Grand Tour had traditionally taught the superiority of
English over continental ways, but the younger radical poets had been too
attracted to a cosmopolitan rather than a distinctly English vision – they
organize these things better in France or Italy. Although I have spent more
time on learning to look and learning to quote, I do not think we can doubt
that, for Wordsworth, the final purpose of these poems has more to do with
governing. While he may worry here, in a sequence of sonnets, about
modern history's tendency to dispel those "old credulities" that inspired

the imagination, there is no doubt that, as he puts it in "Musings," the goal of poetry is to "irradiate" (284) history: an aesthetic power that has no power to shape history is, for Wordsworth, no power at all. If we find late Wordsworth unlovely, we need to remember that for him the goal of his poetry was not simply aesthetic pleasure but political insight.

II

While I believe that the growing popularity of Shelley and Keats after their deaths and the continuing cultural importance of Byron provide an important context for Wordsworth's final independent volume and represent an implicit influence on his poems, Wordsworth's *explicit* goals in the "Memorials" involve his own evolving religious feelings. For example, "The Cuckoo at Laverna. May 25, 1837" – again, the one poem written on the tour – seems in its opening lines to echo Shelley's "To a Sky-lark," which, as we have seen, Wordsworth admired. A number of words from Shelley's fourth stanza appear in Wordsworth's poem:

> The Pale purple even
>   Melts around thy flight;
> Like a star of Heaven,
>   In the broad day-light
> Thou art unseen, – but yet I hear thy shrill delight
>
> (*SPP*, 16–20)

Wordsworth hears his Cuckoo with "delight," even though it is "faint, and *melt*ing into air" (1, 3; emphasis added). It is "invisible" (6) like Shelley's "unseen" bird. Again, Shelley closes with the hope that he might learn from the bird so that "The world should listen then – as I am listening now" (105); Wordsworth opens his poem with one of his typical calls for us to halt and "LIST" (1). However, Wordsworth is not going to follow Shelley's speculations about a "Sprite or Bird" (61) that may not truly be of this earth. Wordsworth's bird is important exactly because it is of *this* earth, and its creaturely presence allows the poet to link, as we have seen, Italy and England, "new and old" (25), but, most importantly, earth and heaven.

The poem's central section, which recounts Wordsworth's experience of the monastery of Laverna, offers an appreciation of St. Francis of Assisi, a very early celebration of the then controversial monk, as Batho and Moorman note.[95] The monastery, a "Christian Fortress, garrisoned / In faith and hope, and dutiful obedience" (not faith, hope, and love), was founded on binding "rules / Stringent as flesh can tolerate" (32–33, 40–41), but St. Francis is seen as possessing a "milder Genius" (42) that enables him still to delight in the natural world: "For earth through heaven, for heaven, by changeful earth, / Illustrated, and mutually endeared" (47–48). Francis' "baptized imagination" (71) allowed him "to catch from Nature's humblest monitors / Whate'er they bring of impulses sublime" (72–73). This living natural supernaturalism, this ability to see glimpses of the divine in any corner of nature, drew "every shape of creature" (53) to Francis's side in order "to hold companionship so free, / So pure, so fraught with knowledge and delight" (60–61). Francis may be bound by the rules of his order, but he also bonds with nature so thoroughly that his followers find him experiencing earth in a way similar to how Adam and Eve found "all Kinds in Eden's blissful bowers" (65). While Wordsworth admits that he, unlike Francis and his followers, "walk[s] in the world's ways" (92), the poet gets his own intimation of immortality when he links the startling eruption of the cuckoo's song to the "Voice of One / Crying amid the wilderness" (93–94): if looking at the great artifice of St. Peter's causes him to think of Peter's denial of Christ, hearing this bird's natural song leads him to think of the advent of Christ. Nature is for him almost literally God's second book; natural experiences map onto Biblical ones.

What stands in the way of our appreciating such poems? In part, perhaps, it is the difficulty of this poetry. If, for example, we read Browning's poem entitled "Italy" (the poem we know as "My Last Duchess"), also published in 1842 as part of the *Bells and Pomegranates* series brought out by Wordsworth's publisher Moxon, we are immediately captured by the speaker's strong dramatic voice; we have to figure out how the Duke is using this speech in this dramatic situation, but we do not have difficulty in unraveling the description. Wordsworth's lyrical shifts are harder to follow, and that is as true of "The Cuckoo of Laverna" as it is of the famous turns in the "Intimations Ode." And, perhaps, it is the very retrospective nature of this poetry that makes it seem "late," even tired. The insistence on creating "assemblages new and old" urges the new back into the boundaries of the old. Where John Rudy finds in this poem a "revolutionary sympathy with a kindred spirit in a moment of sublime recognition beyond the discriminating intellect's categories of definition,"[96] we are likely to see a conservative reworking of Wordsworth's revolutionary experience of nature independent of religion. Although much work on late Wordsworth wants to rescue the aesthetic power of this verse, it does so by finding a revolutionary religiosity, or a questioning of authority, or a rejection of a masculinist eroticism. Beauty is found in this late poetry when it accords with our truths, but I want, as I have attempted throughout this study, to do justice to the rich flavor of Wordsworth's late poetry even as it asserts positions we find unpalatable.

Perhaps "The Cuckoo at Laverna" is finally and simply a poem of old age: Robinson reports that Wordsworth could not, at first, catch the cuckoo's song as his hearing was not what it had been, and Wordsworth confirmed to Fenwick that there is a "melancholy" aspect to this poem for "I was first convinced that age had rather dulled my hearing."[97] Perhaps this aging poet is to be dismissed in the same way that the "old women" Looser takes up are; her comment on reactions to Barbauld's great *Eighteen Hundred and Eleven* might apply to responses to late Wordsworth: "The implication seems to have been that reading *Eighteen Hundred and Eleven* was like being disappointed by an old friend, an old teacher – or simply an old woman writer."[98] We want the Wordsworth of "Tintern Abbey" not of the "Cuckoo at Laverna."

Wordsworth tackles old age directly in one of the other longer lyrics in the collection, "At Vallombrosa."[99] As in "Musings near Aquapendente," Wordsworth engages in a complicated act of double quotation. Given the connection of Vallombrosa with Milton – he refers to it in *Paradise Lost* and was presumed to have visited the monastery – Wordsworth offers the Miltonic lines on the "autumnal leaves that strew the brooks / In Vallombrosa" as his epigraph. He then begins his poem with two lines from his earlier "Stanzas composed in the Simplon Pass": "VALLOMBROSA – I longed in thy shadiest wood / To slumber, reclined on the moss-covered floor!"[100] That poem describes another moment of touristic disappointment, when Wordsworth's party, having reached the Simplon Pass, the main post-Napoleonic route into Italy, turned back. The poem in the Italian "Memorials" celebrates the fact that he has finally made the pilgrimage to this site that, for him, is deeply connected with Milton. Wordsworth suggests that Milton drew upon his experiences at this place in depicting the landscape of Eden, finding that the landscape at Vallombrosa "would yield him fit help while prefiguring that Place / Where, if Sin had not entered, Love never had died" (15–16). As in "The Cuckoo and Laverna" the physical world, approached properly, mutually illustrates Paradise and heaven. Wordsworth imagines Milton in old age returning in memory to this place:

> When with life lengthened out came a desolate time,
> And darkness and danger had compassed him round,
> With a thought he might flee to these haunts of his prime,

> And hence again a kind of shelter be found.
> And let me believe that when nightly the Muse
> Would waft him to Sion, the glorified hill,
> Here also, on some favoured height, they would choose
> To wander, and drink inspiration at will.   (17–24)

If we imagine this passage as rewriting the second verse paragraph of "Tintern Abbey," we have Milton – with the "darkness" of his "blind man's eye" living in a danger that echoes the "din" of the lyrical ballad – able to envision the landscape that, though long absent, still remains available to him through memory and imagination. As in "Tintern Abbey," the ability to return in memory to the "haunts of his prime" enables Wordsworth to see into – or perhaps *through* – the "life of things," as the natural world now stands in for Sion.

Like Milton, Wordsworth – now, too, in "the winter of age" (27) – finds that Vallombrosa still has a "musical charm" (27) that aging's "changes . . . had no power to unbind" (28). Finally reaching Vallombrosa, he, for once, does not experience touristic disappointment but instead finds that as he "repose[s]" at Vallombrosa he is not "forced from sweet fancy to part" (30), finding "the realised vision is clasped to my heart" (32). The imaginative expectation, the experience, and the memory – divided from one another across the Yarrow poems – here form an assemblage that more than comforts; it inspires him as he closes the poem:

> Even so, and unblamed, we rejoice as we may
> In Forms that must perish, frail objects of sense;
> Unblamed – if the Soul be intent on the day
> When the Being of Beings shall summon her hence.
> For he and he only with wisdom is blest
> Who, gathering true pleasures wherever they grow,
> Looks up in all places, for joy or for rest,
> To the Fountain whence Time and Eternity flow.   (33–40)

The emphasis here is clearly on a Christianized sense of the "motion and a spirit, that impels / All thinking things, all objects of all thought, /And rolls through all things" ("Tintern Abbey," 101–103). Yet, for all the transcendental language of "Being of Beings" and "the Fountain whence Time and Eternity flow," "all things" – the "frail objects of sense" – are here preserved and celebrated.

However, this binding of nature and the human imagination is different from that explored so powerfully by Hartman. What old age has no power to unbind is God's connection with everything, the fountain from which both nature and the imagination flow. Whether it is the powerful personal inter-action with nature recorded in "spots of time" as in *The Prelude* or the cultural production of myth in discovering meaning in the physical world as in *The Excursion*, Wordsworth now, long before Eliot and *Four Quartets*, presents a Christian frame for moments of mythopoesis. For Wordsworth's younger contemporaries, the foundational, revolutionary move that the Lake Poet made in his early poetry was to allow humanity and nature to stand by themselves – to become, in the words of that later inheritor of Wordsworth and Keats, Wallace Stevens, an "adventurer / In humanity," imagining "a race / Completely physical in a physical world."[101] Or as Stevens writes in "Sunday Morning," we must move beyond "the dark / Encroachment of that old catastrophe" that took place in "silent Palestine / Dominion of the blood and sepulcher" (stanza I: 6–7, 14–15) to discover a new "boisterous devotion to the sun, / Not as a god, but as a god might be," and "They shall know well the heavenly fellowship / Of men that perish and of summer morn" (stanza vii: 3–4, 12–13). Where Keats might find strength in sensations, what Wordsworth sees as "frail objects of sense," where Byron might seek an eros liberated from any encroachment from cant, and where Shelley might want to imagine the unbinding of humanity through imagination and love, Wordsworth increas-ingly binds the "life of things" from "Tintern Abbey" "to the "Being of Beings." In finding God behind nature – not to mention behind the proper workings of the state and the victory at Waterloo – Wordsworth sustained his love of nature by grounding it in a love of God. It is a vision that differs from his contemporaries – one that they rejected and one that Wordsworth honed in competition with them – but it does not so much betray or swerve from the early verse as recenter the experiences of the "Great Decade" in religious belief. This is not, however, simply a case of a completely internal development of a poet engaging in retrospection and re-collection. The poetry of Wordsworth after Waterloo evolves in constant debate with his younger contemporaries, as he asserts his sense of his own legacy against what they would make of it. Long after Keats, Shelley, and Byron were dead, he continued to contest with them over the nature of poetry and the power of poetry to shape our lives.

Wordsworth in 1850
The Prelude, *"this posthumous yet youthful work"*

This is a voice that speaks to us across a gulph of nearly fifty years. A few months ago, Wordsworth was taken from us at the ripe age of fourscore, yet here we have him addressing the public, as for the first time, with all the fervour, the unworn freshness, the hopeful confidence of thirty. We are carried back to the period when Coleridge, Byron, Scott, Rogers and Moore were in their youthful prime.... This is to renew, to antedate, the youth of a majority of the living generation. But only those whose memory still carries them so far back can feel within them any reflex of that eager excitement with which the news of battles fought and won, or mail-coach copies of some new work of Scott, or Byron, or the *Edinburgh Review*, were looked for and received in those already old days.

Review of Wordsworth, *The Prelude*, *The Examiner*
(July 27, 1850): 478

Wordsworth died on April 13, 1850, from pleurisy brought on by walking outside on a cold evening without a coat (Gill, pp. 422–23). The poet spent his last years still quite active, seeing many visitors in the Lake District and visiting others in London in 1842, 1845, and 1847, as both Gill and Moorman make clear. The year 1845 had also seen his last major editing effort for a one-volume edition of his works, reprinted in 1847. He had not published an original volume of poetry since 1842; he was made the poet laureate in 1843 but wrote no laureate poems.

However, Wordsworth had one more poetic card up his sleeve. *The Prelude* was published in July 1850, three months after his death. The reviewer for *Ainsworth's Magazine* found reading the poem similar to standing over Wordsworth's tombstone: "A work like this, published so soon after the demise of its author, cannot be approached but with feelings of reverence, somewhat akin to what we should experience on contemplating the simple marble slab and brief inscription which now mark the spot where repose the mortal remains of the poet" (July 1850: 558).[1] This analogy suggests that Wordsworth's long-delayed poem entombed his long poetic career, but, in the end, it reinvigorated it.

The Prelude, read during Wordsworth's lifetime only by his family and privileged friends such as Coleridge and De Quincey, became, of course, a central poem in the Wordsworth canon, often seen as the most important long poem of the period, challenged only by Blake's prophecies, which were similarly masked to most readers in the first half of the nineteenth century, if for different reasons. When I was taught romantic poetry, in another century, we did not read *The Excursion*. We did not read Scott's romances or Southey's epics. We glanced at *The Revolt of Islam* and *Endymion*, and we did not even read all of *Don Juan* in its incomplete totality. But we did read *The Prelude*, and in its multiple versions, from 1799, 1805, and 1850. It gave us the French Revolution and Wordsworth's discontent with it; it combined autobiography, history, philosophy, and visionary poetry; it provided the lived and poetic frame for Matthew Arnold's "great decade"; and it even allowed us to situate Wordsworth with other romantic writers who died too young, as when Johnston claims that "Wordsworth the Romantic poet 'died' when he read the recently completed *Prelude* to Coleridge in January 1807."[2] Shaping the long poems of Tennyson, Eliot, Pound, and Williams, as well as the novels of writers from Eliot to Joyce, it at times belonged as much to modernism as to the romantic era in which it was written or to the Victorian age when it was published.[3] It was *our* epic poem.

It was obviously not an epic poem read by Byron or Shelley or Keats. Wordsworth seems to have withheld the poem from readers for a number of complex reasons. As it was supposed to preface *The Recluse* once it was finished, he thought it inappropriate to release his autobiographical poem until the philosophical one was done (Gill, p. 145); perhaps he did not want to supply fodder to critics who might again call out the "egotistical sublime." He also seemed loathe to release key facts about his early life while he was alive, perhaps because his revolutionary youth increasingly did not accord with his later revered status as a spokesperson for a particular kind of spirituality; maybe he did not want to fall into the trap that had been laid for Southey with the publication of *Wat Tyler*.[4] There is also the possibility, given his concerns about both his poetic legacy and the financial legacy he could leave to his family, that he delayed publication to protect its copyright: as Susan Eilenberg argues, Wordsworth's interest in copyright suggests not only a desire to extend the financial benefits of his poetic corpus to his inheritors but also a drive "to pronounce from beyond the grave a controversion of his own mortality."[5] The delayed *Prelude* reanimated him as a provider and a poet.

The posthumous release of *The Prelude* had the additional unintended effect of once again erasing the younger poets who had, in various ways, challenged and changed Wordsworth's poetry. As in the postscript to the 1820 *River Duddon* sequence where Wordsworth evokes his interactions with Coleridge in 1797 or in the 1835 "Yarrow Revisited" where he echoes the 1803 "Yarrow Unvisited" with his companion Dorothy as his *"winsome Marrow"* (6), Wordsworth, in publishing in 1850 *The Prelude*, addressed to Coleridge, with its account of his life up until 1805, engages in a kind of time travel, creating not so much spots of time as time warps, where he invites the reader to revisit earlier moments with his fellow Lakers. This leap returns Wordsworth to a time before he had to contend with rival poets, at which point, in Matthew Arnold's words, "Scott effaced him before this [poetry-reading] public. Byron effaced him."[6] Offering "this posthumous yet youthful work," as the *Gentleman's Magazine* (November 1850: 459) put it, Wordsworth bounds back beyond all the younger poets who predeceased him, managing to come both before and after them; again, in the words of the *Gentleman's Magazine*, "the Prelude is elder than ... the poetry and the prose of Byron, Shelley, Southey, and Carlyle" (459). It is interesting to note how often the reviews of *The Prelude* resituate Wordsworth's poetry in the cultural battles of the 1790s: he is seen as "the demolisher of Darwin and the silencer of Hayley" (*Prospective Review* 25 [January 1851]: 97) and as the vanquisher of the Della Cruscans and their "laborious nonsense" (*Sharpe's London Journal* 12 [July 1850]: 186). The reviewers also work to reunite Wordsworth with Coleridge, who, of course, had long ago announced the existence of *The Prelude* when he celebrated its "orphic song" in his poem on hearing Wordsworth read *The Prelude*.[7]

Not that the reviews ignore comparisons with Wordsworth's other, more challenging contemporaries, particularly Scott and Byron, with some, such as *The Palladium* (September 1850: 215) and *Fraser's Magazine* (44 [July 1851]: 102) arguing that Wordsworth stands above Scott, Byron, Shelley, and Keats, while others praise his rivals, as the *North British Review* (13 [August 1850]: 503) places Byron – and Burns – above Wordsworth and argues that had "Shelley and Keats lived longer" they would have rivaled the "Patriarch of the Lakes."[8] The poet who is most often preferred to Wordsworth is Tennyson with his *In Memoriam*, where he is seen as offering a superior kind of meditative, spiritual verse that had come to be the hallmark of "late" Wordsworth. We get adumbrations of a great tradition that will move from Wordsworth to Keats to Tennyson and that will set aside Byron and Scott, not to mention Hunt.

The actual list of writers and preferences was not, in the end, the most important feature of these reviews of *The Prelude* and the retrospectives on Wordsworth's poetic work: what stands out in these reviews is the extent to which the poetry of the first half of the nineteenth century comes to be understood in relation to Wordsworth's efforts in the subjective lyric rather than in the epic or narrative poetry or public poetry more generally; these reviewers are already restructuring romanticism as offering a poetry about inner reflection on nature, memory, and the past rather than an outward revisioning of human relations.[9] We see this in the review of *The Prelude* in *Sharpe's London Journal* (12 [July 1850]: 186), which turns from Wordsworth's longer poems to celebrate "The Lines on Tintern Abbey, a large proportion of the Sonnets, the ode on the Intimations of Immortality in Early Childhood, and, above all, Laodamia." With the exception of the last poem, these selections approximate the Wordsworthian canon I was taught. Arnold would solidify this list of great poems, turning from Wordsworth's *Excursion* and even *The Prelude* to pronounce, "His best work is in his shorter pieces . . . . Wordsworth composed verses during a space of some sixty years, and it is no exaggeration to say that within one decade, between 1798 and 1808, almost all his really first-rate work was produced" (p. 336).

The embrace of this supposed great decade of lyric poetry changed how romantic literature as a whole was read. The poetical and political struggles that had actually created romanticism in the first half of the nineteenth century were set aside to follow Wordsworth in leaping beyond them. Wordsworth was no longer seen as competing with Byron and Scott to be the narrative poet of his day. Accounts of romanticism increasingly turned from historical, satirical, and political romances to an internalized quest romance. Wordsworth no longer spoke to and against Hunt or Hazlitt, Byron or Shelley about the key public issues of his day. He was instead the poet of private, philosophical contemplation. Where Ryan's Wordsworth, speaking to the Church of Wordsworth, might be a religious poet many today find less interesting than the radical of the 1790s, he was still very much a poet speaking to key issues such as the debates around Darwin. In the end, when due to the efforts of scholars such as Emile Legouis and A. C. Bradley, *The Prelude* came to find its place (or at least the place of its lyric "spots of time") in the Wordsworth canon, we do not get Ryan's religious poet but M. H. Abrams' secular, apolitical poet of natural supernaturalism, as "faith in an apocalypse by revelation had been replaced by faith in an apocalypse by revolution, and this now gave way to faith in an apocalypse by imagination or cognition."[10] Whatever the ideology of romantic poets, Jerome McGann's "romantic ideology" had been firmly planted in romantic scholarship.

Perhaps most significantly, Wordsworth finally displaced Byron as the central poet of the early nineteenth century. Byron as a political poet addressing a large public gave way to Wordsworth as a spiritual poet speaking to, essentially, Coleridge's clerisy of Ryan's Church of Wordsworth.[11] However, the great erasure of a politically and historically engaged romanticism did as much damage to our understanding of Wordsworth's poetry as it did to our take on Byron's. Not only were Byron and Scott set to the side of the romantic canon until quite recently, Wordsworth's goal of writing a poetry that would inspire and guide the body politic of the nation – not just the self in nature – was also elided. Our recovery of *The Prelude*, then, oddly enough helped to create "late" Wordsworth: after *The Prelude*, the deluge of dull poetry.

The "late" Wordsworth I have tried to recover in this book believed – along with Byron or Shelley or Hunt – that poetry could do real, tangible, political work in the world, whether in regard to our relationship to the environment or our attitudes toward war, our conceptions of sexuality or our vision of sociality. To be clear once again: this is not to reduce poetry to politics but to say that poetry matters in cultural combats and that those combats, defined in part by the conversations and contestations between poets, play out in the poetry itself. The conflicts I have tried to trace *among* authors occur *in* the interior of their texts, in the play of echoes and indirect rewritings that make, say, the *River Duddon* sonnets speak to Shelley or *Peter Bell* stand against the Byronic. As Wordsworth continued to reshape his poetry in part through confronting the challenges posed by the verse of his younger contemporaries, he joined those poets in asserting culture's power to reflect upon the past, speak to the present, and shape the future. The Wordsworth I was taught was silenced after 1814. I have tried to hear him, as he continued to develop as a writer, debating about poetry and politics with Byron, Shelley, and Keats. I believe we will read "late" Wordsworth correctly only when we see him as, in his own unique way, a second-generation romantic.

Notes

Introduction

1. Ralph Ellison, *The Collected Essays of Ralph Ellison*, ed. John F. Callahan (New York: The Modern Library, 1995), p. 165.
2. Geoffrey Hartman, *Wordsworth's Poetry 1787–1814* (New Haven, CT: Yale University Press, 1977), p. 338.
3. Harold Bloom, *The Anxiety of Influence* (New York: Oxford University Press, 1973), p. 5.
4. Kenneth R. Johnston, *The Hidden Wordsworth: Poet, Lover, Rebel, Spy* (New York: W. W. Norton & Co., 1998), p. 11
5. As in Canto I of *Don Juan*: "Thou shalt believe in Milton, Dryden, Pope, / Thou shall not set up Wordsworth, Coleridge, Southey; . . . . / Thou shalt not steal from Samuel Rogers, nor – / Commit – flirtation with the muse of Moore" (205.1633–34, 1639–40); *Lord Byron: The Complete Poetical Works*, vol. 5, ed. Jerome J. McGann (Oxford: Clarendon Press, 1986); canto, stanza, and line numbers will be given in the text.
6. Throughout this book I use these two poems as touchstones for the younger poets. Michael Gamer reminds me (email, February 9, 2020) that Wordsworth himself highlighted these poems in his 1815 collected poems, with Wordsworth placing "Tintern Abbey" at the end of the vital group of "Poems of the Imagination" and the "Intimations Ode" as the final poem.
7. Quoted in *The Prose Works of William Wordsworth*, 3 vols., ed. Alexander B. Grosart (London: Moxon, 1876), 3: 463.
8. On the shape of Wordsworth's later career, see in particular William H. Galperin, *Revision and Authority in Wordsworth: The Interpretation of a Career* (Philadelphia: University of Pennsylvania Press, 1989), but also Willard L. Sperry, *Wordsworth's Anti-Climax*, Harvard Studies in English, Volume XIII (Cambridge, MA: Harvard University Press, 1935).
9. Among numerous other examples, see G. Kim Blank, *Wordsworth's Influence on Shelley: A Study of Poetic Authority* (New York: St. Martin's, 1988); Beth Lau, *Keats's Reading of the Romantic Poets* (Ann Arbor: University of Michigan Press,

1991); Jack Stillinger, "Wordsworth and Keats," *The Age of William Wordsworth*, ed. Kenneth R. Johnston and Gene W. Ruoff (New Brunswick: Rutgers University Press, 1987), pp. 173–95; and Jerome McGann, *Byron and Wordsworth* (Nottingham: School of English Studies, University of Nottingham, 1999).

10. I am indebted to many other superb scholars who have sought to illuminate the later Wordsworth, including Geoffrey Hartman and Stephen Gill, William Galperin, James Garrett, Bruce Graver, Alan Hill, Theresa Kelley, Judith Page, Daniel Robinson, Philip Shaw, Eric Walker, and John Wyatt – and the editors of the Cornell Wordsworth. Perhaps most influential on my own way of thinking about Wordsworth has been Peter Manning, who, in a serious of brilliant articles, gives our best sense of how the later Wordsworth reinvents himself through a deep engagement with history and literary culture. As I was wrapping up this project, I received a copy of Jonathan Bate's *Radical Wordsworth: The Poet Who Changed the World* (New Haven, CT: Yale University Press, 2020), so I was not able to take full advantage of this new take on the poet's life and its useful treatment of his afterlife (pp. 459–91). I should also point to Jeffrey C. Robinson's *Poetic Innovation in Wordsworth's Poetry, 1825–1833: Fibres of These Thoughts* (London: Anthem Press, 2019), which offers an experimental reading of a key late Wordsworth manuscript.

11. Tim Fulford, *The Late Poetry of the Lake Poets* (Cambridge: Cambridge University Press, 2013).

12. Tim Fulford, *Wordsworth's Poetry 1815–1845* (Philadelphia: University of Pennsylvania Press, 2019), p. 175. Eric C. Walker, *Marriage, Writing, and Romanticism: Wordsworth and Austen After War* (Stanford, CA: Stanford University Press, 2009) also sees Wordsworth in *The Excursion* responding to Keats's eroticism in the "Hymn to Pan" from *Endymion* that Keats read to Wordsworth (pp. 202–10).

13. Fulford, *The Late Poetry of the Lake Poets*, p. 18.

14. Fulford, *Romantic Poetry and Literary Coteries: The Dialect of the Tribe* (New York: Palgrave Macmillan, 2015).

15. Nicholas Roe, *John Keats: A New Life* (New Haven, CT: Yale University Press, 2012), p. 196. See also Jack Stillinger, "Wordsworth and Keats," pp. 173–95.

16. On Haydon, see David Bleney Brown, Robert Woof, and Stephen Hebron, *Benjamin Robert Haydon, 1786–1846: Painter and Writer, Friend of Wordsworth and Keats* (Kendal: Wordsworth Trust, 1996); Eric George, *The Life and Death of Benjamin Robert Haydon: Historical Painter, 1786–1846*, 2nd ed. (Oxford: Clarendon, 1967).

17. *The Life of Benjamin Robert Haydon*, ed. Tom Taylor, 3 vols. (London: Longman, Brown, Green, and Longmans, 1853), 1: 123; quoted in Brown et al., *Haydon*, p. 25.

18. *The Diary of Benjamin Robert Haydon*, ed. Willard Bissell Pope, 5 vols. (Cambridge: Harvard University Press, 1960–63), 1: 446, 450.

19. Haydon, *Diary*, 2: 147, 171.

20. Haydon, *Diary*, 2: 173–76.

21. See Penelope Hughes-Hallet, *The Immortal Dinner* (New York: Vintage Books, 2012).

22. Haydon to Edward Moxon, November 29, 1845, *The Keats Circle*, ed. Hyder Edward Rollins, 2 vols. (Cambridge: Harvard University Press, 1948) 2: 143–44.

23. Roe, *John Keats, A New Life*, p. 196.

24. See Wordsworth's letter to Reynolds, November 28, 1816; *WLMY*, 2: 345–46. See also Leonidas M. Jones, *The Life of John Hamilton Reynolds* (Hanover: University Press of New England, 1984), pp. 68–74. A good selection of Reynolds's criticism is reprinted in *Selected Prose of John Hamilton Reynolds*, ed. Leonidas M. Jones (Cambridge, MA: Harvard University Press, 1966).

25. Reynolds, *Selected Prose*, p. 258.

26. See Michael Foot, "Hazlitt's Revenge on the Lakers," *Wordsworth Circle* 14 (Winter, 1983): 61–68.

27. See Lamb, letter to Wordsworth, August 9, 1814, full of praise for the poem, and his letter to Wordsworth, September 19, 1814, where he discusses Hazlitt's attack on the passage on Voltaire in *The Excursion*, 2: 479–86 and asks "are you a Xtian? Or is it the Pedlar & the Priest that are?"; see *The Letters of Charles and Mary Lamb*, Vol. 3, ed. Edwin W. Marrs, Jr. (Ithaca, NY: Cornell University Press, 1978): pp. 95–96, 112. As Marrs notes, Lamb would take up their disagreement over Voltaire again at the "immortal dinner."

28. Haydon, *Diary*, 2: 372–73.

29. Haydon, *Diary*, 2: 148–66.

30. Haydon, *Diary*, 2: 46–47.

31. June 12, 1815; they would meet again on June 15; Haydon, *Diary*, 1: 451; F. B. Pinion, *A Wordsworth Chronology* (Boston: G. K. Hall, 1988), p. 98.

32. *The Autobiography of Leigh Hunt*, ed. Edmund Blunden (Oxford: Oxford University Press, 1928), pp. 304–305. Of course, Wordsworth may have hoped for additional appreciation, including a positive review of his 1815 volume in *The Examiner*, as Moorman suggests (p. 279).

33. Clarke Olney in *Benjamin Robert Haydon, Historical Painter* (Athens: University of Georgia Press, 1952) indicates the painting is owned by *The Times* (192n.). See also catalogue number 28, p. 151 in Brown et al., *Haydon*.

34. Robert Woof, "Haydon, Writer and Friend of Writers," in Brown et al., *Haydon*, p. 32.

35. Haydon, *Diary*, 2: 63.

36. These quotations come from, in order, *The Satirist* 12 (February 1813): 188; the *Theatrical Inquisitor* 4 (February 1813): 57; *The Times* (January 25, 1813); the *Theatrical Inquisitor* 2 (March 1813): 111; and then again the *Theatrical Inquisitor* 4 (February 1813): 62; both *The Times* and the *Theatrical Inquisitor* raise questions about the play's moral vision. All of these reviews can be found in *Coleridge: The Critical Heritage*, ed. J. R. de J. Jackson (New York: Barnes and Noble, 1970).

37. In a review of *Thalaba the Destroyer* in *Edinburgh Review* 1 (October 1802): 66.

38. The attacks began in *Blackwood's* 2 (October 1817) and would continue there and elsewhere. See Nicholas Roe, *Keats and the Culture of Dissent* (Oxford: Oxford University Press, 1997) and Cox, *Poetry and Politics in the Cockney School: Keats, Shelley, Hunt and Their Circle* (Cambridge: Cambridge University Press, 1998), esp. pp. 16–37.

39. The younger writers would launch an additional counterattack, as we can see the three Lake Poets being read as a group on the pages of Hunt's *Examiner*, in Byron's *Don Juan* (see n.5), or in Hazlitt's evocation of three poets, "one with a receipt-stamp in his hand, the other with a laurel on his head, and the third with a symbol we could make nothing of, for it was neither literal nor allegorical," all "following in the train of the Pope and the Inquisition and the Bourbons" (*CWWH*, 7: 152).

40. Coleridge, *Biographia Literaria*, ed. James Engell and W. Jackson Bate, 2 vols. (Princeton, NJ: Princeton University Press, 1983), 1: 5.

41. Letter, March 30, 1815, to Byron, *Collected Letters of Samuel Taylor Coleridge*, ed. Earl Leslie Griggs, 6 vols. (Oxford: Oxford University Press,1956–71), 4: 563, quoted in Holmes, *Coleridge: Darker Reflections, 1804–1834* (New York: Pantheon Books, 1998), p. 377.

42. See "Editor's Introduction," *Biographia Literaria*, 1: li–lviii.

43. Lapp sees Hazlitt combining a "politicized Romanticism of dissident protest with the skillful articulation of the collective voice of 'public opinion,'" while Coleridge promotes a "Romanticism of withdrawal into visionary idealism that locates cultural authority in the attractive figure of the poet-prophet." Together they provide an "instructive epitome of much larger patterns of conflict: the political struggle between reaction and reform, marketplace competition over new reading audiences, and the friction between competing genres and modes of discursive performance in the public sphere." *Contest for Cultural Authority: Hazlitt, Coleridge, and the Distresses of the Regency* (Detroit, MI: Wayne State University Press, 1999), p. 12.

44. On Southey, see, for example, the *Examiner* review of Southey's *Lay of the Laureate. Carmen Nuptiale* (July 7, 1816) and the satire on that poem, "The Laureate Laid Double" (August 4, 1816); *The Examiner* also began on

August 11, 1816, to publish "Acanthologia. Specimens of Jacobin Poetry" as part of the wider attempt to embarrass Southey through the reproduction of his early works. There is another satiric poem, "A Dream" by "Night Mare," that uses the figure of Queen Mab to imagine a "topsy-turvy" world where "The Rich will be generous, the Liberal scurvy; Each Placeman be honest, and Minister wise" (August 25, 1816); Southey is attacked along with Scott, Canning, Castlereagh, and Ellenborough. This all predates Hazlitt's stronger attacks upon Coleridge, Southey, and even Wordsworth in the fall.

45. Keats, letter to Haydon, January 10, 1818; *KL*, 1: 203. See also Mary Shelley, *The Journals of Mary Shelley 1814–1844*, ed. Paula R. Feldman and Diana Scott-Kilvert, 2 vols. (Baltimore, MD: Johns Hopkins University Press, 1987), September 14, 1814, 1: 25.

46. James K. Chandler, "'Wordsworth' after Waterloo," *in The Age of William Wordsworth: Critical Essays on the Romantic Tradition*, ed. Kenneth R. Johnston and Gene W. Ruoff (New Brunswick: Rutgers University Press, 1987), pp. 84–111.

47. Hubbell, "*Laon and Cythna*: A Vision of Regency Romanticism," *Keats-Shelley Journal* 51 (2002): 174–97.

48. Byron, *Letter to John Murray Esq.*, in *Lord Byron: The Complete Miscellaneous Prose*, ed. Andrew Nicholson (Oxford: Clarendon Press, 1991), p. 135. Nicholson has a fine review of the controversy, pp. 399–410.

49. Byron, "Addenda," *Letter to John Murray Esq.*, p. 156.

50. Byron, "Addenda," *Letter to John Murray Esq.*, pp. 155–56.

51. Reiman, headnote to review, *Romantics Reviewed, Lake Poets*, 2: 469.

52. This review is taken up by Coleridge in the "conclusion" to his *Biographia Literaria*, 2: 239, and then Jeffrey responds in a long note to a passage where Hazlitt refers to future "publications from the Lake school" in his review of *Biographia Literaria, Edinburgh Review* 27 (August 1817): 509.

53. See "Life and Writings of Thomas Warton," in *The Poetical Works of the Late Thomas Warton*, ed. Richard Mant, 5th ed. (London: F. & C. Rivington, 1802), pp. lxii–lxiii.

54. Interestingly enough, Southey in a review of an edition of Johnson's *Lives of the Most Eminent English Poets* uses the phrase "metaphysical school" (*Quarterly Review* 12 [October 1814]: 82).

55. Bloom, *Anxiety of Influence*, p. 95.

56. See, among others, Susan Eilenberg, *Strange Power of Speech: Wordsworth, Coleridge, and Literary Possession* (Oxford: Oxford University Press, 1992), esp. pp. 192–212; Mark Rose, *Authors and Owners* (Cambridge, MA: Harvard University Press, 1993); Thomas Pfau, *Wordsworth's Profession: Form, Class and the Logic of Early Romantic Cultural Production* (Stanford, CA: Stanford University Press, 1997); and Michael Gamer, *Romanticism,*

Self-Canonization, and the Business of Poetry (Cambridge: Cambridge University Press, 2017).

57. See Cox, *Poetry and Politics in the Cockney School*, esp. pp. 16–81; Roe, *Keats and the Culture of Dissent*, esp. pp. 1–26.

58. Peter Manning, *Reading Romantics: Text and Context* (Oxford: Oxford University Press, 1990), pp. 195–215.

59. See, for example, Daniel Robinson, "*The River Duddon* and Wordsworth, Sonneteer," in *The Oxford Handbook of William Wordsworth*, ed. Richard Gravil and Daniel Robinson (Oxford: Oxford University Press, 2015), pp. 289–308.

60. See Philip Shaw, "Commemorating Waterloo: Wordsworth, Southey, and the 'Muses Page of State,'" *Romanticism* 1.1 (1995): 50–67 and "Wordsworth after Peterloo: The Persistence of War in *River Duddon . . . and Other Poems*," in *Commemorating Peterloo: Violence, Resilience and Claim-making during the Romantic Era*, ed. Michael Demson and Regina Hewitt (Edinburgh: Edinburgh University Press, 2019), pp. 250–70; and James Garrett, *Wordsworth and the Writing of the Nation* (Burlington, VT: Ashgate, 2008).

61. Matthew Arnold, "Preface," *The Poems of William Wordsworth*, ed. Matthew Arnold (London: Macmillan and Co., 1879), p. xii.

62. Sperry, *Wordsworth's Anti-Climax*, p. v.

63. H. W. Garrod, *Wordsworth* (Oxford: Clarendon Press, 1923), p. 138.

64. Fulford, *The Late Poetry of the Lake Poets*, p. 20.

65. Fulford, *The Late Poetry of the Lake Poets*, p. 2.

66. See "Great Sex and Great Decades," Siskin, *The Historicity of Romantic Discourse* (New York: Oxford University Press, 1988), pp. 164–78.

67. Sperry, *Wordsworth's Anti-Climax*, p. 38.

68. Sperry offers his quotations without notes for the most part. He quotes from De Quincey, "Lake Reminiscences, from 1807 to 1830, No. 1: William Wordsworth," *Tait's Edinburgh Magazine* 6 (January 1839): 9.

69. Devoney Looser, "Age and Aging," in *Women's Writing in the Romantic Period*, ed. Devoney Looser (Cambridge: Cambridge University Press, 2015), pp. 170, 177. Looser draws on other accounts of aging such as Philippe Ariès, *Centuries of Childhood: A Social History of Family Life*, trans. Robert Baldick (New York: Knopf, 1962) and Susannah R. Ottaway, *The Decline of Life: Old Age in Eighteenth-Century England* (Cambridge: Cambridge University Press, 2007). See also Margaret Morganroth Gullette, *Aged by Culture* (Chicago, IL: University of Chicago Press; 2004). This is a burgeoning field with professional organizations – the North American Network in Aging Studies and the European Network in Aging Studies – and a journal, *Age, Culture, Humanities: An Interdisciplinary Journal.*

70. Edith Batho 's *The Later Wordsworth* (Cambridge: Cambridge University Press, 1933) also takes a largely biographical approach to the "late" work. More recent scholars such as Hartman and Judith Page (see n.72 and n.73) have been more interested in Wordsworth's relation to his daughter, Dora, than in his affair with Annette Vallon.

71. Sperry, *Wordsworth's Anti-Climax*, pp. 122–43.

72. Hartman, *The Unremarkable Wordsworth* (Minneapolis: University of Minnesota Press, 1987), p. 14.

73. Hartley Coleridge, August 21, 1836, *The Letters of Hartley Coleridge*, ed. Grace Evelyn Griggs and Earl Leslie Griggs (New York: Oxford University Press, 1936), p. 196; quoted in Judith Page, *Wordsworth and the Cultivation of Women* (Berkeley: University of California Press, 1994), p. 114. See also Peter Manning, "Wordsworth at St. Bees: Scandals' Sisterhoods, and Wordsworth's Later Poetry," *ELH* 52 (Spring 1985): 33–58.

74. Galperin, *Revision and Authority in Wordsworth*, p. 2.

75. Charles Mahoney, *Romantics and Renegades: The Poetics of Political Reaction* (New York: Palgrave Macmillan, 2003), p. 2.

76. First published in *The Friend* (1809) and then in the 1815 collected poems and ultimately placed in *The Prelude* (1850), II: 142–44.

77. Hazlitt, "Letter-Bell," in *William Hazlitt: Metropolitan Writings*, ed. Gregory Dart (Manchester: Carcanet, 2005), p. 178.

78. Thompson, "Disenchantment or Default? A Lay Sermon," in *Power and Consciousness*, ed. Conor Cruise O'Brien and William Dean Vanech (London: University of London Press; New York: New York University Press, 1969), pp. 152–53.

79. Thompson, "Disenchantment or Default," p. 152.

80. Thompson, "Disenchantment or Default," p. 177.

81. Thompson, "Disenchantment or Default," p. 173.

82. Mahoney, *Romantics and Renegades*, p. 7. See also Lapp, *Contest for Cultural Authority*, pp. 88–91.

83. Jonathan Sachs, *Romantic Antiquity* (Oxford: Oxford University Press, 2010) provides an insightful, contextualized reading of Hazlitt's review as engaging in particular with the ways in which John Philip Kemble's portrayal of Coriolanus had marked Shakespeare's tragedy as setting forth an "imperial" or "legitimate" vision (pp. 179–220).

84. Scrivener, *Radical Shelley: The Philosophical Anarchism and Utopian Thought of Percy Bysshe Shelley* (Princeton, NJ: Princeton University Press, 1982), pp. 120–22.

85. Jay Cantor, *The Space Between: Literature and Politics* (Baltimore, MD: Johns Hopkins University Press, 1981), p. 11.

86. See Timothy J. Wandling 's very useful "Early Romantic Theorists and the Fate of Transgressive Eloquence: John Stuart Mill's Response to Byron," in *Nervous Reactions: Victorian Recollections of Romanticism*, ed. Joel Faflak and Julia M. Wright (Albany: State University of New York Press, 2004), pp. 123–40; also Mill, *Autobiography of John Stuart Mill*, 2nd ed. (London: Longmans, Green, Reader, & Dyer, 1873), ch. 5, esp. p. 150.

1 Cockney Excursions

1. Letter 2529, *The Collected Letters of Robert Southey*, Part IV, ed. Ian Packer and Lynda Pratt, https://romantic-circles.org/editions/southey_letters/Part_Fou r/HTML/letterEEd.26.2529.html.
2. C. Mahoney, *Romantics and Renegades: The Poetics of Political Reaction* (New York: Palgrave Macmillan, 2003), p. 83.
3. Wordsworth was preparing a fair copy for the printer in February 1814. Dorothy Wordsworth was waiting for the proof-sheets on April 24. Wordsworth asked Lord Lonsdale's permission to dedicate the poem to him on June 4. See F. B. Pinion, *A Wordsworth Chronology* (Boston: G. K. Hall, 1988), pp. 94–95; letter to Lord Lonsdale, June 14, 1814, *WLMY*, 2: 148–49.
4. Kenneth Johnston, *Wordsworth and "The Recluse,"* (New Haven, CT: Yale University Press, 1984), p. 290.
5. Byron, "Don Juan," in *Lord Byron: The Complete Works*, Volume 5, ed. Jerome J. McGann (Oxford: Clarendon Press, 1986); canto, stanza, and line numbers will be given in the text.
6. Duncan Wu, *William Hazlitt: The First Modern Man* (Oxford: Oxford University Press, 2008), p. 168.
7. Moorman, 2: 260.
8. Mary Shelley, *The Journals of Mary Shelley*, ed. Paula R. Feldman and Diana Scott Kilvert, 2 vols. (Baltimore, MD: Johns Hopkins Press, 1987), 1: 25.
9. Cox, *Romanticism in the Shadow of War: Literary Culture in the Napoleonic War Years* (Cambridge: Cambridge University Press, 2014), pp. 161–64.
10. Hazlitt makes an explicit link between *The Excursion* and these celebrations in his "Character of Mr. Wordsworth's new poem, The Excursion," in *The Examiner*, where, after noting that Wordsworth's "mind is . . . coeval with the primary forms of things," he complains of the "Regent's Fair" that "Every one wishes to get rid of the booths and bridges in the Park, in order to have a view of the ground and water again" (*CWWH*, 19: 10&n.).
11. Johnston, *Wordsworth and "The Recluse,"* p. 291.
12. On links between the Solitary and Wordsworth's contemporaries such as Thelwall and Fawcett, see Kenneth Johnston, *Wordsworth and "The Recluse,"* pp. 383–84n. See also Coleridge's letter to Wordsworth, September 1799, in

The Collected Letters of Samuel Taylor Coleridge, ed. E. L. Griggs, 6 vols. (Oxford: Oxford University Press, 1956–71), 1: 527: "I wish you would write a poem, in blank verse, addressed to those, who, in consequence of the complete failure of the French Revolution, have thrown up all hopes of the amelioration of mankind, and are sinking into an almost epicurean selfishness."

13. Thomas Noon Talfourd, *Final Memorials of Charles Lamb*, 2 vols. (London: E. Moxon, 1848), 2: 170.

14. Sally Bushell, James A. Butler, and Michael C. Jaye, eds., the Cornell Wordsworth *Excursion* (Ithaca, NY: Cornell University Press, 2007), p. 8; book and line numbers for poetry and page numbers for prose will be given in the text.

15. William Galperin, *Revision and Authority in Wordsworth: The Interpretation of a Career* (Philadelphia: University of Pennsylvania Press, 1989), pp. 29–63.

16. Alison Hickey, *Impure Conceits: Rhetoric and Ideology in Wordsworth's Excursion* (Stanford, CA: Stanford University Press, 1997).

17. See also Frances Ferguson, *Wordsworth: Language as Counter-Spirit* (New Haven, CT: Yale University Press, 1977); Geoffrey Hartman, *Wordsworth's Poetry 1787–1814* (New Haven, CT: Yale University Press, 1964); Susan J. Wolfson, *The Questioning Presence: Wordsworth, Keats, and the Interrogative Mode in Romantic Poetry* (Ithaca, NY: Cornell University Press, 1986); and Jonathan Wordsworth, *William Wordsworth: The Borders of Vision* (Oxford: Clarendon, 1982). Most recently, Brandon C. Yen, in *"The Excursion" and Wordsworth's Iconography* (Liverpool: Liverpool University Press, 2018), takes up the "iconography of landscape images" in the poem, tracing them to visual sources and through allusions to other Wordsworth poems (p. 36).

18. Beth Lau, *Keats's Reading of the Romantic Poets* (Ann Arbor: The University of Michigan Press, 1991), pp. 48–59.

19. Paul Mueschke and Earl L. Griggs, "Wordsworth as the Prototype of the Poet in *Alastor*," *PMLA* 49 (1934): pp. 229–45.

20. Hartman, *Wordsworth's Poetry*, pp. 292–323.

21. Favret, *War at a Distance: Romanticism and the Making of Modern Wartime* (Princeton, NJ: Princeton University Press, 2010), pp. 25–30.

22. Kenneth Johnston, *Wordsworth and "The Recluse,"* pp. 273, 264.

23. Hill, "Wordsworth, Boccaccio, and the Pagan Gods of Antiquity," *Studies in English Literature, 1500–1900* 45 (February 1994): p. 36. Hill cites a note by Haydon in his copy of *The Excursion* held at Cornell.

24. Blake, *Marriage of Heaven and Hell*, in *The Complete Poetry and Prose of William Blake*, ed. David V. Erdman, rev. ed. (Berkeley: University of California Press, 1982), plate 11, p. 38.

25. Hazlitt, "Character of Mr. Wordsworth's new Poem, The Excursion," "The Same Subject Continued," *The Examiner*, August 28, 1814; *CWWH*, 19: 13.
26. Johnston, *Wordsworth and "The Recluse,"* p. 320.
27. Philip Connell, *Romanticism, Economics and the Question of "Culture"* (Oxford: Oxford University Press, 2001), p. 173. He is quoting C. A. Bayley, *Imperial Meridian: The British Empire and the World 1780–1830* (New York: Routledge, 1989). For moments, such as the attack upon child labor and the harshness of industrialization in Book VIII, that would have appealed more to the younger writers, see Carl Woodring, *Politics in English Romantic Poetry* (Cambridge, MA: Harvard University Press, 1970), pp. 134–36. See also James Garrett, *Wordsworth and the Writing of the Nation* (Burlington, VT: Ashgate Publishing Company, 2008), pp. 96–102, 108–109.
28. Johnston, *Wordsworth and the Recluse*, p. 323.
29. Thomas Medwin, *The Life of Percy Bysshe Shelley*, ed. H. Buxton Forman (London: Oxford University Press, 1913), pp. 178–79.
30. See Ben W. Griffith, Jr., "The Keats–Shelley Poetry Contests," *Notes and Queries* 199 (1954): 359–60; Clayton W. Hudnall, "John Hamilton Reynolds, James Rice, and Benjamin Bailey in the Leigh Browne-Lockyer Collection," *Keats-Shelley Journal* 19 (1970): 21; and Walter Edwin Peck, *Shelley: His Life and Work* (rpt. New York: Burt Franklin, 1969), pp. 49–51.
31. John Kinnaird, *William Hazlitt: Critic of Power* (New York: Columbia University Press, 1978), p. 228.
32. See Kevin Gilmartin's important reading of Hazlitt's review in *William Hazlitt, Political Essayist* (Oxford: Oxford University Press, 2015), pp. 97–100, 233–37.
33. See Earl Wasserman, *Shelley: A Critical Reading* (Baltimore, MD: Johns Hopkins University Press, 1971), pp. 19–21; Yvonne M. Carothers, "Alastor: Shelley Corrects Wordsworth," *Modern Language Quarterly* 42 (1981): 21–47; and Paul Mueschke and Earl L. Griggs, "Wordsworth as the Prototype of the Poet in *Alastor*," *PMLA* 49 (1934): 229–45. A good account of the poem's relations to *The Excursion*, which also uses Shelley's response to *Peter Bell*, is Martyn Crucefix, "Wordsworth, Superstition, and Shelley's *Alastor*," *Essays in Criticism* 2 (April 1983): 126–47. A somewhat differing view is found in Christopher Heppner, "Alastor: The Poet and the Narrator Reconsidered," *Keats-Shelley Journal* 37 (1988): 91–109. See also Francesca Cauchi, "A Rereading of Wordsworth's Presence in Shelley's *Alastor*," *Studies in English Literature, 1500–1900* 50 (Autumn, 2010): 759–74, where Shelley is found analyzing Wordsworth's decline as arising from an over-speculative idealism.
34. See Marilyn Butler, *Peacock Displayed: A Satirist in His Context* (London: Routledge and Kegan Paul, 1979), pp. 106–108.

35. See the preface to the poem in *The Garden of Florence; and Other Poems* by "John Hamilton" (London: John Warren, 1821), pp. 32–33, where he connects it with the "Immortality Ode," as he explains why an unfinished poem is being offered to the public; stanza numbers will be given in the text. See also my "John Keats, Medicine, and Young Men on the Make," in *John Keats and the Medical Imagination*, ed. Nicholas Roe (Cham, Switzerland: Palgrave Macmillan, 2017), pp. 121–22.

36. Although we cannot be certain how he would have completed the poem, Reynolds indicates that he would "have shown how ruthlessly discontent and a connexion with the world mar all the beauty and bloom of youth" ("Preface," p. 33). He gave further hints in a statement copied into two of the commonplace books kept by the Leigh women:

> The Romance of Youth dissolves with gathering years and the bright and glowing colours which dazzled at that period are now no more to be discovered, but a steady, a lambent flame remains which is far more calculated to produce lasting happiness than that visionary perspective which was only descried on the horizon. (London Metropolitan Archive, Keats House Collection, K/MS/01/047)

Reynolds's poem would have been content to lose "splendour in the grass" and "glory in the hour" to experience the glories and splendor that can be the produce of the everyday. The projected shape of Reynolds's fable is thus closer in certain ways to Wordsworth than to his fellows in the Hunt circle.

37. See Beth Lau's chapter on Shelley in *Keats's Reading of the Romantic Poets*, pp. 147–72, esp. 160–66; Stuart Sperry, *Keats the Poet* (Princeton, NJ: Princeton University Press, 1973), pp. 94–95; Miriam Allot, "Keats's *Endymion* and Shelley's 'Alastor,'" in *Literature of the Romantic Period 1750–1850*, ed. R. T. Davies and B. G. Beatty (Liverpool: Liverpool University Press, 1976), pp. 151–70; Leonard Brown, "The Genesis, Growth, and Meaning of *Endymion*," *Studies in Philology* 30 (1933): 618–53; A. C. Bradley, *Oxford Lectures on Poetry* (1909 rpt. London: Macmillan, 1965), pp. 240–44. I have learned much from Daniel P. Watkins's contexualized reading of *Endymion* in *Keats's Poetry and the Politics of the Imagination* (Rutherford, NJ: Fairleigh Dickinson University Press, 1989), pp. 35–53, but I disagree with his view that Keats's poem "displays the disintegration of public hope and social possibility and at the same time seeks an alternative possibility of value in the mind and in transcendental redemptive powers" (p. 37); I find this a good description of what Keats is writing against in the poem but not of its solutions.

38. Watkins, *Keats's Poetry and the Politics of the Imagination*, pp. 40–41: "The problem is not simply Endymion's apparent unhappiness ... but rather a general sense of death and decay permeating the entire community, even

while the institutional rhetoric (in the form of the priest's encomium) celebrates community well-being."

39. Deven Parker, in email comments on July 20, 2019, points out that Shelley's and Keats's depictions of the Arab Maiden and the Indian Maid draw upon orientalist fantasies that could undermine the idea that these women offer some "real" solution for the "Alastor" poet or Endymion. I would stress their status as actual human beings rather than dreams or goddesses, but their connection with eroticizing fantasies may also aid in the slippage between the "real" and the "ideal."

40. Letter of Benjamin Bailey to John Taylor, August 29, 1818; *The Keats Circle*, ed. Hyder Edward Rollins, 2 vols. (Cambridge: Harvard University Press, 1984), 1: 35.

41. Lionel Trilling, "The Poet as Hero: Keats in his Letters," in *The Opposing Self* (New York: Harcourt Brace Jovanovich, 1979), pp. 3–43.

42. Cox, *Poetry and Politics in the Cockney School*, pp. 112–22.

43. *The Poems of John Keats*, ed. Miriam Allot (Harlow: Longman, 1970), p. 121.

44. See Woodhouse's report in *The Manuscripts of the Younger Romantics: John Keats*, ed. Jack Stillinger; General Editor Donald H. Reiman, 7 vols. (New York: Garland Press, 1985–88), 3: 220; *Blackwood's Edinburgh Magazine* 3 (August 1818): 524; Reiman, *Keats*, 1: 95; *British Critic* 9 (June 1818): 652; Reiman, *Keats*, 1: 212.

45. *Poems of John Keats*, ed. Allot, p. 206.

46. Medwin, *The Life of Percy Bysshe Shelley*, ed. H. Buxton Forman (London: Oxford University Press, 1913), p. 148. Interestingly, Wordsworth had heard that *Childe Harold III* was indebted to him: he writes to Henry Crabb Robinson (June 24, 1817, *WLMY*, 2: 394) that "I am told he has been poaching on my Manor" – an intriguing description of his relationship to other poets. See Jane Stabler's fine account of the back and forth between the two poets, "Byron and *The Excursion*," *Wordsworth Circle* 45 (Spring 2014): 137–47.

47. Jerome McGann, *Fiery Dust: Byron's Poetic Development* (Chicago, IL: University of Chicago Press, 1968), pp. 305–306.

48. Keats also echoes this passage (*Excursion*, 4.681–717; noted by Lau and Bush) in *Endymion*, as he suggests that the imposing mythology of autocratic Babylon or Chaldea – as opposed perhaps to that of "democratic" Greece – should be linked to contemporary attempts to impress the people with the trappings of political power:

> Ah! how all this hums,
> In wakeful ears, like uproar past and gone –
> Like thunder clouds that spake to Babylon,
> And set those old Chaldeans to their tasks. –
> Are then regalities all gilded masks? (*KPP*, 3.18–22)

49. *Lord Byron: The Complete Poetical Works*, vol. 2, ed. Jerome J. McGann (Oxford: Clarendon Press, 1980); stanza and line numbers will be given in the text.

50. It is interesting that in a letter where he awaits the publication of *Childe Harold IV*, Keats mentions he is reading Voltaire and Gibbon (to George and Tom Keats, February 21, 1818, *KL*, 1: 237). The figure of Voltaire was clearly a contentious one, attacked by Wordsworth, defended by Byron. Haydon, who included a portrait of Voltaire in his painting *Christ's Entry into Jerusalem* as an emblem of the scoffer, often debated with Hunt over the French thinker; see Haydon, *The Diary of Benjamin Robert Haydon*, ed. Willard Bissell Pope, 5 vols. (Cambridge, MA: Harvard University Press, 1960–1963), 2: 54–60, 80–81. Haydon tells us that Keats once approached his painting with bowed head; "'there is the being I will bow to,' said he – he stood before Voltaire!" (2: 317). At the "immortal dinner," Lamb teased Wordsworth about attacking Voltaire in *The Excursion* and proposed a toast: "Here's Voltaire, the Messiah of the French nation, & a very fit one" (2: 173). Hazlitt also objected to Wordsworth's criticisms of Voltaire: "Whatsoever savours of a little, narrow, inquisitorial spirit, does not sit well on a poet and a man of genius" (*CWWH*, 19: 15).

51. See Shelley's "Preface" to *Laon and Cythna* in *The Complete Works of Percy Bysshe Shelley*, ed. Roger Igpen and Walter E. Peck, 10 vols. (1926; rpt. New York: Gordian Press, 1965), pp. 239–47. References to *Laon and Cythna* given in the text are to this edition.

52. Anahid Nersessian, in *Utopia Limited: Romanticism and Adjustment* (Cambridge, MA: Harvard University Press, 2015), finds romanticism as a whole offering a way beyond absolute oppositions between utopia and despair: noting that Hunt saw the era to be "dogmatic" in its despair, she writes "*Utopia, Limited* tarries with another kind of Romanticism by insisting that divestment from regimes of absolute, comprehensive gratification may be a source of politically efficacious joy" (p. 13). Her analysis of a positive vision of limits, divestment, even renunciation might be usefully applied to Byron in this poem.

53. The piece on *Coriolanus* appeared first in *The Examiner* December 15, 1816, then in an expanded version in the *Characters of Shakespear's Plays* (1817) and again in *A View of the English Stage* (1818), *CWWH*, 5. The essays on *The Times* first appeared in *The Examiner*, December 15 and 22, 1816, January 12, 1817, and were reprinted in Hazlitt's *Political Essays* published by William Hone in 1819 (*CWWH*, 7). Page numbers from Howe's edition will be given in the text. Hazlitt links the *Coriolanus* review to the series he was writing on *The Times* in the third of those pieces, "THE TIMES NEWSPAPER. ON THE

CONNECTION BETWEEN TOAD-EATERS AND TYRANTS" in *The Examiner* January 12, 1817: "We some time ago promised our friend, Mr. Robert Owen, an explanation of some of the causes which impede the natural progress of liberty and human happiness. We have in part redeemed this pledge in what we said about *Coriolanus*, and we shall try in this article to redeem it still more" (some phrases are in fact repeated from one piece to another). The centrality of the *Coriolanus* review was seen by William Gifford at the time (see his review in the *Quarterly Review*, 18 [1818]: 458–66 as well as Hazlitt's *Letter to William Gifford* [1818]) and by scholars such as Jonathan Bate, *Shakespearean Constitutions: Politics, Theatre, Criticism 1730–1830* (Oxford: Clarendon Press, 1989), pp. 164–69, John Kinnaird, *Hazlitt: Critic of Power* (New York: Columbia University Press, 1978), pp. 110–12, and Gilmartin, *William Hazlitt*, pp. 17–26, 123–27, 307–308.

54. Hazlitt's vitriolic pieces would soon lead to Stoddart's dismissal and replacement by Thomas Barnes who had connections to Hunt and his circle. Stoddart would go on to found the *New Times*. See Stanley Morison, *The History of The Times, vol. 1: "The Thunderer" in the Making, 1781–1841* (London: *The Times*, 1935); and Derek Hudson, *Thomas Barnes of the "Times"* (Cambridge: Cambridge University Press, 1944).

55. The phrase echoes the title of Coleridge's "Once a Jacobin always a Jacobin" in the *Morning Post* (1802) and reprinted in *The Friend* and *Essays on his Own Times*.

56. From a review of *Comus*, originally published in *The Examiner*, June 11, 1815, and reprinted in *A View of the English Stage* (1818), *CWWH*, 5: 230–33. Hazlitt misquotes (p. 233) line 7 of "November, 1813" ("Now that all hearts are glad, all faces bright"): "regal fortitude." Wordsworth's sonnet celebrates the defeat of Napoleon at Leipzig along with George III; the poet's celebratory depiction of the king as old, blind, and mad may be answered in Shelley's "England in 1819."

57. Scrivener, *Radical Shelley: The Philosophical Anarchism and Utopian Thought of Percy Bysshe Shelley* (Princeton, NJ: Princeton University Press, 1982), pp. 120–22.

58. Marilyn Butler suggests that "Ahrimanes" was a kind of collaborative project for Peacock and Shelley that led ultimately to *Laon and Cythna,* a poem like the proposed "Ahrimanes" in Spenserian stanzas that took up many of the same themes; see Butler, *Peacock Displayed*, pp. 66, 99. See also Kenneth Neill Cameron, "Shelley and *Ahrimanes*," *Modern Language Quarterly* 3 (June 1942): 287–95.

59. The unfinished "Ahrimanes" was probably begun in 1813, but Peacock continued to work on the piece during 1814 before abandoning it in 1815. Even though the poem was begun before the publication of *The Excursion*,

work continued on it during the early months of the epic's public life and can be considered as part of the effort to respond to that poem. There are two extant versions/plans of "Ahrimanes," but there is some dispute about the order of their composition. One (in *Shelley and His Circle, 173–1822*, vol. 3, ed. Kenneth Neill Cameron [Cambridge: Harvard University Press, 1970], pp. 211–242) contains some stanzas and is related to a two-part version of the poem; the other (British Museum, "Letters and Literary Remains of Thomas Love Peacock," Add MS 36816) contains the first and part of the second canto and is linked to a twelve-canto plan for the poem. Both are included in Vol. 7 of *The Works of Thomas Love Peacock*, ed. H. F. B. Brett-Smith and C. E. Jones (London: Constable, 1931), pp. 265–88, 420–32, and see note, pp. 513–18; stanza numbers or page numbers for prose summaries in the fragmentary twelve-canto version will be given in the text. Brett-Smith argues that the more despairing twelve-canto version with which I will be concerned is the latter version. For a different view of the order of composition and an excellent account of the relation of the fragments to Shelley's poetry, see Cameron's commentary in *Shelley and His Circle*, cited in this note.

60. As in *The Excursion* (IV, 671–680), the Persian religion of Oromazes is seen as taking place in nature, requiring no temples: "No pillared fanes to Oromazes rose" (XXII).

61. Scrivener, *Radical Shelley*, pp. 128–29.

62. See Scrivener, *Radical Shelley*, pp. 119–33; P. M. S. Dawson, *The Unacknowledged Legislator: Shelley and Politics* (Oxford: Clarendon Press, 1980), pp. 68–75; Kyle Grimes, "Censorship, Violence, and Political Rhetoric: *The Revolt of Islam* in Its Time," *Keats-Shelley Journal* 43 (1994): 98–116.

63. Scrivener, *Radical Shelley*, esp. pp. 122–23; Stephen C. Behrendt, *Shelley and His Audiences* (Lincoln: University of Nebraska Press, 1989), pp. 15–38. See also David Duff, *Romance and Revolution: Shelley and the Politics of a Genre* (Cambridge: Cambridge University Press, 1994), pp. 154–216; Yasmin Solomonescu, "Percy Shelley's Revolutionary Periods," *ELH* 83 (Winter, 2016): 1105–33.

64. Though, see Douglas Bush, *Mythology and the Romantic Tradition in English Poetry* (New York: Cooper Square Publishers, 1963), pp. 176–77; Clarence DeWitt Thorpe, "The Nymphs," *Keats-Shelley Memorial Bulletin* 10 (1959): 33–47; and James R. Thompson, *Leigh Hunt* (Boston, MA: Twayne, 1977), pp. 36–39.

65. I make some similar observations in my essay on Hunt's *Foliage* volume, "Leigh Hunt's *Foliage*: A Cockney Manifesto," in *Leigh Hunt: Life, Poetics, Politics*, ed. Nicholas Roe (London: Routledge, 2003), pp. 58–77.

66. Shelley would later write to Hunt that he wished he had not undertaken his translation of Tasso's *Amyntas* so that he might write another poem such as the "Nymphs," "which is a poem original and intense, conceived with the clearest sense of ideal beauty and executed with the fullest and most flowing lyrical power, and yet defined with the most intelligible outline of thought and language"; then, comparing it to Hunt's *Story of Rimini*, Shelley finds that [*Rimini*] "affects the passions and searches the understanding more completely, but" "The Nymphs" "appeals to the Imagination, who is the master of them both, their God, and the Spirit by which they live and are" (letter to Hunt, November 14–18, 1819, *SL*, 2: 152).

67. Quoted in Edmund Blunden, *Leigh Hunt: A Biography* (London: Cobden and Sanderson, 1930), p. 134.

68. Bush, *Mythology and the Romantic Tradition,* p. 176.

69. Thompson, *Leigh Hunt,* p. 38.

70. August Wilhelm von Schlegel, *Sämmtliche Werke,* 12 vols. (New York: G. Olms, 1971), 10: 85ff.

71. From *Horae Dramaticae* No. 3, originally published in *Fraser's Magazine,* October 1857, p. 485; in Henry Cole, ed. *The Works of Thomas Love Peacock,* Vol. III (London: Richard Bentley and Son, 1875): pp. 378–79; quoted in Suzanne Barnett, *Romantic Paganism: The Politics of Ecstasy in the Shelley Circle* (Cham, Switzerland: Palgrave Macmillan, 2017), p. 85.

72. Eric C. Walker, *Marriage, Writing, and Romanticism: Wordsworth and Austen After War* (Stanford: Stanford University Press, 2009), pp. 202–210. Fulford, *Wordsworth's Poetry, 1815–1845* (Philadelphia: University of Pennsylvania Press, 2019), pp. 181, 185.

73. Haydon to Edward Moxon, November 29, 1845, *The Keats Circle,* ed. Hyder Edward Rollins, 2 vols. (Cambridge, MA: Harvard University Press, 1948) 2: 143–44.

74. Hartman, "Words, Wish, Worth: Wordsworth," in *Deconstruction and Criticism,* eds. Harold Bloom et al. (New York: Seabury Press, 1979), p. 183. Judith Page, "Judge Her Gently': Passion and Rebellion in Wordsworth's 'Laodamia,'" *Texas Studies in Literature and Language* 33 (Spring 1991): 24–39; included in *Wordsworth and the Cultivation of Women* (Berkeley: University of California Press, 1994), pp. 79–93. Manning, "Cleansing the Images: Wordsworth, Rome, and the Rise of Historicism Manning," *Texas Studies in Literature and Language* 33 (Summer 1991): 306–15. Marilyn Butler, *Romantics, Rebels and Reactionaries: English Literature and its Background, 1760–1830* (Oxford: Oxford University Press, 1981), pp. 113–37.

75. John Paul Pritchard, "On the Making of Wordsworth's 'Dion,'" *Studies in Philology* 49 (January, 1952): 66–74.

76. Jane Worthington, *Wordsworth 's Reading of Roman Prose* (New Haven, CT: Yale University Press, 1946). On "Dion," see pp. 40–42.
77. See Sharon M. Setzer, "Sicilian Daydreams and Parisian Nightmares: Wordsworth's Representations of Plutarch's Dion," *Studies in English Literature, 1500–1900* 32 (Autumn 1992): 607–24.
78. Page, "Passion and Rebellion in 'Laodamia,'" p. 25.
79. We have a number of subtle readings of Wordsworth's poem. For example, William Galperin, *Revision and Authority in Wordsworth: The Interpretation of a Career* (Philadelphia: University of Pennsylvania Press, 1989), pp. 213–14, has argued that "Laodamia" is part of Wordsworth's ongoing project to ironize authority, beginning with the poet's own imaginative authority; "Laodamia" suggests to Galperin that both the "humanistic authority" voiced by Laodamia and "a sententious, Evangelical authority" are equally incapable of controlling the world: "No longer signifying fate or some overarching providence, the pagan apparatus of 'Laodamia' recovers a world whose very recalcitrance should be sufficient to discourage woman's (and man's) attempts to see themselves reflected." Garrett, *Wordsworth and the Writing of the Nation*, p. 52, offers a political reading of the poem, in which individual passions and problems must be "overcome . . . for a greater national good." He sees the poem treating a "time of great national sacrifice" – the Trojan War – parallel to the sacrificial moment of the Napoleonic Wars. Page, as mentioned, has a persuasive reading of the ongoing revisions to the poem as evidencing Wordsworth struggle with his own passions and with Annette Vallon. Other fine readings of "Laodamia" include Richard D. McGhee, "'Conversant with Infinity': Form and Meaning in Wordsworth's 'Laodamia,'" *Studies in Philology* 68 (July 1971): 357–69; Lawrence Lipking, *Abandoned Women and Poetic Tradition* (Chicago, IL: University of Chicago Press, 1988), pp. 137–44; and Eugene L. Stelzig, in "Mutability, Ageing, and Permanence in Wordsworth's Later Poetry," *Studies in English Literature, 1500–1900* 19 (1979): 623–44, who sees the poem taking up not passion versus reason but the need to confront time and death. Also interesting for this discussion (though not on "Laodamia" or "Dion") is Philip Shaw, "Wordsworth's 'Dread Voice': Ovid, Dora, and the Later Poetry," *Romanticism* 8 (2002): 34–48.
80. Christopher Wordsworth, *Memoirs of William Wordsworth*, 2 vols. (London: Edward Moxon, 1851), 2: 67.
81. For the text of "Laodamia" and the history of its revisions, see the Cornell Wordsworth edition of Wordsworth, *Shorter Poems, 1807–1820*, ed. Carl H. Ketcham (Ithaca, NY: Cornell University Press, 1989), pp. 142–52, 529–30. I cite Reading Text 2 and will give line numbers to that 1815 version.

82. It is interesting to think of Keats's famous statement about the afterlife as a repetition of this one "in a finer tone" in contrast to a statement by Protesilaus: Wordsworth has him speak "of a second birth / For all that is most perfect upon earth: / Of all that is most beauteous – imaged there in / Happier beauty" (101–104). In Wordsworth's poem, this happier afterlife is granted only to those who follow virtue, but, for Keats, the happiness we enjoy in the hereafter, which will be repeated in a finer tone, "can only befall those who delight in sensation rather than hunger as you do after Truth" (to Benjamin Bailey, November 22, 1817, *KPP*, p. 103).

83. See *The Diary of Benjamin Robert Haydon*, ed. Willard Bissell Pope, 5 vols. (Cambridge, MA: Harvard University Press, 1960), 2: 464; and Wordsworth's letter to Landor, January 21, 1824, *WLLY*, 1: 244–45. Landor's comments came in his imaginary conversation between Southey and Porson published in the *London Magazine* for July 1823. I will take up a later critical dispute between Landor and Wordsworth in Chapter 5.

84. There is a question of what Wordsworth knew of Keats's poetry and when (see summary of evidence in Hill, "Wordsworth, Boccaccio," p. 39–40). At least one review, *London Magazine* (August 2, 1820: 169), refers to the "Lamia" passage and quotes the lines on Ariadne before Wordsworth recorded the changed lines in a letter to Haydon in November of that year (see n.83).

85. Cox, *Romanticism in the Shadow of War: Literary Culture in the Napoleonic War Years* (Cambridge: Cambridge University Press, 2014), pp. 205–206.

86. Cited in Edith Batho, *The Later Wordsworth* (Cambridge: Cambridge University Press, 1933), pp. 101–102.

87. Quotations from the poems are taken from *SWLH*, 5. It is worth noting that Wordsworth had sent a copy of the 1815 *Poems* that included "Laodamia" to Hunt; see Wordsworth's letter to Hunt, February 12, 1815, *WLMY*, 2: 195.

88. Lawrence Lipking, *Abandoned Women and Poetic Tradition*, pp. 137–44.

89. Pritchard, "On the Making of Wordsworth's 'Dion,'" p. 68. Setzer, "Sicilian Daydreams and Parisian Nightmares," p. 614. Eric C. Walker, *Marriage, Writing, and Romanticism,* reads Dion in relation to Wellington and to questions of how to be a good husband, pp. 79–82.

90. Setzer, "Sicilian Daydreams and Parisian Nightmares," p. 612. Pritchard, "On the Making of Wordsworth's 'Dion,'" p. 68, hears a reference to Christ's entry into Jerusalem, which Haydon was painting with Wordsworth appearing as a devout worshipper; see Figure 0.1.

91. Landor, "Imaginary Conversation between Mr. Southey and Professor Porson," *London Magazine* 8 (July 1823): 5–9.

92. The Cornell Wordsworth *Thirteen Book Prelude*, Vol. 1, ed. Mark L. Reed (Ithaca, NY: Cornell University Press, 1991).

93. Alan Liu, *Wordsworth: The Sense of History* (Stanford, CA: Stanford University Press, 1989), pp. 23–31.

94. Hartman, "Words, Wish, Worth: Wordsworth," in *Deconstruction and Criticism*, eds. Harold Bloom et al. (New York: Seabury Press, 1979), p. 183.

95. Hartman, "Words, Wish, Worth," p. 183.

96. Hartman, "Words, Wish, Worth," p. 183.

97. Connell, *Romanticism, Economics*, p. 177.

98. Hartman, *Wordsworth's Poetry 1787–1814* (New Haven, CT: Yale University Press, 1977), pp. 331–33; Manning, "Cleansing the Images," 306–15.

99. Hill, "Wordsworth, Boccaccio, and the Pagan Gods of Antiquity," p. 39, suggests that the note is either an acknowledgement that Shelley and Keats followed in Wordsworth's footsteps in writing mythological poems or a warning to younger writers that they, unlike Wordsworth, are misusing the classics.

100. Hartman, "Words, Wish, Worth," p. 150. Quotation is from line 50 of "A little onward lend thy guiding hand," in Cornell Wordsworth *Shorter Poems, 1807–1820*, ed. Carl H. Ketcham (Ithaca, NY: Cornell University Press, 1989).

101. Hartman, "Words, Wish, Worth," p. 183.

102. Worthington, *Wordsworth's Reading of Roman Prose,* p. 42.

103. *The Prose Works of William Wordsworth*, eds. W. J. B. Owen and Jane Worthington Smyser, 3 vols. (Oxford: Clarendon Press, 1974), I: 309.

104. See Saint-Juste, "Fragments d'institutions républicaines," in *Oeuvres Complètes de Saint-Juste*, ed. Michèle Duval (Paris: G. Lebovici, 1984), p. 978.

105. I should note that Hunt praised the poem in the 1815 *Feast of Poets* and that Medwin claims that Shelley particularly liked Wordsworth's sonnets, "Tintern Abbey," and "Laodamia" (see *William Wordsworth: The Critical Heritage*, Vol. I: 1793–1820 [London: Routledge, 2001], p. 995). "Dion" is a "classical gem" according to the *European Magazine* 77 (July 1820): 525; Reiman, *Lake Poets*, 2: 519.

106. Thomas Noon Talfourd, "On the Genius and Writings of Wordsworth" (continuation), *New Monthly Magazine* 14 (December 1, 1820): 875.

2 Wordsworth's "Thanksgiving Ode"

1. All quotations from Wordsworth's *Thanksgiving Ode, January 18, 1816. With Other Short Pieces, Chiefly Referring to Recent Public Events* (1816) are from the Cornell Wordsworth *Shorter Poems, 1807–1820 by William Wordsworth*, ed. Carl H. Ketcham (Ithaca, NY: Cornell University Press, 1989); line numbers will be given in the text.

2. On the response of the younger writers to this line, see Duncan Wu, "Wordsworthian Carnage," *Essays in Criticism* 66 (July 2016): 341–59.

3. Byron, *Don Juan*, in *Lord Byron: The Complete Works*, vol. 5, ed. Jerome J. McGann (Oxford: Clarendon Press, 1986); canto, stanza, and line numbers will be given in the text.

4. Leigh Hunt, "Young Poets," *Examiner* (December 1, 1816); reprinted in *SWLH*, 2: 72–75.

5. It is exactly this attempt to address public issues that Geoffrey Hartman finds to be the problem with the late poetry; see *The Unremarkable Wordsworth* (Minneapolis: University of Minnesota Press, 1987), p. 15.

6. Philip Shaw, *Waterloo and the Romantic Imagination* (Basingstoke and New York: Palgrave Macmillan, 2002), p. 6. See also his "Leigh Hunt and the Aesthetics of Post-War Liberalism," in *Romantic Wars: Studies in Culture and Conflict, 1793–1822*, ed. Shaw (Burlington, VT: Ashgate, 2000), pp. 185–207, for a fine account of Hunt's response to Waterloo.

7. *The Diary of Benjamin Robert Haydon*, ed. Willard Bissell Pope, 5 vols. (Cambridge: Harvard University Press, 1960–63), 1: 458.

8. Simon Bainbridge, *Napoleon and English Romanticism* (Cambridge: Cambridge University Press, 1995), p. 153.

9. Duncan Wu, *William Hazlitt: The First Modern Man* (Oxford: Oxford University Press, 2008), pp. 179–80. Quotations from *The Life of Benjamin Robert Haydon*, ed. Tom Taylor, 3 vols. (London: Longman, Brown, Green, and Longmans, 1853), 1: 269; Thomas Noon Talfourd, *Final Memorials of Charles Lamb*, 2 vols. (London: E. Moxon, 1848), 2: 170; and P. G. Patmore, *My Friends and Acquaintances*, 3 vols. (1854), 2: 323.

10. See F. Darrell Munsell, *The Victorian Controversy Surrounding the Wellington War Memorial: The Archduke of Hyde Park Corner* (Lewisten: Edwin Mellen, 1991).

11. On the 1814 celebrations, see Edward Orme, *An Historical Memento, Representing the Different Scenes of Public Rejoicing Which Took Place the First of August, in St. James and Hyde Parks London, in Celebration of the Glorious Peace of 1814 and the Centenary of the Accession of the Industrious House of Brunswick to the Throne of the Kingdoms* (1814); and Cox, *Romanticism in the Shadow of War: Literature Culture in the Napoleonic War Years* (Cambridge: Cambridge University Press, 2014), pp. 160–64.

12. Bainbridge, *Napoleon and British Romanticism*, p. 155. See also Betty Bennett, *British War Poetry in the Age of Romanticism 1793–1815* (New York: Garland, 1976).

13. *Morning Post* (November 30, 1815): [1]. See also David Hughson (pseudonym of Edward Pugh), *Walks through London*, 2 vols. (London: Sherwood, Neely, and Jones, 1817), 2: 329–30. Richard Altick, *The Shows of London* (Cambridge, MA: Harvard University Press, 1978), pp. 239–40.

14. Printed in *Theatrical Inquisitor* 7 (July 1815): 40.

15. Anonymous, *The Duke's Coat; or, The Night After Waterloo, A Dramatick Anecdote* (London: John Miller, 1815), p. iii.

16. This reference is taken from *The Songs Etc. in the Pantomime Called Harlequin Brilliant; or, The Clown's Capers. Now Performing at the Aquatic Theatre, Sadler's Wells* (London: Glendinning, 1815). All subsequent references from this edition will be given in the text.

17. Cox, *Romanticism in the Shadow of War*, pp. 62–66; "'Illegitimate' Pantomime in the 'Legitimate' Theater: Context as Text," *Studies in Romanticism* 14 (Summer 2015): 159–86.

18. Charles Farley, *The New Pantomime of Harlequin and Fortunio, or, Shing-Moo and Thun-ton; With a Sketch of the Story* (London: John Miller, 1815); licensing manuscript, Larpent Collection, Henry Huntington Library, LA 1893. Page numbers will be given in the text.

19. Mary Favret, *War at a Distance: Romanticism and the Making of Modern Wartime* (Princeton, NJ: Princeton University Press, 2010).

20. All references to the play, given in the text, are taken from Thomas John Dibdin, *Songs, Chorusses, &c. in the New Comic Pantomime Called Harlequin & Fancy; or, The Poet's Last Shilling* (London: C. Lowndes,1815).

21. Byron, "Detached Thoughts," in *BLJ*, 9: 36–37.

22. Wordsworth, letter to Benjamin Robert Haydon, January 13, 1816, *WLMY*, 2: 273; letter to R. P. Gillies, April 9, 1816, *WLMY*, 2: 299. See also Nicholas Roe, "Leigh Hunt and Wordsworth's *Poems*," *Wordsworth Circle* 12 (Winter 1981): 89–91. Wordsworth was also reading Scott's *Paris Revisited* at this time (see letter to Scott, February 22, 1816, *WLMY*, 2: 280).

23. Strachan, "Headnote," *SWLH*, 5: 22.

24. Kucich, "Headnote," *SWLH*, 1: 269.

25. Lynda Pratt, Daniel E. White, Ian Packer, Tim Fulford, and Carol Bolton, "Introduction," *Robert Southey: Later Poetical Works, 1811–1838*, gen. ed. Tim Fulford and Lynda Pratt, 4 vols. (London: Pickering and Chatto, 2012), 3: 6–7. See also Michael Gamer, "Robert Southey's Laureate Policy," in *Romanticism, Self-Canonization, and the Business of Poetry* (Cambridge: Cambridge University Press, 2017), pp. 156–96.

26. Pratt et al., "Introduction," 3: 6–7.

27. Southey, letter to Neville White, December 12, 1813, *Collected Letters of Robert Southey*, www.rc.umd.edu/editions/southey_letters, # 2345; cited by Pratt et al., "Introduction," 3: 3.

28. Hunt, "The New Year's Ode," *The Examiner*, January 16, 1814; reprinted in *SWLH*, 1: 309–13. I have reproduced Hunt's version of lines 214–29. For Southey's text, see *Carmen Triumphale* in *Robert Southey: The Later Poetical Works*, 3: 23–38. Line numbers will be given in the text.

29. Ironically enough, Hunt and the Cockneys were also attacked for combining simplicity and affectation, as we saw in the Introduction.

30. Magnuson, *Reading Public Romanticism* (Princeton, NJ: Princeton University Press, 1998), pp. 122–66.

31. Hunt, "Ode for the Spring of 1814," first published in *The Examiner,* April 17, 1814, and then with *The Descent of Liberty: A Mask* (London: Gale, Curtis and Fenner, 1815); "Ode" reprinted in *SWLH,* 5: 22–24, and *The Descent,* 5: 83–122. Line and scene numbers will be given in the text.

32. Cox, *Poetry and Politics in the Cockney School: Keats, Shelley, Hunt and Their Circle* (Cambridge: Cambridge University Press, 1998), pp. 125–30.

33. Wordsworth, letter to Robert Southey, probably June 1816, *WLMY,* 2: 324–25.

34. Bainbridge, *Napoleon and English Romanticism,* pp. 156–57. I have also learned much from Philip Shaw's *Waterloo and the Romantic Imagination,* cited earlier, and his "Wordsworth, Waterloo, and Sacrifice," in *Sacrifice and Modern War Literature,* ed. Alex Houen and Melissa Schramm (Oxford: Oxford University Press, 2018), pp. 20–33. See also see Woodring, *Politics in English Romantic Poetry* (Cambridge: Harvard University Press, 1970), pp. 124–25, 140–41; Richard Gravil, *Wordsworth's Bardic Vocation, 1787–1842* (Basingstoke: Palgrave MacMillan, 2003); J. R. Watson, *Romanticism and War: A Study of British Romantic Writers and the Napoleonic Wars* (Basingstoke: Palgrave Macmillan, 2004), pp. 174–82; and James M. Garrett, *Wordsworth and the Writing of the Nation* (Burlington, VT: Ashgate, 2008), pp. 81–89. Garrett sees the same tensions I do in the poems but finds a different resolution: "A careful examination of these commemorative poems of 1816 reveals a poet intent on writing the nation but unable to overcome the internal divisions … that everywhere fractures the nation. Ultimately, the victor proves to be Nature, an abstraction as well, but one capable of annihilating the grids of the mapmakers and the identity of nations, and it is clearly no accident that the volume opens with a paean to the sun and closes in 'darkness infinite'" (p. 82).

35. *Form of Prayer and Thanksgiving to Almighty God; To be used in all Churches and Chapels throughout those Parts of the United Kingdom called* England *and* Ireland*, on* Thursday *the Eighteenth Day of* January *1816, being the Day appointed by Proclamation for a General THANKSGIVING to Almighty God: For His great Goodness in putting an End to the War in which we were engaged against* France*. By Special Command* (London: George Eyre and Andrew Stahan, 1816), p. 6.

36. Ketcham, "Introduction," *Shorter Poems,* p. 15.

37. Garrett, *Wordsworth and the Writing of the Nation,* p. 83

38. Wordsworth, letter to Robert Southey, probably June 1816, *WLMY,* 3: 325.

39. Elmes, "The Most Proper Mode of Commemorating the Great Victories of the Late Wars," *Annals of the Fine Arts* 2 (1818): 33. We find the sermon

preached at St. Paul's calling for a monument but perhaps only an internal one similar to Wordsworth's "labour of the soul": "So great an instance of His timely aid should never be forgotten by us. A monumental memorial of the great deeds achieved on the field of Waterloo, should, as it were, be inscribed on the heart of every British subject." George Ferne Bates, *A Sermon Preached in the Cathedral Church of St. Paul... On Thursday, the Eighteenth of January, 1816, Being the day appointed for A General Thanksgiving on the late Peace* (London: Rider and Weed, 1816), p. 17.

40. Bates's *A Sermon Preached in the Cathedral Church of St. Paul* makes a similar claim, arguing that true faith "regards all the direful effects of war as specially under the superintendence of Divine Providence" (p. 19). Again, *Mont St. Jean, A Poem* by William Liddiard (London: Longman, Hurst, Rees, Orme, and Browne, 1816) offers an epigraph that finds that during the battle "Oh Heaven, thy arm was there!" C. F. Warden has perhaps the most extreme view in his *The Battle of Waterloo; A Poem; In Two Parts* (London: Dean and Munday, 1817), where he finds the victory "consolidating the peace of the world, as to be unparalleled in the records of past ages; and to almost require, in a sublime point of view, all ulterior circumstances to be dated from its period" (p. 1). Waterloo here becomes as important as the birth of Jesus.

41. See also *A Letter from the Right Honourable William Pitt in the Shades to the Allied Sovereigns in the Sunshine* (perhaps by William Playfair) that warns Napoleon is still like a Bengal tiger let loose in Europe (London: Blacklock, 1814).

42. Moorman, 2: 288; J. R. Watson, *Romanticism and War*, p. 178.

43. See Moorman, 2: 292; Robinson, *Diary, Reminiscences, and Correspondence of Henry Crabb Robinson*, ed. Thomas Sadler, 3 vols. (London: Macmillan, 1869), 1: 331.

44. On the publication of Wordsworth's sonnets and Hunt's response, see B. Bernard Cohen, "Haydon, Hunt, and Scott and Six Sonnets (1816) by Wordsworth," *Philological Quarterly* 19 (October 1950): 434–37.

45. Hunt, "Account of the remarkable rise and downfall of the late Kan of Tartary, with the still more remarkable fancies that took possession of the heads of some of his antagonists," *The Examiner* (January 13, 1816) in *SWLH*, 2: 40–49; *The Champion* (January 7, 1816).

46. Wordsworth was, of course, not alone in finding a moral message in Waterloo. For example, Henry Davidson in *Waterloo, A Poem. With Notes* (London: John Murray, 1816) argues that "those great moral and political principles which have been prominently brought forward by the present war" have been "decidedly proved" (p. 110).

47. Byron, *The Complete Poetical Works*, vol. 3, ed. Jerome J. McGann (Oxford: Oxford University Press, 1981). Line numbers are given in the text. Given the

dueling translations of Filicaia by both Wordsworth and Hunt, it is worth noting that Byron also praises him in *Childe Harold IV*, stanza 42. It is also interesting that Wordsworth clearly knew Byron's earlier "Ode to Napoleon Buonaparte" (1814); see Wordsworth's letter to John Scott, April 18, 1816; *WLMY*, 2: 304.

48. Hunt, "To the Right Honourable Lord Byron on his Departure for Italy and Greece," *The Examiner* (April 28, 1816); *SWLH*, 5: 115–16.

49. *Lord Byron: The Complete Poetical Works*, vol. 2, ed. Jerome J. McGann (Oxford: Clarendon Press, 1980); stanza and line numbers will be given in the text.

50. Leslie A. Marchand, *Byron, A Portrait* (Chicago, IL: Chicago University Press, 1970), p. 236. See, also, Donald Sultana, *From Abbotsford to Paris and Back* (Bristol: Sutton, 1993). We need to take seriously Byron's sense that Napoleon is preferable to the Allied sovereigns, just as we cannot doubt the Hunt circle's commitment to radical, revolutionary action. In a section of Haydon's *The Life of Benjamin Robert Haydon*, ed. Tom Taylor, 3 vols. (London: Longman, Brown, Green, and Longmans, 1853) where he discusses reactions to the fall of Napoleon (he praises Hunt's while berating Hazlitt's), Haydon writes: "Napoleon's system was inspired by all the genius and energy of a demon. Gradual progress and gradual enlightenment might have reformed the rottenness of corrupt theories. Hazlitt and Hunt, and Byron and Shelley, wished their ends to be brought about by means which would have entailed consequences more dreadful to human liberty and intellect than the extreme of corruption in old governments" (1: 270).

51. See Martin Kelsall, *Byron's Politics* (Totowa, NJ: Barnes & Noble Books, 1987), pp. 57–81; Philip Shaw, "Leigh Hunt and the Aesthetics of Post-War Liberalism," esp. pp. 191–93.

52. On Byronic lightning, see Susan Wolfson, "'This is my Lightning'; or, Sparks in the Air," *Studies in English Literature, 1500–1900* 55 (Autumn 2015): 751–86.

53. McGann sees Hunt as the "likely catalyst" for Byron's more ideological turn in the War Cantos. He notes that Canto VI was probably begun in January, with Byron making little progress on the canto until the summer, around the time of Leigh Hunt's arrival in Italy and Shelley's death; *The Complete Works*, 5: 715.

54. Simon Bainbridge, *British Poetry and the Revolutionary and Napoleonic Wars* (Cambridge: Cambridge University Press, 2003), p. 197.

55. Jerome McGann, *The Romantic Ideology: A Critical Investigation* (Chicago, IL: University of Chicago Press, 1983), p. 1.

3 "This Potter-Don-Juan"

1. *Memoirs of Edward Vaughan Kenealy*, ed. Arabella Kenealy (London: John Long, 1908), p. 239.

2. In a letter to Catherine Clarkson of April 24, 1814 (*WLMY*, 2: 140), Dorothy wrote that Wordsworth had plans, in addition to publishing *The Excursion* and his collected works, to release "shortly after – Peter Bell, The White Doe, and Benjamin the Waggoner." The delay until 1819 seems to have arisen because of Wordsworth's disappointment over the reception of *The Excursion* and *The White Doe of Rylstone*.

3. See Peter Manning, *Reading Romantics: Text and Context* (Oxford: Oxford University Press, 1990), pp. 195–215.

4. Chandler, "'Wordsworth' after Waterloo," in *The Age of William Wordsworth: Critical Essays on the Romantic Tradition*, ed. Kenneth R. Johnston and Gene W. Ruoff (New Brunswick: Rutgers University Press, 1987), p. 100. The moment of *Peter Bell*'s first conception is also intriguing. The poem was begun on April 20, 1798, six days after Wordsworth received a shipment of books, including Mary Wollstonecraft's *Memoirs*. In the middle of May 1787, Wordsworth, after seeing Lewis's *The Castle Spectre*, read a draft of *Peter Bell* to Hazlitt and Coleridge on the same day that Hazlitt and Wordsworth conducted the debate that led to "Expostulation and Reply" and "The Tables Turned." The poem's creation is hedged round with the controversy over Wollstonecraft, the popularity of Lewis's Gothic play, and debates with Hazlitt. See F. B. Pinion, *A Wordsworth Chronology* (Boston: G. K. Hall, 1988), pp. 31–32.

5. Byron, "Epilogue," 9–10, 11–12, 16–20; in *Lord Byron: The Complete Poetical Works*, vol. 4, ed. Jerome J. McGann (Oxford: Clarendon Press, 1986), p. 286.

6. Tim Fulford, *Wordsworth's Poetry 1815–1845* (Philadelphia: University of Pennsylvania Press, 2019), offers a much more nuanced account of Wordsworth's engagement with his patrons but still sees his turn to Beaumont and the Lowthers as altering his "politics of landscape" (pp. 41–89).

7. Scrivener, *Radical Shelley: The Philosophical Anarchism and Utopian Thought of Percy Bysshe Shelley* (Princeton, NJ: Princeton University Press, 1982), p. 220.

8. Martyn Crucefix, in the interesting "Wordsworth, Superstition, and Shelley's *Alastor*," *Essays in Criticism* 33 (April 1983): 126–47, argues that Hunt's review, with its mocking of Wordsworth's dedication, its conflation of Wordsworth and Peter Bell, and its attacks upon Wordsworth's methodistical moralizing, helped to shape Shelley's *Peter Bell the Third*, as we again find Hunt setting the agenda for the poetry of others in the group.

9. On Reynolds's satire, see, in particular, Brian Bates, *Wordsworth's Poetic Collections, Supplementary Writing, and Parodic Reception* (London: Pickering & Chatto, 2012), pp. 121–39. Wordsworth pointed to Reynolds's satire in a letter to Lowther (May 22, 1819, *WLMY*, 2: 542), writing that *Peter Bell* "has furnished abundant employment to the Witlings and the small critics, who have been warring with me for more than 20 years." In addition to the

lines in *Don Juan* and some scattered prose comments, Byron wrote in 1819 an unpublished satiric "epilogue" for *Peter Bell* (already quoted) that largely belittles Wordsworth's dedication. In April 1819, Keats offered in "The House of Mourning written by Mr. Scott" a critique of Wordsworth's sonnet "Composed in the Valley near Dover, on the Day of Landing" (1807). In "Wordsworth and Keats" in *The Age of William Wordsworth*, ed. Kenneth R. Johnston and Gene W. Ruoff (New Brunswick, NJ: Rutgers University Press, 1987), pp. 192–95, Jack Stillinger argues for the impact of *Peter Bell* on Keats's Spring odes. I should also note that Bernard Barton praised *Peter Bell* in "To William Wordsworth on his Peter Bell" in *Poems* (1819).

10. From Moore's diary, quoted in Markham L. Peacock, Jr., *The Critical Opinions of William Wordsworth* (1950; rpt. New York: Octagon Books, 1969), p. 203.

11. Robinson, *On Books and Their Writers*, ed. Edith J. Morley, 3 vols. (London: J. M. Dent and Sons, 1938), 1: 85.

12. Quoted in Peacock, *Critical Opinions*, p. 203.

13. The poem is reprinted with indications of Wordsworth's contributions in the Cornell Wordsworth *Shorter Poems 1807–1820*, ed. Carl H. Ketcham (Ithaca, NY: Cornell University Press, 1989), pp. 600–607. On Wordsworth's involvement in writing it, see *WLMY*, 2: 175–76, 204–205. Jalal Uddin Khan finds Wordsworth taking up Byron in a number of other poems written in the years running up to the publication of *Peter Bell*, poems which then appeared in the *River Duddon* volume; see "Wordsworth's *River Duddon* Volume: A Response to Coleridge and Byron," *Critical Review* 36 (January 1, 1996): 80–82. Wordsworth also included, in a letter to Southey, four epigrams satirizing Byron's *Cain*. See the Cornell Wordsworth *Last Poems, 1821–1850*, ed. Jared Curtis, April Lea Denny-Ferris, and Jillian Heydt-Stevenson (Ithaca, NY: Cornell University Press, 1999), pp. 25–26.

14. See G. L. Marsh, "The Peter Bell Parodies of 1819," *Modern Philology* 40 (1943): 267–74.

15. See Ketcham, *Shorter Poems*, p. 600 for the story that Hogg told Wordsworth that Byron had called the Lakers "Pond Poets." For a sense of what Byron might have said to Hogg, see Byron's letter of March 24, 1814, *BLJ*, 4: 84–85.

16. It is also clear that what the authors object to is the critical acclaim granted Byron, particularly the fact that he has been praised by the *Edinburgh Review* and Jeffrey (30–35), who had of course attacked Wordsworth. See, also, Coleridge's attack in the *Biographia Literaria* upon the Byronic hero of Maturin's *Bertram* and of the Don Juan tradition as "jacobinical," an attack which McGann suggests inspired Byron 's *Don Juan* (*Lord Byron: The Complete Poetical Works*, vol. 5, ed. Jerome J. McGann [Oxford: Clarendon Press, 1986], p. 668]. *Blackwood's*, in a generally favorable set of "Essays on the

Lake School of Poetry" that stands in marked contrast to the set on the Cockney School, praised Wordsworth for breaking with the tradition of exhibiting "the strength of the human energies, which, in our most esteemed poems and plays, are frequently not even elevated by self-devotion; witness Coriolanus, Richard the Third, Satan in Paradise Lost, the Giaours and Corsairs, &c. of modern days" (4 [December 1818]: p. 257).

17. The *Edinburgh [Scots] Magazine*, 2nd series, 4 (May 1819) has two interesting reviews, one of Reynolds's parody of Wordsworth and of Polidori's attempt to pass off *The Vampyre* (1819) as Byron's and the other of Wordsworth's *Peter Bell*. The reviews thus bring together Wordsworth and Byron, going so far as to suggest that when Wordsworth states in his dedication that the poem remained for nineteen years in manuscript and thus "nearly survived its *minority*" he is making a "hit at Lord Byron when he was a *minor* poet" (429; Reiman, *Lake Poets*, 2: 863).

18. Quotations from the first edition of *Peter Bell* are from the Cornell Wordsworth volume, ed. John E. Jordan (Ithaca, NY: Cornell University Press, 1985); line numbers will be given in the text.

19. See, for example, the reviews by the *British Critic* 9 (May 1816): 452–69 and the *Anti-Jacobin Review* 45 (August 1811): 127–38 and 46 (March 1814): 209–37, reprinted in Reiman, *Byron*, 2: 30–50, 428–37.

20. Manning provides these lines as they were misquoted during the trial in his "The Hone-ing of Byron's *Corsair*," in *Reading Romantics: Texts and Contexts* (Oxford: Oxford University Press, 1990), p. 221. See *The Trials of Jeremiah Brandreth, William Turner, Isaac Ludlam . . . Taken in Shorthand by William Brodie Gurney* (London: Butterworth, 1817). See also David Erdman, "Byron and Revolt in England," *Science and Society* 11 (1947): 234–48; and Carl Woodring, *Politics in English Romantic Poetry*, pp. 164–80.

21. *Peter Bell, The 1819 Texts*, ed. Carlo M. Bajetta, 2nd rev. ed. (Milan: Edizioni C.U.S.L., 2005), p. 151n. See *Don Juan*, Canto 1, stanzas 6 and 7.

22. Wordsworth wrote in his dedication to Southey: "The Poem of Peter Bell, as the Prologue will shew, was composed under a belief that the Imagination not only does not require for its exercise the intervention of supernatural agency, but that, though such agency be excluded, the faculty may be called forth imperiously, and for kindred results of pleasure, by incidents, within the compass of poetic probability, in the humblest departments of daily life" (p. 41).

23. See, for example, Jonathan Wordsworth, "Introduction," *Peter Bell, 1819* (Oxford: Woodstock Books, 1992), np.

24. Bajetta, "Introduction," *Peter Bell, The 1819 Texts*, p. 61; Leah S. Marcus, "Vaughan, Wordsworth, Coleridge, and the *Encomium Asini*," *ELH* 42 (1975): 224–41.

25. It is worth noting with Bajetta that Southey, to whom *Peter Bell* is dedicated, was at this time writing a biography of Wesley. Bajetta, "Introduction," p. 62.

26. As Reiman and Fraistat note, Shelley uses the same punctuation as Hunt did in *The Examiner*; see *SPP*, p. 339n. Some have felt that Shelley knew Hunt's review but not Wordsworth's poem; on this debate, see Jack Benoit Gohn, "Did Shelley Know Wordsworth's *Peter Bell*?" *Keats-Shelley Journal* 28 (1979): 20–24.

27. Dan White suggested to me (email, July 13, 2019) Taylor's poem as a contrast to the Cockney take on Methodism. "Poetry and Reality" appeared in Taylor's *Essays in Rhyme, on Morals and Manners* (London: T. Miller, 1816). White has edited an excerpt in "Contexts: British Romanticism and the Religious World," *The Broadview Anthology of British Literature*, Vol. 4, 3rd edn. (Peterborough: Broadview Press, 2018). I quote from White's version.

28. The manuscript of Smith's poem is held at the Essex County Record Office (D/DR Z11). He loaned the ms. to Keats who excerpted it in a letter to his brothers (February 14 [?], 1818, *KL*, 1: 229–30). Portions appear in the *London Magazine* 3 (February, March, June, 1821): 200–202, 280–82, 648–50.

29. Scrivener, *Radical Shelley*, p. 220.

30. On Wordsworth's engagement with Methodism, see Richard E. Brantley, *Wordsworth's "Natural Methodism"* (New Haven, CT: Yale University Press, 1975). "Natural Methodism" is Lamb's not particularly flattering phrase from his review (revised by Gifford) of *The Excursion* for the *Quarterly Review* 12 (October 1814): 105; Reiman, *Lake Poets*, 2: 828.

31. Gill, p. 357, notes that even Wordsworth, in telling Basil Montagu of his continual traveling, labeled himself "as much a Peter Bell as ever."

32. Timothy Morton shows how Shelley works out part of Wordsworth's moral collapse through his changed relationship to nature; Shelley objected to the passage in *The Excursion* describing the death of a trout (8.568–71) both in conversation and in *Peter Bell the Third* (584–88 &n.). See Morton, *Shelley and the Revolution in Taste: The Body and the Natural World* (Cambridge: Cambridge University Press, 1994), pp. 102–104.

33. Byron would parody these lines in his "Epilogue," quoted earlier: "There's something in a Stupid Ass, / And something in a heavy Dunce" (1–2), as would Reynolds (though some believe Lockhart wrote it) in his second parody of Wordsworth, *Benjamin the Waggoner* (London: Baldwin, Cradock and Joy, 1819): "There's something in a glass of ale .... There's something in a velocipede" (p. 44). See Brian Rejack, "Nothings of the Day: The Velocipede, the Dandy, and the Cockney," *Romanticism* 19 (2013): 291–309; and Richard Marggraf Turley, "Keats on Two Wheels," *Studies in Romanticism* 57 (Winter 2018): 601–25.

34. See Jeffrey, "Byron's *The Corsair: a Tale* and *Bride of Abydos: A Turkish Tale*," *Edinburgh Review* 23 (April 1814): 200; Reiman, *Byron*, 2: 849). See also

Gerard Cohen-Vrignaud, "Becoming Corsairs: Byron, British Property Rights and Orientalist Economics," *Studies in Romanticism* 50 (Winter 2011): 685–714.

35. Byron ultimately focuses upon a contrast between Wordsworth and Pope both here and in his comments on *Peter Bell* in his "Some Observations Upon An Article in *Blackwood's Edinburgh Magazine*" (1821; in *Lord Byron: The Complete Miscellaneous Prose*, ed. Andrew Nicholson [Oxford: Clarendon Press, 1991], pp. 105, 107, 109). Given Byron's joke about a balloon, it is interesting to note that another 1819 poem, Hans Busk's *Vestriad* (London: Sherwood, Neely, and Jones), describes a flight in a balloon that Wordsworth admired. In a letter to Busk of July 6, 1819, Wordsworth praises the *Vestriad,* particularly the "descents into the submarine regions, and the infernal" (*WLMY*, 2: 546). He also states that "throughout the whole of your productions is an air of lively novelty that most honourably distinguishes you among the multitude of candidates for poetic celebrity" (547), a hit at other contemporary poets. Wordsworth's comment on Busk's use of a balloon is particularly interesting: "I noticed in your Vestriad with particular pleasure, your flight in the Balloon. Rich in bold fictions as your Poem is, you were not called upon to make more of that vehicle than you have done – Judgement is shown in nothing more than the power to resist temptations of Fancy, especially where, as in your case, the gratification lies within easy reach" (547). Here are Busk's lines: "Oh ! give the bard the air-impell'd balloon, / Majestic rising like the orbed moon! / Thus seated in a nobler, steadier car, / Ride o'er a jarring world, nor feel a jar!" (267–70).

36. It is interesting to note a growing critical discourse within Wordsworth's lifetime that puts Shelley into contrast with Byron, to the latter's detriment. Wordsworth himself found Shelley "decidedly superior" to Byron (quoted in Peacock, *Critical Opinions*, p. 203). Wordsworth's friend and defender Henry Taylor has a critical account of both younger poets in the preface to his *Philip Van Artevelde: A Dramatic Romance. In Two Parts* (London: Edward Moxon, 1834), in which Taylor finds Byron, marked by "an absorbing and contracting self-love" (xiv), losing popularity among younger writers to Shelley, who heads a "PHANTASTIC SCHOOL, [who] labour to effect a revolution in this order of things. They would transfer the domicile of poetry to regions where reason, far from having any supremacy or rule, is all but unknown" (xxv–xxvi). Charles Kingsley in "Thoughts on Shelley and Byron," published in *Fraser's Magazine* 48 (November 1853), contends that the problems with modern poetry, which have been blamed upon Byron, should instead be seen as rising from the popularity of Shelley: "it is worth remarking, that it is Shelley's form of fever rather than Byron's, which has been of late years the prevailing epidemic ... The private tippling of eau-de-cologne, say the London physicans, has increased mightily of late; and so has the reading of Shelley" (p. 570).

4 Thinking Rivers

1. While I will have a few words to say about the *Topographical Description*, my main interest is in the Duddon sonnets themselves rather than the entire volume. Which is not to say that this is not an interesting collection. "Vaudracour and Julia," of course excerpted from the *Prelude*, links these poems to Wordsworth's great unpublished masterpiece, to which I will return briefly at the close of this chapter. Gill suggests that Wordsworth, preparing to visit Europe and to see Annette Vallon, wanted to "extract ... the poem from the autobiographical context" in order to connect the present to the past without revealing any intimate details (p. 340). Again, one might take up a number of the odes to relate them not only to Wordsworth's most famous major lyrics but also to pieces from the "Thanksgiving Ode" volume. Gill argues that these poems, when published with the *Topographical Description*, "proclaimed once again Wordsworth as poet, celebrant of a particular, blessed region" (p. 334), thus establishing them as key statements of the Lake School. Philip Shaw, in his fine essay "Wordsworth after Peterloo: The Persistence of War in *River Duddon ... and Other Poems*," in *Commemorating Peterloo: Violence, Resilience and Claim-making during the Romantic Era*, ed. Michael Demson and Regina Hewitt (Edinburgh: Edinburgh University Press, 2019), pp. 250–70, discusses the volume as a whole, and Jalal Uddin Khan has devoted a number of essays to this volume and largely to poems outside the sonnet sequence. See in particular "Publication and Reception of Wordsworth's 'The River Duddon' Volume," *Modern Language Studies* 32 (Autumn, 2002): 45–67; and "Wordsworth's *River Duddon* Volume: A Response to Coleridge and Byron," *Critical Review* 36 (January 1, 1996): 62–82. A useful reading of the organization of the volume and the place of the sonnets within it can be found in John Wyatt, *Wordsworth's Poems of Travel, 1819–42: "Such Sweet Wayfaring"* (New York: St. Martin's Press, 1999), pp. 30–54. The *Wordsworth Circle*'s special issue on "Wordsworth and the River Duddon: Bicentenary Readings" 55.1 (Winter, 2020) arrived too late to shape my reading.

2. Brian R. Bates, *Wordsworth's Poetic Collections, Supplementary Writing, and Parodic Reception* (London: Pickering & Chatto, 2012), pp. 141–59. See also Shaw, "Wordsworth after Peterloo," esp. pp. 264–66.

3. Hunt, "Literary Notices. No. 55," *The Examiner* (May 9, 1819): 302–303; *SWLH*, 2: 192.

4. *Eclectic Review*, 2nd series, 14 (August 1820): 172; Reiman, *Lake Poets*, 1: 394–401. See also the *Monthly Review*, 2nd series, 93 (October 1820); Reiman, *Lake Poets*, 2: 766: "It is impossible to restrain a passing smile at the *fineness* of the title 'Vaudracour and Julia,' when contrasted with 'Peter Bell,' and 'The Waggoner.'"

5. Benjamin Kim stresses the nationalist strain in the sequence; *Wordsworth, Hemans, and Politics, 1800–1830* (Lewisburg, PA: Bucknell University Press, 2013), pp. 75–97.

6. Jackson, "Introduction," *Sonnet Series*, p. 15.

7. This passage can be found in *The River Duddon, A Series of Sonnets: Vaudracour and Julia: and Other Poems. To Which is Annexed a Topographical Description of the Country of the Lakes in the North of England* (London: Longman, Rees, Orme, and Brown, 1820), pp. 217–18; see the edited version in *The Prose Works of William Wordsworth*, ed. W. J. B. Owen and Jane Worthington Smyser, 3 vols. (Oxford: Clarendon Press, 1974), 2: 171–72. Alan Bewell pointed out to me that Wordsworth both contrasts and links rivers and lakes. For example, Wordsworth writes, "The form of the lake is most perfect when . . . it least resembles that of a river"; but he goes on to say that larger lakes "such as Winandermere, Ulswater, Hawswater, do, when the whole length of them is commanded from an elevated point, lose somewhat of the peculiar form of the lake, and assume the resemblance of a magnificent river" (231–32, 232–33; 2: 179). Bewell sees this oscillation from lake to river in parallel with the movement from individual poem to sequence. It also indicates why sonnets on the River Duddon fit within the work of the Lake School.

8. The 1820 first edition of the Duddon sonnets included a title page to be used in binding together various poems. It is for Volume III of "Poems by William Wordsworth: Including The River Duddon; Vaudracour and Julia; Peter Bell; The Waggoner; A Thanksgiving Ode; and Miscellaneous Pieces."

9. Hunt, "Literary Notices. No. 55," *The Examiner* (May 9, 1819): 302–303; *SWLH*, 2: 192.

10. Peter J. Manning, *Reading Romantics: Text and Context* (Oxford: Oxford University Press, 1990), pp. 195–215.

11. It is interesting to note that David Carey in his 1820 *Beauties of Modern Poets* (2nd ed.; London: William Wright, 1820) prefaces his anthology with a piece entitled "The Mansion of the Poets," where Thomas Campbell is the first poet recognized, receiving "a laurel crown of perennial green" (xv). Next to appear is Byron, who gets a mixed reception and is given "a wreath composed of the laurel and the cypress tree" (xvii). Scott, Moore, and Southey all precede Wordsworth, treated more briefly, who is given a "chaplet of lilies and daises" (xx).

12. Jackson, "Introduction," *Sonnet Series*, p. 15.

13. Jackson provides a "History of Composition," *Sonnet Series*, pp. 49–55. One of the included poems was written in 1802, one in 1804–1806, one between 1807 and 1814, and one between 1815 and 1819. The bulk were written in 1818, though composition continued until the publication of the sequence in 1820.

Kim points out that the sonnets were written during periods of political activity for Wordsworth, with the earlier poems coming during the Peninsular Wars that called forth his *Convention of Cintra* and the bulk of the later poems being written during the 1818 Westmorland election; *Wordsworth, Hemans, and Politics,* p. 76.

14. Wilcox, "Wordsworth's River Duddon Sonnets," *PMLA* 69 (March 1954): 131–41; Phelan, *The Nineteenth-Century Sonnet* (Basingstoke: Palgrave Macmillan, 2005), pp. 64–65; Johnson, *Wordsworth and the Sonnet* (Copenhagen: Rosenkilde and Bagger, 1973), pp. 120–44; Wyatt, *Wordsworth's Poems of Travel,* pp. 34–37; Garrett, *Wordsworth and the Writing of the Nation* (Aldershot: Ashgate, 2008), pp. 128–29. These and other critics have offered various organizational schemes for the sequence, finding differing breaks in the flow of the river, the development of the individual, and the course of history. Taking an opposite position, Kim finds a "lack of a governing consciousness, and the sonnets seem to have only a vague thematic connection"; *Wordsworth, Hemans, and Politics,* p. 84. Eric C. Walker, *Marriage, Writing, and Romanticism: Wordsworth and Austen after War* (Stanford, CA: Stanford University Press, 2009), offers an intriguing reading of the sequence in relation to trauma and marriage (pp. 185–89).

15. Wilcox, "Wordsworth's River Duddon Sonnets," p. 136.

16. *Blackwood's* 7 (May 1820); Reiman, *Lake Poets,* 1: 101. Mary Wordsworth made a similar observation in a letter to Sara Hutchinson, December 1, 1818; *Letters of Mary Wordsworth, 1800–1855,* ed. Mary E. Burton (Cambridge: Clarendon Press, 1958), p. 41.

17. Johnson, in *Wordsworth and the Sonnet,* notes: "The sequence abounds in circular images: pools, caves, spots of ground, stones, religious structures" (p. 143).

18. Daniel Robinson, "'Still Glides the Stream': Form and Function in Wordsworth's *River Duddon* Sonnets," *European Romantic Review* 13 (2002): 449–64. See also his "*River Duddon* and Wordsworth, Sonneteer," in *The Oxford Handbook of William Wordsworth,* ed. Richard Gravil and Daniel Robinson (Oxford: Oxford University Press, 2015), pp. 289–308

19. Robinson, "'Still Glides the Stream.'"

20. Galperin, *Revision and Authority in Wordsworth: The Interpretation of a Career* (Philadelphia: University of Pennsylvania Press, 1989), p. 217.

21. Daniel Robinson, "'Still Glides the Stream,'" p. 450.

22. See Wordsworth's letter to Alexander Dyce, *c.* April 22, 1833, *WLLY,* 2: 603–605; and comments to Fenwick in "Note to 'Miscellaneous Sonnets,'" *FN,* p. 73.

23. Daniel Robinson, "'Still Glides the Stream,'" p. 449. Johnson, *Wordsworth and the Sonnet,* pp. 128–29, tracks various direct echoes of Milton in the

sonnets. For an excellent account of the development of the sonnet in the romantic period, see Stuart Curran, *Poetic Form and British Romanticism* (Oxford: Oxford University Press, 1986), pp. 29–55.

24. In the *Memoirs of Edward Vaughan Kenealy*, ed. Arabella Kenealy (London: John Long, 1908), Wordsworth is quoted as saying, "Do you call that [*The Prisoner of Chillon*] beautiful? . . . Why, it's nonsense . . . " (p. 239).

25. Khan in "Wordsworth's *River Duddon* Volume: A Response to Coleridge and Byron" explores a complex dialogue between Wordsworth and Coleridge's poetry as well as Coleridge's critique of Wordsworth in the *Biographia Literaria*.

26. Tim Fulford, *The Late Poetry of the Lake Poets: Romanticism Revised* (Cambridge: Cambridge University Press, 2013), p. 125; he sees Coleridge rejecting the "Jacobin poetics" of *Lyrical Ballads* and struggling to distance himself not only from Wordsworth but also from Byron as a patron and Scott as an admired poet (p. 131).

27. Holmes, *Coleridge: Darker Reflections, 1804–1834* (New York: Pantheon Books, 1998), p. 404.

28. Johnston, *Unusual Suspects: Pitt's Reign of Alarm and the Lost Generation of the 1790s* (Oxford: Oxford University Press, 2013), p. 231.

29. Coleridge's comment on Rousseau comes from an article in *The Friend* (5 October 1809), in *Coleridge's Responses: Selected Writings on Criticism, the Bible and Nature, Volume I: Coleridge on Writers and Writing*, ed. Seamus Perry (London: Continuum, 2008): 382. The swipe at Byron occurs in Marginalia to Pepys' *Memoirs*, in Perry, p. 162. On the composition dates for "Mont Blanc," see *SPP*, p. 96. Richard Holmes, *Shelley, the Pursuit* (New York: Penguin Books, 1974), has Shelley reading Coleridge's "Christabel" volume around that time (p. 345).

30. See the annotations to "Mont Blanc" in *The Poems of Shelley. Volume 1: 1804–1817*, ed. Geoffrey Matthews and Kelvin Everest (London: Longman, 1989), 142, for "The Aeolian Harp," and 122 for "Kubla Khan." The editors also note various echoes of Byron's *Childe Harold III* at lines 44–47, 49–57, and 71–74. Charles Robinson speculates that Shelley could have known "Kubla Khan" in manuscript through Byron (who also recited "Christabel" to him). See Robinson, *Shelley and Byron: The Snake and Eagle Wreathed in Fight* (Baltimore, MD: Johns Hopkins University Press, 1976), pp. 36–7.

31. In her "Note on the Early Poems," Shelley writes that this poem "was addressed in idea to Coleridge, whom he never knew; and at whose character he could only guess imperfectly, through his writings, and accounts he heard of him from some who knew him well. He regarded his change of opinion as rather an act of will than conviction, and believed that in his inner heart he would be haunted by what Shelley considered the better and

holier aspirations of his youth"; *Complete Works of Percy Bysshe Shelley*, ed. Roger Igpen and Walter E. Peck, 10 vols. (1926; rpt. New York: Gordian Press, 1965), 3: 15–16. Matthews and Everest, *The Poems of Shelley. Volume 1: 1804–1817*: 448, point to parallels between this lyric and the portrait of Coleridge in *Peter Bell the Third*.

32. Robinson, *Shelley and Byron*, pp. 36–7.
33. Richard Adelman, "Idleness and Vacancy in Shelley's 'Mont Blanc,'" *Keats-Shelley Journal* 62 (2013): 62–79.
34. *Morning Post* (September 11, 1802); see *CPP*, p. 195n. It is interesting to note Hazlitt's comments on religious reactions to Mont Blanc in his "On the Jealousy and the Spleen of Party": "crossing the Alps has, I believe, given some of our fashionables a shivering-fit of morality, as the sight of Mont Blanc convinced our author of the Being of a God – they are seized with an amiable horror and remorse for the vices of others" (*CWWH*, 12: 368).
35. Stuart Curran, *Poetic Form and British Romanticism*, p. 61.
36. Colin Jager, *Unquiet Things: Secularism in the Romantic Age* (Philadelphia: University of Pennsylvania Press, 2014), p. 242.
37. Keats, letter to Bailey, November 3, 1817, in *KPP*, p. 100.
38. See Susan Wolfson, *The Questioning Presence: Wordsworth, Keats, and the Interrogative Mode in Romantic Poetry* (Ithaca, NY: Cornell University Press, 1986), and Charles Rzepka, *The Self as Mind: Vision and Identity in Wordsworth, Coleridge, and Keats* (Cambridge, MA: Harvard University Press, 1986).
39. Gilmartin, *William Hazlitt, Political Essayist* (Oxford: Oxford University Press, 2015).
40. Letter to Robinson, June 24, 1817, *WLMY*, 2: 393. It is interesting to note that at the end of this letter (394) Wordsworth makes reference to Moore's *Lalla Rookh* and Byron's *Manfred* and *Childe Harold III* "where I am told he has been poaching on my Manor."
41. *Journals of Dorothy Wordsworth*, ed. E. de Selincourt, 2 vols. (London: Macmillan, 1941), 2: 23.
42. Chester Shaver and Alice Shaver, *Wordsworth's Library: A Catalogue* (New York: Garland, 1979).
43. Email, August 1, 2013. As we will see in Chapter 5, Wordsworth became increasingly aware of Shelley's poetry.
44. Colbert, "Contemporary Notice of the Shelleys' *History of a Six Weeks' Tour*: Two New Early Reviews," *Keats-Shelley Journal* 48 (1999): 22–29.
45. Wordsworth to Haydon, January 16, 1820 (*WLMY*, 2: 578). Robert Perceval Graves, the curate at Windermere for around thirty years, reports that Wordsworth was pleased to note the similarities between his own "Praised be the Art" and Keats's "Ode on a Grecian Urn." Graves, "Recollections of

Wordsworth and the Late Country," in *The Afternoon Lectures on Literature and Art* (Dublin: William McGee; London: Bell and Daldy, 1869), pp. 301–2; cited in Markham L. Peacock, Jr., *The Critical Opinions of William Wordsworth* (1950; rpt. New York: Octagon Books, 1969), p. 290.

46. Jackson, "History of Composition," in *Sonnet Series*, 51–52; interestingly, he thinks Wordsworth may be echoing Coleridge's *Monody on the Death of Chatterton* (1796).

47. *Poetical Works of William Wordsworth*, ed. Ernest de Selincourt and Helen Darbishire, 5 vols. (Oxford: Oxford University Pres, 1940–49; rev. 1952–59), 3: 523. Moorman, 2: 378.

48. Wordsworth included "Guilt and Sorrow" in his *Poems, Chiefly of Early and Late Years*; these lines occur on p. 17. They are lines 208–209 in the Cornell Wordsworth edition of *The Salisbury Plain Poems of William Wordsworth*, ed. Stephen Gill (Ithaca, NY: Cornell University Press, 1975).

49. Khan finds Wordsworth in conversation with Byron in a number of poems outside the sonnet sequence; "Wordsworth's *River Duddon* Volume: A Response to Coleridge and Byron," pp. 78–80.

50. The reference to Horace was emphasized by the 1836 rewrite of the first line as "Latian shades." On the Horatian and other allusions, see Shaw, "Wordsworth after Peterloo," pp. 257–59.

51. Or perhaps we only need hear Byron, who wrote of the East, Italy, and the Alps and was the poet who worried Wordsworth the most. We can find most of the imagery in the first eight lines of the sonnet in *Childe Harold IV*, where we find both Horace's Bandusian spring and the later "Latian" ("temple of Latian Jupiter") together in a note to stanza 174; there is also a passage on mountain torrents with a note about rainbows, referring back to an Alpine scene in *Manfred* (stanza 72&n.). *Lord Byron: The Complete Poetical Works*, vol. 2, ed. Jerome J. McGann (Oxford: Clarendon Press, 1980).

52. Coleridge wrote to William Sotheby that, having "involuntarily poured forth" the "Hymn" on Scafell, "afterwards I thought the Ideas &c disproportionate to our humble mountains–& accidentally lighting on a short Note in some swiss Poems, concerning the Vale of Chamouny, & its Mountain, I transferred myself thither, in the Spirit, & adapted my former feelings to these grander external objects"; *Collected Letters of Samuel Taylor Coleridge*, 6 vols., ed. Earl Leslie Griggs (Oxford: Clarendon Press, 1956–71), 2: 864–65; see *CPP*, p. 195n.

53. Russett, *Fictions and Fakes: Forging Romantic Authenticity, 1760–1845* (Cambridge: Cambridge University Press, 2006). See also Tilar Mazzeo, *Plagiarism and Literary Property in the Romantic Period* (Philadelphia: University of Pennsylvania Press, 2006).

54. Hazlitt, "Character of Mr. Wordsworth's New Poem, The Excursion," *The Examiner* 21 August 21, 1814; *CWWH*, 19: 10.

55. Wordsworth translated Catullus 3 on the death of Lesbia's sparrow ("The Death of a Starling") among other Catullus poems; see Henry Stead, *A Cockney Catullus: The Reception of Catullus in Romantic Britain, 1795–1821* (Oxford: Oxford University Press, 2016), pp. 165–77.

56. Garrett, *Wordsworth and the Writing of the Nation*, pp. 145–48; also Shaw, "Wordsworth after Peterloo," pp. 260–64.

57. The comment is recorded by John Cairns in Alexander R. Macewen, *The Life and Letters of John Cairns* (London: Hodder and Stoughton, 1895), p. 315.

58. Robert Ryan, *Charles Darwin and the Church of Wordsworth* (Oxford: Oxford University Press, 2016), p. 24. Gill (p. 398) makes the important point that, while Wordsworth was a strong supporter of the Church of England, he was not particularly concerned with parsing particular doctrines.

59. See, for example, the *Eclectic Review*, 2nd series 14 (August 1810); Reiman, *Lake Poets*, 1: 395–97; *Gentleman's Magazine* 90 (October 1820); Reiman, *Lake Poets*, 2: 563–64; and *Literary and Statistical Magazine* 4 (August 1820); Reiman, *Lake Poets*, 2: 577–79.

60. Hazlitt, in his review of *The Excursion*, printed in *The Examiner* (August 21, 28, 1814) and reprinted in *The Round Table*, has a long diatribe against life in the country that opens: "All country people hate each other. They have so little comfort, that they envy their neighbours the smallest pleasure or advantage, and nearly grudge themselves the necessaries of life. From not being accustomed to enjoyment, they become hardened and averse to it – stupid, for want of thought – selfish, for want of society. There is nothing good to be had in the country, or, if there is, they will not let you have it" *(CWWH*, 4: 116). See also John Kinnaird, *William Hazlitt, Critic of Power* (New York: Columbia University Press, 1978), p. 228.

61. *The Excursion* seems present again in Sonnet XXX on the Kirk of Ulpha where he delights "'mid that wave-washed Church-yard to recline, / From pastoral graves extracting thoughts divine" (10–11), though, as Daniel Robinson notes, Wordsworth also buries a reference to Smith's sonnet "Written in the church-yard at Middleton in Sussex," as Robinson finds Wordsworth replacing "the anxious and morbid imagination" of Smith with his more tranquil vision ("'Still Glides the Stream,'" p. 460).

62. See Jackson's note on p. 107.

63. Cornell Wordsworth *Thirteen Book Prelude*, Vol. 1, ed. Mark L. Reed (Ithaca, NY: Cornell University Press, 1991).

64. Geoffrey Hartman also finds an apocalyptic turn in this poem, also known as "After Thought"; he links the sonnet to "Tintern Abbey." Hartman, *Wordsworth's Poetry, 1787–1814* (1964; rpt. Cambridge, MA: Harvard University Press, 1987), p. 336.

65. Wordsworth is reported as saying, "The danger for both Keats and Tennyson . . . was overlusciousness"; Peacock, *Critical Opinions*, p. 290.

5 Late "Late Wordsworth"

1. Among other fine works in the field, see Karen Chase, *Victorians and Old Age* (Oxford: Oxford University Press, 2009), Kathleen Woodward, *Age and Its Discontents: Freud and Other Fictions* (Bloomington; Indiana University Press; 1991), and Helen Yallop, *Age and Identity in Eighteenth-Century England* (London: Pickering & Chatto, 2013). Closest to my time period and interests is Devoney Looser, *Women Writers and Old Age in Great Britain, 1750–1850* (Baltimore, MD: Johns Hopkins University Press, 2008). Susannah R. Ottaway, *The Decline of Life: Old Age in Eighteenth-Century England* (Cambridge: Cambridge University Press, 2004), provides a history of the demography and conceptualization of old age in the period leading up to Wordsworth. See also Judith Page, *Wordsworth and the Cultivation of Women* (Berkeley: University of California Press, 1994), pp. 112–45, on "Wordsworth as Paterfamilias" in his later poetry.
2. See Eugene L. Stelzig, "Mutability. Ageing, and Permanence in Wordsworth's Later Poetry," *Studies in English Literature, 1500–1900* 19 (1979): 623–44.
3. Text from the Cornell Wordsworth *Shorter Poems, 1807–1820*, ed. Carl H. Ketcham (Ithaca, NY: Cornell University Press, 1989). There are fine readings of this poem by Geoffrey Hartman, "Words, Wish, Worth: Wordsworth," in *Deconstruction and Criticism*, eds. Harold Bloom et al. (New York: Seabury Press, 1979), and Philip Shaw : "Wordsworth's 'Dread Voice': Ovid, Dora, and the Later Poetry," *Romanticism* 8 (2002): 34–48.
4. Cornelius Webb called Keats the "Muses' son of Promise" in lines quoted and mocked in *Blackwood's Edinburgh Review* 2 (October 1817): 38; Reiman, *Keats*, 1: 49.
5. Looser, *Women Writers and Old Age*, p. 19.
6. Hartman, *Wordsworth's Poetry 1787–1814* (New Haven, CT: Yale University Press, 1977), pp. 285–86.
7. Of course, many writers issued new collections of their developing corpus. If we look at 1842, the year of Wordsworth's *Poems, Chiefly of Early and Late Years* to which I will be turning, Samuel Rogers issued with Wordsworth's publisher Edward Moxon *Poems*, which opens with Rogers's famous *Pleasures of Memory* and includes poems dated in the 1830s. Again, Tennyson also published with Moxon *Poems by Alfred Tennyson. In Two Volumes*. However, Gill seems correct in stressing how unusual was Wordsworth's obsessive revisions of earlier poems.

8. Gamer, *Romanticism, Self-Canonization, and the Business of Poetry* (Cambridge: Cambridge University Press, 2017), pp. 39, 47. See also Charles Mahoney, *Romantics and Renegades: The Poetics of Political Reaction* (New York: Palgrave Macmillan, 2003), p. 84, for an account of how Wordsworth reworked the collection of "Sonnets, dedicated to Liberty," later connecting them with the "Thanksgiving Ode" volume; and Tim Fulford, *The Late Poetry of the Lake Poets* (Cambridge: Cambridge University Press, 2013), esp. pp. 1–8.

9. Gill argues that the 1820 trip to the continent was a self-conscious attempt by Wordsworth to relive prior European trips, a "re-enactment of formative experience" (Gill, p. 338), so that Wordsworth's retrospective approach was lived as well as written.

10. Quotations from the various sonnet and travel sequences are from the Cornell Wordsworth edition of *Sonnet Series and Itinerary Poems, 1820–1845*, ed. Geoffrey Jackson (Ithaca, NY: Cornell University Press, 2004); line numbers for the poems and page numbers for prose will be given in the text.

11. See Jackson's note, p. 236n, where he also cites Milton's *Paradise Lost*, 3: 353–59, as a possible source.

12. In the Cornell Wordsworth *Poems in Two Volumes, and Other Poems, 1800–1807*, ed. Jared Curtis (Ithaca, NY: Cornell University Press, 1983), p. 198.

13. Looser, *Women Writers and Old Age*, p. 19.

14. Cornell Wordsworth *Thirteen Book Prelude by William Wordsworth*, vol. 1, ed. Mark L. Reed (Ithaca, NY: Cornell University Press, 1991).

15. Rubenstein, "Wordsworth and 'Localised Romance': The Scottish Poems of 1831," *Studies in English Literature, 1500–1900* 16 (Fall 1976): 590.

16. Cornell Wordsworth, *Lyrical Ballads, and Other Poems, 1797–1800*, ed. James Butler and Karen Green (Ithaca, NY: Cornell University Press, 1992).

17. Peter J. Manning, "Cleansing the Images: Wordsworth, Rome, and the Rise of Historicism," *Texas Studies in Language and Literature* 33 (Summer 1991): 293.

18. Nanora Sweet offers an account of a "culture of disestablishment" in "'Lorenzo's' Liverpool and 'Corinne's' Coppet: The Italianate Salon and Romantic Education," in *Lessons of Romanticism*, ed. Thomas Pfau and Robert F. Gleckner (Durham, NC: Duke University Press, 1998), pp. 244–60.

19. Cox, "The Living Pantheon of Poets in 1820," in *Cambridge Companion to Romantic Poetry*, ed. James Chandler and Maureen Mclean (Cambridge: Cambridge University Press, 2008): "This attempt to reconstruct a pantheon frames writing in a different way than efforts to define either a limited or expanded canon, for a 'heathen' pantheon unlike a 'sacred' canon seeks to include all the 'gods' of poetry, no matter how minor, how disparate, how heterodox" (p. 12).

20. Browning, "The Lost Leader," 19–20, quoted in John Hadyn Baker, "Wordsworth's 'The Warning': A New Source for Browning's 'The Lost Leader,'" *Notes and Queries* 44 (September 1997): 340–41.
21. Rubenstein, "Wordsworth and 'Localised Romance," p. 579.
22. Manning, "The Persian Wordsworth," *European Romantic Review* 17 (2006): 194.
23. Gill, *Wordsworth and the Victorians* (Oxford: Clarendon Press, 1998), p. 3; see also pp. 10–39.
24. Henry Crabb Robinson, *Diary, Reminiscences, and Correspondence of Henry Crabb Robinson*, ed. Thomas Sadler, 2 vols. (Boston: Fields, Osgood, & Co., 1869), 2: 243.
25. Robert M. Ryan, *Charles Darwin and the Church of Wordsworth* (Oxford: Oxford University Press, 2016), p. 8.
26. John Wyatt in *Wordsworth's Poems of Travel, 1819–42: "Such Sweet Wayfaring"* (New York: St. Martin's Press, 1999) takes up the organization of the entire volume, pp. 119–21. All quotations of the "Memorials of a Tour of Italy, 1837" are from the Cornell Wordsworth *Sonnet Series and Itinerary Poems, 1820–1845*, ed. Geoffrey Jackson (Ithaca, NY: Cornell University Press, 2004); line numbers for the poems and page numbers for prose will be given in the text. We see in this volume the constant regrouping discussed by Gill: in the first edition (British Library), the first title page is *Poetical Works of William Wordsworth, Vol. VII* before the title page for the new volume; since the 1837 collected works had been six volumes, this new work is seen as connected to it. There would be a further regrouping of these poems in 1845.
27. Wyatt, in *Wordsworth's Poems of Travel*, also stresses the social and political thrust of this poem and of the collection as a whole (pp. 118–36, esp. p. 131).
28. *The Prose Works of William Wordsworth*, eds. W. J. B. Owen and Jane Worthington Smyser, 3 vols. (Oxford: Clarendon Press, 1974), 1: 124.
29. Walter Jackson Bate, *The Burden of the Past and the English Poet* (Cambridge: Belknap Press, 1970).
30. Christopher Wordsworth, *Memoirs of William Wordsworth*, 2 vols. (London: Moxon, 1851), 2: 329.
31. See, for example, Buzard's analysis of the differences between the Grand Tour and nineteenth-century travel in *The Beaten Track: European Tourism, Literature, and the Ways to Culture, 1800–1918* (Oxford: Clarendon Press, 1993), pp. 97–130. See also Ernest Giddey, "1816: Switzerland and the Revival of the 'Grand Tour,'" *Byron Journal* 19 (1991): 17–25.
32. Buzard, *Beaten Track*, pp. 120–21.
33. Buzard, *Beaten Track*, p. 121.
34. Redford, *Venice and the Grand Tour* (New Haven, CT: Yale University Press, 1996), p. 105.

35. J. R. Hale, "Introduction," *The Italian Journal of Samuel Rogers* (London: Faber and Faber, 1956), p. 69.

36. Peter J. Manning, "The Other Scene of Travel: Wordsworth's 'Musings Near Aquapendente,'" in *The Wordsworthian Enlightenment: Romantic Poetry and the Ecology of Reading*, ed. Helen Reguiro Elam and Frances Ferguson (Baltimore, MD: The Johns Hopkins University Press, 2005), p. 206.

37. Redford, *Venice and the Grand Tour*, pp. 28–39.

38. Redford, *Venice and the Grand Tour*, p. 115.

39. Martin Kelsall, *Byron's Politics* (Totowa, NJ: Barnes & Noble Books, 1987), pp. 73–78, analyzes the ways in which Hobhouse's notes radicalize Byron's poem.

40. Henry Crabb Robinson, *Diary*, 2: 241, 242.

41. See Manning's "The Other Scene of Travel" and "Cleansing the Images"; and James Chandler, *Wordsworth's Second Nature: A Study of the Poetry and Politics* (Chicago, IL: University of Chicago Press, 1984), pp. 176–81.

42. Redford, *Venice and the Grand Tour*, pp. 35–39.

43. Buzard, *The Beaten Track*, pp. 19–30, has argued that Wordsworth is a key figure in the development of modern tourism. Geoffrey Jackson goes further in his edition of the poems, calling Wordsworth a "cultural colonist intent on engraving foreign (and Scottish) landmarks on his own Anglocentric cultural map" ("Introduction," p. 16).

44. Coe, *Wordsworth and the Literature of Travel*, pp. 101–107, provides a list of sixty-four travel books.

45. Dean MacCannell, *The Tourist: A New Theory of the Leisure Class* (New York: Schocken Books, 1976), p. 10.

46. The note, tying the experience to Rome, states more fully: "Sight is at first a sad enemy to imagination . . . nothing perhaps brings this truth home to the feelings more than the city of Rome . . . . [W]hen particular spots or objects are sought out, disappointment is, I believe, invariably felt. Ability to recover from this disappointment will exist in proportion to knowledge & the power of the mind to reconstruct out of fragments & parts & to make details in the present subservient to more adequate comprehension of the past" (pp. 180–81). This problem is pursued in the following three poems, where we discover that historical knowledge is one barrier to aesthetic appreciation of the sights of Rome; as the title of the first of these poems puts it, "At Rome – Regrets. – In Allusion to Niebuhr, and Other Modern Historians." Wordsworth regrets that "old credulities" are being unveiled by history, "stript naked as a rock / 'Mid a dry desert" (1, 3–4) History would seem to preclude our ability to delight any longer in a place such as Rome, for the "glory of Infant Rome must disappear," as "Truth" "must steer / Henceforth a humbler course perplexed and slow" (5, 7–8). Wordsworth,

however, is happy in the thought that he learned of Rome when "story lacked / Severe research"; troubled by the modern historians' debunking of legendary history, Wordsworth knows "in our hearts" that "Assent is power, belief the soul of fact" (12, 14). This would seem to be the position of Coleridge in his *Lay Sermon* (1817): "principles, as taught in the Bible, . . . are understood in exact proportion as they are believed and felt . . . For the words of the apostle are literally and philosophically true: WE (that is, the human race) LIVE BY FAITH" (pp. 17–18, quoted in Jerome McGann, *The Romantic Ideology: A Critical Investigation* (Chicago, IL: University of Chicago Press, 1983), p. 6). Where the enlightened historian pits old beliefs against new facts, Wordsworth would recover the power lost by the disillusioning experiences of confronting the facticity of Rome by assenting to what he famously calls elsewhere an "outworn creed." Imaginative power is still, as Liu has shown of the early poetry, linked to a denial of history, but this is an oddly historicized antihistoricism, as Manning has shown in a different way.

47. Ironically, the disappointment Wordsworth feels in the touristic visit to the Tarpeian rock is itself a recurring theme in travel texts. For example, in *Bishop Burnet's Travels Through France, Italy, Germany and Switzerland* (London, 1750), which was a source for Wordsworth's poem – see Charles N. Coe, "A Source for Wordsworth's Sonnet, 'At Rome'," *Notes and Queries* 193 (1948): 430–31 – the author states that the "*Tarpeian* Rock is now so small a Fall, that a Man would think it no great Matter, for his Diversion, to leap over it" (p. 231). In Samuel Laing's 1842 *Notes of a Traveler, on the Social and Political State of France, Prussia, Switzerland, Italy, and Other Parts of Europe, During the Present Century* (London: Longman, Brown, Green, and Longmans, 1842), we learn: "A fall from the Tarpeian rock might have broken a man's neck sufficiently well, if the ground below was clear, and originally it was, perhaps, hollowed out, or naturally lower, as ground at the foot of a steep precipice usually is" (p. 413).

48. Letter to Dorothy Wordsworth, Mary Wordsworth, and Dora Wordsworth, April 27 or 28, 1837; *WLLY*, 3: 396; see Moorman, 2: 523, and *FN*, p. 180.

49. In fact, he told Isabella Fenwick that he was "somewhat disappointed at Vallombrosa" (*FN*, p. 182).

50. Redford, *Venice and the Grand Tour*, pp. 28–32.

51. See Charles N. Coe, "A Source for Wordsworth's Sonnet, 'At Rome'," *Notes and Queries* 193 (1948): 430–31.

52. Redford, in *Venice and the Grand Tour*, quotes Robert Molesworth saying in 1694, "An *English-Man* should be shewn the misery of the enslaved Parts of the World, to make him in love with the happiness of his own Country" (pp. 17–18).

53. Robinson, letter to Landor, December 7, 1836, in *The Correspondence of Henry Crabb Robinson with the Wordsworth Circle (1806–1866)*, ed. Edith J. Morley, 2 vols. (Oxford: Clarendon Press, 1927), 1: 328.

54. Graver, "Sitting in Dante's Throne: Wordsworth and Italian Nationalism," in *Dante and Italy in British Romanticism*, ed. Frederick Burwick and Paul Douglass (New York: Palgrave Macmillan, 2011), p. 35. See also Joseph Luzzi, *Romantic Europe and the Ghost of Italy* (New Haven, CT: Yale University Press, 2008), for Wordsworth's shifting responses to a politicized reading of Dante (pp. 141–59).

55. Rogers, *Italy, A Poem* (London: Edward Moxon, 1839), p. 119.

56. John Chaloner, *Rome; A Poem. In Two Parts* (London: Longman, Hurst, Rees, Orme, and Brown, 1821). James Edmund Reade, *Italy: A Poem, In Six Parts* (London: Saunders and Otley, 1838): for the passage on Byron, see Canto II, stanzas xxxvi–xlii; for Hunt, p. 456n; for Shelley, 382n. Interestingly, he attaches to Shelley the line about Keats's name "being writ on water." He also has a Vallombrosa poem addressed to Milton, pp. 59–60.

57. William Edmondstoune Aytoun, *Poland, Homer, and Other Poems* (London: Longman, Rees, Orme, Brown, Green, and Longman, 1831), pp. 95–108.

58. Margaret Keogh, *Herculaneum, Pompeii, and Other Poems* (London: J. L. Cox and Sons, 1842). Keogh appears in Jennifer Wallace's *Digging the Dirt: The Archeological Imagination* (London: Duckworth, 2004), p. 86, where the poet is seen to experience a "kind of Byronic melancholia" brought on by her inability as a woman to travel: "Men could travel to Pompeii and include it on their Grand Tour, while women had to stay at home and read about it."

59. Alexander Andrew Knox, *Giotto and Francesca, And Other Poems* (London: Edward Bull, 1842). On Knox and the Shelleys, see Mrs. Andrew Crosse (Cornelia Augusta Hewett Crosse), "Alexander Knox and His Friends," *Temple Bar* 94 (1892): 495–517. To be fair, "M." in *Poems Written Chiefly Abroad* (London: Saunders & Otley, 1842), while at times sounding Byronic, compares Wordsworth favorably to Catullus, calling the English poet "Nature's . . . favourite" as "The poet of his own dear lake" (p. 35).

60. Henry Crabb Robinson, during his trip to Italy in 1831, talks of the "insignificant stones raised to Keats and Shelley" in Rome; he mentions Byron's theory that Keats was killed by a bad review, an idea picked up by Landor. Robinson would next go on to Florence where he met Landor, where among other things they discussed Hazlitt. These writers are clearly present to Robinson on Italian soil. Robinson, *On Books and Their Writers*, ed. Edith J. Morley, 3 vols. (London: J. M. Dent and Sons, 1938), 1: 389–90.

61. Peter J. Manning, "The Other Scene of Travel," pp. 191–211. Tim Fulford also takes up this poem in *Wordsworth's Poetry, 1815–1845* (Philadelphia: University of Pennsylvania Press, 2019), pp. 292–96.

62. Curtis, in his note to the poem, indicates that he thinks Hunt was Wordsworth's source for this story (p. 354). Manning, "The Other Scene of Travel," finds him relying on Tom Moore's *Life of Byron* (1834).

63. Robinson, *Diary*, 2: 243; Moorman, 2: 524; he also met with Richard Monckton Milnes in London in 1836 (Gill, p. 392).

64. See Chester L. Shaver and Alice C. Shaver, *Wordsworth's Library, A Catalogue* (New York: Garland, 1979), pp. 62, 144, 234.

65. Of course, Wordsworth did not need to *own* the younger writers' books to have read their poetry, as he could have encountered it in books belonging to others or in reviews. It is also interesting to note that Barron Field, in his manuscript *Memoirs of the Life and Poetry of William Wordsworth, with Extracts from his Letters to the Author, by Barron Field, Esqr. late Chief Justice of Gibraltar, in twelve chapters and three appendices* ... (British Library, ADD MS 41325–41327) – which Wordsworth read and commented on – quotes the famous passage on the rainbow from "Lamia," has an extensive discussion of Byron, quotes Hunt, and mentions Shelley.

66. Wordsworth, letter to Landor, April 20, 1822, *WLLY*, 1: 124; quoted in Robert Super, *Walter Savage Landor, A Biography* (1954; rpt. Westport, CT: Green Wood Press, 1977), p. 161; Robinson, *Books and Their Writers*, 3: 854.

67. Graves, "Recollections of Wordsworth and the Lake Country," in *The Afternoon Lectures on Literature and Art* (Dublin: William McGee; London: Bell and Daldy, 1869), pp. 279, 301–302.

68. *Memoir and Letters of Sara Coleridge, Edited by Her Daughter*, ed. Edith Coleridge, 2 vols. (London: H. S. King, 1873), 1: 224. Cited in Edith C. Batho, *The Later Wordsworth* (Cambridge: Cambridge University Press, 1935), p. 101.

69. *Memoir and Letters of Sara Coleridge*, 1: 409–10.

70. Edward Trelawney, *Recollections of the Last Days of Shelley and Byron* (1858; rpt. Williamstown, MA: Corner House Publishers, 1975), pp. 13–14. See David Crane, *Lord Byron's Jackal: A Life of Edward Trelawney* (New York: Four Walls Eight Windows, 1999), pp. 34–37.

71. Batho, *Later Wordsworth*, p. 100.

72. John Morley, *Life of William Ewart Gladstone*, 3 vols. (New York: Macmillan, 1903), 1: 136.

73. Recorded in the *Prose Works of William Wordsworth*, ed. Alexander B. Grosart, 3 vols. (London: Edward Moxon, Son, and Company, 1876), 3: 463.

74. Robinson, *Books and Their Writers*, 1: 409. The comments on Shelley's poem are gathered by Peacock, *Critical Opinions*, p. 349.

75. Robinson, *Books and Their Writers*, 2: 485. Wordsworth puts Byron and Ebenezer Elliott in the same category. The second comment was reported by Hartley Coleridge and included in Peacock, *Critical Opinions*, p. 349.

76. Pinion, *Wordsworth Chronology*, p. 190.

77. Peacock, *Critical Opinions*, pp. 202–207.

78. Manning, "The Other Side of Travel," p. 204.

79. The "Evening Voluntaries" are quoted from the Cornell Wordsworth edition of *Last Poems, 1821–1850*, ed. Jared Curtis, Apryl Lea Denny-Ferris, and Jillian Heydt-Stevenson (Ithaca, NY: Cornell University Press, 1999). "Not in the lucid intervals of life" was probably composed between April 1833 and January 1835. The lines on Byron (7–15) do not appear in the earliest manuscript version. Byron's letters were published in 1830 and 1832. For a similar critique of Byron by Wordsworth's friend and supporter Henry Taylor, see his *Philip Van Artevelde: A Dramatic Romance. In Two Parts* (London: Edward Moxon, 1834), xiii–xxi. On Taylor, see Lawrence Poston, "Wordsworth among the Victorians: The Case of Henry Taylor," *Studies in Romanticism* 17 (1978): 293–305.

80. Robinson, *Diary*, 2: 240–41.

81. Robinson, *Diary*, 2: 238, 240–41; letters to Landor, December 7, 1836, December 17, 1836; *Correspondence ... with the Wordsworth Circle*, 1: 326–33. See Robert H. Super, *Walter Savage Landor*, pp. 275–77.

82. That attempt failed, though Landor allowed Robinson to "intercept the copy of the *Satire* intended for Southey"; Super, *Walter Savage Landor*, p. 276.

83. Field, *Memoirs of the Life and Poetry of William Wordsworth*, p. 315 opposite. Geoffrey Little has edited a partial transcription of *Barron Field's "Memoirs of Wordsworth"* (Sydney: Sydney University Press, 1975), p. 129.

84. Robinson, *Diary*, 2: 246.

85. Robinson points out parallels between Byron's and Landor's attacks in his letter to Landor, December 17, 1836; *Correspondence ... with the Wordsworth Circle*, 1: 329–33. When Landor later published an additional attack in a conversation between Southey and Porson – *Blackwood's* 52 (December 1842): 687–715 – Wordsworth's son-in-law Edward Quillinan would respond to Landor in "Imaginary Conversation, Between Mr. Walter Savage Landon and the Editor of Blackwood's Magazine," *Blackwood's* 53 (April 1843): 518–36. It is interesting to note that Landor in his imaginary conversation has Porson describe Wordsworth and Byron as secret sharers, "condemned to a Siamese-twinship" (p. 687). Manning, "The Other Scene of Travel: Wordsworth's 'Musings Near Aquapendente," p. 204, points out a similar linking of Wordsworth and Byron in Hazlitt's *Spirit of the Age*.

The two poets seem to offer connected yet contrasting versions of a potentially debilitating inward turn.

86. Super, *Landor*, pp. 275, 265, n.78. Landor acknowledges Brown without naming him in a note to the poem, p. 221n.

87. Chandler, "Lines Crossed: Walter Savage Landor and Wordsworth," *Charles Lamb Bulletin* 159 (March 2014): 53.

88. Wordsworth, letter to Robinson, March 13, 1821, in Robinson, *Correspondence . . . with the Wordsworth Circle*, 1: 99–100.

89. Jane Spencer, *Literary Relations: Kinship and the Canon, 1660–1830* (Oxford: Oxford University Press, 2005). To be fair, Dennis Low, in *The Literary Protégés of the Lake Poets* (Aldershot: Ashgate, 2006), has shown how Southey in particular, but also Coleridge and Wordsworth, mentored a number of women writers in the 1820s and onward; Low discusses how Wordsworth aided Maria Jane Jewsbury, for example, by recommending her to the editor of *The Keepsake* (p. 143).

90. The poem begins in the Apennines, near Aquapendente. It glances back to Savona, Genoa, and Pisa and looks forward – via a series of classical allusions – to the Southern part of the journey, which was not in the end taken because of a cholera epidemic at Naples. It closes by a turn to Rome, the poem ending after a series of evocations of Rome with the cry, "Let us now / Rise, and to-morrow greet magnificent Rome" (371–72). Although the poem thus, in one sense, organizes itself along Wordsworth's and Robinson's projected itinerary, with Rome as its central focal point, these verses are more strongly ordered by an argument about the relationship between sights, historical memory, and poetic inspiration.

91. Manning, "The Other Scene of Travel," p. 206.

92. Manning, "The Other Scene of Travel," p. 209.

93. See Curtis's note at 796n. Also, see AB-Stage Reading Text in the Cornell Wordsworth *Thirteen Book Prelude*, vol. 1, ed. Mark L. Reed (Ithaca, NY: Cornell University Press, 1991), Book 8: 236–37; "The Matron's Tale," in the Cornell Wordsworth *"Lyrical Ballads," and Other Poems, 1797–1800*, ed. James Butler and Karen Green (Ithaca, NY: Cornell University Press, 1992), p. 336, lines 24–26.

94. We might see a similar replacement of Shelley by Coleridge in the Fenwick Note on Shelley's "court[ing] agitation" in rough seas: "of all the men I have ever known Coleridge had the most passive courage in bodily peril" (*FN*, p. 178).

95. Batho, *The Later Wordsworth*, pp. 296–98; Moorman, 2: 526.

96. John Rudy, "Wordsworth's St. Francis and the Baptized Imagination," *Renascence: Essays on Values in Literature* 40 (Summer 1988): 277.

97. Robinson, letter to Christopher Wordsworth, October 18, 1850, *Memoirs of William Wordsworth*, ed. Christopher Wordsworth, 2 vols. (London: Moxon, 1851), 2: 330. *FN*, p. 182.
98. Looser, *Women Writers and Old Age*, p. 134. For a similar set of issues, see Jonathan Shears, "'Old Men – and Women – May be Permitted to Speak Long': Samuel Taylor Coleridge and the Voice of Experience," *Romanticism* 25.3 (2019): 249–260.
99. While he does not tackle this poem, Eugene Stelzig, in "Mutability. Ageing, and Permanence in Wordsworth's Later Poetry," *Studies in English Literature* 19 (1979): 623–44, offers a strong reading of Wordsworth's writings on age; he sees Wordsworth moving away from a poetry of recollected experience to a more abstract musing on a religiously tinged notion of mutability.
100. The significance of these double echoes is taken up by Robin Jarvis, "Shades of Milton: Wordsworth at Vallombrosa," *Studies in Romanticism* 25 (Winter, 1986): 483–504.
101. Wallace Stevens, "Esthétique du Mal," stanza xv, lines 7–9, in *The Palm at the End of the Mind*, ed. Holly Stevens (New York: Vintage Books, 1972).

Postscript Wordsworth in 1850

1. It would be worth exploring more broadly all the retrospective work on romanticism done around this moment with the publication in 1847 of Medwin's *Life of Percy Bysshe Shelley*, in 1848 of Milnes's *Life, Letters, and Literary Remains of John Keats*, and in 1850 of both Hunt's *Autobiography* and the final volume of *The Life and Correspondence of the late Robert Southey*.
2. Kenneth R. Johnston, *The Hidden Wordsworth: Poet, Lover, Rebel, Spy* (New York: W. W. Norton & Co., 1998), p. 11.
3. As Herbert Lindenberger suggests in "The Reception of *The Prelude*," *Bulletin of the New York Public Library* 64 (1960): 205.
4. For a recent account of how the *Wat Tyler* text was released, see Daniel White, "The Case of the Nocturnal Amanuenses: New Evidence in the Wat Tyler Affair," *Modern Philology* 118 (November 2020): 277–303. Both the *British Quarterly Review* 12 (1850): 570 and *The Athenaeum* (August 3, 1850): 807 suggest *The Prelude* was held back to mask Wordsworth's revolutionary views. See Lindenberger, "The Reception of *The Prelude*," p. 198. Jaspar Cragwall, in "Wordsworth and the Ragged Legion; or, the Lows of High Argument," in *Romantic Autobiography in England*, ed. Eugene Stelzieg (London: Routledge, 2016), pp. 179–93, finds that Wordsworth wanted to avoid linkages between his sense of himself as a poet-prophet and the enthusiasm exhibited by Methodist preachers.

5. Eilenberg, *Strange Power of Speech: Wordsworth, Coleridge, and Literary Possession* (Oxford: Oxford University Press, 1992), p. 212. On Wordsworth and the attempt to reform copyright laws, see Moorman, 2: 552–54; Gill, pp. 391–92; and Michael Gamer, *Romanticism, Self-Canonization, and the Business of Poetry* (Cambridge: Cambridge University Press, 2017), pp. 41–47.

6. Mathew Arnold, "Preface," *The Poems of William Wordsworth*, ed. Matthew Arnold (London: Macmillan and Co., 1879), p. v.

7. Coleridge published his response as "To a Gentlemen" in *Sibylline Leaves* (1817): *CPP*, p. 200–203. There are many references to his poem in reviews; for example, see *Ainsworth's Magazine* (18 [July 1850]: 558) and the *Leader and Saturday Analyst* (August 17, 1850: 496).

8. We may now be surprised to see how Shelley stands above Keats in many of these evaluative exercises; Joanne Wilkes has shown the extent to which the attacks on Keats during his lifetime – for obscurity, vulgarity, lack of masculinity – continued into the reviewing culture at mid-century, in "Snuffing out an Article: Sara Coleridge and the Early Victorian Reception of Keats," in *Nervous Reactions: Victorian Recollections of Romanticism*, ed. Joel Faflak and Julia M. Wright (Albany: State University of New York Press, 2004), pp. 189–206.

9. It is worth mentioning that, at the time, David Macbeth Moir in his *Sketches of The Poetical Literature of the Past Half-Century* (published by Blackwood in 1851) still conveys a very eclectic and catholic pantheon of poets, spending considerable time on women writers such as Smith and Baillie, taking up Broomfield and Campbell, and praising Hunt as the leader of a "fourth school" of English poetry following upon the Lake School.

10. M. H. Abrams, *Natural Supernaturalism: Tradition and Revolution in Romantic Literature* (New York: W. W. Norton & Company, 1971), p. 334.

11. Timothy J. Wandling has tracked the changes in critical responses to Byron in his helpful "Early Romantic Theorists and the Fate of Transgressive Eloquence: John Stuart Mill's Response to Byron," in *Nervous Reactions: Victorian Recollections of Romanticism*, ed. Joel Faflak and Julia M. Wright (Albany: State University of New York Press, 2004), pp. 123–40.

Select Bibliography

Abrams, M. H. *Natural Supernaturalism: Tradition and Revolution in Romantic Literature.* New York: W. W. Norton & Company, 1971.

Adelman, Richard. "Idleness and Vacancy in Shelley's 'Mont Blanc.'" *Keats-Shelley Journal* 62 (2013): 62–79.

Allot, Miriam. "Keats's *Endymion* and Shelley's 'Alastor.'" In *Literature of the Romantic Period 1750–1850.* Ed. R. T. Davies and B. G. Beatty, pp. 151–70. Liverpool: Liverpool University Press, 1976.

Altick, Richard. *The Shows of London.* Cambridge, MA: Harvard University Press, 1978.

Arnold, Matthew. "Preface." In *The Poems of William Wordsworth.* Ed. Matthew Arnold, pp. v-xxvi. London: Macmillan and Co., 1879.

Ariès, Philippe. *Centuries of Childhood: A Social History of Family Life.* Trans. Robert Baldick. New York: Knopf, 1962.

Aytoun, William Edmondstoune. *Poland, Homer, and Other Poems.* London: Longman, Rees, Orme, Brown, Green, and Longman, 1831.

Bainbridge, Simon. *Napoleon and English Romanticism.* Cambridge: Cambridge University Press, 1995.

British Poetry and the Revolutionary and Napoleonic Wars. Cambridge: Cambridge University Press, 2003.

Barnett, Suzanne. *Romantic Paganism: The Politics of Ecstasy in the Shelley Circle.* Cham, Switzerland: Palgrave Macmillan, 2017.

Bate, Jonathan. *Shakespearean Constitutions: Politics, Theatre, Criticism 1730–1830.* Oxford: Clarendon Press, 1989.

Radical Wordsworth: The Poet Who Changed the World. New Haven, CT: Yale University Press, 2020.

Bate, Walter Jackson. *The Burden of the Past and the English Poet.* Cambridge: Belknap Press, 1970.

Bates, Brian. *Wordsworth's Poetic Collections, Supplementary Writing, and Parodic Reception.* London: Pickering & Chatto, 2012.

Batho, Edith. *The Later Wordsworth.* Cambridge: Cambridge University Press, 1933.

Behrendt, Stephen C. *Shelley and His Audiences.* Lincoln: University of Nebraska Press, 1989.

Bennett, Betty. *British War Poetry in the Age of Romanticism 1793–1815.* New York: Garland, 1976.

Blank, G. Kim. *Wordsworth's Influence on Shelley: A Study of Poetic Authority.* New York: St. Martin's, 1988.

Bloom, Harold. *The Anxiety of Influence.* New York: Oxford University Press, 1973.

Blunden, Edmund. *Leigh Hunt. A Biography.* London: Cobden and Sanderson, 1930.

Bradley, A. C. *Oxford Lectures on Poetry.* 1909; reprint, London: Macmillan, 1965.

Brantley, Richard E. *Wordsworth's "Natural Methodism."* New Haven, CT: Yale University Press, 1975.

Brown, David Bleney, Robert Woof, and Stephen Hebron, eds. *Benjamin Robert Haydon, 1786–1846: Painter and Writer, Friend of Wordsworth and Keats.* Kendal: Wordsworth Trust, 1996.

Brown, Leonard. "The Genesis, Growth, and Meaning of *Endymion.*" *Studies in Philology* 30 (1933): 618–53.

Bush, Douglas. *Mythology and the Romantic Tradition in English Poetry.* New York: Cooper Square Publishers, 1963.

Butler, Marilyn. *Peacock Displayed: A Satirist in His Context.* London: Routledge and Kegan Paul, 1979.

    Romantics, Rebels and Reactionaries: English Literature and its Background, 1760–1830. Oxford: Oxford University Press, 1981.

Buzard, James. *The Beaten Track: European Tourism, Literature, and the Ways to Culture, 1800–1918.* Oxford: Clarendon Press, 1993.

Cameron, Kenneth Neill. "Shelley and *Ahrimanes.*" *Modern Language Quarterly* 3 (June 1942): 287–95.

    ed. *Shelley and His Circle, 1773–1822.* 7 vols. Cambridge, MA: Harvard University Press, 1961–86.

Cantor, Jay. *The Space Between: Literature and Politics.* Baltimore, MD: Johns Hopkins University Press, 1981.

Carothers, Yvonne M. "Alastor: Shelley Corrects Wordsworth." *Modern Language Quarterly* 42 (1981): 21–47.

Chaloner, John. *Rome; A Poem. In Two Parts.* London: Longman, Hurst, Rees, Orme, and Brown, 1821.

Chandler, David. "Lines Crossed: Walter Savage Landor and Wordsworth." *Charles Lamb Bulletin* 159 (March 2014): 46–60.

Chandler, James K. *Wordsworth's Second Nature: A Study of the Poetry and Politics.* Chicago, IL: University of Chicago Press, 1984.

    "'Wordsworth' after Waterloo." In *The Age of William Wordsworth: Critical Essays on the Romantic Tradition.* Ed. Kenneth R. Johnston and Gene W. Ruoff, pp. 84–111. New Brunswick, NJ: Rutgers University Press, 1987.

Chase, Karen. *Victorians and Old Age.* Oxford: Oxford University Press, 2009.

Cauchi, Francesca. "A Rereading of Wordsworth's Presence in Shelley's *Alastor.*" *Studies in English Literature, 1500–1900* 50 (Autumn 2010): 759–74.

Coe, Charles Norton. "A Source for Wordsworth's Sonnet, 'At Rome.'" *Notes and Queries* 193 (1948): 430–31.

Wordsworth and the Literature of Travel. New York: Bookman Associates, 1953.

Cohen, B. Bernard. "Haydon, Hunt, and Scott and Six Sonnets (1816) by Wordsworth." *Philological Quarterly* 19 (October 1950): 434–37.

Cohen-Vrignaud, Gerard. "Becoming Corsairs: Byron, British Property Rights and Orientalist Economics." *Studies in Romanticism* 50 (Winter 2011): 685–714.

Colbert, Benjamin. "Contemporary Notice of the Shelleys' *History of a Six Weeks' Tour*: Two New Early Reviews." *Keats-Shelley Journal* 48 (1999): 22–29.

Coleridge, Hartley. *The Letters of Hartley Coleridge*. Ed. Grace Evelyn Griggs and Earl Leslie Griggs. New York: Oxford University Press, 1936.

Coleridge, S. T. *Biographia Literaria*. Ed. James Engell and W. Jackson Bate. 2 vols. Princeton, NJ: Princeton University Press, 1983.

Collected Letters of Samuel Taylor Coleridge, Ed. Earl Leslie Griggs. 6 vols. Oxford: Clarendon Press, 1956–71.

Coleridge, Sara. *Memoir and Letters of Sara Coleridge, Edited by Her Daughter*. Ed. Edith Coleridge. 2 vols. London: H. S. King, 1873.

Connell, Philip. *Romanticism, Economics and the Question of "Culture."* Oxford: Oxford University Press, 2001.

Cox, Jeffery N. *Poetry and Politics in the Cockney School: Keats, Shelley, Hunt and Their Circle*. Cambridge: Cambridge University Press, 1998.

"The Living Pantheon of Poets in 1820." In *Cambridge Companion to Romantic Poetry*. Ed. James Chandler and Maureen McLane, pp. 10–34. Cambridge: Cambridge University Press, 2008.

Romanticism in the Shadow of War: Literary Culture in the Napoleonic War Years. Cambridge: Cambridge University Press, 2014.

"'Illegitimate' Pantomime in the 'Legitimate' Theater: Context as Text." *Studies in Romanticism* 14 (Summer 2015): 159–86.

"John Keats, Medicine, and Young Men on the Make." In *John Keats and the Medical Imagination*. Ed. Nicholas Roe, pp. 109–28. Cham, Switzerland: Palgrave Macmillan, 2017.

Cragwall, Jaspar. "Wordsworth and the Ragged Legion; or, the Lows of High Argument." In *Romantic Autobiography in England*. Ed. Eugene Stelzieg, pp. 179–93. London: Routledge, 2016.

Crane, David. *Lord Byron's Jackal: A Life of Edward Trelawney*. New York: Four Walls Eight Windows, 1999.

Crosse, Cornelia Augusta Hewett. "Alexander Knox and His Friends." *Temple Bar* 94 (1892): 495–517.

Crucefix, Martyn. "Wordsworth, Superstition, and Shelley's *Alastor*." *Essays in Criticism* 2 (April 1983): 126–47.

Curran, Stuart. *Poetic Form and British Romanticism*. Oxford: Oxford University Press, 1986.

Davidson, Henry. *Waterloo, A Poem. With Notes*. London: John Murray, 1816.

Dawson, P. M. S. *The Unacknowledged Legislator: Shelley and Politics*. Oxford: Clarendon Press, 1980.

Duff, David. *Romance and Revolution: Shelley and the Politics of a Genre*. Cambridge: Cambridge University Press, 1994.

Ellison, Ralph. *The Collected Essays of Ralph Ellison*. Ed. John F. Callahan. New York: The Modern Library, 1995.

Eilenberg, Susan. *Strange Power of Speech: Wordsworth, Coleridge, and Literary Possession*. Oxford: Oxford University Press, 1992.

Erdman, David. "Byron and Revolt in England." *Science and Society* 11 (1947): 234–48.

Farley, Charles. *The New Pantomime of Harlequin and Fortunio, or, Shing-Moo and Thun-ton; With a Sketch of the Story*. London: John Miller, 1815.

Favret, Mary. *War at a Distance: Romanticism and the Making of Modern Wartime*. Princeton, NJ: Princeton University Press, 2010.

Ferguson, Frances. *Wordsworth: Language as Counter-Spirit*. New Haven, CT: Yale University Press, 1977.

Foot, Michael. "Hazlitt's Revenge on the Lakers." *Wordsworth Circle* 14 (Winter 1983): 61–68.

Fulford, Tim. *The Late Poetry of the Lake Poets*. Cambridge: Cambridge University Press, 2013.

Romantic Poetry and Literary Coteries: The Dialect of the Tribe. New York: Palgrave Macmillan, 2015.

Wordsworth's Poetry 1815–1845. Philadelphia: University of Pennsylvania Press, 2019.

and Lynda Pratt, gen. eds. *Robert Southey: Later Poetical Works, 1811–1838*. 4 vols. London: Pickering and Chatto, 2012.

Gamer, Michael. *Romanticism, Self-Canonization, and the Business of Poetry*. Cambridge: Cambridge University Press, 2017.

Galperin, William H. *Revision and Authority in Wordsworth: The Interpretation of a Career*. Philadelphia: University of Pennsylvania Press, 1989.

Garrett, James. *Wordsworth and the Writing of the Nation*. Burlington, VT: Ashgate, 2008.

Garrod, H. W. *Wordsworth*. Oxford: Clarendon Press, 1923.

George, Eric. *The Life and Death of Benjamin Robert Haydon: Historical Painter, 1786–1846*. 2nd ed. Oxford: Clarendon, 1967.

Giddey, Ernest. "1816: Switzerland and the Revival of the 'Grand Tour.'" *The Byron Journal* 19 (1991): 17–25.

Gill, Stephen. *Wordsworth and the Victorians*. Oxford: Clarendon Press, 1998.

Gilmartin, Kevin. *William Hazlitt, Political Essayist*. Oxford: Oxford University Press, 2015.

Gohn, Jack Benoit. "Did Shelley Know Wordsworth's *Peter Bell*?" *Keats-Shelley Journal* 28 (1979): 20–24.

Graver, Bruce. "Sitting in Dante's Throne: Wordsworth and Italian Nationalism." In *Dante and Italy in British Romanticism*. Ed. Frederick Burwick and Paul Douglass, pp. 29–37. New York: Palgrave Macmillan, 2011.

Graves, Robert Perceval. "Recollections of Wordsworth and the Late Country." In *The Afternoon Lectures on Literature and Art*, pp. 277–321. Dublin: William McGee; London: Bell and Daldy, 1869.

Gravil, Richard. *Wordsworth's Bardic Vocation, 1787–1842*. Basingstoke: Palgrave MacMillan, 2003.

Griffith, Ben W., Jr. "The Keats-Shelley Poetry Contests." *Notes and Queries* 199 (1954): 359–60.

Grimes, Kyle. "Censorship, Violence, and Political Rhetoric: *The Revolt of Islam* in Its Time." *Keats-Shelley Journal* 43 (1994): 98–116.

Griggs, Earl L., and Paul Mueschke. "Wordsworth as the Prototype of the Poet in *Alastor*." *PMLA* 49 (1934): 229–45.

Gullette, Margaret Morganroth. *Aged by Culture*. Chicago, IL: University of Chicago Press, 2004.

Hale, J. R., ed. *The Italian Journal of Samuel Rogers*. London: Faber and Faber, 1956.

Hamilton, John [John Hamilton Reynolds]. *The Garden of Florence; and Other Poems*. London: John Warren, 1821.

Hartman, Geoffrey. *Wordsworth's Poetry 1787–1814*. New Haven, CT: Yale University Press, 1977.

    "Words, Wish, Worth: Wordsworth." In *Deconstruction and Criticism*, eds. Harold Bloom et al, pp. 177–216. New York: Seabury Press, 1979.

    The Unremarkable Wordsworth. Minneapolis: University of Minnesota Press, 1987.

Haydon, Benjamin Robert. *The Life of Benjamin Robert Haydon*. Ed. Tom Taylor. 3 vols. London: Longman, Brown, Green, and Longmans, 1853.

    The Diary of Benjamin Robert Haydon. Ed. Willard Bissell Pope. 5 vols. Cambridge: Harvard University Press, 1960–63.

Hazlitt, William. *William Hazlitt: Metropolitan Writings*. Ed. Gregory Dart, Manchester: Carcanet, 2005.

Heppner, Christopher. "Alastor: The Poet and the Narrator Reconsidered." *Keats-Shelley Journal* 37 (1988): 91–109.

Hickey, Alison. *Impure Conceits: Rhetoric and Ideology in Wordsworth's Excursion*. Stanford, CA: Stanford University Press, 1997.

Hill, Alan G. "Wordsworth, Boccaccio, and the Pagan Gods of Antiquity." *Studies in English Literature, 1500–1900* 45 (February 1994): 26–41.

Holmes, Richard. *Shelley, the Pursuit*. New York: Penguin Books, 1974.

    Coleridge: Darker Reflections, 1804–1834. New York: Pantheon Books, 1998.

Hubbell, Andrew. "*Laon and Cythna*: A Vision of Regency Romanticism." *Keats-Shelley Journal* 51 (2002): 174–97.

Hudson, Derek. *Thomas Barnes of the "Times."* Cambridge: Cambridge University Press, 1944.

Hughes-Hallet, Penelope. *The Immortal Dinner*. New York: Vintage Books, 2012.

Hunt, Leigh. *The Autobiography of Leigh Hunt*. Ed. Edmund Blunden. Oxford: Oxford University Press, 1928.

Hughson, David [Edward Pugh]. *Walks through London.* 2 vols. London: Sherwood, Neely, and Jones, 1817.

Hudnall, Clayton W. "John Hamilton Reynolds, James Rice, and Benjamin Bailey in the Leigh Browne-Lockyer Collection." *Keats-Shelley Journal* 19 (1970): 11–39.

Jackson, J. R. de J., ed. *Samuel Taylor Coleridge: The Critical Heritage.* New York: Barnes and Noble, 1970.

Jager, Colin. *Unquiet Things: Secularism in the Romantic Age.* Philadelphia: University of Pennsylvania Press, 2014.

Jarvis, Robin. "Shades of Milton: Wordsworth at Vallombrosa." *Studies in Romanticism* 25 (Winter 1986): 483–504.

Jones, Leonidas M. *The Life of John Hamilton Reynolds.* Hanover: University Press of New England, 1984.

Johnson, Lee M. *Wordsworth and the Sonnet.* Copenhagen: Rosenkilde and Bagger, 1973.

Johnston, Kenneth R. *Wordsworth and "The Recluse."* New Haven, CT: Yale University Press, 1984.

The Hidden Wordsworth: Poet, Lover, Rebel, Spy. New York: W. W. Norton & Co., 1998.

Unusual Suspects: Pitt's Reign of Alarm and the Lost Generation of the 1790s. Oxford: Oxford University Press, 2013.

Kelsall, Martin. *Byron's Politics.* Totowa, NJ: Barnes & Noble Books, 1987.

Kenealy, Edward Vaughan. *Memoirs of Edward Vaughan Kenealy.* Ed. Arabella Kenealy. London: John Long, 1908.

Keogh, Margaret. *Herculaneum, Pompeii, and Other Poems.* London: J. L. Cox and Sons, 1842.

Khan, Jalal Uddin. "Wordsworth's *River Duddon* Volume: A Response to Coleridge and Byron." *Critical Review* 36 (January 1, 1996): 62–82.

"Publication and Reception of Wordsworth's 'The River Duddon' Volume." *Modern Language Studies* 32 (Autumn 2002): 45–67.

Kim, Benjamin. *Wordsworth, Hemans, and Politics, 1800–1830.* Lewisburg, VA: Bucknell University Press, 2013.

Kinnaird, John. *William Hazlitt: Critic of Power.* New York: Columbia University Press, 1978.

Knox, Alexander Andrew. *Giotto and Francesca, And Other Poems.* London: Edward Bull, 1842.

Lamb, Charles, and Mary Lamb. *The Letters of Charles and Mary Lamb.* Vol. 3. Ed. Edwin W. Marrs, Jr. Ithaca, NY: Cornell University Press, 1978.

Lau, Beth. *Keats's Reading of the Romantic Poets.* Ann Arbor: University of Michigan Press, 1991.

Lindenberger, Herbert. "The Reception of *The Prelude.*" *Bulletin of the New York Public Library* 64 (1960): 196–208.

Lipking, Lawrence. *Abandoned Women and Poetic Tradition.* Chicago, IL: University of Chicago Press, 1988.

Little, Geoffrey, ed. *Barron Field's "Memoirs of Wordsworth."* Sydney: Sydney
    University Press, 1975.
Liu, Alan. *Wordsworth: The Sense of History*. Stanford, CA: Stanford University
    Press, 1989.
Looser, Devoney. *Women Writers and Old Age in Great Britain, 1750–1850*.
    Baltimore, MD: Johns Hopkins University Press, 2008.
    "Age and Aging." In *Women's Writing in the Romantic Period*. Ed.
    Devoney Looser, pp. 169–82. Cambridge: Cambridge University Press, 2015.
Low, Dennis. *The Literary Protégés of the Lake Poets*. Aldershot: Ashgate, 2006.
Luzzi, Joseph. *Romantic Europe and the Ghost of Italy*. New Haven, CT: Yale
    University Press, 2008.
MacCannell, Dean. *The Tourist: A New Theory of the Leisure Class*. New York:
    Schocken Books, 1976.
Macewen, Alexander R. *The Life and Letters of John Cairns*. London: Hodder and
    Stoughton, 1895.
Magnuson, Paul. *Reading Public Romanticism*. Princeton, NJ: Princeton
    University Press, 1998.
Mahoney, Charles. *Romantics and Renegades: The Poetics of Political Reaction*.
    New York: Palgrave Macmillan, 2003.
Manning, Peter. "Wordsworth at St. Bees: Scandals' Sisterhoods, and
    Wordsworth's Later Poetry." *English Literary History*. 52 (Spring 1985):
    33–58.
    Reading Romantics: Text and Context. Oxford: Oxford University Press, 1990.
    "Cleansing the Images: Wordsworth, Rome, and the Rise of Historicism."
    Texas Studies in Literature and Language 33 (Summer 1991): 306–15.
    "The Other Scene of Travel: Wordsworth's 'Musings Near Aquapendente." In
    *The Wordsworthian Enlightenment: Romantic Poetry and the Ecology of
    Reading*. Ed. Helen Reguiro Elam and Frances Ferguson, pp. 191–211.
    Baltimore, MD: Johns Hopkins University Press, 2005.
    "The Persian Wordsworth." *European Romantic Review* 17 (2006): 189–96.
Mant, Richard. "Life and Writings of Thomas Warton." In *The Poetical Works of
    the Late Thomas Warton*. 5th ed. Ed. Richard Mant. London: F. &
    C. Rivington, 1802.
Marchand, Leslie A. *Byron, A Portrait*. Chicago, IL: Chicago University Press,
    1970.
Marcus, Leah S. "Vaughan, Wordsworth, Coleridge, and the *Encomium Asini*."
    English Literary History 42 (1975): 224–41.
Marsh, G. L. "The Peter Bell Parodies of 1819." *Modern Philology* 40 (1943):
    267–74.
Mazzeo, Tilar. *Plagiarism and Literary Property in the Romantic Period*.
    Philadelphia: University of Pennsylvania Press, 2006.
McGann, Jerome. *Fiery Dust: Byron's Poetic Development*. Chicago, IL: University
    of Chicago Press, 1968.
    The Romantic Ideology: A Critical Investigation. Chicago, IL: University of
    Chicago Press, 1983.

Byron and Wordsworth. Nottingham: School of English Studies, University of Nottingham, 1999.

McGhee, Richard D. "'Conversant with Infinity': Form and Meaning in Wordsworth's 'Laodamia.'" *Studies in Philology* 68 (July 1971): 357–69.

Medwin, Thomas. *The Life of Percy Bysshe Shelley*. Ed. H. Buxton Forman. London: Oxford University Press, 1913.

Morley, John. *Life of William Ewart Gladstone*. 3 vols. New York: Macmillan, 1903.

Morison, Stanley. *The History of The Times*. Vol. 1: *"The Thunderer" in the Making, 1781–1841*. London: The Times, 1935.

Morton, Timothy. *Shelley and the Revolution in Taste: The Body and the Natural World*. Cambridge: Cambridge University Press, 1994.

Munsell, F. Darrell. *The Victorian Controversy Surrounding the Wellington War Memorial: The Archduke of Hyde Park Corner*. Lewisten: Edwin Mellen, 1991.

Nersessian, Anahid. *Utopia Limited: Romanticism and Adjustment*. Cambridge: Harvard University Press, 2015.

Nicholson, Andrew, ed. *Lord Byron: The Complete Miscellaneous Prose*. Oxford: Clarendon Press, 1991.

Olney, Clarke. *Benjamin Robert Haydon, Historical Painter*. Athens: University of Georgia Press, 1952.

Ottaway, Susannah R. *The Decline of Life: Old Age in Eighteenth-Century England*. Cambridge: Cambridge University Press, 2007.

Page, Judith. "'Judge Her Gently': Passion and Rebellion in Wordsworth's 'Laodamia.'" *Texas Studies in Literature and Language* 33 (Spring 1991): 24–39.

Wordsworth and the Cultivation of Women. Berkeley: University of California Press, 1994.

Patmore, P. G. *My Friends and Acquaintances*. 3 vols. [np]: Saunders and Otley, 1854/5.

Peacock, Thomas Love. *The Works of Thomas Love Peacock*. Eds. H. F. B. Brett-Smith and C. E. Jones. 10 vols. London: Constable & Company, Limited, 1924–1934.

Peacock, Markham L., Jr. *The Critical Opinions of William Wordsworth*. 1950; reprint, New York: Octagon Books, 1969.

Peck, Walter Edwin. *Shelley: His Life and Work*. 1927; reprint, New York: Burt Franklin, 1969.

Pfau, Thomas. *Wordsworth's Profession: Form, Class and the Logic of Early Romantic Cultural Production*. Stanford, CA: Stanford University Press, 1997.

Phelan, Joseph. *The Nineteenth-Century Sonnet*. Basingstoke: Palgrave Macmillan, 2005.

Pinion, F. B. *A Wordsworth Chronology*. Boston: G. K. Hall, 1988.

Poston, Lawrence. "Wordsworth among the Victorians: The Case of Henry Taylor." *Studies in Romanticism* 17 (1978): 293–305.

Pritchard, John Paul. "On the Making of Wordsworth's 'Dion.'" *Studies in Philology* 49 (1952): 66–74.

Reade, James Edmund. *Italy: A Poem, In Six Parts*. London: Saunders and Otley, 1838.

Redford, Bruce. *Venice and the Grand Tour*. New Haven, CT: Yale University Press, 1996.

Rejack, Brian. "Nothings of the Day: The Velocipede, the Dandy, and the Cockney." *Romanticism* 19 (2013): 291–309.

Reynolds, John Hamilton. *Selected Prose of John Hamilton Reynolds*. Ed. Leonidas M. Jones. Cambridge: Harvard University Press, 1966.

Robinson, Charles. *Shelley and Byron: The Snake and Eagle Wreathed in Fight*. Baltimore, MD: Johns Hopkins University Press, 1976.

Robinson, Daniel. "'Still Glides the Stream': Form and Function in Wordsworth's *River Duddon* Sonnets." *European Romantic Review* 13 (2002): 449–64.

"*The River Duddon* and Wordsworth, Sonneteer." In *The Oxford Handbook of William Wordsworth*. Ed. Richard Gravil and Daniel Robinson, pp. 289–308. Oxford: Oxford University Press, 2015.

Robinson, Henry Crabb. *Diary, Reminiscences, and Correspondence of Henry Crabb Robinson*. Ed. Thomas Sadler. 2 vols. Boston, MA: Fields, Osgood, & Co., 1869.

The Correspondence of Henry Crabb Robinson with the Wordsworth Circle (1806–1866). Ed. Edith J. Morley. 2 vols. Oxford: Clarendon Press, 1927.

On Books and Their Writers. Ed. Edith J. Morley. 3 vols. London: J. M. Dent and Sons, 1938.

Roe, Nicholas. "Leigh Hunt and Wordsworth's *Poems*." *Wordsworth Circle* 12 (Winter 1981): 89–91.

Keats and the Culture of Dissent. Oxford: Oxford University Press, 1997.

ed. *Leigh Hunt: Life, Poetics, Politics*. London: Routledge, 2003.

John Keats: A New Life. New Haven, CT: Yale University Press, 2012.

Rogers, Samuel. *Italy, A Poem*. London: Edward Moxon, 1839.

Rollins, Hyder Edward, ed. *The Keats Circle*. 2 vols. Cambridge: Harvard University Press, 1948.

Rose, Mark. *Authors and Owners*. Cambridge, MA: Harvard University Press, 1993.

Rubenstein, Jill. "Wordsworth and 'Localised Romance': The Scottish Poems of 1831." *Studies in English Literature, 1500–1900* 16 (Fall 1976): 579–90.

Rudy, John. "Wordsworth's St. Francis and the Baptized Imagination." *Renascence: Essays on Values in Literature* 40 (Summer 1988): 268–78.

Russett, Margaret. *Fictions and Fakes: Forging Romantic Authenticity, 1760–1845*. Cambridge: Cambridge University Press, 2006.

Ryan, Robert. *Charles Darwin and the Church of Wordsworth*. Oxford: Oxford University Press, 2016.

Rzepka, Charles. *The Self as Mind: Vision and Identity in Wordsworth, Coleridge, and Keats*. Cambridge, MA: Harvard University Press, 1986.

Sachs, Jonathan. *Romantic Antiquity*. Oxford: Oxford University Press, 2010.

Saint-Juste, Louis Antoine Léon de. "Fragments d'institutions républicaines." *Oeuvres Complètes de Saint-Juste*. Ed. Michèle Duval. Paris: G. Lebovici, 1984.

Scrivener, Michael. *Radical Shelley: The Philosophical Anarchism and Utopian Thought of Percy Bysshe Shelley*. Princeton, NJ: Princeton University Press, 1982.

Setzer, Sharon M. "Sicilian Daydreams and Parisian Nightmares: Wordsworth's Representations of Plutarch's Dion." *Studies in English Literature, 1500–1900* 32 (Autumn 1992): 607–624.

Shaver, Chester, and Alice Shaver. *Wordsworth's Library: A Catalogue.* New York: Garland, 1979.

Shaw, Philip. "Commemorating Waterloo: Wordsworth, Southey, and the 'Muses Page of State.'" *Romanticism* 1.1 (1995): 50–67.

"Leigh Hunt and the Aesthetics of Post-War Liberalism." In *Romantic Wars: Studies in Culture and Conflict, 1793–1822.* Ed. Philip Shaw, pp. 185–207. Burlington, VT: Ashgate, 2000.

"Wordsworth's 'Dread Voice': Ovid, Dora, and the Later Poetry." *Romanticism* 8 (2002): 34–48.

Waterloo and the Romantic Imagination. Basingstoke and New York: Palgrave Macmillan, 2002.

"Wordsworth, Waterloo and Sacrifice." In *Sacrifice and Modern War Literature.* Ed. Alex Houen and Melissa Schramm, pp. 20–33. Oxford: Oxford University Press, 2018.

"Wordsworth after Peterloo: The Persistence of War in *River Duddon . . . and Other Poems.*" In *Commemorating Peterloo: Violence, Resilience and Claim-Making during the Romantic Era.* Ed. Michael Demson and Regina Hewitt, pp. 25–70. Edinburgh: Edinburgh University Press, 2019.

Shelley, Mary. *The Journals of Mary Shelley 1814–1844.* Ed. Paula R. Feldman and Diana Scott-Kilvert. 2 vols. Baltimore, MD: Johns Hopkins University Press, 1987.

Shelley, Percy Bysshe. *The Complete Works of Percy Bysshe Shelley.* Ed. Roger Igpen and Walter E. Peck. 10 vols. 1926; reprint, New York: Gordian Press, 1965.

Siskin, Clifford. *The Historicity of Romantic Discourse.* New York: Oxford University Press, 1988.

Solomonescu, Yasmin. "Percy Shelley's Revolutionary Periods." *English Literary History* 83 (Winter 2016): 105–33.

Southey, Robert. *The Collected Letters of Robert Southey,* Part IV. Ed. Ian Packer and Lynda Pratt. Adelphi, MD: Romantic Circles, 2013.

Spencer, Jane. *Literary Relations: Kinship and the Canon, 1660–1830.* Oxford: Oxford University Press, 2005.

Sperry, Stuart. *Keats the Poet.* Princeton, NJ: Princeton University Press, 1973.

Sperry, Willard L. *Wordsworth's Anti-Climax.* Harvard Studies in English, Volume XIII. Cambridge: Harvard University Press, 1935.

Stabler, Jane. "Byron and *The Excursion.*" *Wordsworth Circle* 45 (Spring 2014): 137–47.

Stead, Henry. *A Cockney Catullus: The Reception of Catullus in Romantic Britain, 1795–1821.* Oxford: Oxford University Press, 2016.

Stelzig, Eugene L. "Mutability, Ageing, and Permanence in Wordsworth's Later Poetry." *Studies in English Literature, 1500–1900* 19 (1979): 623–44.

Stevens, Wallace. *The Palm at the End of the Mind.* Ed. Holly Stevens. New York: Vintage Books, 1972.

Stillinger, Jack. "Wordsworth and Keats." In *The Age of William Wordsworth*. Ed. Kenneth R. Johnston and Gene W. Ruoff, pp. 173–95. New Brunswick, NJ: Rutgers University Press, 1987.

——— ed. *The Manuscripts of the Younger Romantics: John Keats*. Gen ed. Donald H. Reiman. 7 vols. New York: Garland Press, 1985–88.

Sultana, Donald. *From Abbotsford to Paris and Back*. Bristol: Sutton, 1993.

Super, Robert. *Walter Savage Landor, A Biography*. 1954; reprint, Westport, CT: Green Wood Press, 1977.

Sweet, Nanora. "'Lorenzo's' Liverpool and 'Corinne's' Coppet: The Italianate Salon and Romantic Education." In *Lessons of Romanticism*. Ed. Thomas Pfau and Robert F. Gleckner, pp. 244–60. Durham, NC: Duke University Press, 1998.

Talfourd, Thomas Noon. *Final Memorials of Charles Lamb*. 2 vols. London: E. Moxon, 1848.

Taylor, Henry. *Philip Van Artevelde: A Dramatic Romance. In Two Parts*. London: Edward Moxon, 1834.

Taylor, Jane. *Essays in Rhyme, on Morals and Manners*. London: T. Miller, 1816.

Thompson, E.P. "Disenchantment or Default? A Lay Sermon." In *Power and Consciousness*. Ed. Conor Cruise O'Brien and William Dean Vanech, pp. 149–81. London: University of London Press, 1969.

Thompson, James R. *Leigh Hunt*. Boston, MA: Twayne, 1977.

Thorpe, Clarence DeWitt. "The Nymphs." *Keats-Shelley Memorial Bulletin* 10 (1959): 33–47.

Trelawney, Edward. *Recollections of the Last Days of Shelley and Byron*. 1858; reprint, Williamstown, MA: Corner House Publishers, 1975.

Trilling, Lionel. *The Opposing Self*. New York: Harcourt Brace Jovanovich, 1979.

Turley, Richard Marggraf. "Keats on Two Wheels." *Studies in Romanticism* 57 (Winter 2018): 601–25.

Walker, Eric C. *Marriage, Writing, and Romanticism: Wordsworth and Austen After War*. Stanford, CA: Stanford University Press, 2009.

Wallace, Jennifer. *Digging the Dirt: The Archeological Imagination*. London: Duckworth, 2004.

Wandling, Timothy J. "Early Romantic Theorists and the Fate of Transgressive Eloquence: John Stuart Mill's Response to Byron." In *Nervous Reactions: Victorian Recollections of Romanticism*. ed. Joel Faflak and Julia M. Wright, pp. 123–40. Albany: State University of New York Press, 2004.

Warden, C. F. *The Battle of Waterloo; A Poem; In Two Parts*. London: Dean and Monday, 1817.

Wasserman, Earl. *Shelley: A Critical Reading*. Baltimore, MD: Johns Hopkins University Press, 1971.

Watkins, Daniel P. *Keats's Poetry and the Politics of the Imagination*. Rutherford, NJ: Fairleigh Dickinson University Press, 1989.

Watson, J. R. *Romanticism and War: A Study of British Romantic Writers and the Napoleonic Wars*. Basingstoke: Palgrave Macmillan, 2004.

White, Daniel. "The Case of the Nocturnal Amanuenses: New Evidence in the *Wat Tyler* Affair." *Modern Philology* 118 (November 2020): 277–303.

Wilcox, Stewart. "Wordsworth's River Duddon Sonnets." *PMLA* 69 (March 1954): 131–34.

Wilkes, Joanne. "Snuffing out an Articles: Sara Coleridge and the Early Victorian Reception of Keats." In *Nervous Reactions: Victorian Recollections of Romanticism*. Ed. Joel Faflak and Julia M. Wright, pp. 189–206. Albany: State University of New York Press, 2004.

Wolfson, Susan J. *The Questioning Presence: Wordsworth, Keats, and the Interrogative Mode in Romantic Poetry*. Ithaca, NY: Cornell University Press, 1986.

"'This is my Lightning'; or, Sparks in the Air." *Studies in English Literature, 1500–1900* 55 (Autumn 2015): 751–86.

Woodring, Carl. *Politics in English Romantic Poetry*. Cambridge, MA: Harvard University Press, 1970.

Woodward, Kathleen. *Age and Its Discontents: Freud and Other Fictions*. Bloomington: Indiana University Press, 1991.

Wordsworth, Christopher. *Memoirs of William Wordsworth*. 2 vols. London: Moxon, 1851.

Wordsworth, Dorothy. *Journals of Dorothy Wordsworth*. Ed. E. de Selincourt. 2 vols. London: Macmillan, 1941.

Wordsworth, Mary. *Letters of Mary Wordsworth, 1800–1855*. Ed. Mary E. Burton. Cambridge: Clarendon Press, 1958.

Wordsworth, Jonathan. *William Wordsworth: The Borders of Vision*. Oxford: Clarendon, 1982.

"Introduction." *Peter Bell, 1819*. Oxford: Woodstock Books, 1992.

Worthington, Jane. *Wordsworth's Reading of Roman Prose*. New Haven, CT: Yale University Press, 1946.

Wu, Duncan. *William Hazlitt: The First Modern Man*. Oxford: Oxford University Press, 2008.

"Wordsworthian Carnage." *Essays in Criticism* 66 (July 2016): 341–59.

Wyatt, John. *Wordsworth's Poems of Travel, 1819–42: "Such Sweet Wayfaring."* New York: St. Martin's Press, 1999.

Yallop, Hellen. *Age and Identity in Eighteenth-Century England*. London: Pickering & Chatto, 2013.

Yen, Brandon C. *"The Excursion" and Wordsworth's Iconography*. Liverpool: Liverpool University Press, 2018.

Index

CAMBRIDGE STUDIES IN ROMANTICISM

General Editor

JAMES CHANDLER, University of Chicago